ARCHAEOLOGY AND BIBLE HISTORY

ARCHAEOLOGY AND BIBLE HISTORY

Joseph P. Free

REVISED AND EXPANDED BY

Howard F. Vos

ZondervanPublishingHouse
Academic and Professional Books
Grand Rapids, Michigan

A Division of HarperCollinsPublishers

Library of Congress Catalog Cataloging-in-Publication Data

Free, Joseph P.
  Archaeology and Bible history / Joseph R. Free; revised by Howard F. Vos.
    p.   cm.
  Includes bibliographical references and index.
  ISBN 0-310-47961-4
    1. Bible–Antiquities.   2. Bible–History of Biblical events.   I. Vos, Howard Frederic,
1925-   .   II. Title.
  BS621.F7   1992
  220.9'3–dc20

                                                                    92-6108
                                                                    CIP

Edited by Gerard Terpstra
Cover design by Church Art Works
Cover photos: left and center by Daniel Blatt; right by Shlomo Arad, SIPA

Printed in the United States of America

92   93   94   95   96   97 / ML / 10   9   8   7   6   5   4   3   2   1

CONTENTS

CHART, MAPS, AND ILLUSTRATIONS

CHART

MAPS

ILLUSTRATIONS

TO THE READER

The Subject Matter and Development of This Book

This book deals with archaeology and Bible history, and not merely with archaeology and the Bible. Too often books on archaeology and the Bible contain a heterogeneous amount of material that lacks a unifying element. In this book I follow the sequence of Bible history as a unifying thread and show how archaeological discoveries illuminate and confirm the successive events of biblical history. Thus the following chapters serve as a summary of Bible history as well as a source of information on the bearing of archaeology on the Bible. This book is not exhaustive in any particular field but is rather introductory to many fields.

The Scope of This Book

Because the chief aim throughout the book is to be practical and helpful, I have not always limited myself to the most narrow interpretation of archaeology, which often restricts itself merely to data from the excavation of buried cities; nor have I necessarily broadened this study to its wide interpretation, which defines archaeology as "the study of ancient things." In general, the definition of archaeology followed here is that of the *Century Dictionary*, which describes archaeology as "that branch of knowledge which takes cognizance of past civilizations, and investigates their history in all fields, by means of remains of art, architecture, monuments, inscriptions, literature, language, implements, customs, and all other examples which have survived."[1] Occasionally I have departed from this definition when I felt that it would be helpful to deal with matters concerning chronology, supposed biblical contradictions and difficulties, and other topics chiefly relating to the validity and accuracy of the Scriptures.

The Author's Theological Position

My position is that of the Bible believer. Although in college days I came to the place where I wondered whether God existed, I now hold to the historic and traditional position of the Christian church, not merely because it is

---

[1]*Century Dictionary*, 1903 ed., 1:293; cited in G.A. Barton, *Archaeology and the Bible*, 7th ed. (Philadelphia: American Sunday School Union, 1937), xxxiii.

historic or traditional, but because I became convinced that it is true. The evidences from archaeology, fulfilled prophecy, Christian experience, and many other areas left me with no other choice than to acknowledge the Bible as the Word of God in the most complete sense.

Until recent years, the term "evangelical" or "conservative" could have adequately, or at least almost adequately, described my position. With the frequent appropriation of these terms by those who are neither evangelical nor conservative, their usefulness has been greatly diminished. Therefore, throughout this book the position that used to be designated "conservative" or "evangelical" will more often be designated by such phrases as "Bible believer's position," "orthodox position," "view of those who hold to the fundamentals of the faith," and, occasionally, "very conservative."

While I hold a very conservative position, I wish to emphasize that I always seek to be aware of what is going on in radical, liberal, and neo-orthodox circles, as well as developments in conservative and fundamentalist areas. We are counseled, "Test everything. Hold on to the good" (1 Thess. 5:21).

Bibliographical References and Footnotes

Each bibliographical reference is given in full the first time it appears, together with an abbreviation. For example, when the first reference is made to Chester C. McCown's book *The Ladder of Progress in Palestine* (New York: Harper, 1943), the author and title are given in full, followed by the letters, MLPP. Each successive reference is indicated only by the abbreviation followed by the page number. A list of abbreviations and the books they represent appear at the end of this book.

Bibliographical references include general works and secondary sources as well as primary sources. General works, such as Barton (BAB), Finegan (FLAP), and Price (PMOT), are included in the bibliographical material, inasmuch as source materials, such as Breasted's *Ancient Records of Egypt* (BARE), are not always available to many who will use this book.

It is helpful to remember that the documentation and additional information in the footnotes in a carefully prepared book often contain material that is as important as, and in some cases even more important than, the material in the text. Such material has been placed in footnotes in order to avoid breaking the line of thought but is available for those who wish "to know the reason why" or wish to pursue the matter further in other sources.

How to Use This Book

Those who are primarily interested in seeing how archaeology illuminates and confirms the Bible will find it profitable to read this book from beginning to end. Also, those who wish to get a sweep of biblical history will do well to read the book through, inasmuch as it summarizes the main sequence of events in the Scriptures, both Old and New Testaments, as well as the intertestamental period.

This book may also be used as a compendium on the subject "How Archaeology Confirms the Bible" by reading those sections whose headings contain the words "Archaeological Confirmation Concerning. . ." or some similar phrase. Likewise, this book may also be used as a compendium on the subject "How Archaeology Illuminates the Bible" by reading those sections that contain the phrase "Archaeological Light on. . ." or some similar expression. Many sections of this book give material that both illuminates *and* confirms the Bible.

Sunday school teachers who wish to use an example of archaeological illumination or confirmation to enliven a lesson will often find it profitable to check the section of this book that corresponds to the portion of the Scriptures from which the lesson is taken—they may find some archaeological material that will fit a point in the lesson or may be adapted to the lesson.

In my lifetime I have heard many messages or sermons that could have had some point driven home by the effective use of some archaeological item. While we are not called to "preach archaeology," we are responsible for getting our messages across, and the materials from archaeological discoveries constitute one of several useful areas from which progressive servants of God may draw material to bring home their message more effectively.

This book will be useful either as a text or as collateral reading in academic courses that deal with Bible survey, Bible history, or Bible archaeology.

It will also be useful for Sunday school and Bible class teachers who wish to have a series of lessons on the subject "Through the Bible." For the students in such classes this book will serve as a lesson help.

In the various uses made of this book, may it make more real the great events and the great truths of the Scriptures as they are illuminated and confirmed by archaeological discoveries.

Joseph P. Free

REVISER'S PREFACE

Joseph P. Free profoundly influenced a whole generation of students and laypersons alike. As professor or archaeology at Wheaton College in Wheaton, Illinois, he had an extensive outreach to the general public through articles in Sunday school quarterlies and other publications, and through public appearances and study tours to Bible lands. To us, his students, he did not merely impart information but challenged us to know what we believed and why. And he helped us to think perceptively about attacks on the Scriptures and to answer those attacks. Moreover, with the new insights that kept coming from research in Near Eastern studies, he helped to bring a new excitement to Bible study.

Not only was it my privilege to study with Dr. Free, but I also prepared the first edition of this book for the publisher. Now it has been my privilege to produce this new edition, which is based on the fourteenth printing of 1976. There have been some minor revisions along the way. I have followed Dr. Free's outline, his theological position, and his chronological framework. I have sought to bring the archaeological and historical material up to date and have modified the archaeological interpretation where necessary. The bibliography has required almost total replacement. It is my hope that this book will now continue to make the impact for which it was designed. May another generation of Bible students benefit from the profound insights of this dedicated scholar.

Howard F. Vos

Chapter 1

Bible Archaeology, Bible History, and Buried Cities

The Functions of Bible Archaeology

A friend once asked me, "What is the value of archaeology for biblical study, anyway?" I pointed out that numerous passages of the Bible that long puzzled the commentators have readily yielded up their meaning when new light from archaeological discoveries has been focused on them. In other words, archaeology illuminates the text of the Scriptures and so makes valuable contributions to the field of biblical interpretation and exegesis. In addition to illuminating the Bible, archaeology has confirmed countless passages that have been rejected by critics as unhistorical or contradictory to known facts. This aspect of archaeology forms a valuable part of the defense of the Scriptures—a discipline commonly known as apologetics. In summary it may be said that two of the main functions of Bible archaeology are the illumination and the confirmation of the Bible.

The Bible, a Historical Book

The Bible is a historical book, and the great truths of Christianity are founded on the historic facts revealed in it. If the fact of the Virgin Birth, the fact of the

Crucifixion, and the fact of the Resurrection are set aside, our faith is without foundation. Since the New Testament revelation stands upon the foundation of the Old Testament, the accuracy of the Old Testament is of great importance to us.

Although confirmation of one kind of truth (historical) does not demonstrate the validity of another kind of truth (theological), the veracity of the historical narrative of Scripture lends credence to the theological message. Those who do not accept the historical accuracy of the Bible find it easier to dismiss its theological claims. The accuracy and historicity of the Scriptures as God's Word and as his unique revelation has been denied by the destructive critic who has set aside the full validity of the Bible at point after point. For example, certain critics have said that the accounts of Abraham are legendary, that Mosaic legislation was formulated hundreds of years after the time of Moses, that such people as the Hittites were either legendary or insignificant, that the book of Judges was composed of "good stories" and not really historical accounts, and that various people ranging from Sargon to Sanballat were unhistorical. Yet archaeological discoveries have shown that these critical charges and countless others are wrong and that the Bible is trustworthy in the very statements that critics have set aside as untrustworthy.[1]

The Purpose and Nature of Bible History; Verbal Inspiration

Bible history is not primarily a record of humanity's seeking after God. It is rather a record of *God's revelation to humanity*. Pagan religions deal with humanity's seeking after God or gods, but the Scriptures are God's own revelation to us, telling how from the beginning in Eden God spoke to Adam and Eve and how he later directed Noah, called Abraham from Ur, spoke through the prophets, and finally gave the supreme revelation in his Son Jesus Christ.

Bible believers hold that this record of God's revelation is not only vital for all humankind but is accurate in all respects. We also hold that the Bible writers exercised their own personality, used their own vocabulary, and drew on their own memories, intuitions, and judgments and that at the same time they were prevented from making errors and were so guided by God that they expressed exactly what God wished to make known. This guidance was not so vague that it assured merely the general idea or concept that God wished to convey, but rather it extended even to the choice of words when it would be essential to convey his message. The foregoing description sets forth my view of "verbal inspiration,"

namely, that God guided even to the choice of words[2] when necessary. On the other hand, I reject the dictation theory of inspiration, which makes the process a mere mechanical operation, robs a writer of his personality, and makes him a mere machine. In summary, I agree with Gaussen's definition of inspiration, which holds that inspiration is "that inexplicable power which the divine Spirit put forth of old on the authors of Holy Scripture, in order to their guidance[3] even in the employment of the words they used, and to preserve them alike from all error and all omission."[4]

The Bible is not a textbook on science, yet when it speaks of matters relating to science, it is accurate. The Scriptures, for example, do not claim to be, nor are they, a treatise on astronomy, yet when Job speaks of the Bear (Job 38:32), he writes in accord with known astronomical facts. As has been said, "The Scriptures were written not primarily to tell us how the heavens go, but to tell us how to go to heaven." Yet the content of all Scripture is scientifically and historically accurate, and the scientific and historical allusions of the Bible are constantly illuminated and confirmed by modern discoveries.

Accuracy of the Text of the Bible

Bible believers do not hold that the translations of the Bible into English and other languages are inerrant. Nor do we maintain the inerrancy of existing manuscripts. But as believers in the fundamentals of the faith, we do hold that the *original* manuscripts were absolutely ac-

---

[1]For archaeological light on Abraham, see chapter 4; on Mosaic legislation, see chapter 9; on the Hittites, see chapter 10; on the book of Judges, see chapter 11; on Sargon, see chapter 17; on Sanballat, see chapter 22.

[2]The Latin word *verba* means "words"; hence the term "verbal inspiration" indicates that God guided even to the extent of the choice of the words when necessary. "Verbal inspiration" does not mean that God dictated the contents of the books of Scripture *verbatim*, or word for word.

[3]This expression "in order to their guidance" is probably a literal translation of the French original. In idiomatic English one would say "in order to guide them."

[4]L. Gaussen, *Theopneustia: The Plenary Inspiration of the Holy Scriptures* (Chicago: Bible Institute Colportage Association, n.d.), 34 [GT].

curate and without error. The question arises, "If we do not have the original manuscripts, how can we be sure of the accuracy of the manuscripts we do have?" In reply it should be said that hundreds of manuscripts have come down to us and that the variations in these manuscripts are so slight that none of them alter any vital Christian truth. Through the science of textual study, scholars are able to reconstruct a text so close to what the original text must have been that it is satisfactory to scholars of almost every degree of liberalism and conservatism. Hort, the great New Testament scholar of the nineteenth century, pointed out that "only about one word in every thousand has upon it substantial variation supported by such evidence as to call out the efforts of the critic in deciding between the readings."[5] The statement of Bentley, made many years ago, is still valid, that "the real text of the sacred writings is competently exact, nor is one article of faith or moral precept either perverted or lost, choose as awkwardly as you will, choose the worst by design, out of the whole lump of readings."[6]

Hort's statement that only about one word in one thousand in the New Testament would call out the efforts of scholars, is significant when we realize that the Westcott and Hort Greek New Testament is about five hundred pages long and that one one-thousandth of it would be only half a page. This does not mean that such an amount of the New Testament is necessarily inaccurate or wrong; it means merely that one one-thousandth of the material would require scholarly study to ascertain what were likely the original words.[7]

The surviving Hebrew Old Testament manuscripts show very little variation. A careful scholar of an earlier generation, William Henry Green said, "The Hebrew manuscripts cannot compare with those of the New Testament either in antiquity or number, but they have been written with greater care and exhibit fewer various readings."[8] In regard to the accuracy of the text of the Old Testament, Green concluded, "It may be safely said that no other work of antiquity has been so accurately transmitted."[9]

Light on Bible History From Buried Cities

A century and a half ago many familiar biblical cities such as Jericho, Samaria, Bethel, Shiloh, Bethshan, Gezer, Nineveh, Babylon, and Ur were shapeless mounds, the very identity of which, in some cases, had been forgotten.

Skepticism had been expressed concerning the details of the capture of Jericho; the ivory palace of Ahab at Samaria (1 Kings 22:39) was a puzzling reference in the Scriptures; the Wellhausen school of criticism doubted the actual existence of the tabernacle and minimized the importance of Shiloh, where the biblical record locates the setting up of the tabernacle in Palestine (Josh. 18:1); and the boasted glories of Nineveh and Babylon seemed more in keeping with the glowing reports of an overenthusiastic chamber of commerce than with sober historic fact.

Within the past hundred and fifty years, however, all of these cities have been uncovered, some receiving additional archaeological attention in recent

[5]B. F. Westcott and F. J. A. Hort, *The New Testament in the Original Greek* (New York: Harper, 1882), 2:2.

[6]Article on "Text," *International Standard Bible Encyclopedia* (Grand Rapids: Eerdmans, 1929), 2955 [ISBE].

[7]H. C. Thiessen, *Introduction to the New Testament* (Grand Rapids: Eerdmans, 1943), 77 [TINT].

[8]W. H. Green, *General Introduction: Text* (New York: Scribner, 1899), 179 [GIT].

[9]Ibid., 181.

years.[10] The importance of the discoveries is apparent when we realize that the excavation of these cities, and dozens more, has produced material that confirms the Scriptures at point after point. In addition to confirming the Bible, the excavations in the Near East have brought much illumination to the pages of Scripture. This phase of modern archaeological investigation is well summarized by Ira Maurice Price, late professor in the field of Old Testament at the University of Chicago: "The Old Testament is fast acquiring a fresh significance. Old Testament history has become incandescent with the wondrous archaeological discoveries in Bible lands. Almost every period of that old Book has been flooded with new light out of the ruins of the past."[11]

How Are Cities Buried?

Laypeople often ask, "How were these cities in the Bible lands buried?" They might suppose that the natural drifting of sands covered them over; and it did. But other processes were far more important in building up the mounds that represent the remains of Near Eastern cities. The repeated destruction and rebuilding of a city, a process that often went on during the course of many centuries, resulted in the formation of an artificial mound that may range from fifty to one hundred feet in elevation. Such a mound is known to archaeologists as a "tell," from the Arabic word for "hill."

The recurrent cycle is as follows: An invader captures a town, destroys many of the buildings, and possibly kills or carries off the inhabitants. In the course of time, some of the original inhabitants or perhaps another group level off the old ruins and build new buildings on the site of the old city. The layer of remains and debris from the first city forms a stratum that often measures from one to five feet in depth. During the course of many centuries, such a city is likely to go through many destructions and rebuildings, each one leaving what is called a "layer of occupation."

Some fourteen miles south of the Sea of Galilee, where the Jezreel and Jordan valleys meet, stands the mound that represents the biblical city of Beth Shan (called Tell el-Husn today, located near the modern town of Beisan, which retains the handed-down form of the name Beth Shan). Beth Shan is significant in biblical history as the place to which Saul's body was taken after he died in the battle against the Philistines at Mount Gilboa (1 Sam. 31:8–10). This site was excavated (1921–1933) by the University of Pennsylvania. The excavators went down over seventy feet through eighteen distinct strata.[12] Beneath them they found pits of unknown origin. The history of the city began perhaps as early as 3500 B.C. and continued down into the Christian era, with a possible gap that shows no evi-

[10]For archaeological light and confirmation concerning Jericho, see chapter 10; for Samaria, see chapter 15; for Shiloh, see chapter 12; for Babylon, see chapter 20.

[11]Ira Maurice Price, *The Dramatic Story of Old Testament History*, 2nd ed. (New York: Revell, 1935), 7 [POTH].

[12]Fitzgerald, reporting on the excavation, pointed out that by the end of 1931 they had gone through ten levels, measuring thirteen meters (43 feet). In resuming the work in 1933, they dug an area 24 x 16 meters through another eight definite levels (numbered XI to XVIII), measuring eight and one-half meters (about 28 feet), and then came to pit dwellings dug in the virgin soil by the earliest inhabitants of the site. Cf. Gerald M. Fitzgerald, "The Earliest Pottery of Bethshan," *Museum Journal* (University of Pennsylvania) 24, 1 (1935). See also, Michael Avi-Yonah, ed., *Encyclopedia of Archaeological Excavations in the Holy Land* (Englewood Cliffs, N.J.: Prentice Hall, 1975 for Vol. 1), 1:207–29 [EAEHL].

dence of occupation from 1000 to 300 B.C.[13] The stratification at Beth Shan of nearly twenty levels shows how cities of biblical times were built up through successive destructions and rebuildings. It is not uncommon to find remains of ten cities, one on top of the other.[14]

Invasion, however, was not the only cause of the destruction of a city in the Near East. Earthquake and fire struck from time to time, leaving a ruined site that may later have been rebuilt; pestilence sometimes decimated the inhabitants of a town to such an extent that it was abandoned and later reoccupied by others. Moreover, ordinary refuse and debris tended to accumulate in the streets of an oriental town and so added to the stratification. If a house (commonly made of mud brick) collapsed, much of the debris may have remained to form the base on which a new house was built. All of these causes of accumulation and stratification combined to make the city mounds of Bible lands grow upward, in many cases at the rate of about five feet per century.[15] City mounds or tells can usually be distinguished from natural hills because they tend to be more flat-topped. Such a configuration occurs because ancient city walls helped to hold debris in place and give definition to a mound.

Present-Day Archaeological Techniques

Modern archaeological method has been developed during the past one hundred years. In 1838 Edward Robinson, Professor of Biblical Literature at Union Theological Seminary, New York, went to Palestine and during a brief visit of only a few weeks, identified scores of biblical sites, many of which were excavated in the following years of the nineteenth and twentieth centuries. Not much actual excavating was done in Palestine until the Palestine Exploration Fund of England was formed in 1865 to foster research in Palestine. A few years earlier, in the 1840s, Nineveh was excavated in Mesopotamia. Much of the work done early in the nineteenth century consisted of "treasure hunts" rather than real scientific work. Even during the latter part of the nineteenth century, many excavations tended to be hunts for museum pieces.

Today the picture is entirely different. An archaeological excavation is a carefully planned scientific expedition. The governments of Near Eastern countries require prospective excavators to secure a government permit, which is granted only to competent individuals and recognized institutions. The staff of an archaeological expedition is ordinarily made up of a director and several assistants, including a photographer, a pottery expert, and, if possible, an architect.

The director of the "dig" lays out the surface of the buried city in squares, often ten meters on a side, with a narrow strip of soil known as a *balk* between. The balk serves as a walkway and a path on which wheelbarrows may be moved toward the dump. Each square has its own number, and all of the objects found in it are entered in the record book according to the number of the square and the depth at which they are found. This organization of a site is part of an excavation procedure developed by British archaeologists Sir Mortimer Wheeler and Kathleen

---

[13]Chester C. McCown, *The Ladder of Progress in Palestine* (New York: Harper, 1943), 152, 168, 169, 180 [MLPP].

[14]Melvin G. Kyle, *Excavating Kirjath-Sepher's Ten Cities* (Grand Rapids: Eerdmans, 1934), told of the excavation of ten levels at the mound of Tell Beit Mirsim, believed to represent the biblical town of Kiriath Sepher, mentioned in Joshua 15:15–16; Judges 1:11–12.

[15]For chart and information on levels of Beth Shan, cf. Alan Rowe, "The Discoveries at Beth Shan During the 1926 Season," *Museum Journal* 18,1 (March 1927): 12; Fitzgerald, "Earliest Pottery," 7–8, 15; J. McKee Adams, *Ancient Records and the Bible*, (Nashville: Broadman, 1946), 80 [AARB].

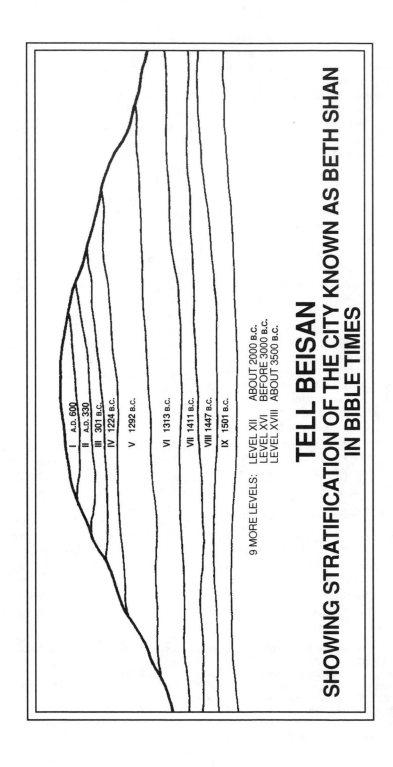

TELL BEISAN

SHOWING STRATIFICATION OF THE CITY KNOWN AS BETH SHAN
IN BIBLE TIMES

I   A.D. 600
II   A.D. 330
III   301 B.C.
IV   1224 B.C.
V   1292 B.C.
VI   1313 B.C.
VII   1411 B.C.
VIII 1447 B.C.
IX   1501 B.C.

9 MORE LEVELS: LEVEL XII   ABOUT 2000 B.C.
                 LEVEL XVI   BEFORE 3000 B.C.
                 LEVEL XVIII   ABOUT 3500 B.C.

Kenyon.[16] The actual digging is done by national workers or foreign students supervised by trained archaeologists of the staff. Surface soil is loosened with a pick. Then oversized hoes, about three or four times the size of a garden hoe, are used to scrape loosened soil into rubber buckets, made from old automobile tires, or baskets and then emptied into wheelbarrows. Wheelbarrow operators carry on a constant shuttle service to the dump. Workers use small hand picks, ice picks, trowels, and brushes to uncover and free objects as they surface.

As each layer of the mound is systematically cleared, every object is carefully recorded, and the more important objects are photographed in the actual position where they are found (in situ). No object is too insignificant to be recorded by the modern archaeologist, for all objects, large and small, combine to give a picture of the nature of ancient life. Archaeologists take note of everything, whether coins, seals, scarabs, pottery vessels, tools, statuettes, lifesize statues, or the foundations of houses and temples, and even the plan of the entire town.

The field archaeologist does not go out with a primary aim of illuminating some point in history or of confirming some biblical passage, but rather to find out what secrets the mound will yield. Needless to say, his discoveries often do illuminate some historical point or confirm some disputed reference in the Bible.

As archaeologists excavate, they are concerned about dating their finds. One of the most useful ways of doing so involves study of the pottery found in each level. Down through the centuries there were changes in the shape, decoration, type of clay, style, and other features of ancient bowls, jars, and dishes. The principle of dating levels by pottery found in them was first developed by pioneer Egyptologist Sir Flinders Petrie at the end of the nineteenth century. And during more recent decades archaeologists have further refined the classification of the various types of pottery according to the periods in which they were used.[17]

Some of the generally accepted cultural periods (for Palestine) readily discernible by pottery chronology are as follows:

Neolithic Period, 6000–4300 B.C.
Chalcolithic Period, 4300–3300 B.C.
Early Bronze Period, 3300–2000 B.C.
Middle Bronze Period (age of Abraham, Isaac, etc.), 2000–1550 B.C.
Late Bronze Period (time of Moses, Joshua, Judges), 1550–1200 B.C.
Iron I Period (end of Judges, time of David, Solomon), 1200–1000 B.C.
Iron II Period (kings of Israel and Judah), 1000–586 B.C.
Iron III or Persian Period (end of Old Testament), 586–300 B.C.
Hellenistic Period (Intertestamental Period), 300–50 B.C.

After World War II another aid to the establishment of Near Eastern chronology appeared on the scene, this time as something of a by-product of atomic science. Willard F. Libby of the Institute for Nuclear Studies at the University of Chicago developed the Carbon 14 technique. Basic to this procedure are certain assumptions:

1. Carbon 14 (radioactive) ceases to be taken in by an organism when it dies.

2. After the organism dies, Carbon 14 disintegrates at a constant rate and has a half-life of 5,730 years. That is to say, an ounce of it would reduce to a half ounce in 5,730 years.

3. In the living organism, Carbon 14 and Carbon 12 have a constant proportion; after the death of the organism,

[16]See Mortimer Wheeler, *Archaeology from the Earth* (Baltimore: Penguin Books, 1954).

[17]An important book for the classification of Palestinian pottery is Ruth Amiran, *Ancient Pottery of the Holy Land* (Jerusalem: Massada Press, 1969).

Carbon 12 remains stable whereas Carbon 14 disintegrates.

In testing an object (which must be burned) the amount of Carbon 14 remaining can be measured against the Carbon 12 in the object in order to gain an indication as to how long the living organism has been dead. Charcoal, among other things, has proved to be very useful in Carbon 14 tests. Usually the Carbon 14 method yields dates valid within 5 to 10 percent of the time involved.[18] A discussion of the variables in the system and the doubts some scholars have expressed concerning it is beyond the scope of this book.

A third method of dating especially useful to archaeologists has come into its own during the last couple of decades, though the method was actually under development about the time of World War I. Known as Dendochronology, it seeks to establish a chronology by means of tree-ring dating.[19]

During the past three decades or so underwater archaeology has been scientifically developed. The basic principles are similar to those used on land. The excavation is divided into squares for record keeping (a grid of iron pipes commonly being used for the purpose), and excavation proceeds to go down stratum by stratum.[20]

[18]See Willard F. Libby, *Radiocarbon Dating*, 2nd ed. (Chicago: University of Chicago Press, 1955).
[19]A useful book on this subject is M. G. L. Baillie, *Tree-Ring Dating and Archaeology* (Chicago: University of Chicago Press, 1982).
[20]One of the authorities in this field is George F. Bass. See his *Archaeology Under Water* (Baltimore: Penguin, 1966).

Chapter 2

Creation

(Genesis 1–3: Creation, Fall, Promise of a Redeemer)

Two-Point Outline of the Book of Genesis

Genesis falls into two general parts: (1) chapters 1–11, which treat universal history and deal with Creation, the Fall, the Flood, and the tower of Babel, and (2) chapters 12–50, the patriarchal period, dealing with the lives of Abraham, Isaac, Jacob, and Joseph.

Treatment of the Material in the First Part of Genesis

Because of the nature of the material in the early chapters of Genesis, several subjects that lie at the fringe and sometimes beyond the limits of "Archaeology and Bible History" will be considered. One of my purposes in this book is to make departures from the immediate subject of archaeology and Bible history whenever I feel it will be helpful. Therefore I will briefly discuss such matters as the critical view of Genesis 1 and 2, the documentary theory, the time of the creation of man and the universe, gaps in genealogies, and, just now, the record of the creation of the universe and its implications.

Creation of the Universe, the World, and Its Inhabitants (Genesis 1)

One may speculate as to the origin of the world, but God has provided the eternal answer to the question in the opening verse of the Bible. "In the beginning God created the heaven and the earth" (Gen. 1:1). This verse answers unscriptural human theories and explanations concerning the creation or origin of the world. It answers *atheism*, which holds that there is no God, by setting forth the existence and work of God; it answers *agnosticism*, which asserts that we cannot know how things began, by stating that God did the creating; it answers *polytheism*, which holds that there were many gods, by setting forth God, not many gods, as the Creator.

The first chapter of Genesis records the creation of the universe, the world, and the inhabitants of the world. The second chapter develops certain points given in chapter 1, adding details concerning the manner of the creation of man, the nature of his surroundings (Eden), and the beginning of human activity.

Critical View of Genesis 1 and 2; Documentary Theory

According to the critical view of the Bible, Genesis 1 is ascribed to one writer and Genesis 2 to another. Genesis 2 supposedly represents a different and somewhat contradictory version of Creation. An examination of the details of this critical view shows that Genesis 1 is assigned to the so-called "priestly" writer, usually referred to as "P," who is supposed to have written about 500 B.C.[1] Genesis 2 is assigned to the writer (or school of writers) called "J," supposedly writing about 850 B.C.

This type of critical analysis of the Bible, usually known as the Documentary Hypothesis, is sometimes referred to popularly as the JEDP theory. This view holds that Moses (c. 1500–1400 B.C.) did not write the Pentateuch, but that it is made up of four main documents, written long after his time: J in the ninth century (c. 850 B.C.), E in the eighth century (c. 750 B.C.), D in the seventh century (621 B.C.), and P in the sixth to the fifth century (500–450 B.C.).

The J document was originally so designated because it supposedly used the name "Jehovah" for God, and the E document because of its use of "Elohim" for God. The document now called P was originally considered to be a part of the E document (until 1853), and one would expect it to use Elohim as the word for God. Subsequent studies have shown, however, that the use of Jehovah in the J document and of Elohim in the E and P documents did not always hold true.[2] In view of such difficulties in using the criterion of the divine names for dividing up the Pentateuch into documents, liberal scholars now lean more heavily on supposed differences in diction and style in assigning one part to J, another to P, and so forth. By way of answer to the critical view, it should be pointed out that when the writer of the Pentateuch moves from one subject to another, he would of necessity use different words. In short, one would expect differences in diction, vocabulary, and even style when the subject matter changes. Further demonstration of the many ways in which the critical criteria break down is given by Oswald Allis (AFBM, 40ff.), James Orr,[3] Robert Dick Wilson,[4] and other scholars.[5] In view of the many evidences for the unity of Genesis and of the Pentateuch, I can see no valid reason for denying the Mosaic authorship of the Pentateuch and for assigning it to various documents and writers in the late period (ninth to fifth centuries B.C.).

As a matter of fact, in recent decades scholars within the Wellhausen circle have questioned and repudiated almost every tenet of Wellhausen's system. The results of their study have not led them back to a Mosaic origin of the Pentateuch, however. They tend to make the whole Pentateuch postexilic (after 535 B.C.). Gleason Archer has provided an excellent survey of the development of recent pentateuchal scholarship and arguments for

[1]Robert H. Pfeiffer, *Introduction to the Old Testament* (New York: Harper, 1941), 139 [PIOT].

[2]Oswald T. Allis, *The Five Books of Moses* (Philadelphia: Presbyterian and Reformed, 1943), 25, 32, 38 [AFBM].

[3]James Orr, *The Problem of the Old Testament* (New York: Scribner, 1917) [OPOT].

[4]Robert Dick Wilson, *A Scientific Investigation of the Old Testament* (Philadelphia: Sunday School Times, 1926) [WSI]. Revised by Edward J. Young (Chicago: Moody, 1959).

[5]Cf. William Henry Green, *The Higher Criticism of the Pentateuch* (New York: Scribner, 1896) [GHCP]. The place of archaeology in answering the critical view is developed in M. G. Kyle, *The Deciding Voice of the Monuments in Biblical Criticism* (Oberlin: Bibliotheca Sacra, 1924) [KDVM], and in his *Moses and the Monuments: Light from Archaeology on Pentateuchal Times* (Oberlin: Bibliotheca Sacra, 1920) [KMM]. Edward J. Young, *An Introduction to the Old Testament* (Grand Rapids: Eerdmans, 1949) [YIOT], contains a concise history of the literary criticism of the Pentateuch from a conservative standpoint (109–53).

the Mosaic authorship of the first five books of the Old Testament.[6]

Answer to the Critical View of Genesis 1 and 2

An examination of Genesis 1 and 2 shows that they are not two divergent accounts of Creation. Genesis 1 is the record of the creation of the universe, the world, and the inhabitants of the world. Genesis 2, on the other hand, gives further details. It tells how man was created, describes the nature and location of his surroundings (Eden), records the test of obedience (not to eat of the Tree of Knowledge of Good and Evil), and relates the details of the creation of Eve (vv. 21–22). The two sections are not contradictory nor divergent, but the second supplements the first, and together they form an overall view of the broad sweep of Creation, along with the essential details.

In any modern book that gives a running narrative, one may find that a particular chapter will refer to a certain character in a passing remark, while a succeeding chapter will take up that character and give further details concerning him or her. The two chapters, written by the same author, are not contradictory but supplementary. In just such a way, Genesis 2 elaborates and supplements Genesis 1. Those who wish to see the unity of the first chapters of Genesis should read Genesis 1 and then skip to Genesis 3; they will notice that the preparation for Genesis 3 is lacking. Or if they begin with chapter 2, they will find that many essentials are missing, which are given only in Genesis 1. Genesis 1 is obviously an integral and essential part of the whole record of Creation. The unity of the book

of Genesis was well demonstrated by a scholar of the last century, William Henry Green.[7] Oswald T. Allis, formerly professor at Princeton Theological Seminary, subsequently demonstrated the Mosaic authorship, the unity, and the validity of Genesis and the other books of the Pentateuch in his *Five Books of Moses* (AFBM).

Time of the Creation of Humankind

In the margin of many Bibles the date 4004 B.C. is given for Genesis 1. This date was computed about 350 years ago by an Irish clergyman, Archbishop Ussher (*Annals*, 1650), who used some of the indications of Scripture and research available to him at that time. Ussher's system is often referred to as the "short chronology" system. Essentially, his method was to add up all the genealogical figures in the Bible, assuming that they were complete. In the early nineteenth century Hales published a system (1809–1814), in which he took the Greek translation of the Hebrew Old Testament (known as the Septuagint, abbreviated LXX) as the basis for the patriarchal generations and computed the date of Creation as 5411 B.C.[8]

There are, however, many other systems of biblical chronology. Over 250 years ago (1738) Des Vignolles, a member of the Royal Society of Berlin, knew of some two hundred attempts to compute the earliest biblical date, ranging from 3483 B.C. to 6984 B.C.[9] Thus, if the computations of various scholars range from about 3500 to 7000 B.C., it is evident that the long-accepted date of 4004 B.C. is not in any sense final and absolute. We must remember that the Bible is not a textbook on chronology any more than it is a textbook on astronomy. The main pur-

[6]Gleason L. Archer, Jr., *A Survey of Old Testament Introduction*, rev. ed. (Chicago: Moody, 1974), 81–118 [ASOTI].

[7]William Henry Green, *The Unity of the Book of Genesis* (New York: Scribner, 1910) [GUG].

[8]William Smith, "Chronology," in *Dictionary of the Bible* (New York: Hurd and Houghton, 1871), 1:446–47 [SDB].

[9]*Cambridge Ancient History*, 2nd ed., "Chronology of Old Testament" (New York: Macmillan, 1924), 1:158 [CAH].

pose of the Bible is to give God's revelation to human beings and to show them their relation to God; nevertheless, when it speaks on matters relating to chronology or astronomy, or any other field, it is true and accurate.

However, the fact that the Bible was not written primarily to give chronological data does not mean that chronological indications are lacking in the Bible. The very fact that the suggested dates for the beginning, noted by Des Vignolles, range approximately from 3500 to 7000 B.C. shows that definite calculations are possible. But why are there such variations? The differences between the Hebrew and Greek texts of the Old Testament gave Ussher a date of 4004 B.C., based on the Hebrew, and Hales a date of 5411 B.C., based on the Greek. Some of the figures given in the Greek translation differ from those given in the Hebrew text. But variations in the interpretation of the Hebrew text make it possible to have other dates than either 4004 or 5411 B.C. In addition, we must entertain the possibility that there are gaps in the genealogies of Genesis.

Possibilities of Gaps in Biblical Genealogies

Genesis 5 and 11 give the genealogy of the descendants of Adam. The usual method of computing the date of Adam is to add the ages of all of his descendants, using the figures given for the age of each at the time of the birth of the son who carried on the line. Bishop Ussher's computation resulted in the date 4004 B.C., but others have arrived at different figures. This does not mean that there is any error in the Bible; it means rather that we do not know all the factors involved in computation. One pertinent question is whether these genealogies are complete or whether they give only the main characters.

B.B. Warfield pointed out that there may be gaps in the biblical genealogies. This is not mere theory but is given possible support by the fact that certain genealogies omit some of the generations. The genealogy in Matthew 1:1–17 omits three kings (Ahaziah, Jehoash, and Amaziah) and indicates that Joram begat Uzziah, who was his great-great-grandson (Matt. 1:8)[10] One of the illustrations of a compressed genealogy in the Old Testament is found in Ezra 7:3, where six generations are omitted (which are given in a more complete genealogy in 1 Chronicles 7:7ff.). Such occurrences indicate that the Bible may not give a complete record in a genealogy but rather an indication of the line of descent.

The question arises: When the Bible states that one person begat another, must not the second person be the son or daughter of the first one, with no gaps in between? The possibility of a gap even in such cases is shown by Matthew 1:8, the text which states that Joram begat Uzziah. The term "son" is also used in the sense of "descendant," shown by the fact that some of those referred to in Genesis 46:18 as the "sons of Zilpah" were actually her grandchildren, and furthermore it is said that they were "born" by her. Thus we see that the expression "born by" may sometimes mean "had as a descendant."[11]

In addition to Warfield and Raven, more recent writers who hold to the fundamentals of the faith have pointed out this possibility of gaps in the genealogies. Oswald T. Allis deals with the problem involved in genealogical notations such as "After Terah had lived 70 years, he became the father of Abram. . ." (Gen. 11:26). Would we not have to allow just seventy years? An examination of the biblical text shows that the whole context

---

[10]B.B. Warfield, "On the Antiquity and Unity of the Human Race," in *Studies in Theology* (New York: Oxford University Press, 1932), 235–58 [WST].

[11]John Raven, *Old Testament Introduction* (New York: Revell, 1910), 134–35 [ROTI].

reads, "After Terah had lived 70 years he became the father of Abram, Nahor and Haran." As Allis points out, it seems improbable that all three of these sons were born the same year, and a comparison of scriptural references (Acts 7:4; Gen. 12:4) shows that actually Abraham was born sixty years later. The words of the verse apparently mean that at the age of seventy, Terah became a father. This does not accord with the theory that we are dealing with a rigid chronology (AFBM, 262). In view of such evidence of compression of genealogies, it seems safe to conclude that the creation of man took place probably sometime between 4000 and 8000 B.C.,[12] or perhaps somewhat earlier, although some conservatives have no hesitancy in allowing a very high age for man.[13]

Date of the Creation of the Universe

The date of the creation of the universe is an entirely different question from the date of the creation of man. The universe may have been created shortly before the creation of man or long before, depending on whether a long period of time is involved in the first two verses of Genesis and whether the days of Creation were twenty-four-hour days or long periods of time. I incline to the view that the days of Creation were literal twenty-four-hour days, but that a long period of time may have elapsed during the era described in Genesis 1:1–2. I recognize, however, the possibility of a second and third view that are sometimes set forth. The second holds that the days of Genesis were long periods of time, while the third states that no long period of time is involved in either the first two verses of Genesis or the creative days. All three views are discussed in the following paragraphs.

According to the first theory, the original creation of the universe and the earth is described in Genesis 1:1, "In the beginning God created the heavens and the earth." Then a period of time followed during which "the earth was formless and empty" (Hebrew, "the earth was desolation and waste," Genesis 1:2a). This period of time may have been of any length, from a few thousand to a few million years, and could include the geological ages observable in the earth's surface. During this period the fall of the angels (2 Peter 2:4; Jude 6), and the fall of Satan (Isa. 14:12–14) may have occurred. After this cataclysmic period, the putting of the world in order is described in Genesis 1:2b, 3ff., "And the Spirit of God was hovering over the waters, and God said, 'Let there be light,' and there was light." The succeeding creative acts took place in six days of twenty-four hours each and included the creation of plants, animals, and man. This view, in my opinion, is best supported by internal biblical evidence as well as by the external evidence from the world itself. Fur-

[12]For additional discussion of gaps in the biblical chronology see AFBM, 261–64; ASOTI, 185–89; Merrill F. Unger, *Introductory Guide to the Old Testament* (Grand Rapids: Zondervan, 1951), 192–94.

[13]Such a "limitless view" is set forth by Byron Nelson, who refers to the glacial age, which he says began to end "some twenty thousand years ago," and then asks, "Why should man not be very, very old, if that is the case? What is there in the Christian religion against it? What doctrine is in any way changed? Six thousand or sixty thousand or six hundred thousand years affect the fundamental situation set forth by the message of the gospel not a whit. Rather, the older man is the greater is the significance of the statement of the New Testament that Christ appeared in the 'last time,' and that we are now living in 'the last times.' " Byron Nelson, *Before Abraham: Prehistoric Man in Biblical Light* (Minneapolis: Augsburg, 1948), 95 [NBA]. Not all Christian scholars are convinced that there is conclusive evidence for placing man's beginning in remote antiquity. It is reassuring, however, to know that any future discoveries, pointing to an extremely early date for man's creation, can easily harmonize with the Scriptures, as shown by Byron Nelson's book.

ther reasons for assigning a long period of time to the first two verses of Genesis and taking the days as twenty-four-hour days will be discussed later when we consider the other two theories.

In the nineteenth century George H. Pember, in his book *Earth's Earliest Ages*, popularized this view that there may have been a long period or gap between Genesis 1:1 and 1:2, and it is sometimes charged that the whole idea is due merely to his book.[14] The possibility of such a gap has, however, been held by many competent theologians, including Hengstenberg (1802–1869), a German Lutheran scholar who became professor of theology at the University of Berlin in 1828; Franz Delitzsch (1813–1890), professor at Erlangen in Germany and an outstanding Old Testament scholar; and others such as Boehme, Oetinger, F. von Meyer, Stier, Keerl, and Kurtz.[15]

According to the second theory, the days of Genesis were long periods of time, perhaps corresponding to the various geological ages. This is sometimes referred to as the "day-age" theory. It is said that this view was held by Josephus, the Jewish historian of the first century A.D., by many rabbis, and by some early Christian fathers, including Irenaeus (2nd century), Origen (3rd century), and Augustine (4th century). Bible believers who hold this view today are not necessarily theistic evolutionists, inasmuch as the latter usually hold that God used evolution as a means of finally producing human beings, and they often attempt to fit the evolutionary process into the creative days of Genesis. On the contrary, most Bible believers who hold the view that the days of Genesis are long periods of time reject the theory of evolution.

I believe that a reasonable literal interpretation of the Bible does not give as much justification to an acceptance of the day-age theory of Creation as to the twenty-four-hour day theory (though I recognize that the day-age theory can be and often is held by a Bible believer who is true to the fundamentals of the faith). It is a principle of literal interpretation that we take a word in its usual sense unless there is definite evidence to show that it is used figuratively. Until rather conclusive evidence to the contrary is forthcoming, I prefer to take the days of Genesis as literal twenty-four-hour days because (1) this is the natural and usual use of the word; (2) the delimiting of the day by "evening and morning" (Gen. 1:5, 8, 13, etc.) would point to a literal day (holders of the day-age theory point out that "and there was evening and there was morning" may be figurative also, indicating the beginning and the end of an era, but this usage would seem a little strained in the light of the context); (3) the reference to the Sabbath day in the Ten Commandments refers to the six creative days and the seventh day of God's rest in such a way as to imply literal twenty-four-hour days (Exod. 20:11). An alternative to the day-age theory as usually stated is the idea that the creative days were literal days, but they were separated by extended periods of time.

According to the third view, the creation of the earth was followed immediately or at least very soon by the creation of plants, animals, and man during creative days of twenty-four hours. This view places the creation of the universe and the earth, as well as man and animal life, all within a brief period, perhaps since 10,000 B.C. Such a view is tenable, but there are factors that point to the possibility of a period of time between the creation of the earth and the creation of man: (1) In warning Israel of God's judg-

---

[14]George H. Pember, *Earth's Earliest Ages* (New York: Revell, c. 1876) [PEEA].

[15]A list of those holding the view that there was a gap is given by George Trumbull Ladd, *The Doctrine of Sacred Scripture* (1883), 1:265 [LDSS]. Ladd himself rejected the view but pointed out those who held it.

ment on backsliding, the prophet Jeremiah presented his vision of the earth as being "formless and empty" (Jer. 4:23), using the same Hebrew words as those applied to the earth in Genesis 1:2. Jeremiah was apparently led to think back to the desolation of the earth before the creation of man and compare it with the cataclysmic state that would result if God's judgment should fall on unrepentant Israel. This use of the very same words could point to a cataclysmic period in Genesis 1:2, which perhaps followed the sinning of the angels and Satan. (2) The geologic ages seem to give evidence of a period longer than a few thousand years. In some areas, several petrified forests have been found superimposed on one another. God could have created them this way, but it is possible that he permitted them to be formed over an extended period of time. Of course, natural scientists generally assign extended billions of years to the age of the earth, with no real degree of unanimity among them as to an approximate age.

Events of the Creation Days

The main events of the creative days may be easily summarized as follows:

First day: Light	Fourth day: Light bearers
Second day: Sky	Fifth day: Marine and aerial life
Third day: Dry land	Sixth day: Land animals and man

There is an orderly progression in the process of creation. The light of the first day corresponds to the light bearers of the fourth day; the sky ("expanse") is established on the second day, and the life that peoples the sea and the sky is brought forth on the fifth; the dry land is made to emerge on the third day, and the inhabitants of the dry land are created on the sixth.

On the first day, God spoke and there was light (Gen. 1:3). Skeptics like Voltaire have inquired, "How could there be light before there was any sun?" Modern science has shown the existence of light apart from the sun, as in the case of phosphorescence and the phenomenon of the Aurora Borealis (northern lights). Furthermore, the sun could have been created in the creative activity in Genesis 1:1-2, and could have already been in existence before the first day (or during the first day; cf. discussion of the fourth day). Sir James Jeans, a British physicist, referring to the words of Genesis that give the explanation of the origin of light, says, "The whole story of its creation can be told with perfect accuracy and completeness in the six words, 'God said, Let there be light.' "[16]

On the second day, God made the expanse of the sky, dividing the earthly from the celestial waters (Gen. 1:6-8). The word *firmament* (kjv) may seem to imply that the Bible writer conceived of the sky as a solid vault ("something firm") in which the sun, moon, and stars are fixed like light bulbs. The liberal writer Skinner held that this was the unscientific view of the ancient Hebrew writers; he says, "The firmament is the dome of heaven, which to the ancients was no optical illusion, but a material structure. . . ."[17] A further analysis gives us the answer to the charge that the Bible is unscientific in this regard. The "firmament" is a mistranslation due to the false astronomy of the Greeks of the third century b.c., who believed that the sky was a solid crystalline sphere. Hence the Hebrew work *rakia'* was ren-

[16]*The Mysterious Universe*, cited in D.E. Hart-Davies, *The Genesis of Genesis* (London: James Clarke, 1932), 32 [HDGG].

[17]John Skinner, *Genesis*, International Critical Commentary (New York: Scribner, 1910), 21 [SG].

dered *stereoma* in the Greek translation of the Old Testament.[18] Then when Jerome translated the Old Testament into Latin,[19] he used the Latin word *firmamentum*, which in turn was rendered by the English word "firmament" in KJV. The original word in the Hebrew, *rakia'*, does not have the idea of something "firm" but comes from a root meaning that which is "stretched out," "attenuated," or "extended," and is best translated "expanse," as in the NIV. It perfectly describes the expanse of the atmosphere of our earth. In summary, the word "firmament" is faulty translation arising from the false science of the third century B.C. and incorrectly translates the original word. Hart-Davies well comments, "Thus, what has been frequently exhibited as a blunder in the Biblical narrative proves to be the product of a mistake in the realm of science; or, shall we say, a misguided attempt on the part of the modernists of two thousand years ago to 'restate' the ancient faith in terms of modern thought?" (HDGG, 39).

On the third day, God caused the waters of the earth to be gathered together, perhaps by the depressing of low places and the elevation of solid ground. The earth was now ready for vegetation, and God said, "Let the land produce vegetation: seed-bearing plants and trees. . . that bear fruit with seed in it" (Gen. 1:11).

On the fourth day, God said, "Let there be lights in the expanse of the sky. . . . God made two great lights. . . ." (Gen. 1:14, 16). There are two main views as to the instituting of the sun, moon, and stars. One view holds that the sun, moon, and stars were created in the original creation of Genesis 1:1ff., but that their

light did not penetrate through the mists to the earth until the fourth day. This view is expressed by Jamieson, Fausset, and Brown: "The sun, moon, and stars were for the first time unveiled in all their glory in the cloudless sky."[20] It might be objected that God is said to have "*made* two great lights" (Gen. 1:16). The word rendered "made" (*'asah*), however, does not necessarily imply a creative act, being different from the word "create" (*bara'*) used in Genesis 1:1. Furthermore, in the next verse (v. 17) it says that God "set them [*nathan*] in the expanse of the sky," employing the Hebrew word usually translated "gave" (*nathan*), which is often used in the sense of "institute." Taking *nathan* in this sense of "institute," we could translate verse 17, "And God instituted [i.e., appointed] them in the expanse of the sky to give light on the earth." Hence this passage may refer to God's declaration of the function of the heavenly bodies rather than to their creation. The word "create" (*bara'*) is not used here. A second view holds that while light was created on the first day, it was concentrated in the sun on the fourth day; that is, at the word of God, the heavenly bodies came into operation as lights of the universe.[21]

On the fifth day, God caused the waters to bring forth marine life and the air to swarm with birds (Gen. 1:20). Why were birds and fish created on the same day? Older commentators (Calvin, Luther) explained it on the ground of their similarity, fins being like wings. It seems likely, however, that it is due to the fact that Creation proceeded from the lower to the higher; fish and birds occupy a lower place in the scale of life than land ani-

---

[18]The Greek translation of the Hebrew Old Testament is called the Septuagint, abbreviated LXX (probably made in the third or second century B.C.).

[19]The Vulgate translation, 4th century A.D.

[20]*A Commentary Critical and Explanatory on the Whole Bible*, single-vol. ed. (Grand Rapids: Eerdmans, 1935), 17 [JFB].

[21]C.F. Keil and F. Delitzsch, *Biblical Commentary on the Old Testament* (Edinburgh: T. & T. Clark, 1872), vol. 1, The Pentateuch, 56 [KD].

mals, especially the mammals (KD, 60–61).

On the sixth day, God made land animals and man (Gen. 1:24–27). Why does the creation of land animals and man fall on the same day? Lange points out that man has his being, as to his bodily appearance, from the earth in common with the animals; the land emerged on the third day of Creation, and now in the corresponding day in the second group of three, that is, the sixth day, the creatures that inhabit the earth were formed.[22] However, there is a great gulf between the animals and man, and one of the prime reasons is the fact that God created man in his own image, in his spiritual likeness (Gen. 1:26). This divine likeness was marred by the Fall, shattered by sin; but when a person puts his trust in Christ he becomes a new creation (2 Cor. 5:17) and "participate[s] in the divine nature" (2 Peter 1:4).

On the seventh day, God rested from his creative work and blessed the seventh day and sanctified it (Gen. 2:2–3). This shows that the sabbath principle of setting apart one day in seven existed from the beginning.

Critical View of Sabbath; Pan-Babylonian Theory

The Babylonian records tell of a certain special day that was observed on the seventh, fourteenth, twenty-first, and twenty-eighth of the month. Another special Babylonian day called shabatum was observed on the fifteenth of the month; shabatum is etymologically the same as the Hebrew sabbath.[23] The critical school has tended to hold that the Hebrew Sabbath was derived from these Babylonian special days. This whole critical tendency to trace the early records of

Genesis back to Babylonian religion and folklore, known as "Pan-Babylonianism," was forcefully presented to the world by Friedrich Delitzsch in his work Babel und Bibel (Babel and Bible), 1902, first given in the form of two lectures before the German emperor, Kaiser Willhelm II.[24] It made such a stir in Germany that even the cab drivers were discussing Delitzsch's ideas. It is said that a cartoon was published showing a dog baying at the moon, with the words coming out of his mouth, "Is Delitzsch right?" The emperor wrote a public letter proclaiming the need of orthodoxy. The evidence shows that the emperor was justified in his rebuke of Delitzsch, as we will see in the next section.

Answer to the Critical View of the Sabbath

An examination of some of the details of the Pan-Babylonian theory shows that it is not supported by the facts. The Babylonian special day differs from the biblical Sabbath in several ways: (1) The Babylonian special day was observed not only on the seventh, fourteenth, twenty-first, and twenty-eighth day, but also on the fifteenth and nineteenth days, and only the last was called shabatum. (2) The tablets call the seventh day "an evil day" or "an unlucky day," whereas Scripture describes it as "a holy day." (3) The restrictions on that day applied only to certain specified individuals, such as the king (shepherd of the great peoples), the seer, and the physician, whereas the Old Testament makes the Sabbath binding on everyone. (4) There was no cessation of business activity on Babylonian special days, in contrast to the Hebrew Sabbath. (5) Although Babylonians had special regard for days that were multiples of

---

[22]John Peter Lange, Genesis (New York: Scribner, 1870), 172 [LCG].

[23]George A. Barton, Archaeology and the Bible, 7th ed. (Philadelphia: American Sunday School Union, 1937), 310 [BAB].

[24]Article on Friedrich Delitzsch, in Encyclopedia Britannica, 14th ed., 7:168.

seven, those days rarely ever fell on the seventh day of the week in their lunar calendar and thus were not equivalent to the Hebrew Sabbath.[25] It does not seem, therefore, that there was any necessary connection between the Hebrew Sabbath and Babylonian special days.

Babylonian Creation Tablets

In the excavation of Nineveh by Layard and Rassam (1850–1854), the library of King Ashurbanipal (ruled 688–626 B.C.) was uncovered, with its multitudes of clay tablets.[26] Among these tablets was found the so-called Babylonian account of Creation, which tells of the conflict between the great god Marduk and the goddess of the deep, Tiamat. Marduk emerged from the conflict triumphant and was adored by both gods and men. During the course of the epic, reference is made to the creation of man.[27]

An examination shows some similarities between the Babylonian epic and the Genesis record of the creation of man: (1) The Babylonian account was written on seven tablets, perhaps corresponding to the seven days of creation. (2) The account of man's creation is found in the sixth tablet, parallel to the Bible's story of the Creation of man on the sixth day (BAB, 296).

The differences, however, are even more pronounced than the similarities: (1) The polytheistic Babylonian account with its many gods is in striking contrast to the majestic record of Creation by the one true and living God. (2) Mythology abounds in the Babylonian account, overlaid with fantastic ideas; Marduk, for example, cut Tiamat into two pieces and used one half as a covering for the heavens. (3) The order is different in many respects: in the Babylonian account the mention of the formation of the world does not occur until the fourth tablet, whereas in the biblical record the world appears early in the creation work of God. (4) A multitude of details is entirely different in the Babylonian account; e.g., Marduk and the lesser deities are all pagan inventions. (5) The whole nature of the Babylonian account is different, since it is basically a hymn to Marduk and has a political purpose. By portraying the preeminent place of her patron deity (Marduk) among the gods, Babylon could advance her cause in her bid for supremacy in Mesopotamia.

Connection Between Creation Tablets and the Bible

If there is any connection between the Babylonian tablets and the true account of Creation given in the Bible, it is likely that the facts regarding Creation were handed down and diffused among many peoples and finally appeared in this variant form in Babylonia with the addition of many legendary and polytheistic features. Our examination shows that the Pan-Babylonian theory of origins is not borne out.

Nature of Genesis 2; Location of Eden

Adam and Eve were placed in a "garden in the east, in Eden" (Gen. 2:8). The second chapter of Genesis, which tells of Eden, is not a variant account of the first, but gives additional details not recorded in Genesis 1. A careful examination shows that Genesis 1 and 2 harmonize. Some

---

[25]I.M. Price, O.R. Sellers, and E. Leslie Carlson, *The Monuments and the Old Testament* (Philadelphia: Judson, 1958), 109–11 [PMOT].

[26]H.V. Hilprecht, *Explorations in Bible Lands During the 19th Century*, (Philadelphia: Holman, 1903), 132, 133 [HEBL].

[27]Alexander Heidel has provided a translation and commentary in his book *The Babylonian Genesis*, 2nd ed. (Chicago: University of Chicago Press, 1951) [HBG]. See also James B. Pritchard, ed., *Ancient Near Eastern Texts Relating to the Old Testament*, 2nd ed. (Princeton: Princeton University Press, 1955), 60–70 [PANET].

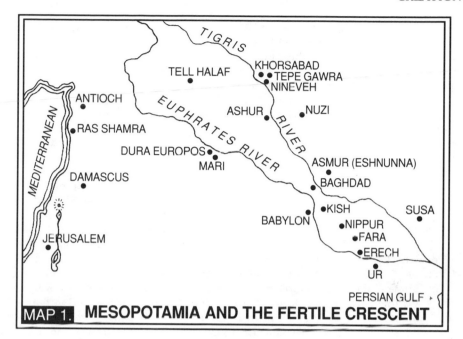

MAP 1. **MESOPOTAMIA AND THE FERTILE CRESCENT**

modern books are misleading when they suggest that there are "inconsistencies in details" between these two chapters.

One of the main purposes of Genesis 2 is to describe the nature of Adam and Eve's environment and the events leading up to the Fall. All of the essential facts are carefully recorded. Even the general location of the Garden of Eden may be ascertained from the facts given. The Bible records that two of the four rivers connected with the Garden of Eden are the Euphrates and the Hiddekel (Gen. 2:14). The Hiddekel River is the river we now call the Tigris. This is demonstrated by Babylonian clay tablets that apply the name Idiglat (of which Hiddekel is a variation) to the Tigris.

Thus we see that Eden was in the region of the Tigris and Euphrates, the area known geographically as Mesopotamia (Greek, meaning "between the rivers"), which today is the country known politically as Iraq.

Identification of the Pison and Gihon is a subject of conjecture. To say that they were ancient irrigation canals does not seem to solve anything. The irrigation culture of ancient Mesopotamia did not develop until the fourth and especially the third millennia B.C., long after the Flood. Irrigation canals would not have existed as early as the Garden of Eden. The precise location of Eden within Mesopotamia is also a subject of pure conjecture. Probably we will never be sure exactly where it was located. The effects of the Noahic flood on the topography of the Near East may have been devastating, making it impossible to determine geographical locations in earliest times on the basis of present conditions. The courses of rivers could have been greatly altered, and some rivers could have disappeared entirely.

That there was such a place of perfection as the Garden of Eden seems to be reflected in the Sumerian account of the land of Dilmun, which was pure, clean, and bright, where "the lion kills not, the wolf snatches not the lamb," where there was no disease or pain, deceit, or guile [ANET, 38].

The land of Dilmun was both a paradise and a real land. In the minds of many, Bahrain Island in the Persian Gulf has been connected with the land of Dilmun even since Henry Rawlinson made the identification in 1861. A Danish expedition under the leadership of Geoffrey Bibby worked on the island for more than fifteen years (beginning in 1953) and believed it to have been the seat of power in a fairly extensive empire. Dilmun reached its zenith as a sea-trading power about 2000 B.C.[28]

Features of Mesopotamia
(Physical, Political)

Since the Garden of Eden was in the vicinity of Mesopotamia, it may be helpful to note some of the main features of this area, even though there has likely been some change since early time. The two main rivers of Mesopotamia are the Euphrates and Tigris. The Euphrates, meaning "that makes fruitful," is 1,780 miles long, and the Tigris, meaning "arrow," is 1,060 miles long. These rivers carry down mud or silt and deposit it along their banks and at the head of the Persian Gulf. Much of southern Mesopotamia consists of this fertile silt. In ancient times canals were maintained between the Euphrates and the Tigris in order to supplement the rainfall, which averages about ten inches per year. The main part of Mesopotamia measures about six hundred by three hundred miles. The terrain gently rises from sea level at the Persian Gulf to about a thousand feet above sea level at Haran in the north.

The earliest inhabitants of this area that can be described with certainty from the archaeological discoveries are the Sumerians, who came on the scene about 3000 B.C. or a little before. A high point of Sumerian culture is illustrated by the materials that Sir C. Leonard Woolley found in his excavation of the cemetery at Ur. These materials are now dated about 2500 B.C.[29] After the middle of the third millennium, Semites filtered into Mesopotamia, apparently coming from the Arabian Peninsula. They reached a prominent position under Sargon of Akkad about 2350. Sargon built the first Mesopotamian empire. From then on, there was a general decline in Sumerian civilization, except for some revival during the Ur III period (c. 2000). During the period 2000–1700, the city of Babylon became very important and gave the name of Babylonia to the area of Mesopotamia that it controlled; Hammurabi was the great king of this era. Following a period of Babylonian decline, the Assyrians emerged in Northern Mesopotamia. Although Old and Middle Assyrian empires may be identified and discussed, the Neo-Assyrian Empire (c. 900–612) is the Assyrian period most significant for biblical study.[30] The years 612–539 B.C. marked the period of Babylonian rule,[31] with Babylon and southern Mesopotamia coming into prominence; this is usually known as the Neo-Babylonian period. It was followed by the domination of the

[28]See Geoffrey Bibby, *Looking for Dilmun* (New York: New American Library, 1969).

[29]C. Leonard Woolley, *Ur of the Chaldees*, rev. by P.R.S. Moorey (London: Herbert Press, 1982) [WUC].

[30]The great kings of the Assyrian Empire included Shalmaneser III (858–824 B.C.), Tiglath-pileser III (745–427), Shalmaneser V (727–722), Sargon II (721–705), Sennacherib (704–681), Esarhaddon (680–669), and Ashurbanipal (668–627); see chapters 17–18. Most of these kings of Assyria came in contact with certain of the kings of Israel and Judah: Shalmaneser III received tribute from Jehu, the tenth king of Israel (for archaeological light, see "Archaeological Confirmation of Jehu," in chapter 16); Tiglath-pileser III received tribute from Menahem, the sixteenth king of Israel (see chapter 17); for other contacts between Assyria and Israel, see chapters 17–18.

[31]The great king of this period was Nebuchadnezzar II (605–562 B.C.). See chapter 20 for the section "Nebuchadnezzar's Control of Judah; Archaeological Evidence of His Building Activity in Babylon."

Persians,[32] 539–331. Alexander the Great brought the Persian Empire to an end in 331 B.C. But let us return to ancient Mesopotamia and Eden.

The Fall of Man (Genesis 3)

God placed Adam and Eve in an ideal environment, where they were tested in regard to obedience. Eve disobeyed, choosing her own self-interest in yielding to Satan's temptation to "be like God" (Gen. 3:5); Adam also sinned, likewise partaking of the Tree of the Knowledge of Good and Evil. When God questioned them, Adam sought to shift the responsibility to Eve (v. 12), and in turn, Eve said, "The serpent deceived me" (v. 13). The consequences of the Fall included the cursing of the ground, the requiring of exhausting labor to gain one's livelihood, and the imposition of temporal death; and in the spiritual realm, the Fall brought about the loss of innocence, the realization of guilt, and finally spiritual death (vv. 16–24).

Temptation Seals

At Tepe Gawra, a few miles north of Nineveh, where excavations were made in 1930–1932 by E.A. Speiser of the University of Pennsylvania, a seal was found that depicted a man, a woman, and a serpent. Since it was found in the level antedating 3000 B.C., Barton remarks, "It strongly suggests that the story of the temptation is very old" (BAB, 46; a picture is found in illustration 176½ in the back of Barton). In earlier excavations, made at Nineveh, another seal was found, now in the British Museum, showing a tree in the center, a man on the right, a woman on the left plucking fruit, and a serpent behind her standing erect (for a picture of this, see PMOT, 116). The significance of these seals lies in the fact that they may point back to the actual temptation in Eden.

Prophecy of Christ; God-Men of Pagan Religions

A prophecy of Christ is implied in the reference to the seed of the woman who would bruise the head of the serpent (Gen. 3:15). The fact that this coming One would be the seed of the woman rather than the seed of the man is an implied prophecy of the virgin birth of Christ, the One "born of a woman" (Gal. 4:4).

Critics have pointed out that pagan religions contain legends of supernatural men who were a combination of god and man. They often try to reduce the position of Christ to the level of the demi-gods of these pagan legends, citing as examples such heroes as the Babylonian Gilgamesh, who was two-thirds god and one-third man.[33] However, Christ was entirely different, because his being comprised no such proportion as two-thirds God and one-third man. Christ was completely God and completely man; all that God was, Christ was; all that man was, Christ was. This is an entirely different concept than the pagan fractional combinations.

---

[32]Cyrus was the first king of the Persian Empire, ruling 539–530 B.C., followed by Cambyses II (529–522). Cyrus gave the Jews permission to return from captivity, a policy illuminated by archaeological discovery (see "Archaeological Light on Cyrus' Policy" in chapter 21). For the other Persian kings, see chapter 22.

[33]James C. Muir, *His Truth Endureth* (Philadelphia: National, 1937), 15 [MHTE]. Muir does not hold this critical view; he merely describes the nature of Gilgamesh.

Chapter 3

Early Civilization

(Genesis 4–11: Cain and Abel, Flood, Babel)

Cain and Abel (Genesis 4:1–15)

After God cast Adam and Eve out of the Garden of Eden, Eve "gave birth to Cain. . . . Later she gave birth to his brother Abel" (Gen. 4:1–2). The Hebrew literally reads, "and she added to bring forth." On the basis of the Hebrew, many commentators believe that Cain and Abel were twins (JFB, 20; SG, 103).[1] Abel became a shepherd and Cain engaged in agriculture. It is evident that they had been instructed, probably by God, in the principle of sacrifice. Each brought an offering. Abel brought of the firstborn of his flock, and "the LORD looked with favor on Abel and his offering," but when Cain brought the products of the ground, the Lord was not pleased (Gen. 4:3–5).

Why was Abel's sacrifice acceptable? Some have thought that it was a matter of material, Abel's offering being animal, or that it was a matter of quality, Cain bringing something inferior, perhaps the first thing he laid his hands on. However, the divine commentary in Hebrews 11:4 shows that Abel's sacrifice was acceptable because his heart was right: "*By faith* Abel offered God a better sacrifice. . ." (MNG, 124). By implication, it is evident that Cain's offering was not acceptable because his heart was not right, for he had not truly trusted in God *by faith*. An external ritual, whether it be sacrifice, baptism, or church attendance, has little or no meaning unless one by faith has trusted in the Lord.[2]

When Cain became angry, God said, "If

[1]John Calvin, *Commentaries on the First Book of Moses, Called Genesis*, trans. from original Latin and compared with the French edition by John King (Edinburgh: Calvin Translation Society, 1847), 189 [CG].

[2]It is sometimes stressed that Abel's sacrifice was acceptable because, being a lamb, its blood was shed and this shedding of blood pointed forward to Christ. This is of course quite true, for "without the shedding of blood there is no forgiveness" (i.e., of sins, Heb. 9:22). The mere shedding of an animal's blood, however, could never make real atonement. In later times, when backslidden Israelites offered lambs but had not turned their heart to the Lord, God said through his prophets that he hated the people's sacrifices (Amos 5:21–22; cf. Isa. 1:11–16). God showed that an empty formality, though it included shedding of blood, was an abomination to him. By analogy, the sacrifice of Abel, though one of blood, could not have been acceptable if his heart had not been turned to the Lord.

you do not do what is right, sin is crouching at your door" (Gen. 4:7). The word sin (*hatta'th*) is often used in the sense of "sin-offering" in the Bible.[3] If it is taken in this sense, then God was actually saying, "If you do not do what is right, a sin-offering is lying at the door," which would seem to indicate that Cain's sin might be made right by a sin-offering that showed a change of heart. But Cain did not make things right with the Lord. When he and Abel were alone in "the field," i.e., the open country, he slew Abel. Even in the face of this sin, God did not forsake Cain, but, responding to Cain's words "whoever finds me will kill me" (Gen. 4:14), God put a mark on him that he might not be slain. Dodd, quoted in Clark's Commentary (p. 59), computed that the family of Adam and Eve and their sons could have increased to 32,000 by this time in Cain's life (cited in MNG, 125–26). Thus there could have been many whom Cain feared to meet.

Early Civilization (Genesis 4), Archaeological Light on Early Cities, Music, and Metal

Cain built a city (Gen. 4:17). When and where the earliest village life appeared is debated. Since the work of Kathleen Kenyon on the early levels of Jericho (1952–1958), many have classified Jericho as the oldest city in the world. Kenyon assigned a date of about 8000 B.C. to early village culture there.[4] But Mureybet (Mureybit), located in the bend of the Euphrates east of ancient Antioch (Modern Antakya), is probably fully as old.[5] And dates of 7500 to 6800 have been assigned to early village life at Cayönü, a town located between

the points where the Tigris and Euphrates originate at the north of Mesopotamia.[6] It is not possible, however, to be dogmatic about these dates, which are assigned largely on the basis of Carbon 14 tests, and scholars in the field have reservations about accepting them.[7] Presumably, too, these dates, if correct, have little to do with cities in the days of Cain, for he lived before the Flood. Such dates might do more to give some indication of the date of the Flood than when the earliest village life occurred, because probably the Flood totally wiped out the earliest villages. In any case, numerous early villages dating from 6000 B.C. on down have been excavated in Mesopotamia, where there was a civilization more advanced than anywhere else. Certainly the use of the wheel, writing, and other trappings of civilization appeared first in Mesopotamia, and there is no real debate over where civilization began.

One of Cain's family, a descendant named Jubal, is referred to as the "father of all who play the harp and flute" (Gen. 4:21). This reference implies an early knowledge of various types of instruments, the harp representing stringed instruments, and the flute, wind instruments. Archaeological discoveries have produced much evidence concerning the early development of musical instruments in the Bible lands. Most of the recent books on the history of music devote a large share of their beginning chapters to the evidence of early music found in the excavations, such as the harps and lyres discovered at Ur of the Chaldees and the string and wind instruments pictured on the Egyptian monuments.[8]

---

[3]CG, 202; W.H. Griffith-Thomas, *Genesis* (London: Religious Tract Society, n.d.), 64 [GTG].
[4]Kathleen Kenyon, *Archaeology in the Holy Land*, 3d ed. (New York: Praeger,, 1970), 331.
[5]James Mellaart, *The Neolithic of the Near East* (New York: Scribner, 1975), 45.
[6]Ibid., 52.
[7]See, for example, Hans J. Nissen, *The Early History of the Ancient Near East* (Chicago: University of Chicago Press, 1988), 4.
[8]See WUC; James B. Pritchard, *The Ancient Near East in Pictures*, 2nd ed. (Princeton: Princeton University Press, 1969), pictures 191–219, 794–97 [PANEP]. The article "Musical Instruments of Israel," by Ovid R. Sellers, appeared in the *Biblical Archaeologist* [BA] 4,3 (September 1941). It deals

A tower at Jericho that has been dated to about 8,000 B.C.

knowledge of iron long before 1200. At a site in Mesopotamia about fifty miles northeast of Baghdad, called Tell Asmar today, but known in ancient times as Eshnunna, Henri Frankfort of the Oriental Institute at the University of Chicago found evidence[9] of an iron blade from the level of 2700 B.C. A small steel ax from Ur and other very early objects of iron have also been found.[10] The fact that a greater abundance of iron has not been found seems to indicate that it was not widely used in early times, but another contributing factor may be that iron oxidizes more quickly and completely than copper, and, having disintegrated, would not be as readily detected in excavating. Numerous archaeological discoveries give evidence of the use of copper during the period 4300–3000. In summary, the excavations indicate some knowledge of metal in early times, as implied in the biblical record (Gen. 4).

Another man in the Cainitic civilization, Tubal-cain, is described as one who "forged all kinds of tools out of brass and iron" (Gen. 4:22). This reference reflects the early use of metal. It was formerly believed that the use of metal began very late, and it is certainly true that metal was probably not widely used in early times. Discoveries have shown, however, that metal was known and used much earlier than previously supposed. The usual date formerly given for the beginning of the Iron Age in the Near East was 1200 B.C., and this date is still used for convenience in listing the metal ages. Modern archaeology, however, shows that there was a

The Long-Lived Patriarchs of the Line of Seth (Genesis 5); Possible Reflection in the Clay Tablets

The descendants of Adam and Eve's son Seth were noteworthy for their longevity. Seth himself lived to be 912 years old, and in the seventh generation after Seth, Methuselah reached the greatest age of all—969 (Gen. 5:27). Most of those who came between Seth and Methuselah lived to be between 800 and 900 years of age.

It is reasonable to believe that people lived a long time when humankind was first on the earth. The effects of sin and disease and the debilitating aspects of civilization had not had time to work their full effect. Climate and diet may

primarily with musical instruments in the middle and later part of biblical history, c. 1000 B.C. and later.

[9]Rusted remains of a blade still clinging to a dagger handle were found by laboratory test to be iron. Oriental Institute Communication [OIC], no. 17, pp. 56ff., published by the University of Chicago; HSAB, article by Meek on Mesopotamia, 168.

[10]Millar Burrows, *What Mean These Stones?* (New Haven: American Schools of Oriental Research, 1941), 158 [BWMS].

have been different in antediluvian times. Considering all the factors, it would be rather surprising if the life span had not been considerably greater when the human family was in its infancy.

A possible reflection of the fact that humans did live to greater ages in early times is seen in some of the Babylonian clay tablets, which tell of early kings who ruled for fabulously long periods; one, named Dumuzi, held sway for eighteen thousand years, and another ruled for thirty-six thousand years.[11] These texts are certainly mythological, but they may well be a legendary account of the fact revealed in the Bible that people did live to greater ages in early times.

The Two Lines of Cain and Seth; Their Mingling (Genesis 4–6)

The ungodly line of Cain, described in Genesis 4:17–24, included Lamech, the first recorded polygamist (technically, polygynist; v. 19) and also the second recorded murderer (v. 23). The godly line of Seth, described in Genesis 5, included Enoch, the man who "walked with God; then he was no more, because God took him away" (Gen. 5:24). It is rather striking that the ages of those in the godly line of Seth are recorded, whereas the ages of those in the line of Cain are not.

Many scholars believe that the separation between the godly line of Seth and godless line of Cain broke down and that their intermarriage is described in Genesis 6:2, "The sons of God saw that the daughters of men were beautiful, and they married any of them they chose." It would appear that the "sons of God" were the god-fearing Sethites,[12] God's spiritual children, whereas the "daughters of men" were those of Cain's line who rose only to

the human level and were not God's children (MNG, 154).

There are several places in the world where clear and lucid rivers merge with muddy and murky rivers. As they join, there is at first no intermingling of the clear and muddy waters, but both flow along in the same river bed, the clear water on one side and the muddy water on the other, with almost a noticeable line of division between them. After some distance, however, the two streams begin to intermingle, and it is not long before the muddy water has made the clear water a turbid brown. From then on it is all muddy. So it was with the lines of Seth and Cain. As long as there was separation, the Sethite line brought forth those who walked with God. But after the beginning of intermarriage and the accompanying breakdown in separation, it was not long until "the LORD saw how great man's wickedness on the earth had become, and that every inclination of the thoughts of his heart was only evil all the time" (Gen. 6:5).

The Flood (Genesis 6–8); the Size of the Ark

Because of this culmination of the wickedness of the human race, God sent the Flood upon the earth. Noah and his family were saved from the waters by means of the ark. The ark is a good illustration of Christ, the One who saves us from the waters of judgment.

The size of the ark is given specifically as being three hundred cubits long, fifty cubits wide, and thirty cubits high (Gen. 6:15). We know, from a certain archaeological discovery, that the standard cubit in the days of the kings of Israel and Judah (900–600 B.C.) was about eighteen inches. In the later years of the nine-

---

[11]Stephen Langdon, *Oxford Editions of Cuneiform Texts* 2, 1 (1923) [LCT]; translation appears in BAB, 317, lines 15, 34.

[12]Some have held that the "sons of God" were fallen angels. This seems unlikely, inasmuch as the Bible indicates that there is no marriage among the angels (Matt. 22:30).

teenth century, archaeologists examined a tunnel in Jerusalem that was built in the days of Hezekiah (c. 700). An inscription at the entrance written in the old Hebrew alphabet tells that this tunnel is twelve hundred cubits long. Measurement of the tunnel revealed that it was about eighteen hundred feet long, thus demonstrating that the cubit was about eighteen inches. Cubits varied somewhat in the ancient world. The Egyptian cubit was about 20.5 inches, the Mesopotamian cubit about an inch shorter than the Egyptian. The "long" cubit of Ezekiel 40:5 may have been equal to the Egyptian cubit.

If the minimum length of the cubit (eighteen inches) is used as a basis for calculating the size of the ark, and if it is assumed that the ark was rather squarely built, then the three floors would give a displacement of 43,000 tons (MNG, 159). This would be just a little smaller than the largest of the pre-World War II Italian liners, the Rex, which had a displacement of about fifty thousand tons. By way of comparison, the *Queen Elizabeth*, built after the war had a displacement of 83,673 tons. There would certainly have been plenty of room in the three decks of the ark for Noah, his family, the animals, and their food.[13]

The Flood Tablets; Area Covered by the Flood

The excavation of Nineveh (1850–1854) produced clay tablets that later proved to be the Babylonian account of the Flood. In many ways this account is very similar to the biblical record of the Flood, and it is a definite reflection of the fact that there must have been a flood.[14]

A tablet with a Babylonian flood account, from the library of Ashurbanipal of Assyria. Now located in the British Museum.

There are two main views among conservative Bible scholars as to the area covered by the Flood: (1) It covered the *inhabited* earth, that is, Mesopotamia and perhaps some of the surrounding lands, but not the whole earth, According to this view, there was no need for a worldwide deluge, because a flood over the inhabited earth would have been sufficient to bring life to an end. (2) The Flood covered the *entire* earth. I recognize the possibility of the first view, but I see no reason why the second view of a universal flood should not be adhered to. Scriptural evidence supports the universality of the

[13]Much has been written in recent decades about the search for Noah's ark. If a search is to be launched, it is necessary, first, to decide where to look. Genesis 8:4 says that the ark "came to rest on the mountains of Ararat," on the eastern border of Turkey. Although one peak is identified as the traditional site, there is no absolute certainty on the matter. Dozens of expeditions have ascended the traditional peak since World War II, but the ark has not yet certainly been found, though members of one or two expeditions have claimed a sighting or even brought back some pieces of wood. Carbon 14 tests on these samples have been inconclusive.

[14]For a discussion of the Mesopotamian Flood accounts, a translation of them, and their relation to the biblical account, see Alexander Heidel, *The Gilgamesh Epic and Old Testament Parallels*, 2nd ed. (Chicago: University of Chicago Press, 1949).

Flood: (1) The fact that every living creature was to be destroyed[15] would indicate that the whole earth was subject to the Flood (Gen. 7:4). Probably the animals had scattered over much of the earth; a universal flood would have been needed to destroy them. (2) All the high hills were to be covered (v. 9). (3) After the Flood was over, God referred to having "destroyed all living creatures" (Gen. 8:21); it would seem that a universal flood would be required to bring this result. There is also a physical reason for positing a universal flood: since water seeks its own level, it is difficult to imagine water being at a great height in Asia Minor and Mesopotamia, and not elsewhere over the earth (MNG, 193).

S.R. Driver objected that the covering of all the high hills by the waters of the Flood would imply a depth of five miles of water over all the earth and that it would be impossible to have this much water.[16] This is answered by two considerations: (1) We do not know how high the mountains were at the time of the Flood; the surface of the earth may have been quite different from what it is now. (2) The Flood was a miracle; whether it would be possible for it to occur today is entirely beside the point; it was God who caused it, and he could cause the earth to be covered to any depth that he chose.

The Noahic Covenant (Genesis 9)

After the Flood, God laid down the principles for the continuation of life on the earth: (1) Provision was made for the transmission of life, "Be fruitful and increase in number" (Gen. 9:1). (2) Provision was made for man's dominion over animal life: "The fear and dread of you will fall upon all the beasts of the earth" (v. 2).

(3) Provision was made for the means of sustaining life: "Every thing that lives and moves shall be food for you" (v. 3). (4) Provision for human government was implied in the statement, "Whoever sheds the blood of man, by man shall his blood be shed" (v. 6); if a man's life could be taken, anything less—his liberty, his property—could be taken. Thus the foundation for civil authority and civil government with penal regulation is given here (JFB, 1-vol. ed., 22; large ed., 104–5).

Noah's Drunkenness (Genesis 9:20–23)

After life began in the new period following the Flood, Noah planted a vineyard; and "when he drank some of its wine, he became drunk" (Gen. 9:20–21). Some commentators hold that Noah was ignorant of the effects of wine before he drank (KD, 155), while others hold that he formerly must have been an agriculturalist and would have known the characteristics of the grape. (In their commentary, Jamieson, Fausset, and Brown [JFB] suggest that because Noah was a pious man, his action may have been due to age or inadvertency.[17]

The Table of Nations (Genesis 10)

The descendants of Noah's three sons—Shem, Ham, and Japheth—are listed in Genesis 10, and the part of Shem's line that culminated in Abraham is given at the end of Genesis 11 (vv. 10–27). This list of the peoples living during the early history of humankind indicates the general direction of their migrations and the location of their settlement. *The descendants of Japheth* (Gen. 10:1–5) seem to have gone to the north and northwest in the direction of the Caspian Sea, the Black Sea, Asia Minor, and later

[15]The question has sometimes been raised as to whether all of the present varieties of animals could have developed since the time of the Flood. Certainly all of the main groups of animals were represented on the ark. The variations we observe today within the main groups of animals could have developed since the Flood.

[16]S.R. Driver, *Genesis*, 99ff. [DG], cited in MNG, 163.

[17]Unless otherwise noted, the references to JFB will be in the one-volume edition.

perhaps into Europe; Gomer, for example (v. 2), may have been the progenitor of the later Gimirrai, who came into Asia Minor from north of the Black Sea. *The descendants of Ham* (vv. 6–20) tended to go south and southwest, to Egypt, Africa, the east coast of the Mediterranean, and Arabia. One indication of the direction that Ham's descendants took is implied in the name Mizraim (v. 6), probably the progenitor of the Egyptians, since Mizraim is the Hebrew name for Egypt in the Bible. *The descendants of Shem* (vv. 21–31) settled in the Near East (Mesopotamia), with some groups going south (to Arabia) and southeast (to Persia, whose ancient name was Elam, v. 22). We do not know to which group some of the present-day peoples belong. Whether the Chinese, for example, form a subdivision of one of the Japhetic, Hamitic, or Semitic groups, or perhaps are a combination of two or more groups we do not know.

The table of nations in Genesis 10 is significant because it emphasizes the brotherhood of the human race in the sense that God is the *Creator* of all humankind. Humans are not united in a spiritual fellowship except by being born again of the Spirit of God. But there is a *natural fellowship* of humans implied in this table of nations and further emphasized by Paul in his message on Mars Hill at Athens when he said that "from one man [God] made every nation. . . that they should inhabit the whole earth" (Acts 17:26). The scriptural teaching concerning this natural brotherhood is a forceful answer to race prejudices that have resulted in race riots in various parts of the world. It is also the answer to the erroneous theories of racial superiority promulgated by totalitarian political groups in this century.

Failure of Man Under the Noahic Covenant; Tower of Babel (Genesis 11)

God laid down the principle of human government in the days of Noah. In the ensuing years, humankind increased and seemed to prosper, but all of this ended in a self-exaltation of humans and a forgetting of God. In a great united effort, people began to build a tower and a great city and to exalt *their* name. They urged each other on by saying, "Let *us* build *ourselves* a city, with a tower. . . that *we* may make a name for *ourselves* and not be scattered. . . ." (Gen. 11:4). God's name was conspicuously absent in their carefully laid plans. It was purely a human effort in which no cognizance was taken of God's sovereignty or directive power.

Archaeological Light on the Tower of Babel (Genesis 11)

At the sites of many ancient cities in Mesopotamia stand the remains of towers, built in several stages or stories. In the Babylonian clay tablets they are referred to as ziggurats and represent a part of the religious structures of the ancient dwellers of Mesopotamia. On top of these staged towers there was usually a shrine. Possibly these towers were modeled after the original tower of Babel.[18]

George Smith, the staff member of the British Museum who translated the Babylonian account of the Flood, published the translation of a fragment that tells of the destruction of one of these ziggurats: "The building of this temple offended the gods. In a night they threw down what had been built. They scattered them abroad, and made strange their speech. The progress they impeded."[19] This account may be a later reflection of what actually occurred when God came down

---

[18]Pictures of the ziggurat at Ur appear in WUC, 143, 148, 151–53. Other pictures of ziggurats may be seen in PANEP, pictures 746–48, 755, 759. A reproduction of the ziggurat at Babylon, sometimes referred to as "The Tower of Babel" but certainly not the original tower of Babel, may be seen at the Oriental Institute Museum of the University of Chicago. A picture of this ziggurat appears in this book on page 40.

[19]George Smith, *Chaldean Account of Genesis* (New York: Scribner, 1876) [SCAG], cited in CBS, 29.

A model of one of the ziggurats or staged towers of ancient Babylonia. On the top of this particular tower stood the temple of Marduk, the chief god of Babylon in the time of Nebuchadnezzar (c. 600 B.C.). These ziggurats were likely the later counterparts of the Tower of Babel (See "Archaeological Light on the Tower of Babel," pp. 39). Courtesy of the Oriental Institute of the University of Chicago.

at the time of the building of the tower of Babel and scattered the people abroad by confounding their language.

Original Unity of Language (Genesis 11)

Before the building of the tower of Babel, "the whole world had one language and a common speech" (Gen. 11:1), but after the rebellion, implied in the building of the tower of Babel, the Lord confounded the language of all the earth (v. 9). Max Mueller, a comparative philologist, declared concerning the common origin of speech, "We have examined all possible forms which language can assume, and we now ask, can we reconcile with these three distinct forms, the radical, the terminational, the inflectional, the admission of one common origin of human speech? I answer decidedly, Yes."[20] The linguistic scholar Swadesh stated, "The case for a single beginning seems

---

[20]Max Mueller, *Science of Language*, 329 [MSL], cited in MNG, 215. Mueller, 1823–1900, was born in Germany and later was made professor of comparative philology at Oxford; see *Encyclopedia Britannica* article on Mueller [EB].

fairly strong."[21] Roucek observed, "Scholars speculate that most languages originated in one universal parent language."[22] While some secular scholars still favor polygenesis in the origin of language, the trend is toward monogenesis.

Concerning the origin of language, the well-known philologist Otto Jespersen of the University of Copenhagen wrote, "Some scholars (among them quite recently W. Schmidt) see the insufficiency of the usual theories, and giving up all attempts at explaining it in a natural way fall back on the religious belief that the first language was directly given to the first men by God through a miracle."[23]

I see no reason for doubting the biblical indication concerning the original unity of language, or the implication that humankind had speech from the beginning.[24] No discovery, ancient or modern, has shown otherwise.

The Nature of Genesis 1–11

As we have seen, the first eleven chapters of Genesis deal with universal history, describing the creation of the universe and humankind, the fall of the human race, the Flood, and the tower of Babel. Humans were tested three times during this period, and each test ended in failure: first, in the disobedience in Eden; second, in the sin that brought the judgment of the Flood; and finally in humankind's self-exaltation and the forgetting of God, which culminated in the scattering of the people and the confusion of tongues at Babel.

Humankind as a whole had failed three times, and God now chose one man, Abraham, to be a witness to him and a blessing to the entire human race (Gen. 12:1–3). The call of Abraham and the events of his life are dealt with in the next chapter.

[21]Morris Swadesh, *The Origin and Diversification of Language* (Chicago: Aldine-Atherton, 1971), 215.

[22]Joseph S. Roucek, *The Study of Foreign Languages* (New York: Philosophical Library, 1968), 7.

[23]"Language," EB (1942), 13:702.

[24]Shown by several statements in Genesis 1–3. "The man said, 'This is now bone of my bones. . .' " (2:23); "The man gave names to all the livestock. . ." (2:20); cf. 3:2, 10, 12.

Chapter 4

Abraham's Early Life in Canaan

(Genesis 12–20)

The Time of Abraham

The era of Abraham is frequently thought to have begun about 2000 B.C., and that is a useful approximation. To arrive at a more precise date, it is necessary to work backward, with the use of fairly specific chronological reckonings. In this venture I prefer to stick with the Hebrew text of the Old Testament. Solomon probably began to reign in 970 B.C. According to 1 Kings 6:1, the Exodus took place 480 years before the fourth year of Solomon's reign, or about 1446. Exodus 12:40–41 puts the entrance of the patriarchs into Egypt 430 years earlier—about 1876. From a study of Genesis 12:4; 21:5; 25:26; and 47:9 we can infer that the patriarchs sojourned in Canaan 215 years, entering about 2091.[1] Since Abraham was seventy-five when he entered Canaan, his birth would be pegged at 2166 B.C.

Those who follow the Septuagint, the Greek translation of the Old Testament, arrive at a slightly later date for Abraham,

perhaps about 2085 B.C. for his birth and 2010 as the date for his entrance into Canaan. Many who cut themselves loose from the chronological specifics of the Old Testament text place the patriarchal period in a general way during the first half of the second millennium B.C. Among such there is no unanimity of opinion in regard to the chronology of the patriarchs.

The Genealogical Descent of Abraham
(Genesis 11–12)

Abraham's line of descent from Noah's son Shem appears in Genesis 11. This may be a complete geneaology, but on the other hand it may name only the important people in the line of descendants (See chapter 2, the section entitled "Possibilities of Gaps in Biblical Genealogies," 22–23). Abraham's line of descent from Shem is recorded as follows: Shem, Arphaxad, Salah, *Eber*, Peleg, Reu, Serug, Nahor, Terah, and Abraham (Gen. 11:10–

---

[1]In these references it is clear that Abraham entered Canaan at the age of 75. Isaac was born when Abraham was 100. Isaac was 60 at Jacob's birth, and Jacob was 130 when he stood before Pharaoh. A total of 215 years elapsed, then, between Abraham's entrance into Canaan and Jacob's entrance into Egypt.

26). Since the name *Eber* comes from the same Hebrew root as the word *Hebrew*, many Bible scholars believe that *Hebrew* is derived from *Eber*,[2] and that both the Hebrews of Abraham's line and several other related peoples were descendants of Eber. In the Old Testament, however, the term *Hebrew* is ordinarily applied to the Chosen People only, those descended from Abraham through Isaac and Jacob.[3]

Archaeological Light on the Place of Abraham's Birth

Abraham's father, Terah, lived in Ur of the Chaldees in southern Mesopotamia. Here Abraham grew up and spent his younger days. As a result of the archaeological excavations conducted at Ur (1922–1934) by C. Leonard Woolley, a great deal is now known about this city; in fact, the whole background and environment of Abraham can now be pictured. The type of house of the Abrahamic period was well illustrated at Ur. An average dwelling measured forty by fifty-two feet. The lower walls were built of burned brick, the upper of mud brick, and the whole wall was usually plastered and whitewashed. An entrance lobby led into the central court, onto which all the rooms opened. On the lower floor were located the servants' room, the kitchen, the lavatory, the guest chamber, and also a lavatory and wash place reserved for visitors. Thus all of the first floor was utilized for the servants and guests; the second floor housed the family. The entire house of the average middle-class person had from ten to twenty rooms (WUC, 191–204).

Other discoveries at Ur showed that education was extensive in the days of Abraham. Young scholars learned to write the cuneiform signs as they were demonstrated by the schoolmaster on a flattened lump of soft clay. They also had reading lessons. Other clay tablets showed that in mathematics they learned the multiplication and division tables, and as they progressed they were subjected to working at square and cube roots and simple exercises in geometry. When the results of this part of the excavation are reviewed, one finds that four thousand years ago, in the days of Abraham, the pupils had the same "reading, writing, and 'rithmetic" as their modern counterparts struggle with today.

The degree of literacy in Ur and the number of documents recovered from the site puts the biblical narrative in a new light. As a member of the upper class, Abraham could well have been able to read and write. If he could not, he had sufficient wealth to maintain a scribe to keep business accounts and to record historical events. Usually it is assumed that patriarchal history was passed down through oral tradition, and many doubt the veracity of numerous facets of it. But in the light of newer discoveries, it is entirely reasonable to expect that Abraham passed on written accounts, and Moses had some of those at hand when he wrote Genesis. Moreover, Moses himself was highly educated as a member of the court of Egypt and in later life presumably would have supervised whatever archives existed among the Hebrews at that time.[4]

Even evidence of the far-reaching extent of the commerce of that day was revealed when a bill of lading of about 2040 B.C. was unearthed. It showed that a ship had come up the Persian Gulf to southern Mesopotamia after a two-year cruise. The cargo included copper ore,

[2]The Hebrew word *eber* means "beyond." In this case it would designate the people who came from "beyond" the Euphrates, i.e., Abraham and his people.

[3]See Exodus 1:15–16, 19; 5:3; 10:3; 1 Samuel 4:6, 9; for other references consult a concordance.

[4]For a discussion of Sumerian education, see Samuel N. Kramer, *History Begins at Sumer* (Philadelphia: University of Pennsylvania Press, 1981), chapter 1. See also C.L. Woolley, *Abraham* (New York: Scribner, 1936), 103 [WA].

gold, ivory, hardwoods for the cabinet maker, and diorite and alabaster for making statuary. Several of these imported materials came from quite distant lands. But our knowledge of the business affairs of Ur during her golden age is not dependent on a single bill of lading. Other bills of lading, invoices, letters of credit, court cases, and tax records have also come to light (WA, 118–33).

The Call of Abraham

Terah took his family from Ur and moved to Haran in northern Mesopotamia, about six hundred miles northwest of Ur (ABB, 45). There he died (Gen. 11:32).

While Abraham was still in Mesopotamia, the Lord called him to leave his land and his people and go into the land that God would show him, which proved to be Canaan (Gen. 12:1).

Idolatry and Pagan Worship
in the Days of Abraham;
Light from Archaeology

Abraham was called to go out from the midst of idolatry and paganism. Several hundred years later when Joshua referred to the family of Abraham, he said that they had "served other gods" (Josh. 24:2). C. Leonard Woolley's excavation at Ur (1922–1934) shed much light on the pagan religion that flourished there in the days of Abraham. The chief deity of the city was the moon-god named Nanna (formerly spelled Nannar), whose temple and ziggurat were in a large area measuring 1,200 by 600 feet. The ziggurat was a tower consisting of a solid mass of brick 200 feet long, 150 feet wide, and about 70 feet high. Massive brick stairways led to the upper levels, and on the topmost (the third) rose a temple to the god. At the foot of the ziggurat stood a temple to Nanna, which he apparently shared with his wife,

the moon-goddess Ningal. Adjacent to the temple was a kitchen for the preparation of sacrifices that were shared by the god, the priests, and worshipers (WUC, 137–60). Nearby, excavators uncovered another temple, the Ekhursag, a worship center for the cult of the ruling king. Offerings were also made to the spirit of the king after he died (WUC, 161, 167).

The Abrahamic Covenant
(Genesis 12:1–3)

God's covenant with Abraham included several promises:

1. *"I will make you into a great nation"* (Gen. 12:2). This has been fulfilled numerically.[5] Moreover, this promise has been fulfilled in the influence that both the nation Israel and individual Israelites have had, not only in spiritual spheres but also in the economic, cultural, and political affairs of the secular world.

2. *"I will bless you"* (v. 2). Abraham was blessed temporally (in cattle, silver, and gold—Gen. 13:2) and spiritually. These blessings have been shared by his descendants, particularly when they have kept their eyes on the Lord.

3. *"I will make your name great"* (v. 2). Abraham is revered even today by Jew, Arab, and Christian alike; particularly for the child of God, he is the "father of the faithful."

4. *"You will be a blessing"* (v. 2); this is better translated "Be a blessing," because the verb is in the imperative mood (the same form of the Hebrew verb is used in Genesis 17:1, "Be blameless"). God's command that Abraham be a blessing shows his missionary purpose for Israel. The nation was to give not only a passive testimony to the Lord, but also a positive witness—"Be a blessing."

5. *"I will bless those who bless you, and whoever curses you I will curse"* (v. 3). In

---

[5]In spite of Hitler's efforts to destroy the Jews during World War II, Jewish population worldwide stands at over 17,000,000 in 1991, *World Almanac and Book of Facts 1991* (New York: Pharos Books, 1990), 610.

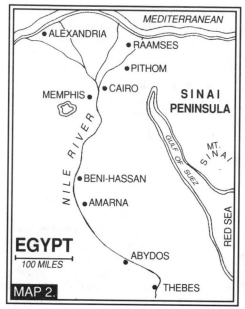

MAP 2.

ration for the Messiah and Savior (Isa. 53), and (4) a channel of blessing for the world (Rom. 15:8–12).

Abraham in Canaan; the Problem Concerning the Existence of Certain Towns in Abraham's Day (Genesis 12)

When Abraham came into Canaan, he lived for a time near Shechem (Gen. 12:6), about thirty miles north of Jerusalem, in a plain within the central mountain ridge of Palestine. Later he moved a few miles to the south and pitched his tent between Bethel and Ai (v. 8), some twelve miles north of Jerusalem. Here he built an altar to the Lord and worshiped.

The results of archaeological excavation seem to conflict with the biblical account at this point because all three of the places mentioned were uninhabited or virtually so when Abraham came through. In his work at Shechem, Wright found that there had been an extensive settlement there in the Chalcolithic period, in the fourth millennium B.C., and that the next major settlement began about 1850 (EAEHL, 4:1086). In his excavations at Et-Tell, identified with Ai, Callaway discovered that the early town there had been destroyed about 2400 B.C. and that the site had been abandoned until about 1200 (EAEHL, 1:49). At Bethel, Kelso found that the village dating to the period 2400–2200 was abandoned about 2200, and around 2000 a new period of occupation began (EAEHL, 1:192). What is one to do with this problem?

In the first place, Et-Tell probably is not to be identified with Ai.[6] Second, although Bethel has long been identified with Beitin, Bimson and Livingston question that conclusion also.[7] Obviously, if we have not yet found the location of either town with certainty, there is no conflict between the discoveries of archaeology and the intimations of Scripture. Third,

Abraham's own life this was observable, and in later years it has been apparent that those countries that have treated the Jews well have prospered.

6. *"All peoples on earth will be blessed through you"* (v. 3). This is messianic in its implications, as shown by the New Testament references to God's promises to Abraham (Gal. 3:8, 16). From Abraham came the line of descent that culminated in the human body of Christ. Through Christ true blessing has come to the earth, a fulfillment of the promise to Abraham that in him all families of the earth would be blessed.

With these promises to Abraham, God began to deal specifically with the Chosen People. His purposes for Abraham and the nation Israel were at least fourfold. Israel was to be (1) a witness to the rest of humankind regarding the reality and nature of God, (2) a depository of God's revelation (Rom. 3:1–2), (3) a prepa-

[6]See the discussion in chapter 10.
[7]See also the discussion in chapter 10.

A high place with altars for sacrifice at Et-Tell.

Abraham stopped only in the vicinity of the "site" of Shechem and at a point between Bethel and Ai. No contact with the inhabitants of these places is indicated, so it does not matter if they were largely deserted. The traditional locations would have been known in his day, and a few inhabitants may have lived in each place. As a matter of fact, in Palestine and much of Syria deurbanization had set in as early as the twenty-fourth century B.C. and certainly characterized the period 2200–2000. Then, gradually and later more rapidly, reurbanization of Palestine began during the twentieth century and was completed during the nineteenth.[8]

This deurbanization process permitted Abraham and Isaac considerable freedom to move about the country, but reurbanization would have restricted or threatened the activities of Jacob and his sons at a later time. Perhaps it is providential that the Hebrews were out of the country and living in Egypt while the Amorites and others were building the kind of power evident when the spies reconnoitered the land after the Exodus. Although there may be some problem connected with the existence of Shechem, Bethel, and Ai in Abraham's day, evidently archaeological discoveries do not show the Bible to be in error; and what we now know about the urbanization process in Palestine indicates that there was a considerable vacuum into which Abraham and Isaac could have moved if they were there in the twenty-second and twenty-first centuries B.C.

[8]See Suzanne Richard, "Toward a Consensus of Opinion of the End of the Early Bronze Age in Palestine-Transjordan," BASOR (Winter 1980), 5–34; Yohanan Aharoni, *The Archaeology of the Land of Israel*, trans. Anson F. Rainey (Philadelphia: Westminster, 1982), 81–97; John Bright, *A History of Israel*, 3rd ed. (Philadelphia: Westminster, 1982), 54–55.

Abraham in Egypt (Genesis 12:10–20); Archaeological Confirmation of "Strangers in Egypt"

The Genesis account declares that when a famine came to Canaan, Abraham went down to Egypt, where the Nile River almost always assured a harvest. The historian Diodorus indicated that Egypt was not open to strangers until about the seventh century B.C., thus seeming to contradict the biblical statement that Abraham went to Egypt.[9] Archaeological discoveries, however, show that people from the region of Palestine and Syria were coming to Egypt in the period of Abraham. This is clearly indicated by a tomb painting at Beni Hassan, dating a little after 2000 B.C. It shows Asiatic Semites who have come to Egypt.[10] Furthermore, the archaeological and historical indications of the coming of the Hyksos into Egypt c. 1900 B.C. provides another piece of evidence showing that strangers were allowed to come into that land (see beginning of chapter 7). Their entrance was almost contemporary with that of Abraham. The Bible is correct in this indication, and Diodorus was wrong.

Many other aspects of Abraham's sojourn in Egypt are illuminated or confirmed by archaeological discoveries. A possible reason for Abraham's saying that Sarah was his sister rather than his wife (Gen. 12:11–13) is furnished by the discovery of a papyrus document relating that Pharaoh had a beautiful woman brought to his court and caused her husband to be murdered. One can see why Abraham wished it to be understood that he was the brother of Sarah rather than her husband.

The Bible enumerates the various possessions that belonged to Abraham while he was in Egypt: "And Abram acquired sheep and cattle, male and female donkeys, menservants and maidservants, and camels" (Gen. 12:16). Archaeological monuments show the presence of sheep, oxen, and donkeys in Egypt. For example, such animals are portrayed on the walls of the beautiful temple of Hatshepsut at

---

[9]Popular books on archaeology in the past have frequently alluded to the critical view that strangers could not have come into Egypt in earlier times, and often traced the basis of such an idea back to the first-century historians Strabo or Diodorus, but ordinarily no further documentation was given. For example, Neatby said that the critic could quote Strabo, the Greek geographer and historian, who stated shortly before the time of Christ that "not till the time of Psammetichus [654 B.C.] did Egypt open its ports to strangers or grant security to foreign traders." T. Miller Neatby, *Confirming the Scriptures* (London: Marshall, Morgan and Scott, n.d.), 24 [NCS].

I have not felt that undocumented statements of this type were adequate. A detailed examination of the writings of Strabo and Diodorus has shown, however, that such an implication was given by Strabo, and a point-blank statement was made by Diodorus. They are provided below.

Strabo: "Now the earlier kings of the Aegyptians, being content with what they had and not wanting foreign imports at all, and being prejudiced against all who sailed the seas, and particularly against the Greeks (for owing to scarcity of land of their own the Greeks were ravagers and coveters of that of others), set a guard over this region and ordered it to keep away any who should approach" (*The Geography of Strabo*, E.T., Horace Leonard Jones, 8 vols. (London: Heinemann; New York: Putnam, 1932), 8:27, 29 (Book 17, 1, 6) [GS]).

Diodorus: "Psammetichus . . . regularly treated with kindness any foreigners who sojourned in Egypt of their own free will . . . and, speaking generally, he was the first Egyptian king to open to other nations the trading-places through the rest of Egypt and to offer a large measure of security to strangers from across the seas. For his predecessors in power had consistently closed Egypt to strangers, either killing or enslaving any who touched its shores" (*Diodorus of Sicily*, E.T., C.H. Oldfather, 10 vols. (London: Heinemann; New York: Putnam, 1933), 1:235 (Book 1, 67, 9, 10) [DS]).

[10]This painting, in the tomb of Khnumhotep at Beni Hassan, portrays the arrival of thirty-seven Semitic tribesmen who apparently came to trade with the local ruler, offering the fragrant cosmetics desired by the Egyptians. J.H. Breasted, *A History of Egypt* (New York: Scribner, 1912), 187 [BAHE].

A painting from the tomb of Khnumhotep at Beni Hassan, showing the arrival of Semitic tribesmen in Egypt shortly after 2,000 B.C.   Lehnert and Landrick, Cairo.

Dôr el Bahri at Thebes (c. 1500 B.C.) and in the tomb of Ti at Saqqarah (c. 2200).

The casual reader usually takes no particular notice of the indication that Abraham had camels among his possessions in Egypt (Gen. 12:16). The critics, however, have set this aside as an error, asserting that camels were not known in Egypt until long after the time of Abraham. A study of archaeological material, however, reveals a knowledge of the camel in Egypt even before the time *MB of Abraham.[11] Archaeological evidence showing early knowledge of the camel in Egypt includes statuettes and figurines of camels, plaques bearing representations of camels, rock carvings and drawings, camel bones, a camel skull, and a camel hair rope. These objects, some twenty in number, range from the seventh century B.C. back to the period before 3000.[12] In recent years numerous indications of the domestication and use of the camel in Mesopotamia and Syria during the patriarchal period have come to light. K.A. Kitchen has collected some of this information.[13] Thus the evidence again shows the authenticity of the record concerning Abraham.

Abraham Again in Canaan; His Separation from Lot (Genesis 13); Archaeological Light

After Abraham returned to Canaan from Egypt, he found that frequently

[11]J.P. Free, "Abraham's Camels," *Journal of Near Eastern Studies* (July 1944), 187–93.

[12]Cf. chapter 14, the section entitled "The Visit of the Queen of Sheba. . . Camels and Sheba," pages 145–46.

[13]K.A. Kitchen, *Ancient Orient and Old Testament* (Chicago: InterVarsity, 1966), 79–80; idem, "Camel," *Illustrated Bible Dictionary* (Downers Grove, Ill.: InterVarsity, 1980), 1:228–30.

there was strife between his herdsmen and those of his nephew Lot. Abraham proposed that they separate and generously offered to have Lot choose any part of Canaan that he might wish (Gen. 13:9). Lot looked about and chose the Plain of Jordan (vv. 10–11), which includes the Jordan Valley and the area around the Dead Sea. Today this whole area is the hottest part of Palestine, with temperatures ranging from 104 to 118 degrees on some August days. The biblical record of Lot's choice of the Jordan Plain might seem to be an error. Why did he not choose the attractive maritime plain, or the hill country, or the central mountain ridge region of Palestine? Excavations at Khirbet Kerak, Beth Shan, Jericho, Teleilat el Ghassul, Bab ed-Dra, and other sites have demonstrated that many people were living in the Jordan Valley and region of the Dead Sea, the area of the "Plain of Jordan," in the third and second millennia B.C.

Some have thought that there may have been a drastic change in climate in the Jordan area during the earliest times, but Nelson Glueck reports that there is no evidence of such a change. Whatever the ultimate explanation, Glueck's explorations both before and after 1940 showed that the area had been "densely inhabited," for he discovered more than seventy ancient sites, many of them founded more than five thousand years ago.[14] Glueck concluded that there should be no more "prattle" of an "emptiness in the Jordan Valley!" Thus the archaeological discoveries have shown that no one who

knows the facts can set aside as inaccurate the biblical record of Lot's choice of the Jordan area.

The Battle of the Four Kings Against the Five (Genesis 14); Archaeological Light and Confirmation

After Lot had moved down to the region of the Plain of Jordan and had established his home at Sodom, a military coalition of four kings from Mesopotamia came to this area and made war with five kings who lived near the Dead Sea, including the king of Sodom and the king of Gomorrah (Gen. 14:1–2). When the Mesopotamian kings started back to their native land, they took Lot along as part of their booty (vv. 11–12). Abraham pursued the army of these kings and recovered Lot (v. 16).

Genesis 14 has been regarded as unhistorical by such critics as Noldeke. These critics have said that (1) the names of the Mesopotamian kings are fictional or unhistorical; (2) in the days of Abraham there was no such extensive travel as indicated by this military expedition; and (3) there was no line of march east of Palestine, as indicated by Genesis 14:5ff.

Archaeological discoveries have helped to confirm the validity of Genesis 14. Inscriptions found in recent years have shown that the names of the Mesopotamian kings may in some cases be identified with names of persons already known from the discoveries, and that, in any case, they fit into the pattern of Babylonian names.[15]

---

[14]Nelson Glueck, *The River Jordan*, (Philadelphia: Westminster, 1946), 73 [GRJ].

[15]The old identification of Amraphel with Hammurabi is no longer held. Albright suggested equating Amraphel with Amud-pi-el ("enduring is the word of El"), a king named in the Mari tablets and powerful in Babylonia in the century before Hammurabi (D.J. Wiseman, "Hammurabi," *Zondervan Pictorial Encyclopedia of the Bible*, ed. Merrill C. Tenney, 5 vols. [Grand Rapids: Zondervan, 1975–1976], 3:26). Although reference to Chedorlaomer has not yet been found in the inscriptions, it is often pointed out that there are two Elamite elements in his name: *Chedor* (*Kudur*), found in various Elamite names; and *laomer*, the softening of the name of an Elamite goddess, Lagamar. Tidal, king of Goiim, has been identified with Tudhalias (several Hittite kings were so named); and Arioch, king of Ellasar, has been identified with Arriwuk (a name appearing in the Mari texts). Whether or not these identifications are accepted, it can readily be seen that

Evidence concerning ancient travel in the days of Abraham has been discovered in a clay tablet found in Babylonia, and also in another group of tablets found at the edge of present-day Syria at the site of the ancient city of Mari. The Babylonian tablet contains a contract stipulating that a wagon was rented on condition that it *not* be driven over to the Mediterranean coastlands. It shows that in the days of Abraham travel from Mesopotamia to the Mediterranean was so common that when a person rented a wagon he ran the risk of having it worn out by being driven several hundred miles to the seacoast in the vicinity of Syria and Palestine. Certainly this gives an answer to any idea that extensive travel was improbable in the days of Abraham.[16] Moreover, as early as 2300 B.C. Sargon of Akkad (near Babylon) made raids on the Amorites of Syria and Palestine. Of particular significance for the present study is the fact that prior to Hammurabi's rule in Babylon, Kudur-Mabug, an Elamite king of Larsa (north of Ur), claimed to be "prince of the land of Amurru," which probably included Palestine and Syria.[17]

Evidence concerning the line of march to the east of Palestine was discovered by the American archaeologist W.F. Albright of Johns Hopkins University. He says he "formerly considered this extraordinary line of march as being the best proof of the essentially legendary character of the narrative."[18] Writers who follow the critical view in part or in whole are now inclined to give more credence to the validity of these events in the life of Abraham. Caiger, who made some con-

cessions to the critical view, came to acknowledge that "there seems to be no reason to question a factual basis of Genesis 14" (CBS, 34).

Abrahamic Covenant Confirmed (Genesis 15)

After Abraham recovered Lot, he might have feared some retaliation on the part of the Mesopotamian kings, but God reassured him with the comforting words, "Do not be afraid, Abram. I am your shield. . ." (Gen. 15:1). This was followed by the promise that Abraham's descendants should be as numerous as the stars of heaven. Abraham "believed the Lord, and he credited it to him as righteousness" (v. 6). This is a very significant verse, for here is the first appearance of the words *believe*, *credit*, and *righteousness*. Any study of the great Bible truths of belief or faith, of imputation, and of righteousness must take into account this important passage. We would call Abraham's belief in God "saving faith," for in all ages, human beings have been saved by faith in the Lord and have had God's righteousness imputed or put to their account. The Old Testament saints looked forward to the coming of the promised Seed (Christ), and they were saved by faith through his shed blood, just as believers today look back to the cross and are saved by faith "just as they are" (Acts 15:11). Old Testament saints, coming before the debt of sin was actually paid on the cross, were in the position of those who have an antedated check, a

---

Genesis 14 does not introduce fictional forms but good Near Eastern names. It may also be interesting to observe, in passing, that Babylonian clay tablets dating to the patriarchal period mention Abarama and Abamrama, very close in form to the Hebrew Abraham and often equated with Abraham, though of course they do not refer to the patriarch himself (FLAP, 73).

[16]A translation of this wagon contract may be found in G.A. Barton, *Archaeology and the Bible*, 7th ed., 346–47.

[17]A.T. Clay, *Light on the Old Testament from Babel*, 2nd ed. (Philadelphia: Sunday School Times, 1907), 137.

[18]W.F. Albright, *The Archaeology of Palestine and the Bible* (Cambridge, Mass.: American Schools of Oriental Research, reprint 1974), 142 [AAPB].

check for which the funds will surely be deposited.

Seeking a Posterity—Ishmael
(Genesis 16)

God's covenant and promise to Abraham that he would have a great posterity (Gen. 15:5), who would possess the Promised Land (vv. 18ff.), seemed to arouse in Sarah a desire to have an heir even though she had no children. Sarah gave her handmaid Hagar to Abraham as a secondary wife, and to Abraham and Hagar was born a son, Ishmael. In seeking posterity by this means, Abraham and Sarah were "running ahead of the Lord." God in his own time allowed them to have their own rightful child, Isaac.

Archaeological Light on Sarah's Giving Hagar to Abraham (Genesis 16)

Nowhere do we read that God instructed Sarah to give Hagar to Abraham as a secondary wife. It was quite evidently her own idea. Archaeological discoveries show us the probable source of the idea. The Code of Hammurabi[19] indicates that in Babylonia a wife might give a servant as a secondary wife to her husband in order to have children by the servant girl. Thus Abraham and Sarah were not following the directive will of God but rather the laws and customs of the old land out of which they had come.[20]

God's Covenant with Abraham; Circumcision and Archaeology
(Genesis 17:1–14)

God next revealed himself to Abraham as El Shaddai, Almighty God (Gen. 17:1). He then changed Abram's name to Abraham (vv. 4–5) as a symbol of the covenant and the new relationship between Abraham and God and ordained circumcision (vv. 11–12) as an external sign of a covenant relation with God. Circumcision did not save Abraham or bring him and his posterity into vital relation with God, any more than baptism today saves a child or an adult; both are external tokens of a covenant with God and a trust in God.

Archaeological discoveries show that the practice of circumcision can be traced back to the days of Abraham. This surgical operation is pictured on the Egyptian reliefs that go back into Old

---

[19]The Code of Hammurabi codified many laws and practices that had been in use for generations. This is demonstrated by the subsequent publication of the Code of Lipit-Ishtar, which contains laws similar to those of the Code of Hammurabi and which antedates it by two centuries (Francis Steele, "The Lipit-Ishtar Law Code," *American Journal of Archaeology* [April-June 1947]:158–64).

Evidence of other early laws has been found in the excavation of Tell Hermel (1945ff.) in the region of modern Baghdad. A quantity of clay tablets was discovered that included many laws of the time of Bilalama (nineteenth century B.C., minimal chronology). One of these laws parallels a law in Exodus 21:35. (Cf. W.F. Albright, "A Decade of Middle Eastern Archaeology, 1939–1948," in *Palestine Affairs*, 4, 2 [February 1949]: 24). The code of Bilalama consists of a preamble and fifty-nine sections, covering business relations, specified prices and wages, penalties for non-fulfillment, trespass, marriage, deposit, sale, and torts and injuries caused by persons, animals, and things. See *Sumer*, 4, 2 (1948): 63–102; cited in AJA, 53, 4 (October–December 1949): 398.

For details of the discovery and nature of the Code of Hammurabi, see chapter 9. From what is said here, evidently the Code of Hammurabi was not the earliest law code, and it was not original. Some scholars now believe that its chief function was to bring up to date the common law of Mesopotamia. Of course it is the longest and most complete early law code of the region, and it antedates the Mosaic code by at least three or four centuries.

[20]This archaeological light is significant in refuting the idea that God sanctioned or even demanded polygyny (plurality of wives) in the Old Testament. The practice of polygamy in the Old Testament period was carried on under the permissive will of God, not under his directive will.

At the top of the Code of Hammurabi, Hammurabi portrays himself standing before the sun god Shamash, god of justice, to receive the laws of his code. This code, from the period 2000–1700 B.C., contains advanced laws similar to some of those in the Mosaic laws (1500–1400). In view of this archaeological evidence, the destructive critic can no longer insist that the laws of Moses are too advanced for his time. (See "Critical View of the Legislation of Deuteronomy . . . ," page 103.)   Located at Louvre Museum

Testament times.[21] Ancient burials in Egypt contain bodies that give evidence of circumcision, further showing the early establishment of this practice.[22]

Announcement of the True Heir— Isaac (Genesis 17:15–27)

Following the institution of circumcision, God announced to Abraham that he

and Sarah would have a son (Gen. 17:16, 19). Abraham laughed (v. 17), probably out of amazement because of his advanced age (one hundred) and that of Sarah (ninety). Later when the angelic visitors came to Abraham at Mamre, near Hebron (twenty miles south of Jerusalem), Sarah also laughed when she overheard their announcement that a son was to be born to her and Abraham (Gen. 18:12). Subsequently, when the child was born, he was named Isaac, meaning "laughter" (Gen. 21:6), because of the laughter of the two parents.

Announcement of Sodom and Gomorrah's Doom; the Angel of the Lord; Abraham's Intercession (Genesis 18)

In connection with the prediction made to Abraham of Isaac's coming birth, announcement was also made concerning the future judgment on the wicked cities of Sodom and Gomorrah (Gen. 18:20ff.). It seems that only one of the three angelic visitors made this announcement about Sodom and Gomorrah, and he is referred to as "the LORD" (v. 17). The other two angels went on to speak with Lot and met with him at the gate of Sodom, as recorded in the beginning of the next chapter (Gen. 19:1). The angel who remained with Abraham and who is referred to as "the LORD" is generally regarded as the "angel of the LORD," who appears throughout the Old Testament and is undoubtedly a preincarnation appearance of Christ.[23]

---

[21]For a picture of a circumcision operation from a tomb relief in Egypt, see PANEP, 206. This relief dates to about 2300 B.C. One of the Megiddo ivories, dating to the thirteenth century B.C., shows the prince of Megiddo, probably celebrating a victory. He drives naked, circumcised captives before his chariot. One is left to speculate whether these captives are Canaanite or Amorite or Hebrew. For a picture see PANEP, 111.

[22]James Henry Breasted, *The Oriental Institute* (Chicago: University of Chicago Press, 1933), 15 [BOI].

[23]An excellent study of the appearances of Christ in the Old Testament, often called "Christophanies" or "Theophanies," is found in E.W. Hengstenberg, *Christology of the Old*

At the Dan gate there is a platform (left) for a god or a king and benches for officials.

Abraham's intercession for the wicked cities is significant, not as an instance of bargaining, but rather as an example of the effect of repeated asking. The same truth is given in the parable of the unjust judge to whom the woman came again and again (Luke 18:1); it is a lesson in persistence in prayer. God has put the world together on the principle of prayer; he has "accorded to a created personality the right to assert itself in faith" (KD, 1:232).

Lot at Sodom; Significance of the Gate; Archaeological Light on Lot's House (Genesis 19)

Lot was sitting at the gate of Sodom when the angels came to the city (Gen. 19:1). Archaeological excavations show that the gates of Palestinian cities often had stone benches or seats as a built-in part of the structure, so that people might sit there and wait for their friends or engage in conversation with those whom they had agreed to meet at the gate. The

excavation by the Pacific School of Religion at Tell en-Nasbeh (1926–1935), believed by the excavators to be the site of the biblical Mizpah, revealed a gate lined with stone benches (MLPP, 211). People would sit at the gate in order to meet their associates, hear the news, and engage in trade. Here it was that legal transactions were carried on, as exemplified in the making of the marriage contract between Ruth and Boaz, which was arranged at the gate of the town (Ruth 4:1–2). The gate was the place of public proclamation; it was at the city gate that David waited to hear the news of Absalom, and then he went to the chamber over the gate to weep for him (2 Sam. 18:24, 33). Likely it was the place where the prophets made their proclamations. The significance of the gate becomes evident if one notes how often it is mentioned in the Old Testament. Archaeological discoveries have given us further light on the size and arrangement of the gates of biblical times and illuminate the importance of this structure in Near Eastern life. A particularly interesting gate, dating to the period of the divided monarchy (ninth–eighth century B.C.), has come to light at Dan as a result of the excavations there since 1966 under the leadership of Avraham Biran of the Israel Department of Antiquities. There a visitor to the site may see a stone bench about fifteen feet long that city fathers may have used for transacting business. Next to it was a canopied structure that may have protected the king's throne or a cult statue (See EAEHL, 1:320).

After meeting the visitors at the gate, Lot brought them to his house. The wicked men of Sodom crowded to the door of Lot's house and pressed heavily against it, but they could not get in (Gen. 19:9). Palestinian excavation has produced interesting information about Lot's mob-proof door. When Kyle and Albright

Testament, trans. Theodore Meyer (Edinburgh: T. & T. Clark, 1863) [HCOT]; pages 119–22 deal with this appearing of the angel of the Lord.

excavated the site of Tell Beit Mirsim (1926–1930ff.), identified with the biblical site of Kirjath-Sepher, they found evidence in the level of the Middle Bronze Age (2200–1600 B.C.) of strong walls and great doors. In one building, the very large door socket was still *in situ*, which shows the heavy construction of doors in the days of Lot. On the other hand, in the level of Early Iron II (900–600 B.C.), many houses and scores of doorways were unearthed, but scarcely a door socket; it was evident that in this late period the inhabitants used only archways or curtains. During this period, the kings of Israel and Judah were ruling; hence there was a strong central government. But in the early period of Abraham and Lot (c. 2000) there was no strong central government, and so sturdy doors and walls were necessary. The smaller the police force, the greater the doors. Lot's heavy door fits precisely in this period. The critics, however, date the writing of the accounts of Abraham in the ninth and eighth centuries B.C. How did the writer know the conditions a thousand years or more before his time? M.G. Kyle commented, "Was he an eminent archaeologist, who, while the Plain of Sodom was still uninhabited yet dug up that ancient civilization and so exactly described the condition that prevailed at that time that the description exactly conforms to the facts as found at Kirjath-Sepher?"[24]

Destruction of Sodom and Gomorrah; Archaeological Light (Genesis 19)

After Lot had been warned by the angels, he and his family left the city of Sodom. God then caused brimstone and fire to come down upon the cities of the plain to destroy them. There were five principal cities in this group, including Sodom and Gomorrah (shown by Genesis 14:2). An indication as to the location of these five cities may be seen in the fact that at the south end of the Dead Sea, there are five streams that may have been the respective sources of water for the five cities. Archaeological explorations at the south end of the Dead Sea, particularly at the site of Bab ed-Dra (possibly the place of pagan worship for the inhabitants of Sodom and Gomorrah), have shown evidence of a break in civilization about 2000 B.C.[25] Researches by Nelson Glueck also have shown a break in culture about 2000 in Transjordan, which he connects with the period of Abraham.[26]

It is possible that the cities of Sodom and Gomorrah are now covered by the shallow waters at the south end of the Dead Sea. There is evidence that the level of the Dead Sea has slowly risen over the centuries. In 1892 Dr. Kyle observed an island at the north end of the Dead Sea. Later, the rising waters caused it to disappear. When he rode over the same island in a motorboat in 1924, it was covered with several feet of water.[27] As a matter of fact, the level of the Dead Sea fluctuates considerably in relation to rainy and dry years and tectonic movements at the bottom of the sea. But it rose thirty-seven feet during the nineteenth century and then fell early in the twentieth century.[28] In recent years it has been visibly shrinking at the southern end because of water use for irrigation farther

[24]*The Evangelical Quarterly* (October 1930) [EQ]; cited in W.W. Prescott, *The Spade and the Bible* (New York: Revell, 1933), 94–95 [PSB]. Cf. Similar development in KEK, 197–98.

[25]See Howard F. Vos, *Archaeology in Bible Lands* (Chicago: Moody, 1977), 148.

[26]Nelson Glueck, *The Other Side of Jordan* (New Haven: American Schools of Oriental Research, 1940), 114 [GOSJ].

[27]W.F. Albright, *Annual of the American Schools of Oriental Research* 6:54–55 [AASOR]; two interesting articles on Sodom and Gomorrah by J. Penrose Harland appeared in BA, May 1942 and September 1943.

[28]Efraim Orni and Elisha Efrat, *Geography of Israel*, 3rd ed. (Jerusalem: Israel Universities Press, 1971), 98.

north in the Jordan Valley, and it may be possible to explore the bottom for location of the cities of the plain at an early date. In Josephus's day, at the end of the first century A.D., evidently the southern end of the Dead Sea did not cover the entire plain, because Josephus, the great Jewish historian, wrote, "Traces of the five cities are still to be seen" (*Wars of the Jews* IV.8.4). Presumably Josephus was an eyewitness to remains of Sodom and Gomorrah.

Chapter 5

Abraham, Isaac, and Jacob

(Genesis 21–37)

Birth of Isaac; Offering of Isaac (Genesis 21–22)

In due time a son was born to Abraham and Sarah (Gen. 21:1–2). He was named Isaac, meaning "laughter," because Abraham and Sarah had laughed in amazement at the Lord's announcment that they should have a son at their advanced ages (Gen. 17:17; 18:12; 21:6–7).

Several years later God tested Abraham, telling him to take Isaac to one of the mountains[1] of the land of Moriah and there offer him (Gen. 22:1–2). That God had no desire to have the child slain is shown by the outcome of the event— Isaac was not put to death. When Abraham went up to the mount and stretched forth his hand, he had already accomplished the sacrifice in his own heart and

had fully met the testing of God. God therefore immediately had the angel of the Lord intervene and show Abraham the ram that was the offering provided by God himself to be sacrificed in place of Isaac (KD, 250). The ram offered in Isaac's stead is a beautiful illustration[2] of Christ's substitutionary death. Christ died on the cross not only to pay for our sins, but actually in our stead, in our place, just as the ram died in the place of Isaac.

Problem of the Philistines (21:34)

At this time, Abraham was living at Beersheba in southern Palestine, in the region of "the land of the Philistines" (Gen. 21:32, 34). Abraham's having contacts with the Philistines in his day is a problem because the Philistines as they

[1]The writer of Chronicles applies the name "Moriah" to the mountain in Jerusalem on which Solomon's temple was built (2 Chron. 3:1). Some believe it is the same as the "land of Moriah" of Abraham's time.

[2]I prefer to call such events "illustrations" rather than "types," reserving the term "type" for Old Testament subjects and events that are specifically pointed out (usually in the New Testament) as types of biblical truth. For example, the veil of the tabernacle, described in the Old Testament, is set forth in the New Testament as a type of the body or flesh of Christ (Heb. 10:20). The rending of Christ's body on the cross opened up a more ready access to God, even as the rending of the veil of the temple (corresponding to the earlier tabernacle) opened in a literal sense the way of access to the inner sanctuary.

are known to archaeologists and historians seem to have entered Palestine in the twelfth century B.C. The common view is that they attacked Egypt by sea during the reign of Ramses III (1198–1167 B.C.),[3] that he repulsed them, and that they then settled in southern Palestine, in what is known as the Plain of Philistia. Subsequently they became a powerful people there and oppressed the Hebrews during the days of the judges and King Saul.[4]

Burrows of Yale says of this problem: "We have seen that the Philistines came into Palestine at the beginning of the Early Iron Age, not far from 1200 B.C. It is quite impossible to date Abraham and Isaac as late as this, yet the book of Genesis represents both as having dealings with the Philistines and their king, Abimelech (Gen. 21:22–32; 26:1–33)." Burrows says that this may be explained as "a convenient and harmless anachronism" and concludes, "At any rate, however the mistake may have come about, it is undoubtedly a mistake" (BWMS, 277). This type of supposed contradiction is often used by critics to support their statements that the Bible has "complicated problems and even direct contradictions in some cases" (BWMS, 278).

To deal with this problem, it is useful to note that the Old Testament says the Philistines came from the island of Caphtor (Jer. 47:4; Amos 9:7), commonly identified as Crete. Moreover, the term *Kherethites* (Cretans) is used to designate the Philistines in 1 Samuel 30:14; Ezekiel 25:16; and Zephaniah 2:5–6.

If the Philistines of about 1200 B.C. came from Crete, they would have been part of the warlike maritime culture known as Mycenean or else of the Sea Peoples who were pushed out of the Aegean by the Mycenean Greeks. And in Palestine they were warlike and a constant threat to the Israelites during the days of the judges and the early monarchy.

These were not the only ancient people to come from Crete, however. Minoan Cretans were establishing trading colonies around the Mediterranean by about 2000 B.C., and evidence of their contact with Palestine and Egypt during this early period is substantial. Moreover, the Philistines of Abraham's day appear to have been peace-loving agricultural people, as were the Minoans.

G. Ernest Wright has pointed out that the Hebrew word translated "Philistine" was used for all "Sea Peoples," of whom the Philistines were the most important for the inhabitants of Palestine.[5] Possibly the reference in Genesis should be translated by some other term. If it is, the problem evaporates completely.

Finally, it should be noted that the Gerar of Abimelech (Gen. 21, 26) has now been identified with Tell Abu Hureira, about eleven miles southeast of Gaza. In 1956 D. Alon excavated there and found that it had been inhabited continually through every period from Chalcolithic times to the Iron Age and was very prosperous during the Middle Bronze (the patriarchal) Age. He also found several smelting furnaces, giving evidence of Philistine iron working.[6] So some evidence of the culture of which Abimelech was a part has been found, but the name "Philistine" has not been connected with it. Clearly there are ways of resolving the problem of the Philistines even now, and it is not necessary to conclude that the Bible is in error. Further discoveries in the Mediterranean world may provide additional solutions.[7]

[3]For a picture of Ramses' great battle with the Philistines as portrayed on his temple at Medinet Habu at Luxor, Egypt, see PANEP, 114.

[4]For a discussion of the Philistines in the later period, see chapter 11.

[5]G. Ernest Wright, "Philistine Coffins and Mercenaries," *Biblical Archaeologist* (September 1959), 61.

[6]Edward E. Hindson, *The Philistines and the Old Testament* (Grand Rapids: Baker, 1971), 72.

[7]Actually, the whole issue of identifying or understanding the Philistines and the Sea Peoples is very unsettled at the present time. Any discussion of it is very technical and involved and far beyond the scope of this book. For two informed studies on this subject, see Alessandra Nibbi,

The mosque of Hebron covers the traditional Cave of Machpelah, burial place of Sarah and some of the patriarchs.

Death of Sarah; Purchase of the Cave of Machpelah (Genesis 23)

Sarah died at the age of 127 (Gen. 23:1). She is the only woman whose age is given in Scripture, perhaps because "as the mother of the promised seed she became the mother of all believers" in a spiritual sense (1 Peter 3:6; KD, 259).

After the death of Sarah, Abraham prepared to purchase the cave of Machpelah at Hebron, some twenty miles south of Jerusalem. The owner of the cave, Ephron, used bargaining tactics that were similar to the methods used even today in Near Eastern countries. By insisting on paying for the cave, Abraham obligated himself and had to consummate the bargain by giving a considerable sum. Actually Ephron was not a philanthropist, even though his words may sound so to the ears of Americans (Gen. 23:15).

When Abraham paid for the cave, he weighed out four hundred shekels of silver (Gen. 23:16). This shows that money was measured by weight in those days and was not yet coined. Archaeological discoveries indicate that the minting of coins began somewhat before 700 B.C. in the kingdom of Lydia in Asia Minor, probably in response to intensive commerce between the Lydians and the Greeks.[8] Thus the implication that the shekel was a weight rather than a coin in the days of Abraham is another indication of the early date of the record concerning Abraham's purchase of Machpelah. A similar indication of the shekel as a weight rather than a coin is seen in the time of Joseph as well (Gen. 37:28, fn).

Abraham's ability to produce four hundred shekels of silver for the purchase of the cave of Machpelah indicates that he was not merely a nomadic sheikh engaging in commercial deals involving barter. He had, after all, come from a brilliant

The Sea Peoples and Egypt (Park Ridge, N.J.: Noyes Press, 1975), and N.K. Sandars, *The Sea Peoples* (London: Thames and Hudson, 1978).

[8]See, e.g., H.W. Perkin, "Money," *International Standard Bible Encyclopedia*, rev. ed., (Grand Rapids: Eerdmans, 1986 for vol. 3), 3:404. Excavations at Sardis, capital of Lydia and one of the seven cities of the Revelation, uncovered King Croesus' gold refinery there during the 1960s. See especially George M.A. Hanfmann, *Sardis from Prehistoric to Roman Times* (Cambridge, Mass.: Harvard University Press, 1983), especially chapter 3.

and highly developed commercial culture in southern Mesopotamia. The Genesis narrative presents him as wealthy and powerful, and numerous scholars not of a particularly evangelical bent have portrayed him in a new and significant light in recent decades. Cyrus Gordon developed the thesis that Abraham was a merchant prince and concluded that

> the patriarchal narratives, far from reflecting Bedouin life, are highly international in their milieu, in a setting where a world order enabled men to travel far and wide for business enterprise. . . . Abraham comes from beyond the Euphrates, plies his trade in Canaan, visits Egypt, deals with Hittites, makes treaties with Philistines, forms military alliances with Amorites, fights kinglets from as far off as Elam, marries the Egyptian Hagar, etc.[9]

Albright argued that Abraham was a "caravaneer," engaged in the rather extensive and lucrative caravan trade between Palestine and Egypt.[10] David Noel Freedman viewed him as a "warrior-chieftain" and a "merchant prince" who "belonged to urban culture and civilization."[11]

Today a Moslem mosque stands over the presumed site of the cave of Machpelah, and entrance into the cave is forbidden. During World War I, when General Allenby's troops were marching to Jerusalem, a British officer, Colonel Meinertzhagen, went into the mosque to seek the Turkish officials of Hebron, who were supposed to have fled there. Passing through a door in the limestone rock interior, the colonel slid down a steep incline and found himself in a cave about twenty feet square. In the cave stood a block of stone about six feet long, three feet wide, and three feet high. The officer, not realizing the significance of the place, left without investigating. Later when Hebron had returned to a normal state, an effort was made to visit the cave, but the guardians of the mosque would not give permission.[12]

A new opportunity to explore the cave of Machpelah occurred in 1967, shortly after the Six-Day War when Moshe Dayan (Israel's Minister of Defense) took advantage of the Israeli victory and lowered a twelve-year-old girl named Michal through the small opening into the cave with a camera. By this means they discovered that the cave is twelve or thirteen feet deep and measures 9.65 by 9.26 feet. From the southeastern wall of this room a sunken step leads down to a doorway, and the doorway to a 57-foot-long corridor, which in turn leads to steps that ascend to another entrance in the floor of the mosque, now blocked. At the northwestern side of the room into which Michal was lowered stand three stone slabs, one of which may be a tombstone, and the others may block the entrance into other grottoes.[13]

Seeking a Bride for Isaac (Genesis 24)

When Abraham was well along in years, he sent his servant back to northern Mesopotamia to take a wife for Isaac from among Abraham's own kindred. The servant departed and went to the city of Nahor (Gen. 24:10). Confirmation of the existence of the city is found in the Mari

---

[9]Cyrus Gordon, "Abraham and the Merchants of Ura," *Journal of Near Eastern Studies* (January 1958), 30.

[10]William F. Albright, *Yahweh and the Gods of Canaan* (Garden City: Doubleday, 1968), 51, 62–73.

[11]David N. Freedman, "The Real Story of the Ebla Tablets," *Biblical Archaeologist* (December 1978), 158.

[12]Charles Marston, *New Bible Evidence* (New York: Revell, 1934–1935), 121–22 [MNBE]; Charles Marston, *The Bible Comes Alive* (London: Eyre and Spottiswoode, 1938), 54 [MBCA].

[13]Nancy Miller, "Patriarchal Burial Site Explored for First Time in 700 Years," *Biblical Archaeology Review* (May/June 1985), 26–43.

Tablets, which frequently mention it as Nakhur.[14]

At the well near Nahor the servant met Rebekah, who took him to the house of her father, Bethuel, a nephew of Abraham (cf. Gen. 11:29 with 24:24). At the home of Bethuel, the servant was well provided for, even being given water for washing his feet (Gen. 24:32). The archaeological discoveries at Ur of the Chaldees show that in the houses there was a drain in the corner of the lobby where a jar would be placed for washing feet (WUC, 198).

When it was proposed to Rebekah that she return with the servant to Canaan to become the bride of Isaac, she readily assented (Gen. 24:58). This beautiful chapter provides an excellent illustration of spiritual truth: Abraham as representing God the Father sent the unnamed servant, typifying the Holy Spirit who speaks not of himself, to seek Rebekah, illustrative of the church, the bride of Christ who is called out. Isaac represents the Bridegroom, Christ, whom the bride, having not seen, loves through the testimony of the servant.

Last Days of Abraham; Isaac's Sons, Jacob and Esau (Genesis 25); Archaeological Light on the Birthright

After the death of Sarah, Abraham married Keturah. Some commentators believe that Keturah was taken as a secondary wife or concubine before the death of Sarah, but I feel that this view is not substantiated by the biblical references. Years later, Abraham died at the advanced age of 175 (Gen. 25:7).

To Isaac and Rebekah were born two sons, Jacob and Esau (vv. 20–26). After the boys had reached maturity, Esau one day sold his birthright to Jacob for some lentil stew (vv. 27–34). Archaeological light on

this instance of selling one's birthright to obtain some desired object is furnished by the Nuzi tablets, found in Mesopotamia and dating from the patriarchal period. In one Nuzi tablet, there is a record of a man named Tupkitilla, who transferred his inheritance rights concerning a grove to his brother, Kurpazah, in exchange for three sheep. Esau used a similar technique in exchanging his inheritance rights to obtain the desired stew.[15]

Isaac and Abimelech (Genesis 26); Critical View and Answer

While Isaac was living at Gerar in the Philistine country, he told the local dwellers that Rebekah was his sister, rather than his wife (Gen. 26:6–7). Several years earlier Abraham had similarly told the people in this same area that Sarah was his sister (Gen. 20:2). The critics have held that this event happened just once, but that two different versions were circulated, one centering around Abraham and the other about Isaac. This theory of "doublets" is described by Knobel, a nineteenth-century German writer, who said, "It is held with good reason that one and the same event lies at the foundation of these. . . narratives" (LCG, 392). Even Sir Charles Marston, usually taking a definite stand against the critical view, said of Genesis 20: "It is probable that this chapter is a duplicate of Genesis 26, and the story really concerns Isaac, his son" (MBCA, 53).

These two chapters, however, deal with different events, one occurring in the life of Abraham and the other in the life of Isaac. The fact that similar incidents are recorded as occurring in the lives of both does not mean that these accounts are "doublets," having a single origin. An

[14]W.F. Albright, "Western Asia in the Twentieth Century B.C.: The Archives of Mari," *Bulletin of the American Schools of Oriental Research* 67 (October 1937): 27 [BASOR].

[15]Cyrus Gordon, "Biblical Customs and the Nuzu Tablets," *Biblical Archaeologist* (February 1940): 5. (Both terms are used, "Nuzu" and "Nuzi.")

One of the Nuzi tablets (1500-1400 B.C.) that describes a land sale in the form of an adoption. Other Nuzi tablets show that the background of the patriarchal records fits into the early period (2000-1500 B.C.), and not in the late period (900-600), as held in the liberal view of former years. For other significances of the Nuzi tablets, see "Last Days of Abraham . . . Archaeological Light on the Birthright," above.

examination of ancient or modern life shows many similar yet distinct events. A press release during World War II told of two Princeton University students who went through similar experiences, yet they were two different individuals:

Amazing is the similarity of events that have happened to two brothers now in the Replacement Center at Fort Bragg, prior to and after the declaration of war. 1. William A. Wood Jr. and Thomas B. Wood were born twins. 2. Attended Princeton together in the class of 1938. 3. Both were active in college athletics. 4. Called to the Army on the same day, same order and sent to the same organization. 5. Held executive officer positions with respective batteries. 6. Both are first lieutenants. 7. Took command of batteries next door to each other. 8. Both are married and were presented with sons during the same month, recently.[16]

Certainly if all of these similar events could occur in the lives of these two boys, then Abraham and Isaac could each try to pass off his wife as his sister.

The Stolen Blessing (Genesis 27); Archaeological Light on Oral Blessing

When Isaac was getting along in years, he planned to bestow his blessing on Esau (Gen. 27:1, 7). Rebekah, however, arranged to have Jacob impersonate Esau and receive the blessing. When Isaac discovered the deception, he was filled with remorse, yet he did not revoke his oral blessing. We might wonder why. Archaeological light on oral blessings is found in the Nuzi tablets. One tablet shows that an oral blessing in patriarchal times had legal validity, even in a law court. This particular document recorded the lawsuit of a certain Tarmiya against his two brothers, who contested the right of the younger brother to take a woman by the name of Zululishtar as his wife. Tarmiya won the case and was awarded his bride because the court recognized the validity of his father's "blessing," which Tarmiya reported in this way: "My father, Huya, was sick and lying in bed and my father seized my hand and spoke thus to me: 'My older sons have taken

[16]Press release from Fort Bragg, N.C., printed in *The Princeton Alumni Weekly* 43,2 (September 25, 1942): 5, 9.

wives but thou hast not taken a wife and I give Zululishtar to thee as wife.' " This text parallels biblical blessings like those of the patriarchs in that it was an oral will, with legal validity, and was made to a son by his father. (In this case the father was dying, as was often the case in biblical blessings.)[17]

Jacob Away from Home (Genesis 28–31); Archaeological Light on the Teraphim

Jacob left home (Beersheba,[18] Gen. 28:10), after receiving the blessing through deception, and went to northern Mesopotamia to the home of his mother's brother, Laban. He served for Laban's daughters fourteen years and another six years for the flocks he was to receive. At the end of the twenty-year period, Jacob and his family prepared to leave Laban's home (Gen. 31:17–18).

Before they left, Jacob's wife Rachel stole the family images (Hebrew *teraphim*) of her father, Laban (Gen. 31:19). After Jacob, Rachel, and the rest of Jacob's family had departed, Laban learned of their unexpected departure and pursued them for seven days, a considerable journey. When Laban overtook them, he searched for the teraphim with great diligence but could not find them because Rachel had put them in a camel saddle and sat on them (v. 34). Why was Laban so anxious to find the teraphim? Certainly a man with his wealth would not need to make such a great commotion about some small idols. Commentators have struggled with this passage, suggesting that perhaps the teraphim were of gold, or had a superstitious value, but none of these explanations seemed to be completely satisfactory. The answer was found in the Nuzi tablets, which show that possession of the father's household gods played an important role in inheritance.[19] One of the Nuzi tablets indicated that in the region where Laban lived, a son-in-law who possessed the family images could appear in court and make claim to the estate of his father-in-law.[20] Since Jacob's possession of the images implied the right to inherit Laban's wealth, one can understand why Laban organized his hurried expedition to recover the images, It also explains why Rachel carefully concealed them in the saddle and sat on them.

Jacob's Return (Genesis 32–37); Archaeology and the Horites

After Laban departed from Jacob, Jacob and his family, continuing on their way, came down to the Jabbok River, which

---

[17]See BA (February 1940), 8.

[18]The biblical town of Beersheba has been located at Tel es-Saba (Tell Beersheba), about two miles northeast of the modern city. Yohanan Aharoni directed a Tel Aviv University excavation there from 1969 to 1976. He discovered that the town had a Hebrew foundation, built in the twelfth or eleventh century B.C. Apparently unwalled, the town probably was the place where the sons of Samuel judged the people (1 Sam. 8:2). Beersheba was fortified with a twelve-foot-thick wall in the tenth century. Aharoni found nothing at Tell Beersheba dating to the patriarchal period, and he concluded that patriarchal Beersheba was located near the valley and the wells, probably at Bir es-Saba, within the area of modern Beersheba (EAEHL, 1:160–68). Subsequent excavations at Tell Beersheba, seeking to find a patriarchal level, dug to bedrock and uncovered nothing earlier than 1250 B.C. See Ze'ev Herzog, "Beer-sheba of the Patriarchs," *Biblical Archaeology Review* (November/December 1980), 12–18.

[19]W.F. Albright, "Recent Discoveries in Bible Lands," supplement to *Young's Analytical Concordance to the Bible* (1936), 26 [ARDBL].

[20]Sidney Smith and C.J. Gadd, *Revue d'Assyriologie* 23 (1928): 126–27; E.A. Speiser, *Mesopotamian Origins* (Philadelphia, 1930), 162; cited by Allan A. MacRae, "The Relation of Archaeology to the Bible" [MRAB], in *Modern Science and Christian Faith* (Wheaton: VanKampen, 1948), 273 [MSCF].

flows through Transjordan[21] into the Jordan River. Here at the Jabbok, Jacob met a man, apparently the angel of the Lord, and they wrestled together. This experience was a spiritual turning point in the life of Jacob; from then on, he not only bore the name Israel ("he struggles with God"), but his self-seeking nature began to fade into the background.

Shortly after his experience at the Jabbok, Jacob met Esau, in reconciliation (Gen. 33), and then returned to a place in central Canaan near the city of Shechem (v. 18), about thirty miles north of Jerusalem. Following the difficulty with the Shechemites (Gen. 34), Jacob moved on south to Bethel (Gen. 35:1). Sometime later Jacob and his family left Bethel and journeyed farther south. Rachel died as they were traveling and was buried near Bethlehem (vv. 19–20). About a mile northwest of Bethlehem is a tomb still pointed out as that of Rachel. Some time later, Jacob's father, Isaac, died at Hebron at the age of 180 (vv. 27–29).

At this point, the genealogy of Esau is given (Gen. 36). One of the groups of people mentioned in connection with Esau is the Horites. Because of the similarity of this word to a Hebrew word for "cave," the term "Horite" was formerly interpreted as "cave-dweller." For some decades it has been popular to identify the Horites with the Hurrians, an important group who entered northwestern Mesopotamia from the region of the Armenian mountains after 2400 B.C. But there are serious problems with that identification, and a recent theory holds that "Horite," Egyptian *Ḥurru*, is a general term the Egyptians applied to southern Transjordan and that the Hebrews adopted it from the Egyptians.[22]

---

[21]Area to the east of the Jordan.

[22]For the problem of identifying Horites with Hurrians and documentation on the current theory, see F.W. Bush, "Horites," ISBE, 2:756–57.

The mound of Dothan

The level of Elisha at Dothan

Chapter 6

Joseph in Egypt

(Genesis 37–50)

Joseph Taken to Egypt (Genesis 37); Dothan; the Pit

After the interlude of Esau's genealogy in Genesis 36, the account of the life of Jacob and his family is resumed in Genesis 37. When Joseph was a lad of seventeen, his father Jacob sent him to find his brothers, who were tending their flocks in the area to the north of Hebron (Jacob was living at this time at Hebron, which is about twenty miles south of Jerusalem). Joseph left the vicinity of Hebron and went to the region of Shechem, some thirty miles north of Jerusalem. Upon inquiry, Joseph learned that his brothers

were about twenty miles still farther north, near a place called Dothan (Gen. 37:17). I began the excavation of the mound of ancient Dothan in 1953 and found specific evidence of the city dating from the time of Joseph, about 1900 B.C.[1]

When Joseph's brothers saw him coming, their jealousy prompted them to make plans to kill him and put him in a pit (Gen. 37:20). At Gezer (between Jerusalem and the Mediterranean coast) Macalister found a number of skeletons in an ancient cistern, illustrating the fact that the use of pits and cisterns was a means of disposing of people in Old Testament

[1]From 1953 to 1962 my wife, Ruby, and I, with our staff, carried on the excavation of the mound of ancient Dothan, some sixty miles by road north of Jerusalem. A deep sounding on the slope during the first season showed that Dothan began some 5000 years ago (3000 B.C.), and had a more or less continuous history until about 700 B.C. Two of the lower levels proved to come from the days of the patriarchs (2000–1600), thus confirming the biblical record of the existence of Dothan in the time of Joseph, 1900–1800 (Gen. 37:17). The upper levels on top of the mound yielded evidence of the city of Elisha's time (850–800), confirming the biblical record of the existence of Dothan in the days of that ancient prophet (2 Kings 6:13). The first eight seasons of excavation (1953–1962) disclosed the streets, the walls, the houses, the pottery and implements, and many other aspects of life at ancient biblical Dothan.

For accounts of the excavation, see Joseph P. Free, "The First Season of Excavation at Dothan," *Bulletin of the American Schools of Oriental Research* 131 (October 1953): 16–20; "The Second Season at Dothan," BASOR 135 (October 1954): 14–20; "The Third Season at Dothan," BASOR 139 (October 1955): 3–9; "Digging Down to Ancient Dothan," *Moody Monthly* (November 1954): 15–17ff.

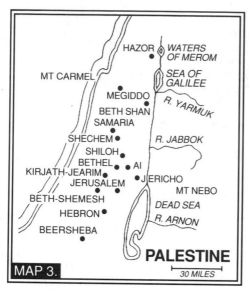

MAP 3.

PALESTINE

30 MILES

"Canaanites" even became a synonym for "slaves" in the Egyptian documents.[3] Joseph's position as overseer in the house of Potiphar also accords with what can be learned from the Egyptian monuments, which frequently mention the *merper*, or superintendent of the house in connection with the large dwellings of important Egyptians.[4]

The fact that Potiphar's wife was able to speak so easily with Joseph might be questioned (Gen. 39:10). Would not Joseph be in the steward's quarters, quite removed from the quarters of Potiphar and his wife? The excavations at Tell el Amarna in central Egypt, however, have revealed a number of house plans showing that the storerooms were at the back of the house and so were reached by going through the main part of the house. It is likely that Potiphar's house followed a similar plan. Thus Joseph, as steward of the house of Potiphar, would have had to pass through the inner apartments daily in order to inspect the storerooms and keep them replenished.[5]

times.[2] Such use of cisterns has also been noted in other places.

Reuben sought to save Joseph's life by suggesting that the lad be put into a pit alive. This they did, but before Reuben could deliver Joseph, the other brothers sold him to a passing caravan of Ishmaelites and Midianites, who took Joseph to Egypt and sold him to Potiphar, an officer of the pharaoh of Egypt (Gen. 37:36).

Joseph in Potiphar's House (Genesis 39); Joseph's Position; Archaeological Light on the Arrangement of Houses

Potiphar's purchase of Joseph is illuminated by the archaeological discoveries of papyrus documents in Egypt, which show that Syrian slaves were highly prized in Egypt. The word "Kan'amu" or

Joseph in Prison (Genesis 39, 40); Egyptian Prisons; the Butler and the Baker

After Potiphar's wife falsely accused Joseph (Gen. 39:17ff.), he was put in prison. Abundant archaeological evidence demonstrates that there were important prisons in Egypt in Joseph's time. Several suggestions have been made as to which of these might be the one where Joseph was confined. The German Egyptologist Ebers identified Joseph's prison with a fortress at Memphis called "White

[2]R.A.S. Macalister, *A Century of Excavation in Palestine* (New York: Revell, 1925), 221 [MCEP]; also R.A.S. Macalister, *The Excavation of Gezer*, 2:429–30; [MEG]; also BAB, 223.

[3]A.H. Sayce, *Expository Times*, 10, 75 [ET], cited in G.A. Frank Knight, *Nile and Jordan* (London: Clarke, 1921), 108 [KN].

[4]A. Erman, *Life in Ancient Egypt*, 187 [ELAE].

[5]A diagram of one of these house plans is found in A. Erman, *Life in Ancient Egypt*, trans. H.M. Tirard (London: Macmillan, 1894), 179 [ELAE]. At the Oriental Institute of the University of Chicago there is a model of a rather elaborate Egyptian villa.

Wall."[6] The word used for the prison where Joseph was placed is the Hebrew term *sohar*, which literally means "house of roundness" and suggests a round tower, used as a state prison. The state prison at Thebes in the south of Egypt where Thothmes III (1501–1477 B.C.) confined his Syrian captives was called *suhan*; Knight suggests that *sohar* may be a Semitic equivalent of the Egyptian term (KNJ, 109). Yahuda notes an Egyptian word, similar to *sohar*, found in many inscriptions as a name of a fortress close to the Palestine frontier to which corrupt officials and notorious criminals were consigned. He believes this fortress is probably the prison where Joseph was held.[7]

Joseph, through God's help, ably interpreted the dreams of Pharaoh's butler and the baker who were confined in the same prison (Gen. 40:1ff.). The Egyptian monuments give abundant evidence of the presence of butlers and bakers in ancient Egyptian life. All of the phases of bread making are portrayed in the tomb paintings. These and other representations show bakers carrying baskets of bread and other baked goods on their heads, just as described to Joseph by the baker (vv. 16–17) (KNJ, 109).

Joseph as the Prime Minister (Genesis 41–42); Possibility of Joseph's Position

After the chief butler was released from prison, he forgot about Joseph until Pharaoh had his dream about the seven cows. Then the butler brought to Pharaoh's attention the fact that Joseph would be able to interpret the dream. Joseph's interpretation of Pharaoh's dream brought him the appointment to the office that we would call the prime minister of Egypt.

Doubt has been cast on the possibility of the promotion of a Canaanite slave such as Joseph to such a high position. Of course God was guiding the destiny of Joseph; but it can be demonstrated, even apart from this factor, that such a rise to power was possible. Egyptian archaeological discoveries tell of foreigners, including Canaanites, who achieved prominence in the course of Egyptian history. Erman points out that "amongst the court officials also we often meet with foreigners who may have been slaves" (ELAE, 106). One such Canaanite was the "first speaker of his Majesty," and at court he assumed the Egyptian name of "Ramses in the temple of Re" (ELAE, 106). This is a significant parallel to the giving of an Egyptian name to Joseph (Gen. 41:45). Also a Canaanite by the name of Dudu[8] rose to high favor in the Egyptian court. His high position is illustrated by a letter written to him by an Amorite, who wrote to Dudu, "Whatever is the wish of Dudu, let me know, and I will do it. . . . Thou sittest in the presence of the King my lord as a high dignitary."[9] Another

---

[6]G.J. Spurrell, *Notes on the Text of the Book of Genesis* (Oxford: Clarendon, 1896), 319 [SNG].

[7]A.S. Yahuda, *The Language of the Pentateuch in Its Relation to Egyptian* (Oxford University Press, 1933), 1:38–42 [YLP]. Albright issued this word of caution on Yahuda's works: "A.S. Yahuda's recent books on the subject of Egyptian materials in the Pentateuch, where the story of Joseph is treated in considerable detail, are unsound," ARDBL, 27. It is quite true that Yahuda does at times see connections between Egypt and the Bible that seem not to exist; however, some of his material is quite useful, when it is based solidly on a valid use of the archaeological materials. The above reference is cited merely as having a possible connection with the place of Joseph's imprisonment.

[8]W.F. Albright has pointed out (by oral communication) that the name Dudu is an Egyptian name but that Dudu's grandfather may have been a Canaanite; this would mean that Dudu was a Canaanite, though he bore an Egyptian name.

[9]CBS, 103–4; also in BAB, 368, lines 11–13, 28, from Winckler and Abel, *Thontafelnfund von El-Amarna*, no. 40. Cf. Knudtzon, *Die El-Amarna Tafeln*, no. 158. This is one of the Amarna Tablets that were found in Egypt by a peasant woman during the winter of 1887–1888. They proved to be

Canaanite by the name of Meri-Ra became armor-bearer to the pharaoh of Egypt (CBS, 61). But probably the position of Yankhamu, also a Canaanite, is even closer to that of Joseph. He acted as the deputy for the pharaoh of Egypt in the grain-growing district of Egypt (CBS, 104). Thus, Joseph's rise to power[10] is shown by the archaeological discoveries to have been entirely possible.

Egyptian Names Mentioned in Connection With Joseph; Critical View and Answer

Several Egyptian names are given in connection with Joseph, including that of his Egyptian wife, Asenath, and her father, Potipherah (Gen. 41:45). The critical view has held that these Egyptian names mentioned in connection with Joseph appear in a later period. Burrows says, "As a matter of fact the Egyptian names given in the Joseph story do not appear in Egypt before the time of the Hebrew monarchy" (BWMS, 53). In support of this idea he cites Albright, who says essentially the same thing (AAPB, 143). This assertion ties in with the critical idea that the Pentateuch was not written by Moses (c. 1500–1400 B.C.), but by late writers (850–450 B.C.), who would be familiar with the names common in the late period of Egyptian history. By way of answer to this contention that the Egyptian names of the Joseph account come in the late period, it is significant to note the acknowledgement of T. Eric Peet, Professor of Egyptology at the University of Liverpool, who was much more radical in his biblical criticism than either Burrows or Albright. Peet said, "Asenath is an

Egyptian name meaning 'Belonging to the goddess Neit.' Names of this type are not absolutely wanting in the earlier periods, but they are extremely rare, and it is only in the XXIst Dynasty [c. 1100–950 B.C.] that they begin to be common."[11] Even though his admission is a grudging one, it is clear that he acknowledges the appearance of such names in the early period. Barton states the fact in more positive language: "The name of Joseph's wife, Asenath (in Egyptian *As-Neit*, 'favorite of the goddess Neith'), occurs from the eighteenth dynasty onward [1600 B.C. and after]" (BAB, 24). This provides another piece of evidence that harmonizes with the conservative view, holding to the early writing of the Pentateuch.

Joseph and His Brothers (Genesis 42–45)

The famine in Canaan caused Jacob to send his sons to Egypt to seek grain. They obtained grain from Joseph, who finally, after testing them, revealed himself to them on their second trip to Egypt. Joseph then instructed his brothers to return to Canaan and to bring their families and their father Jacob down to Egypt. Pharaoh added the provision that wheeled vehicles be sent along to aid in the moving venture.

Joseph's Titles (Genesis 45:8); Archaeological Light

In describing his position in Egypt to his brothers, Joseph referred to himself in a threefold way, as (1) father to Pharaoh, (2) lord of all his entire household, and (3) ruler of all Egypt (Gen. 45:8). The Egyptian monuments show that Joseph

---

letters written by rulers of various cities in Canaan and Syria to two Egyptian kings, Amenhotep III and Amenhotep IV, who ruled about 1400 B.C.

[10]Albright pointed out other evidence showing that Joseph was not the only Semitic prime minister in Egypt; the records tell of one who lived in the seventeenth century, B.C., bearing the good Hebrew name of Hur. Cf. W.F. Albright's article, "The Old Testament and Archaeology" [AOTA], in *Old Testament Commentary*, edited by Herbert C. Alleman and Elmer E. Flack (Philadelphia: Muhlenberg, 1948), 141 [AFOTC].

[11]T. Eric Peet, *Egypt and the Old Testament* (University Press of Liverpool, 1924), 101 [PEOT].

was applying the regular official Egyptian titles to himself.[12] Yahuda believes that "father to Pharaoh" refers to Joseph's position as vizier in its aspect of priestly dignitary, while "lord of his. . . household" describes his position as court chamberlain over the entire court, and "ruler of all Egypt" gives his position as supreme administrator of the entire land. Yahuda observes further that only someone who was familiar with Egypt would have known this.[13]

Jacob in Egypt (Genesis 46–50; Archaeological Light on Jacob's Few Years

When Joseph's message was brought by his brothers to their father, Jacob left for Egypt with all of his family (Gen. 46:1). According to God's provision, the nation Israel was to be blessed if it remained in the Promised Land of Canaan; God expressly stated this to Isaac when he said, "Do not go down to Egypt; live in the land where I tell you to live . . . and I will be with you and will bless you" (Gen. 26:2–3). Even though Jacob was going out of the Promised Land and thus departing from God's appointed place, yet God appeared to Jacob on the way (at Beersheba) and promised not only to go with him and his family, but also to bring them up again from the land of Egypt (Gen. 46:3–4). Scofield points this out as one of the many instances where a distinction between the directive and the permissive will of God must be made. God's directive will indicated Canaan as the place for his people, but God in his tenderness would not forbid the aged Jacob to go to Egypt to be with his family. God's permissive will allowed him to go and be with his

son Joseph (Scofield Reference Bible, note to Gen. 46:3).

When Jacob appeared before Pharaoh, Jacob referred to his own 130 years as "few and difficult" (Gen. 47:9). It strikes the modern occidental mind as somewhat strange to refer to such a goodly number of years as "few." The Egyptian archaeological sources help us understand that Jacob was observing a detail of etiquette in speaking thus to Pharaoh. Since the Egyptian king was regarded as an eternally living god, it was fitting for Jacob to refer to his own 130 years as "few."

The Pharaoh of Joseph's Day

Genesis does not name the Pharaoh before whom Jacob stood and of course whom Joseph served. To discover who he might have been, it is necessary first to establish a time frame for the events recorded. If we follow the chronology proposed at the beginning of chapter 4, the Exodus took place about 1446 B.C., and the children of Israel (Jacob and his sons) entered Egypt 430 years earlier (Exod. 12:40), about 1876. That would have been the era when the Hyksos were beginning to infiltrate from Canaan and when the Middle Kingdom of Egypt was in progress (c. 2000–1780). Politically the Middle Kingdom was very different from the Old Kingdom. In the earlier period (the pyramid age) kings were absolute and the land was apparently more prosperous. During the Middle Kingdom, kings had to contest with the nobles for political control, but by the end of the period they were successful in virtually restoring their absolutism.

Acceptance of 1876 B.C. for Hebrew

---

[12]KNJ, 115, citing Brugsch, *History of Egypt* (1891), 101, 357 [BHE], and Driver, in *Hastings Dictionary of the Bible*, 3:774 [HDB].

[13]A.S. Yahuda, *The Accuracy of the Bible* (London: Heinemann, 1934), 18 [YAB]. Albright's word of caution in regard to Yahuda's works has already been noted (footnotes). In connection with the relationship between Egypt and the Bible, Albright does acknowledge that in the Joseph story "there are many bits of Egyptian colouring in the narrative which have been beautifully illustrated by Egyptological discoveries," ARDBL, 27.

A lintel from a gate showing Sesostris III making an offering to the god Mentou. Sesostris may have been the pharaoh of Egypt in Joseph's day.   Lintel located in Louvre Museum.

entrance into Egypt would place the event during the reign of Sesostris III (or Senwosret or Sen-Usert). Although Egyptian chronologies vary, most Egyptologists conclude that Sesostris's regnal dates were 1878 to 1840. If these dates are right, the seven years of plenty and the beginning of Joseph's administration would have occurred during the reign of the previous pharaoh, Sesostris II (1897–1878). The Bible student will discover no evidence of a change of royal administration in the Genesis narrative, but that fact does not create a serious difficulty. As crown prince, Sesostris III presumably would have acquiesced to the policies inaugurated by his father. And he would have been king when the years of famine set in. An alternate chronology, held by some European scholars, puts the regnal years of Sesostris III at 1887–1850 and would envision him as in full control during the entire period of Joseph's leadership in Egypt. Interestingly, Sesostris III was a vigorous pharaoh who made great

progress in destroying the power of the nobles and in extending the boundaries of Egypt. He also pushed the southern frontier about two hundred miles south of Aswan, to the second cataract, and reconquered Nubia. Perhaps it is legitimate to speculate that he used the famine and the efforts of his prime minister, Joseph, to fasten royal control on all the populace of the land (see Gen. 47:13–26).

Death of Jacob and Joseph (Genesis 49–50); Mummification

After living seventeen years in Egypt, Jacob died at the age of 147 (Gen. 49:28). Before his death, the patriarch gathered his sons before him and bestowed his dying prophetic blessing on each of the individual sons and on the tribes they would beget (Gen. 49).

When Jacob died, his body was mummified, as was Joseph's when he died several years later at the age of 110 (Gen. 50:2, 26). Embalming was practiced generally at least by Egyptian royalty and nobility and is exactly what one would expect in the preparation of the bodies of Jacob and Joseph in Egypt. The elaborate preparation of the body required many days, as evidenced by the biblical statement that forty days were needed in the case of Jacob, with a mourning period of seventy days (Gen. 50:3). Light on the rather long period of time required in Egypt for embalming is furnished by the historian Herodotus, who, living at a later time when embalming had become a very elaborate process, gives seventy days as the period customarily observed; the historian Diodorus gives thirty.[14] The whole subject of embalming has been carefully studied and is not quite so shrouded in mystery as the layman ordinarily believes.[15] Archaeological records from Egypt indicate that the embalmers and undertakers used a liberal supply of fine linen, spice, oils, and rich perfumes.[16] The heart, liver, lungs, and viscera were removed and placed in four vessels known as canopic jars, and the body was soaked in natron before being wrapped in many yards of linen. The dry climate of Egypt was also a significant factor in the preservation of mummies, though this aspect of the matter is often overlooked by the layperson who considers the subject of mummification with some awe.

Time of Patriarchal Events; Accuracy of Patriarchal Accounts

Most current views of biblical chronology place the patriarchal period within the years 2000–1500 B.C., and the more conservative scholars restrict patriarchal activity to the first couple of centuries of that half millennium. Of course events of the period center around the life and times of Abraham, Isaac, Jacob, and Joseph. Although we have tried to refine the chronology of Abraham, 2000 is still a useful date to use for him when dealing in round numbers.

The critical view of past years held that the patriarchal accounts were legendary and included unreliable traditions that lacked historical basis. Julius Wellhausen well expressed this view when he said, "From the patriarchal narratives it is impossible to obtain any historical information with regard to the patriarchs."[17] The archaeological discoveries of recent decades, however, have led to a change of opinion on the part of many liberal scholars. W.F. Albright, trained in a liberal environment but having come to a view he described as neither liberal nor conservative in the usual sense of the word, acknowledged that the conclusion forced on us by recent archaeological discoveries is "that the saga of the patriarchs is essentially historical" (AAPB, 145). The archaeological discoveries that brought about this change of view in Albright include those concerning the cities of Abraham's day,[18] Lot and the Jordan Valley,[19] the line of march taken by the four kings,[20] light on Sodom and Gomorrah,[21] and many similar confirmations of the details and the background of patriarchal times (Albright deals with this line of thought specifically in AAPB, 129–51).

---

[14]KNJ, 117, citing Herodotus 2:86–89; Diodorus 1:91.

[15]For further discussion, see Howard F. Vos, *Genesis and Archaeology* (Grand Rapids: Zondervan, 1985), 106–9; A. Lucas, "Mummification," in his *Ancient Egyptian Materials and Industries*, 3rd ed. (London: Edward Arnold, 1948), 307–90.

[16]J.H. Breasted, *A History of Egypt* (New York: Scribner, 1912), 141 [BAHE].

[17]Julius Wellhausen, *Prolegomena to the History of Israel*, 3rd ed., 331; 1st ed., Edinburgh, 318 [WPHI].

[18]This book, chapter 4, section "Abraham in Canaan."

[19]Ibid., section "Abraham Again in Canaan."

[20]Ibid., section "The Battle of the Four Kings. . . ."

[21]Ibid., section "Destruction of Sodom and Gomorrah."

Chapter 7

Moses in Egypt

(Exodus 1–12)

The King Who "Did Not Know About Joseph" (Exodus 1:8ff.); Archaeological Light

The children of Israel increased in the land of Egypt until finally there arose a king "who did not know about Joseph" (Exod. 1:7–8). This pharaoh determined to prevent further increase of the Israelites by putting to death the male children at birth (vv. 15–16). Though the Bible does not tell which pharaoh this was, enough light has been shed on the general period in which these events occurred to ascertain which of the pharaohs is most likely to be identified with this one.

From historical and archaeological sources, we know that about 1570 B.C. the native Egyptians drove out the Hyksos rulers of Egypt, an Asiatic group that had governed the land for about 150 years, from c. 1730 to c. 1570. The Hyksos had probably begun filtering into Egypt about 1900 and finally gained control of the

country by about 1730. It is generally believed that this pharaoh who did not know Joseph was one of the new line of native Egyptians, probably Ahmose I, who came to the throne when the Hyksos were driven out. Ahmose[1] reigned 1570–1545 B.C.[2]

If Ahmose, or one of the kings of his time, is the pharaoh who "did not know about Joseph" (i.e., who did not know Joseph's people), then the preceding period was that of the Hyksos domination of Egypt. Joseph and his people presumably would have been treated well up to this time, because the Hyksos, another Asiatic group, were in the land and likely would have been well disposed toward the Israelites, also a foreign group. Burrows indicates that this identification of Joseph's period with the Hyksos rule, a view that has long been held, is now generally accepted. He says, "Modern historians agree, on the whole, that the conditions of the Hyksos period afford a

---

[1] Ahmose's name is also spelled Ahmosis, Amosis, Aahmes, and Amasis. Egyptian names have a great variety of spellings, depending on whether they are in the form taken from Greek historians or are transliterated from the hieroglyphic inscriptions of Egypt. In the latter case, the vowels are inserted by conjecture because hieroglyphics are composed only of consonants.

[2] John A. Wilson, *The Burden of Egypt* (Chicago: University of Chicago Press, 1951), viii [WBE].

natural setting for Joseph's rise to power and for the settlement of Israel in Egypt" (BWMS, 71).

The Treasure Cities, Pithom and Raamses (Exodus 1:11); Archaeological Light

Beginning with the king who "did not know about Joseph," this new line of pharaohs put burdensome tasks on the Israelites. They required the people to build treasure cities (or store cities) and made their lives difficult with "hard labor in brick and mortar" (Exod. 1:11, 14). Light on the treasure cities specifically mentioned, Pithom and Raamses (or Ramses), apparently was found in 1883 by the Swiss archaeologist Naville when he excavated a site in the delta of Egypt called Tell el Maskhuta and found inscriptions containing the word *Pi-Tum*, meaning "House of the god Tum." This led Naville to identify Tell el Maskhuta with the Pithom built by the Israelites. He found that some of the bricks were actually made without straw.[3] In the light of more recent studies, however, Albright, among others, expressed the view that Pithom is to be identified with Tell er-Retabeh (ASAC, 194; AOTA, 142), which is eight and one-half miles west of Tell el-Maskhuta. He identified Tell el-Maskhuta with Succoth, which is mentioned in connection with Israel in Egypt (Exod. 13:20). Since these sites are near each other and both are referred to in the portions of Exodus dealing with Israel in Egypt, the brickwork found by Naville at Tell el-Maskhuta could still be connected with Israelite taskwork. Current scholarship is divided over whether Tell er-Retabeh or Tell el-Maskhuta is the site of Pithom, with preference possibly tilting toward the former.

The other treasure city specifically mentioned, Raamses (Exod. 1:11), has usually been identified with Tanis (AOTA, 142; FLAP, 114). The site of Tanis was excavated by Pierre Montet (1929–1932), who strongly maintained that it was the location of Raamses.[4] Tanis is some distance to the north of Tell el-Maskhuta and Tell er-Retabeh (see maps 2 and 4, pages 48 and 91).

Preparation of Moses, the Deliverer (Exodus 2ff.)

During the sojourn of Israel in Egypt, a child was born to an Israelite family, who concealed him at the edge of the Nile River in order to avoid having him put to death by the emissaries of Pharaoh. One day Pharaoh's daughter[5] went down to the river bank and, finding the child hidden in the reeds, took him to rear as her own son. She gave him the name Moses, "because I drew him out of the water" (Exod. 2:10). The name "Moses" could be derived from the Hebrew *masha*, "to draw out" (Gesenius-Robinson *Hebrew Lexicon*). Although it is hardly likely that Pharaoh's daughter, an Egyptian, would give a name based on a Hebrew word, the antecedent of "she" may be Moses' own mother instead of Pharaoh's daughter.[6]

---

[3]Naville, *The Store-City of Pithom and the Route of the Exodus*, 4th ed. (London: 1903), [NPRE], cited BAB, 26–27.

[4]*Revue Biblique* 39 (1930): 15–28; cited in FLAP, 114.

[5]Numerous writers consider Hatshepsut to have been this "Pharaoh's daughter" (e.g., CBS, 66; MNBE, 161; MBCA, 57). If Thutmose III or one of his line was the Pharaoh of the Oppression (see next section), Hatshepsut could have been the princess involved in the rescue of Moses. She was the daughter of Thutmose I, the wife of Thutmose II, and the stepmother of Thutmose III, according to George Steindorff and Keith C. Seele, *When Egypt Ruled the East* (Chicago: University of Chicago Press, 1942), 36–40 [SSWE].

[6]The question of whether Moses' name was derived from Hebrew or Egyptian is often debated and quickly becomes a very technical matter, quite beyond the scope of this book. See, e.g., ISBE, rev. ed., 3:417; *New Bible Dictionary*, 2d ed., 794.

Thutmose III, possibly the pharaoh who oppressed the Israelites   Lehnert and Landrock, Cairo

Gulf of Akabah (the eastern arm of the Red Sea; see maps 2 and 4, pages 48 and 91). While in Midian, Moses married Zipporah, the daughter of Jethro (v. 21). Through tending the flocks of Jethro, Moses became very familiar with the whole region about Horeb (Exod. 3:1), which is the same as Sinai. In this time of preparation he had opportunity to learn all he needed to know about the Sinai area, so that he would be thoroughly ready to lead the children of Israel through Sinai years later when the Exodus from Egypt would take place.[7] Moses' forty years of preparation in the region of Sinai provides an illustration of the fact that God wants the believer to have adequate preparation for his tasks in life.

The Pharaoh of the Oppression (Exodus 2:23); Connection With the Fall of Jericho

While Moses was out in Sinai and Midian, "during that long period, the king of Egypt died" (Exod. 2:23). This particular king is usually known to Bible scholars as the "pharaoh of the oppression," because it was under his rule that the Israelites were particularly oppressed with their labors of making bricks and constructing buildings.

It has been a matter of interest (but not an article of faith) to Bible students to discover the identity of this pharaoh. The question of his identity depends on the date of Israel's Exodus from Egypt, as well as on the date of the fall of Jericho. The archaeological evidence from the pottery and scarabs at Jericho shows that this city fell about the year 1400 B.C. Among the factors supporting this date, John Garstang, the second excavator of Jericho, pointed out that not one piece of Mycenaean ware was found, suggesting that the walls of Jericho fell before the four-

One day when Moses came upon an Egyptian striking a Hebrew, he intervened and killed the Egyptian. When Moses learned that the matter was known, he fled from Egypt, going out to the land of Midian (Exod. 2:15), which is to the east of Egypt, probably on the eastern side of the

[7]At the time of the wilderness journeys, God gave special help by leading Israel with the Cloud. That does not mean God could not also use a well-prepared man who knew the wilderness firsthand.

teenth century had begun.[8] Garstang's claim of an approximate 1400 date for the fall of Jericho seems supported by Kathleen Kenyon's work there (1952–1958), as recent publication of her excavation reports indicates.[9]

If Jericho fell about 1400, at the end of the forty years in the wilderness, then the Exodus occurred about 1440[10] or a little earlier. An examination of the history of Egypt shows that a great king of Egypt, Thutmose III, died in the year 1450 B.C.[11] (His name is also rendered Thutmosis Thothmes). This king could very well fit into the picture as the pharaoh of the oppression. He reigned for thirty-two years (1482–1450),[12] and thus his death came after a long period of rule, as implied in the biblical statement that "during that long period, the king of Egypt died" (Exod. 2:23; CBS, 68ff., has an interesting discussion of Thutmose III as the pharaoh of the Exodus).

It would be helpful, in trying to understand the situation of Israel in Egypt, to know something of this man who may have been the pharaoh of the oppression and who, in any event, was ruling during Israel's sojourn in that land. Thutmose III was one of the greatest, if not the greatest, of all the kings of Egypt. When he came to

the throne, he reorganized the army of Egypt and began a campaign up into Palestine and Syria. When the Egyptian army approached the city of Megiddo in northern Palestine, they had a choice of three routes, one directly through a narrow mountain pass to Megiddo, and the other two less direct but through more open territory (SSWE, 53–54). Thutmose's military officers favored the two open roads, but Thutmose chose the direct route, and, personally leading his own army, he marched through the narrow defile and on into an open place, where early the next morning he formed his battle lines and attacked the Asiatic hosts. The latter fled to the city of Megiddo, but the inhabitants of the city had already closed the gates, making it necessary to haul the Asiatics up over the walls into the city by lowering clothing to them. The Egyptians could have had a striking victory by pursuing the enemy, but they were tempted by the plunder left outside the city by the Asiatic soldiers and stopped to get the horses, chariots of gold and silver, and the other valuables abandoned by the fleeing enemy (BAHE, 287–90). Shortly, however, Thutmose began the siege of the city, and finally those inside the walls surrendered. Still greater

[8]John Garstang, *Joshua Judges* (London: Constable, 1931), 146 [GJJ]. Mycenaean ware began to be imported about 1400 B.C.; see this book, chapter 10, section entitled "Date of the Fall of Jericho," page 112.

[9]See Bryant G. Wood, "Did the Israelites Conquer Jericho?" *Biblical Archaeology Review* (March/April 1990), 57.

[10]Biblical evidence also points to 1440–1450 as the time of the Exodus. 1 Kings 6:1 shows that the Exodus preceded the building of Solomon's temple by 480 years. Since the temple was begun in Solomon's fourth year, 966 B.C. or 967, this biblical reference points to an approximate date of 1446 for the Exodus.

[11]Albright favors a date of c. 1300 for the Exodus, ARDBL, 31; AOTA, 141; BWMS, 75; a large number of Bible scholars subscribe to this late date. For a discussion of this date, see chapter 8, section entitled "Date of the Exodus," pages 86–89.

[12]The dates followed here are those of Steindorff and Seele (George Steindorff and Keith C. Seele, *When Egypt Ruled the East*, rev. ed. [Chicago: University of Chicago Press, 1957], 274). If Thutmose's reign began in 1504, the year of his father's death, he reigned fifty-four years; but his stepmother Hatshepsut controlled the realm from 1504 to 1482. John A. Wilson (WBE, viii) and Alan Gardiner (*Egypt of the Pharaohs* [Oxford: Oxford University Press, 1961], 443) both put the dates of Thutmose III at 1490–1436. Such a chronology would have him ruling and aggressive at the time of the Exodus, if one subscribes to an approximate 1446 date. It seems unlikely that the Hebrews could have been moving around the Sinai when Thutmose III was making constant forays eastward and northward through the region and up into Canaan.

wealth came to Pharaoh from within the city, including 924 chariots, 2,238 horses, 200 suits of armor, 22,500 small cattle, and immense quantities of gold and silver (BAHE, 292; cf. SSWE, 55).

Year after year Thutmose III made expeditions into Palestine and Syria, subjugating the peoples and exacting tribute from them. He made seventeen campaigns in a period of nineteen years, until the people in Syria were quite beaten into submission (BAHE, 316–17). It is little wonder that this king has been called the Napoleon of ancient Egypt.

Moses' Return to Egypt (Exodus 4); His Excuses

At the proper time, God instructed Moses to return to Egypt (Exod. 4:19) to prepare to lead the children of Israel out of the land. Moses had objected when God appointed him to lead Israel from Egypt (3:10), saying that he could not undertake the task because the people would not listen to him (4:1) and because he was not eloquent (v. 10). God answered the first objection by showing Moses that he would be empowered to work miracles so the people would acknowledge him (vv. 2–9); and God answered the second objection by making Aaron, Moses' brother, his spokesman (vv. 11–17).

The Pharaoh of the Exodus (Exodus 5:1); Possible Identity

Moses and Aaron went in before Pharaoh to deliver God's message, "Let my people go" (Exod. 5:1). Bible scholars usually refer to this ruler as the "pharaoh of the Exodus" because it was during his rule that Israel made the Exodus from Egypt. If Thutmose III (1482–1450 B.C.) was the pharaoh of the oppression, then his successor, Amenhotep II (1452–1425, also spelled Amenophis) would have been the pharaoh of the Exodus, the one before whom Moses and Aaron went to deliver

the message that he should let Israel depart from Egypt.

Amenhotep II faced a rebellion of the tributary princes in Syria when they learned of the death of his father, Thutmose III. Marching into the Asiatic territory, he won victory after victory until he finally reached the great Euphrates River. He returned to Egypt with over five hundred north Syrian lords as captives, evidence of his triumphant campaigns to subdue these territorial lands (BAHE, 323–25). Not much is known about the person of Amenhotep II, although it seems that physically he was very strong, inasmuch as he boasts in the archaeological inscriptions that no man could draw his bow (BAHE, 326). The fact that his mummy is now preserved in the Cairo Museum is not an argument against his being the pharaoh of the Exodus, for Scripture does not say Pharaoh was drowned in the Red Sea at the parting of the waters; only part of his army was (Exod. 14:28).

Those who subscribe to a late date of the Exodus (c. 1290–1275 B.C.) will, of course, have a very different idea of who the pharaoh was at that time. An old view held that Ramses II (1299–1232) was the pharaoh of the oppression and Merneptah (1232–1222) the pharaoh of the Exodus. Inasmuch as the Merneptah Stele (now in the Cairo Museum), in which Merneptah records a victory over the Israelites in Palestine, views the Hebrews as settled in Palestine at the time (for inscription see PANET, 378; for picture see PANEP, 115), he could hardly have been the pharaoh of the Exodus. Those who hold to a thirteenth-century date now generally conclude that Ramses II was the pharaoh of the Exodus, and they do not usually concern themselves with identification of a separate pharaoh of the great oppression. Albright considered Seti I (1318–1299) to have been the pharaoh of the oppression (AOTA, 141).

Critical Objection to the Recorded Use of Straw in Brick Making (Exodus 5:13–18); Light From Archaeology and Chemistry

The forced labor of the Israelites was made more difficult when the Egyptian king withheld straw for making brick. The Israelites first had to gather straw for themselves (Exod. 5:7) and finally had to resort to collecting stubble (5:12). On the basis of the biblical record, it has usually been assumed that straw was necessary as binding material, that bricks could not be made satisfactorily without straw, and the Egyptian bricks generally contained a certain amount of straw.

On the contrary, T. Eric Peet, Egyptologist of the University of Liverpool, stated that the use of straw in making bricks was "somewhat rare" in ancient times and that the Nile mud coheres so well that any binding material would be quite unnecessary (PEOT, 99). He added that the reference to the use of straw in brick making is often used to demonstrate the biblical writer's acquaintance with Egyptian customs, but that it actually proves his ignorance of Egyptian practice (PEOT, 100). Peet's treatment of the matter leaves one with the impression that the Bible was wrong in implying that straw was necessary in making bricks.

Archaeological evidence does not bear out Peet's rather extreme assertion that the use of straw in bricks "is somewhat rare, more particularly in ancient times" (PEOT, 99). An ancient Egyptian document, the Papyrus Anastasi, contains the lament of an officer who had to erect buildings on the frontier of Egypt, probably in the region of the present-day Suez Canal. He could not work, he said, explaining, "I am without equipment. There are no people to make bricks, and there is no straw in the district."[13] This document, then, definitely indicates that the overseer of building operations could not progress in his work because of a lack of straw for brick making.

I have examined many mud brick walls surrounding ancient temples in Egypt and have noted the presence of straw in many of the bricks. John Wilson, eminent Egyptologist of the University of Chicago, observed that straw was used as much as it was left out in Egyptian brick making.[14] In summary, it would be fair to state that Peet's extreme view must be definitely modified in view of the archaeological evidence.

There is, however, further evidence from another source. Edward G. Acheson, an American chemist, discovered by observation and experiment that clays were much easier to work when they contained certain organic matter.[15] In a further experiment, he boiled oat straw and added the water from the straw to clay. He found that this clay was much easier to work as a result of the admixture. This likely explains the Israelites' use of straw and, later, stubble, when the straw was not available for their brick making. Without straw or at least the organic material furnished by the stubble, the difficulty of brick making was greatly increased.

This discovery also shows that the presence of some bricks in Egypt containing no straw, as indicated by Peet in an overstatement, in no way detracts from the biblical indication of the desirability of straw in brick making. Lack of visible evidence of straw in bricks means either that straw or stubble was used in small enough quantities in some bricks to be

---

[13]ELAE, English ed., 1927, 204; cf. Alan Rowe, "The Palestine Expedition," *Museum Journal* 20 (1929): 58; also Yahuda, *The Accuracy of the Bible*, 75 [YAB].

[14]Oral communication, 1946.

[15]These findings were presented by Irving A. Cowperthwaite, a Boston industrial engineer, in a paper given at the meeting of the American Scientific Affiliation in 1946. It is concisely summarized by Allan A. MacRae in MRAB, 261, and earlier reported on in *Transactions of the American Ceramic Society*, 6:31.

invisible to the casual observer, or that bricks were made with water in which straw had been soaked, or that the bricks contain no such material and would have given the brick makers more difficulty in forming them. In any event, the basic biblical indication of the desirability of straw for making bricks is fully borne out.

The Hardening of Pharaoh's Heart
(Exodus 4–14)

The statement about the hardening of Pharaoh's heart has sometimes been used in attempting to illustrate the idea that God predestinates certain people to be lost. A study of the event does not support this extreme view of predestination, which seems to set aside man's free will. In analyzing the hardening of Pharaoh's heart, we find the following significant facts:

1. Pharaoh was a wicked man before the Lord dealt with him, for he first *hardened his own heart seven times* before God hardened it once. (Reference to Pharaoh's hardening his own heart may be found in Exodus 7:13, 14, 22; 8:15, 19, 32; 9:7.)

2. Furthermore, his heart was hardened, not with reference to salvation, but in reference to *public policy*. It was a question of whether he would let Israel go. "I will harden his heart so that he will not let the people go" (Exod. 4:21).

3. God predicted that he would harden Pharaoh's heart (4:21; 7:3), but God did not actually do it until after Pharaoh had hardened his own heart seven times. (The first time God hardened Pharaoh's heart is recorded in 9:12.)

4. Pharaoh hardened his own heart *a total of seven times* (7:13, 14, 22; 8:15, 19, 32; 9:7, 34, 35; 13:5), and ten times hardening is referred to God (4:21; 7:3 [predictive]; 9:12; 10:1, 20, 27; 11:10; 14:4, 8, 17).

5. *Three different Hebrew words* are used for "harden," perhaps implying dif-

ferent degrees of resistance on the part of Pharaoh at different times. *Caved* is the weakest of the three words and means "to be dull, heavy"; it is used in 7:14; 8:15, 32; 9:7, 34. *Kashah*, meaning "to be hard," and in the causative stem (Hiph'il) "to make hard," is used in 7:3; 13:15. *Hazak*, the most intensive, implying fixed and stubborn resolution, is used in 4:21; 7:22; 8:19; 9:35.[16]

6. The hardening of Pharaoh's heart does not support the unscriptural and extreme view of predestination that seems to set aside free will. Predestination and free will are both firmly taught in the Scriptures, and both are equally true. If finite minds cannot completely understand the interrelationship between free will and predestination, there is still no justification for emphasizing free will at the expense of the sovereignty of God, or the sovereignty of God at the expense of free will. Free will is clearly taught in such Scripture passages as Matthew 23:37, where Christ said, "How often I have longed to gather my children together. . . but you were not willing," and in Revelation 22:17, "Whoever wishes, let him take the free gift of the water of life." Predestination, having a direct connection with God's foreknowledge, is clearly taught in such passages as Romans 8:29 and 1 Peter 1:2. Let us hold to both of these Scripture truths.

7. Keil and Delitzsch make the following helpful comments on the hardening of Pharaoh's heart: (1) The hardening of Pharaoh was due quite as much to his own act as to the decree of God. (2) After every one of these miracles, it is stated that Pharaoh's heart was *firm*, or *dull*, i.e., insensible to the voice of God and unaffected by the miracles performed before his eyes. (3) Not until after *the sixth plague* is it stated that the Lord made the heart of Pharaoh firm (9:12). (4) This hardening of his own heart was manifested first of all in the fact that he paid no

---

[16]*Pulpit Commentary*, 229 [PC], is helpful on this.

attention to the demand of Jehovah addressed to him through Moses and *would not* let Israel go (KD, 453–54).

The hardening of Pharaoh's heart is a good illustration of the principle laid down in Romans 1, that when people disregard the truth of God continually, God finally gives them up to their own wicked ways ("God gave them over"; cf. Rom. 1:24, 26–28).

The Plagues (Exodus 7–12); Their Significance in the Light of Archaeology

Each time Pharaoh refused to let Israel go, a plague was sent upon the land of Egypt. These plagues were a great nuisance and a great burden to the Egyptians, but more than that, they exposed the powerlessness of their gods. When the first plague struck, the Nile was turned to blood. The Egyptians worshiped the Nile as the source of life. So by the first plague, one of their very own gods was made a plague and a horror to them, and his powerlessness before the true and living God was demonstrated. Likewise other deities were shown to be powerless in the face of the succeeding plagues of frogs, lice, flies, death of cattle, boils, hail, locusts, darkness, and death of the firstborn.

Archaeological discoveries reveal the gross polytheism of the ancient Egyptians. For example, in addition to the Nile god (plague 1), they worshiped the frog god (Heqt, plague 2), the entire bovine family (cow, calf, bull, plague 5), various sun gods (plague 9), and the pharaoh himself as divine and a manifestation of the sun god (plague 10, when the son of Pharaoh died).[17]

Miraculous Nature of the Plagues

Efforts have sometimes been made to explain away the plagues as natural phenomena in Egypt. It is quite true that unusual quantities of frogs and lice, unexpected darkness and the other serious heightening of natural phenomena have been known in Egypt. An examination of the plagues shows, however, that they were miraculous in at least five different ways: (1) *Intensification*—frogs, insects, plagues on cattle, hail, and darkness were all known in Egypt, but now they are intensified far beyond the ordinary occurrence. (2) *Prediction*—the time was set for the coming of the flies ("tomorrow," 8:23), the death of cattle (9:5), the hail (9:18), and the locusts (10:4). The removal time was also set: e.g., frogs (8:10) and thunder (9:29). Modern science cannot accurately predict the cessation of natural phenomena such as hail. (3) *Discrimination*—in Goshen there were no flies (8:22), no death of cattle (9:4), no hail (9:26), and so forth. (4) *Orderliness*—the severity of the plagues increased until they ended with the death of Pharaoh's firstborn. (5) *Moral purpose*—the plagues were not just freaks of nature, but carried a moral purpose in these ways: (a) The gods of Egypt were discredited, a purpose indicated in Exodus 12:12; the Nile-god, frog-god, and sun-god were all shown to be powerless before God. (b) Pharaoh was made to know that the Lord is God, and to acknowledge him (9:27; 10:16). (c) God was revealed as Savior, in rescuing Israel from the hands of the Egyptians (14:30).

---

[17]For an extended discussion of how the plagues attacked the gods and theology of Egypt, see John J. Davis, *Moses and the Gods of Egypt* (Grand Rapids: Baker, 1971).

Chapter 8

Out of Egypt

(Exodus 12–40)

The Passover (Exodus 12:1–11ff.)

At the time when Israel was preparing to leave Egypt, God gave instructions to offer the Passover sacrifice, a lamb for each house, unless the household was too small for one lamb (Exod. 12:3–4). The lamb was a type of Christ; it was to be without blemish (12:5), foreshadowing Christ's sinlessness; it was to be a lamb of the first year, in its prime, as Christ was in his prime at the time of his public ministry and death on the cross; its blood was to be shed by the whole congregation (12:6), symbolic of the fact that the whole world is responsible for the death of Christ; the blood was to be placed on the doorposts (12:7), illustrating the fact that Christ's blood must be appropriated for one to be saved.

Critical View of the Passover; Answer from Archaeology

The critical view has held that the Passover was merely an adaptation of an agricultural feast, presumably a Canaanite pagan feast. This view is widespread, as indicated by older as well as current standard Bible encyclopedias and well-known and accepted works on the Old Testament. Concessions to such a view have been made in the teaching at some seminaries in recent decades.

Archaeological discoveries, however, show the wide gulf between the Canaanite religious practices and the feasts revealed by God to the Israelites. A most striking discovery that throws light on the pagan religious practices of Canaan and Syria is that of the Ras Shamra tablets, found in 1929 after a farmer accidentally uncovered a subterranean passageway on the coast of Syria. These tablets show a sensual paganism, as illustrated in the description of the god El, who had several wives. One of the tablets describing El reads as follows, "Women, each a wife of El, even his servants,—he shall cleanse their lips, shall lift them up; their lips are sweet, sweet like the pomegranate. With them is kissing and conception. . ." (translation in BAB, 355, lines 48–51).

Albright well summarizes the significance of the Ras Shamra tablets in this respect when he says, "Every fresh publication of Canaanite mythological texts makes the gulf between the religions of Canaan and of Israel increasingly clear.[1] Thus the critical idea that the feasts of Israel are to be connected with the pagan Canaanite festivals does not find support, for every essential aspect of Canaanite religion is completely different from that of Israel, as shown by the Ras Shamra tablets. I reject the idea that the Passover was a Canaanite feast.

The Exodus (Exodus 12); the Sojourn and the Monuments; Archaeological Light

After the tenth plague, which resulted in the death of the firsborn, Pharaoh called for Moses and not only gave him permission but even urged him to leave Egypt and take the children of Israel with him (Exod. 12:30–32). They departed from Egypt after a sojourn of 430 years (Exod. 12:40–41). During that time they had increased from some seventy souls (Exod. 1:5) to a large multitude of six hundred thousand men (those over twenty, as indicated in Num. 1:45–46). With women and children, there would have been a total number of at least some two and a half million. (Most estimates of the total range from two to three million.)

Since the Israelites were in Egypt for a long period, one might expect some evidence concerning them on the Egyptian monuments. A study of the monuments, however, shows that the Egyptians did not record matters uncomplimentary to themselves. The plagues and the Exodus of Israel were a national calamity and surely would have been carefully avoided in the monumental records. Furthermore, when something was recorded that proved to be uncomplimentary or distasteful to a later regime, it was effaced at the first opportunity. For example, after the Hyksos were expelled (see chapter 7), their monuments were destroyed. Also, after the death of Hatshepsut (see chapter 7), Thutmose III chiseled away the name and representations of this queen (SSWE, 46; see also figure 5, p. 78). In view of this archaeological evidence of the Egyptian's ability at "chiseling," it is little wonder that nothing has been found on the monuments telling of Israel's sojourn in that land.

Of course there is more to consider than the monuments when explaining why there is no evidence of the Hebrew sojourn in Egypt. First, the Hebrews lived in the eastern delta, which is more moist than the rest of Egypt, and ancient remains decompose more rapidly and more thoroughly there. Second, they had been reduced to slavery, and the people who normally received recognition were royalty, nobility, and the priesthood of the official cults. Third, not many among the Hebrews were educated sufficiently to produce records, and papyrus materials would not have survived long in the delta. Fourth, if they did keep records on papyrus or animal skins, they would have taken them along at the time of the Exodus. Last, the area where they lived is now heavily populated, and early remains that may have survived are not likely to be excavated.

Date of the Exodus

Earlier discussions on biblical chronology have indicated that the Hebrew text of the Old Testament puts the date of the Exodus at about 1446 B.C. This is deduced primarily from 1 Kings 6:1, which says that the Exodus took place 480 years before the dedication of the temple,

---

[1]W.F. Albright, "Recent Progress in North-Canaanite Research," BASOR, 70 (April 1938): 24. Four useful books on Ras Shamra (ancient Ugarit) are Peter C. Craigie, *Ugarit and the Old Testament* (Grand Rapids: Eerdmans, 1983); Adrian Curtis, *Ugarit* (Grand Rapids: Eerdmans, 1985); Charles F. Pfeiffer, *Ras Shamra and the Bible* (Grand Rapids: Baker, 1962); Gordon D. Young, *Ugarit in Retrospect* (Winona Lake, Ind.: Eisenbrauns, 1981).

which occurred in the fourth year of Solomon's reign—967–966. If the Exodus is dated about 1440, the conquest should be placed about 1400, because the Israelites wandered in the wilderness for forty years before crossing the Jordan and beginning the conquest of Canaan.

As also already noted, John Garstang concluded from his excavation at Jericho (1930–1936) that the city fell about 1400 B.C. (GJJ, 147). Although many contested his conclusions, he reaffirmed them in a joint publication with his son after World War II, when he could once more gain access to his stored records.[2] When Kathleen Kenyon conducted the British School of Archaeology excavations at Jericho (1952–1958), she tended to put the fall of the town between 1350 and 1325.[3] But when the final report on her work came out after her death, information in it supported the fall of Jericho about 1400.[4]

Furthermore, an approximate date of 1400 for the beginning of the conquest fits admirably into the context of Egyptian history. At about that time the Amarna Age began and Egyptian control of Canaan rapidly disintegrated, explaining how it would have been possible for the Hebrews to invade a land where powerful Egyptian pharaohs had effectively campaigned. The situation was this. Amenhotep III (1412–1375) and especially Amenhotep IV (1387–1366) launched what is called the Amarna Revolution. This involved moving the capital from Thebes to Amarna (necessitating construction of the latter) and a religious shift to a quasi-monotheism. Instead of worship of the many gods of Egypt, the crown restricted worship to the sun god Aton, but this was

not a true monotheism, because the pharaoh was also considered divine. So during the period roughly from 1400 to 1365 the kings of Egypt were more interested in making religious reforms and expending the energies of the nation on gratifying their personal desires than they were on maintaining a powerful empire. The royal correspondence found at Amarna demonstrates that Egyptian puppet rulers of Palestine sent the pharaohs frequent calls for help during that half century. Local disturbances and the invasion of the Habiru (possibly related in some way to the Hebrews) were the occasions of such requests. But cushioned amid the luxuries of Egypt, the pharaohs chose the path of personal enjoyment rather than royal responsibility. The pleas went unheeded.

The early date of the Exodus is objected to by such scholars as Albright, who pointed out that Glueck's explorations in Edomite territory revealed that this area had no sedentary population until the thirteenth century B.C.[5] Therefore, the Israelites could not have been stopped by them on their way to Palestine at the beginning of the fourteenth century B.C. However, we may suggest with Unger[6] that as nomads the Edomites could have stopped the Israelites; certainly if the nomadic Israelites were able to carry on warfare, nomadic Edomites likewise could have done so. Or we could conjecture that Glueck's assignment of dates may need refinement. It should be pointed out that Glueck's conclusions are based on dates assigned to pottery fragments, and Albright himself stated that pottery evidence for dating some of the

[2]John and J.B.E. Garstang, The Story of Jericho (London: Marshall, Morgan & Scott, 1948), xiv [GSJ].

[3]Kathleen Kenyon, Digging up Jericho (New York: Praeger, 1957), 262.

[4]Bryant G. Wood, "Did the Israelites Conquer Jericho?" Biblical Archaeology Review (March/April 1990), 45–57.

[5]William F. Albright, From the Stone Age to Christianity, 2nd ed. (Baltimore: Johns Hopkins, 1957), 195.

[6]Merrill F. Unger, Archaeology and the Old Testament (Grand Rapids: Zondervan, 1954), 151.

copper mines west and south of Edom was not conclusive.[7]

Another major problem confronting one who accepts the early date of the Exodus is the fact that the Israelites built Pithom and Raamses (Exod. 1:11). Raamses I did not rule until about 1300. Unger suggested the difficulty here may be removed by concluding that Raamses is a modernization or renaming of the ancient place-name Zoan-Avaris. A similar situation occurs in Genesis 14:14, where *Dan* is substituted for the older city name of *Laish*.[8]

Nothing is solved by asserting, as many do, that the Exodus could not have taken place until after 1300 because the store city of Raamses was named after the ruling pharaoh. Moses was eighty at the time of the Exodus (Exod. 7:7). If the date of the Exodus is set at about 1275, Moses would have been born about 1355. The Hebrews built the store city of Raamses before the birth of Moses, long before the reign of the first Raamses (Exod. 1:11). So either Raamses may have been a modernization of Zoan-Avaris, or the town of Raamses may not have been named after the ruling king at all; possibly Raamses was a venerated royal or religious name of centuries' standing.

Third, Yigael Yadin, eminent excavator of Hazor, claimed that Hazor did not fall to the Israelites until the second third of the thirteenth century B.C. (EAEHL, 2:494). But Scripture indicates that Hazor fell to the Israelites twice: in the days of Joshua (Josh. 11:10–11), when Jabin I ruled, and in the days of Deborah and Barak (Judg. 4:2, 23–24), when another Jabin ruled. Yadin assumed that Joshua's conquest is to be related to a thirteenth-century destruction in the lower city of Hazor. There was, however, evidence of destruction at the site around 1400 B.C. or a little later in Areas H and K of the lower city (EAEHL, 2:481–82). What is more natural than to

conclude that the 1400 destruction dates to Joshua's day and the thirteenth-century destruction dates to the period of the Judges?

Fourth, it is argued that the palace's accessibility to Moses militates against the early date of the Exodus. The reasoning is that such accessibility indicates the palace was in the delta region, where the Israelites lived, and the periods when the palace was located in the delta were the days of Joseph and during the thirteenth century B.C. However, the pharaoh of the Exodus could have met Moses at a secondary palace or administrative center. The argument is not conclusive proof for the late date of the Exodus. Moreover, both Thutmose III and Amenhotep II, who together ruled from 1482 to 1425, were active in building projects in the delta.

Fifth, the destruction of Bethel, Lachish, and Debir, presumably by Israelites, is claimed to have occurred about 1230 and therefore to support a late date for the Exodus (see EAEHL, 1:192; 3:743; 1:177). Seemingly, this is strong evidence for the late date of the Exodus, but a second glance puts the matter in a different light. Those cities fell about the same time and near the beginning of the conquest, according to the Joshua narrative. But certainly the conquest did not occur as late as 1230, because the inscription on the Stele of Pharaoh Merneptah represents the Hebrews as settled in Canaan when Merneptah's armies attacked them about 1230. If adjustment in the dates assigned to the destruction of those sites needs to be made, how effective is the use of the evidence in establishing the date of the Exodus? Additionally, it is important to note that while Joshua captured Bethel, Lachish, and Debir, nothing is said about destroying them; he burned only Ai, Jericho, and Hazor (Josh. 6:24; 8:19; 11:13). Some of Joshua's conquests

[7]Albright, *Stone Age*, 195.
[8]Unger, *Archaeology*, 149.

were not permanent. We know that Debir had to be recaptured later (Josh. 15:13–17), and possibly the others did also. If dates of destruction at Bethel, Lachish, and Debir are correct, they may well refer to attacks during the days of the judges instead of to Joshua's conquests.

Finally, Beno Rothenberg, as a result of his excavations in the Timna Valley, south of the Dead Sea (1964–1970), concluded that the copper mining and smelting activity there did not date to Solomon's time but to the fourteenth to twelfth centuries (including the days of Raamses II) instead. This would mean that there was "large-scale Pharaonic industrial enterprise" in this region during the thirteenth century. With hordes of Egyptian troops and workers swarming all over the area during that century, it would seem unlikely that Hebrews in large numbers could have been there at the same time. He felt that his discoveries would require "reconsideration" of the thirteenth-century date of the Exodus, the prevailing view of Israeli scholars.[9]

In conclusion, it seems that archaeological discoveries increasingly support an approximate 1400 date for the conquest and a 1440 date for the Exodus.

Route of the Exodus: Critical View and Answer From Archaeological Evidence

In leaving Egypt, the Israelites went eastward through the delta, from Rameses to Succoth (Exod. 12:37), then to Etham (13:20), and finally to Baal-zephon by the shores of the Red Sea (14:2).

The route of the Exodus has been questioned by the critics. Peet says, "We are not in a position to discover what route the Israelites really followed, except in so far as we may conjecture it by the application of common sense to the problem. All we can hope to recover is the route which the compilers of the ninth century B.C. and onward thought that they followed, which is a very different thing" (PEOT, 126). Caiger reflects this same attitude when he says that "the dotted line showing the 'journey of the Israelites' in most of our Scripture atlases has no real authority" (CBS, 78). It is quite true that many of the sites given in the Bible as lying on the route of the Exodus and the wilderness journeys have not yet been identified.

Archaeological light, however, has been brought to bear periodically so that even Alan Gardiner, the Egyptologist, who long objected to the historicity of the route of the Exodus on topographical grounds, withdrew his objections in 1933. Albright pointed out Gardiner's change of view, and stated:

> With our present knowledge of the topography of the eastern Delta the account of the start of the Exodus given in Exodus 12:37 and 13:20ff. is perfectly sound topographically. . . . Many additional pieces of evidence for the substantial historicity of the account of the Exodus and the wandering in the regions of Sinai, Midian, and Kadesh can easily be given, thanks to our greatly increased knowledge of topography and archaeology. We must content ourselves here with the assurance that there is no longer any room for the still dominant attitude of hyper-criticism toward the early historical traditions of Israel. (ASAC, 194)

M.G. Kyle related that travelers who follow the coast of the Red Sea, along the line of the Exodus, need no other guidebook than the Bible. The whole topography corresponds to that mentioned in the biblical account.[10]

The Parting of the Red Sea (Exodus 14:21ff.)

After Israel had left Egypt, Pharaoh changed his mind and determined to

---

[9]Beno Rothenberg, *Were These King Solomon's Mines?* (New York: Stein & Day, 1972), 184.
[10]Floyd E. Hamilton, *The Basis of Christian Faith*, rev. ed. (New York: Harper, 1933), 172 [HBCF]. A third edition was issued in 1946.

pursue them (Exod. 14:9). When the Egyptians approached the stopping place of the Israelites, "Moses stretched out his hand over the sea, and all that night the LORD drove the sea back with a strong east wind" (Exod. 14:21). It is said that the driving back of water by a wind has been observed in modern times. General Tulloch reported a baring of the sands when a strong east wind drove back the waters of Lake Manzaleh seven miles.[11] Kyle says that such heaping up of waters by the wind is well known and sometimes amounts to seven or eight feet in Lake Erie.[12] The significant thing, however, in the parting of the waters for the Israelites was the time element. This was not just a freak parting of the waters by a chance wind, but rather the intervention of God in sending a wind at the time necessary to save Israel.[13] The time element is sometimes the major factor in a miracle.

Some have argued that *yam sûph* (translated "Red Sea" in KJV and other versions) should be correctly translated "Sea of Reeds" and have sought to relate it to a lake or lakes now part of the Suez Canal system. It is difficult to support such a position effectively, however. The Greek translation of the Old Testament (the Septuagint), Acts 7:36, and Hebrews 11:29 understand *yam sûph* to refer to the Red Sea (NIV mg. of Acts 7:36 and Heb. 11:29 reads, "That is, Sea of Reeds"). Moreover, Exodus 14:27 and 15:5, 8, 10 seem to require something more than one of the lakes of the Suez region. Furthermore, it has been observed that *yam sûph* in Exodus 10:19 would seemingly have to be more than marshy lakes of the Suez region; the Gulf of Suez is large enough to destroy hordes of locusts

and is properly placed for a northwest wind to blow the locusts into its waters. Certainly in Numbers 14:25 *yam sûph* is the Red Sea. Perhaps it is best, then, to conclude that the Hebrews journeyed southward to the west of the present canal system and crossed the Red Sea just south of the modern port of Suez.

The Journey to Sinai (Exodus 15–19)
(See Map 4.)

After the children of Israel had walked across the dry land on the bottom of the Red Sea and had safely reached the other shore (Exod. 14:22), they continued their journey into the Wilderness of Shur (15:22), on the east of the Gulf of Suez (the western arm of the Red Sea). The successive stages of the journey to Mount Sinai may be conveniently summarized as follows:

1. *Desert of Shur* (Exod. 15:22). No water was available there, and so Israel went on to Marah.

2. *Marah* (Exod. 15:23). Here they were unable to drink the bitter waters until the Lord showed Moses a tree that, when cast into the waters, made them sweet (15:25). Marah is sometimes identified with a site now called Huwara, about seven miles east of the Red Sea and about thirty miles south of the place where, according to tradition, the Israelites first stopped after crossing the Red Sea (BBHM, 80). At Huwara there is a basin about five feet in diameter still containing bitter water. The next stop was Elim.[14]

3. *Elim* (Exod. 15:27). Elim is described as having twelve wells of water and seventy palm trees. It is thought by some to be the present-day Wady Ghurundel,

---

[11]*Victoria Institute.*, 28:267, cited in POTH, 100–101.

[12]Article on "Moses," ISBE, 2086, citing Wright, *Scientific Confirmations of the Old Testament*, 106 [WSC].

[13]The Bible specifically states that "The LORD drove the sea back with a strong east wind" (Exod. 14:21).

[14]For an interesting discussion of the vast quantity of fossil water that lies under the Sinai Desert and comes to the surface in springs noted in Scripture, see Arie Issar, "Fossil Water under the Sinai-Negev Peninsula," *Scientific American* (July 1985), 104–10.

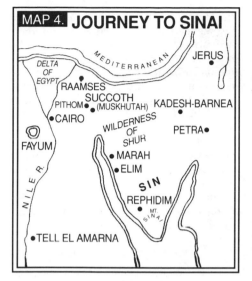

MAP 4. JOURNEY TO SINAI

JERUS
DELTA OF EGYPT
MEDITERRANEAN
RAAMSES
SUCCOTH
PITHOM (MUSKHUTAH)
KADESH-BARNEA
CAIRO
WILDERNESS OF SHUR
PETRA
FAYUM
NILE
MARAH
ELIM
SIN
REPHIDIM
MT. SINAI
TELL EL AMARNA

five miles from Huwarah (possibly Marah), although it may be farther south. *Murray's Handbook* says of Wady Ghurundel:

> This may be safely identified with Elim. The whole desert is almost absolutely bare and barren, but Wady Ghurundel is fringed with trees and shrubs, forming a charming oasis. Here are the stunted palms, with their hairy trunks and dishevelled branches. Here, too, are the feathery tamarisks, with gnarled boughs, their leaves dripping with what the Arabs call manna. And here is the acacia, with its gray foliage and bright blossoms, tangled by its desert-growth into a thicket. Pleasant is the acacia to the sight, wearied by the desert-glare; but it has a higher and holier interest, as the tree of the 'burning bush,' and the 'shittim-wood' of the tabernacle.[15]

4. *Desert of Sin* (Exod. 16:1). The region of Sinai is a rugged area of rocks and ridges, varied in spots with shady nooks and ravines. For much of the way through Sinai, Israel traveled over rocky ascents and through narrow defiles. The Desert of Sin, however, is a contrast to much of Sinai, being an extensive sandy plain,

stretching along the shores of the Red Sea (BBHM, 81).

While Israel was in the Desert of Sin, God sent the manna (Exod. 16;14–15ff.). Attempts to identify the manna of Scripture with the gum of the tamarisk tree and other substances are not successful (see above, the description of Wady Ghurundel, under "Elim"). There are many basic differences between the gum of the tamarisk tree and manna.

5. *Rephidim* (Exod. 17:1). From the Desert of Sin, the Israelites went toward the interior of the Sinai Peninsula, probably going through the valley that today is called the Wady Feiran (BBHM, 81). At the next important stop, Rephidim, Moses smote the rock to bring forth water (17:1, 6), and here also the Israelites were sustained by the Lord in their battle with the Amalekites (17:8).

6. *Mount Sinai* (Exod. 19:1–2), *the Sojourn at Sinai* (Exod. 19–Num. 10). Finally, in the third month after Israel's Exodus from Egypt, they journeyed the fifteen miles from Rephidim to Mount Sinai and camped before the mountain. Israel remained at Mount Sinai for about a year (Cf. Exod. 19:1 with Num. 10:11–12). All of the events in the remainder of Exodus, the material in Leviticus, and the happenings of the first part of Numbers through 10:10 took place at Sinai. In Numbers 10:11–12 we read of Israel's departure from Mount Sinai as they began their journey north to Kadesh.

Identification of Mount Sinai (Exodus 19)

Thirty-five times in the Old Testament Sinai is referred to as a desert or mountain, and seventeen times the same area or mountain is referred to by the name of Horeb. The terms are often used inter-

---

[15]*Murray's Handbook for Syria and Palestine*, [MHSP], 14, cited in BBHM, 80–81.

changeably, and thus it is evident that Sinai and Horeb refer to the same place.

Various locations for Sinai have been suggested, some authorities even placing this mountain far over in Midian, to the east of the Gulf of Akabah (the eastern arm of the Red Sea). The traditional view, however, has always held that Mount Sinai is to be identified with the mountain today called Jebel Musa. Edward Robinson, the pioneer American explorer in Palestine, thought that the peak next to Jebel Musa (called es-Sufsafeh) would fit the conditions better because from here one could see the large plain at the base of the mountain, and this plain was probably the place where the Israelites were encamped.[16]

There is, however, no compelling reason to abandon the traditional identification of Mount Sinai with Jebel Musa (meaning "Mount of Moses" in Arabic), and "it meets all the requirements indicated in the Old Testament" (ABB, 42). Jebel Musa, part of a great range of peaks, rises with imposing grandeur to a height of 7,370 feet. At the base of the mountain is a large plain, about a mile long, which is likely the place where the Israelites camped (RBR, 95).

The Ten Commandments (Exodus 20); the Purpose of the Law

While Israel was at Mount Sinai, Moses went up into the mountain and there received the Ten Commandments and the other laws that God revealed to him. The purpose of the law is at least threefold: (1) To reveal man's sinfulness. Man knows that he is a sinner by the testimony of conscience, but by the published law of God he has an intensified "knowledge of sin" (Rom. 3:19, speaking of what the law says, adds, "that every mouth may be silenced and the whole world held accountable to God"). (2) To reveal God's holiness. The nature of the commandments shows the holiness of God; but the ceremonial law and particularly the tabernacle with its Most Holy Place emphasizes the holiness of God. (3) To lead the sinner to Christ. This aspect of the law is set forth by Paul: "So the law was put in charge to lead us to Christ" (Gal. 3:24).[17] The law pointed to the cross of Christ (by its offerings, priesthood, and tabernacle) as the only way of salvation and access to God. (For development of the preceding material, see TSTS, 113.)

Our Relation to the Law

In the death of Christ the believer is delivered not only from the curse of the law (Gal. 3:13), but also from the law itself (Col. 2:14). May we then break the Ten Commandments? Paul shows that the answer is no, for he refers to being "not free from God's law but. . . under Christ's law" (1 Cor. 9:21). We "belong to another. . . that we might bear fruit to God" (Rom. 7:4). Every commandment of the Decalogue, except the fourth, is reaffirmed and sanctioned in the New Testament. The commandments are repeated in the New Testament for our instruction, that we may know what the will of the Lord is. The mere keeping of the commandments, however, will not save a person; it is only by trusting in Christ as Savior that one is saved. (For further discussion concerning our relationship to the law, see TLST, 170–71.)

Archaeological Light on the Prohibition of Image Worship; Critical View; No Images of Yahweh

The second commandment specifically says, "You shall not make for yourself an

---

[16]Edward Robinson, *Biblical Researches in Palestine*, 3rd ed. (Boston: Crocker and Brewster, 1868), 1:106–7 [RBR].

[17]"Schoolmaster" of the KJV obscures the intent of the Greek and the practices of the Roman world. A *paidagogos* (Greek) was a slave who had supervision of a child and took him to school, i.e., to the schoolmaster. A recent discussion of the term *paidagogos* is found in Norman H. Young, "The Figure of the *Paidagogos* in Art and Literature," BA (June 1990), 80–86.

idol. . ." (Exod. 20:4). The necessity for this commandment is indicated by archaeological discoveries, which show that the Canaanites of Palestine were given to image worship (BWMS, 189). Now that God was preparing Israel for entrance into Canaan, it was particularly fitting to emphasize the prohibition of idol worship, for Israel would be surrounded by idolatry in Canaan. The excavations in Palestine reveal figures of gods on stelae (stone monuments; singular, stele), such as the stele of the god Mekal, found in one of the Late Bronze Age temples of Bethshan (BWMS, 218). Small images in bronze are not uncommon and usually represent gods rather than goddesses. The most common representations of goddesses are the clay plaques or figurines. These figurines may have been household deities, like the teraphim of the Old Testament, or they may have been used in some part of sympathetic magic (BWMS, 219–20).

According to the critical view, the religion of Israel went through an evolutionary development, from animism (worship of spirits) through various stages to polytheism, and finally to monotheism. According to this theory, images were worshiped until the late period, when the prohibition against image worship was supposedly made. Thus the early date and the validity of the second commandment are denied, as seen in Wellhausen's statement that "the prohibition of images was during the older period quite unknown" (WPHI, 439).

If images were worshiped by Israel, as the critics have said, and if the prohibition against images was a late addition to the Scriptures, then we would expect to find images of Yahweh—i.e., the Lord. G. Ernest Wright, an American archaeologist, formerly of Harvard, points out that the excavations have not produced images of the Lord. A great amount of material has been excavated, yet, says Wright, "we can nowhere place our hands on a figure of Yahweh."[18] Thus archaeology does not support the critical idea that images were worshiped by the true followers of the Lord. In fact, this prohibition seems to have been so rigidly ingrained that even backsliders did not make images of the Lord, but contented themselves with statues of Baal and of the fertility goddess.

Directions for Building the Tabernacle (Exodus 25–40)

The last sixteen chapters of Exodus are largely concerned with the directions for building the tabernacle, which was to serve as a meeting place between God and Israel. This purpose of the tabernacle was summarized in God's words to Moses regarding Israel: "Have them make a sanctuary for me, and I will dwell among them" (Exod. 25:8).

When Moses was preparing to direct the construction of the tabernacle, God told him to allow whoever was willing to bring an offering to provide the necessary materials (Exod. 35:4–5). Illumination and confirmation have come from the Near East concerning several of these materials. We will concern ourselves with two of them.

Material for the Tabernacle: The Skins of Sea Cows (Exodus 35:7, 23)

The material referred to as "badgers' skins" was used to make the last of the four coverings for the tabernacle (36:19). One notes, however, that the Hebrew word rendered "badgers' skins" in the KJV is translated "sealskins" in the text of the ASV, and "the hides of sea cows" in the NIV (Exod. 25:5). What reason is there for this variation, and what light is there on this word from a study of the languages and the animals of the Near East?

---

[18]G. Ernest Wright, "The Terminology of Old Testament Religion and Its Significance," *Journal of Near Eastern Studies* 1, 4 (October 1942): 413 [JNES].

The Hebrew word involved is *tahash*. The writers of the Talmud favored the idea that the word meant "badger." Superficially there is a resemblance between *tahash* and the Latin word *taxus* and the German word *Dachs*, both meaning "badger." This derivation was observed by the translators of the kjv. One difficulty with this translation is that badgers probably were not available to the Israelites when they were out in the Sinai wilderness, since this animal does not seem to be found in the region of Sinai nor in Egypt, although it is fairly abundant in Syria, in the Lebanon region to the north of Palestine.[19]

Another difficulty with the "badger" translation lies in the fact that Latin and German belong to families of languages other than Hebrew. Hebrew belongs to the group known as Semitic languages, which includes Arabic. In Arabic a word similar to the Hebrew *tahash* is the word *tuhas*, meaning "dolphin."[20] The Arabic *tuhas* was said by Tristram to be applied also to another marine animal called the dugong, or sea cow, which outwardly resembles dolphins and porpoises.

The dugong averages from five to nine feet in length. It is often found along the shore, where it feeds on seaweed. Since the dugong inhabits the seas in the region of Egypt and Sinai, it is quite likely that the Hebrew word refers to this marine animal. The Hebraist, Gesenius, as well as travelers in the Near East, have pointed out that the Arabs of Sinai wear sandals made of dugong skin.[21] This is significant, since shoes of "leather" (*tahash*) are referred to in Ezekiel 16:10.

While the seal and porpoise, as well as the dolphin and dugong, are all found in the waters near Sinai, and are possible candidates for the *tahash*, most recent writers favor the dugong.[22] The evidence given above would also favor this identification.

Materials for the Tabernacle: the Bronze Mirrors (Exodus 35:5, 24; 38:8); Critical View; Light from Archaeology

Copper was one of the important materials contributed for the construction of the tabernacle (Exod. 25:3; 35:5, 24). We are told that the laver was made of bronze, which was obtained from the contribution of the women's mirrors (Exod. 38:8).

The well-known nineteenth-century biblical critic Julius Wellhausen implied that this record of the laver made of bronze mirrors was a late addition to this part of the Bible when he said that it did not "belong to the original contents of the Priestly Code" (WPHI, 353). Critics usually date the parts of the Pentateuch called the "Priestly Code" (cf. the "P" document[23]) at about 500 b.c.[24] Wellhausen thus puts the record of the tabernacle entirely too late for the time of Moses (c. 1500–1400) and assigns the details concerning the making of the laver to a period even later than the so-called Priestly Code.

There is no valid reason for dating the record of the bronze mirrors in the late period, for it fits into the account as an integral part. Furthermore, the details that can be compared with external evidence are shown to fit into the early period. There is specific archaeological evidence showing the use of such bronze mirrors in the Empire Period of Egyptian

---

[19]A.E. Day, "Badger," ISBE, 1929 ed., 376.

[20]Brown, Driver, Briggs, *A Hebrew and English Lexicon of the Old Testament* (New York: Houghton Mifflin, 1906), 1065 [BDB].

[21]Day, "Badger," 377.

[22]Ibid.

[23]For a brief description of the "P" document, see the section "Critical View of Genesis 1 and 2," in chapter 2.

[24]R.H. Pfeiffer, *Introduction to the Old Testament* (New York: Harper, 1941), 256 [PIOT].

history (c. 1550–1100), the period contemporary with Moses and the Exodus. Excavations in Egypt have produced many bronze mirrors, showing their abundant use in that time. The reason why Israelite women happened to have such mirrors is that they had just come out of Egypt and had these mirrors as part of their possessions. They had even more mirrors than they ordinarily would have possessed, because the Egyptians gave[25] them many gifts at the time of the Exodus (Exod. 12:35–36), apparently because the Egyptians desired them to leave in order to avoid any more plagues. Such bronze mirrors from ancient Egypt may be seen in most of the large museums of the world (see PNEP index for pictures).

Critical View of the Tabernacle and the Lampstand; Archaeological Evidence to the Contrary

The critical view has tended to regard the tabernacle as a late "invention" of priestly writers and to deny, in effect, its existence in the days of Moses. Wellhausen set the critical pattern by denying the authenticity of the description of the tabernacle in Exodus (AAPB, 159), and more recent writers who hold the critical view reflect a similar attitude.

Even some of the details of the tabernacle are held to be late concepts. In recent decades some scholars have held that the seven-branched lampstand of the tabernacle reflects the Babylonian period (c. 600–500 B.C.) or the Persian period (c. 500–300) (AAPB, 161). This explanation fits in with the critical view that Exodus and Leviticus are late writings of about 500–450, assignable for the most part to the so-called "P" writer or school of writers.[26]

Archaeological excavations, however, do not support the critical idea that a sevenfold lamp is a late idea. In the excavations at Tell Beit Mirsim[27] it is precisely in the period of Early Iron I (1200–900 B.C.), never afterward, that we find pottery lamps with seven places for wicks, made by pinching the rim together seven times. Concerning the idea that the sevenfold lampstand reflects Babylonian or Persian times, Albright states, "Unhappily for this a priori conception. . . such lamps are found in Tell Beit Mirsim B, as well as in contemporary deposits elsewhere in Palestine" (i.e., c. 1200). Albright adds that he "wishes to protest most vigorously" against the idea that the priestly sources give "a fanciful account of the tabernacle," reflecting only "priestly ideals of the Exilic Age" (AAPB, 159).

During my sixth, seventh, and eighth seasons at Dothan (1959, 1960, and 1962) activities included the excavation of two tombs that dated to the Late Bronze II Period (1400–1200 B.C.) and the beginning of Iron I (1200–1100). Four different seven-spouted lamps were found in these early tombs, attesting further to the early date of the concept of the sevenfold lamp. For a photo of one of these lamps, see BASOR (December 1960), 14, figure 3.

One does not actually have to unearth the tabernacle and its appurtenances in order to produce evidence that the critical view asserting its lateness is incorrect. The critical argument is subjective. The moment we find one sevenfold lamp in the early period, we have objective evidence to show that the critical view is not sustained, at least at that point.

---

[25]The word really implies the idea of "gave," rather than "lent," in Exodus 12:36. Cf. BDB or any Hebrew lexicon.

[26]For the "P" document, see footnote 20.

[27]Identified as the site of the biblical Kiriath Sepher (cf. Judg. 1:12). This site was excavated by Kyle and Albright, 1926, 1928ff.

Chapter 9

Mount Sinai and the Wilderness

(Leviticus, Numbers, Deuteronomy)

The Book of Leviticus

While the children of Israel were encamped before Mount Sinai, God revealed to Moses the ceremonial laws found in the book of Leviticus. The purpose of Leviticus was to furnish a guidebook for the worship of the LORD and to give instructions to the priests as to the details of this worship. Chapters 1 to 7 give instructions concerning the presentation of five offerings: the burnt, meal, peace, sin, and trespass offerings, all typifying various aspects of the death and ministry of Christ. This section is followed by directions for the consecration of the priests (Lev. 8–10), and the laws of purity (chs. 11–15), which concern the food that might be eaten and the handling of leprosy. Chapter 16 gives the directions for the ceremony of the Great Day of Atonement, in which two goats were brought before the door of the tabernacle of the congregation, the one goat to be sacrificed and the other to be let go into the wilderness, bearing the iniquities of Israel. The two goats were symbolic of Christ's death, which removed transgressions from us. The remainder of Leviticus (chs. 17–27) concerns various laws of holiness, including directions for the place of sacrifice, the significance of blood, the punishment of various sins, the feasts of the Lord (ch. 23), the sabbatical year (ch. 25), conditions of blessing in the Promised Land (ch. 26), and things dedicated to the Lord (ch. 27).

The Critical View of Levitical Laws; Light from Archaeology

The usual critical view holds that the code of Levitical laws was a late development, written down and codified about 500–450 B.C. This view was well expressed by R.H. Pfeiffer of Harvard University when he said concerning the Priestly Code: "It codifies in stereotyped and idealized form the current practices of the Second Temple, about 500 or perhaps in the next half century" (PIOT, 256). Thus, if the critical view were correct, it would mean that these laws are not Mosaic and do not date back to the period 1500–1400 B.C.

However, the fact that the Ras Shamra Tablets, dating back to about 1400 B.C., record several laws similar to those of Leviticus, shows that the critic has no right to deny the possibility of such a code of sacrificial laws as early as the time of Moses. Burrows, a liberal professor at Yale University, pointed out the presence of such offerings in the tablets: "Several of the terms employed in the Hebrew Old Testament for the various types of offering also have appeared in the Ras Shamra tablets, for example, the burnt offering, the whole burnt offering, the guilt offering, and the peace offering" (BWMS, 234).

As to why the Ras Shamra tablets contain references to sacrifices similar to those of the Mosaic laws in Leviticus, there are at least two possible answers. First, they may have been diffused from Israel at the time they were revealed to Moses (about 1450 B.C.) and have come into the practices of the Canaanites and people of Syria, being reflected in the Ras Shamra tablets (1400–1350). Second, the laws and statutes revealed by the LORD at a much earlier time (and later given in a codified form to Moses) were handed down among various peoples and appear in a modified and often corrupted form among such people as those of Ras Shamra. The fact that God gave early revelation of laws and statutes, long before the time of Moses, is shown by his saying to Isaac: "Abraham obeyed me and kept my requirements, my commands, my decrees and my laws" (Gen. 26:5).[1]

The Book of Numbers; Contents; Outline

The fourth book of the Pentateuch is called Numbers because it tells of the two numberings or censuses of the people— one at Sinai, described at the beginning of the book (Num. 1), and the other when Israel was on the plains of Moab at the close of the wanderings (ch. 26). The contents of Numbers include directions for the arrangement of the tribes in the camp of Israel, directions for the service of the Levites in taking care of the taber-nacle, the record of the sending out of the spies (ch. 13), and the events of the forty years in the wilderness, made necessary because of the unbelief of the people in not entering into the land (14:33–34).

The book of Numbers may be conveniently outlined as follows:

1. Israel at Mount Sinai, 1:1–10:10
2. Israel from Mount Sinai to Kadesh, 10:11–12:16
3. Israel at Kadesh, 13:1–19:22
4. Israel's wilderness wanderings, 20:1–33:49
5. Israel on the Plains of Moab, 33:50–36:13

Archaeological Light on the Numbering of the People

A detailed census of Israel, recorded at the beginning of Numbers, was taken while the people were still at Sinai (ch. 1) and another at the close of the wilderness wanderings when they were in the plains of Moab (ch. 26). Moses could easily have learned the methods of census taking during his life in Egypt, for the archaeological discoveries there show that it was a favorite custom of the pharaohs to compile exact statistics. Knight points out that papyri dating back to 3000 B.C. show that even at that early time strict census lists were made up, mention being made of the head of the house, resident female relatives, slaves, and young male children.[2]

Robert Dick Wilson demonstrates the way this material in Numbers fits into the early period of the time of Moses (c. 1500–1400 B.C.), and not into the late period (c. 900–400), to which the critics assign the Pentateuch. In this connection he says, "The form of the numeration of Numbers 1–4 bears many resemblances to those of the Annals of Tahutmes III"

---

[1]For a bibliography on Ras Shamra, see chapter 8, the section entitled "Critical View of the Passover," pages 85–86.

[2]KNJ, 181, citing Griffith, *Law Quarterly Review* (1898), 44–45.

(the same as Thutmose III or Thothmes III; see chapter 7, the section entitled "The Pharaoh of the Oppression," pages 79–81).[3]

From Sinai to Kadesh; Location of Kadesh

After Israel had encamped for nearly a year before Mount Sinai, the Lord directed the people to depart, then guided them with the cloud (Num. 10:11–36). Israel traveled north, finally coming to Kadesh, or Kadesh Barnea, the traditional site of which is about forty miles south of Beersheba.

The view was long held that Kadesh is to be identified with the present site called Ain-Kadis ('Ain Qedeis) in Arabic, forty-nine miles southwest of Beersheba. H. Clay Trumbull, former editor of the *Sunday School Times*, made a complete study of the question and wrote a book of nearly five hundred pages on the subject. He concluded that Kadesh was best identified with Ain-Kadis for several reasons: (1) It is in a region that is a strategic stronghold on the southern border of Canaan, near the principal roads into Canaan. (2) It is at the natural boundary line of southern Canaan. (3) It fits in with the other landmarks mentioned in the biblical text. (4) It integrates best with the journey of Israel after leaving Kadesh. (5) Ain-Kadis best corresponds with the biblical references to Kadesh.[4]

In later years other sites have been proposed as the location of Kadesh. The most important of these involved the work of C. Leonard Woolley and T.E. Lawrence, who in their exploration of the wilderness to the south of Palestine (1913–1914) concluded that 'Ain el-Qudeirat and its nearby Tell el-Qudeirat (five

miles northwest of 'Ain Qedeis) was the site of Kadesh.[5] This identification is now generally accepted. 'Ain el-Qudeirat has the finest spring in the Sinai; it waters the largest oasis in northern Sinai. In 1956 M. Dothan for the Israel Department of Antiquities undertook an exploratory excavation on the tell. The excavation identified three periods of occupation: the first, dated by pottery to the tenth century B.C.; the second, consisting of a substantial fortress, perhaps of the time of Jehoshaphat around the middle of the ninth century; and the third, to the Persian period in the fifth and fourth centuries B.C.[6] Even if 'Ain el-Qudeirat is accepted as the site of Kadesh, it is likely that other springs in the general vicinity (Ain-Kadis, et al.) served the needs of the wandering Israelites.

Supposed Difficulties in Numbers; Formation for Travel; Number of Quail

Critics have often pointed out supposed difficulties and impossibilities in the book of Numbers. For instance, they have said it would have been impossible to get the large numbers of Israelites (two million or more) in formation to travel. According to this objection, the half million Israelites in each of the four main divisions could not have assembled into marching formation in any reasonable time, and after they formed, they would have stretched out a length of twenty-two miles, according to Colenso, or even six hundred miles according to Doughty. This means that it would have taken all day to get into marching formation and then there would not have been any day left in which to travel. An analysis of this situation, however, shows that such a difficulty would not necessarily exist. As

---

[3]Robert Dick Wilson, *A Scientific Investigation of the Old Testament*, with revisions by Edward J. Young (Chicago: Moody, 1959), 43 [WSI], referring to Petrie, *History of Egypt*, 2:103–4.

[4]H. Clay Trumbull, *Kadesh-Barnea* (New York: Scribner, 1884), 311–19 [TKB], summarized in PSB, 107–8.

[5]*The Wilderness of Zin*, Palestine Exploration Fund *Annual*, vol. 3, cited in BAB, 105–6.

[6]M. Dothan, "Kadesh-Barnea," EAEHL, 3:697–98.

Whitelaw points out, two divisions could start formation at six A.M., be ready to move at ten A.M., cover a distance of ten miles in four hours and then stop at two P.M. The other two divisions could fall in line at two P.M., arrive at six P.M. and be settled for the night by ten P.M. Moreover, there is no certain evidence that the Israelites formed a regularly constructed camp every night, and it is likely that this would be done only when they reached a spot where they were to halt for some time. Furthermore, the arranging of the four divisions for marching may have gone on simultaneously, since they were widely separated from each other, with Judah on the east side of the camp, Reuben on the south, Ephraim on the west, and Dan on the north.[7] In case such simultaneous formation occurred, a distance considerably greater than ten miles could have been covered in their daily march. In the absence of more details, the critic has no right to reconstruct a situation that is apparently impossible, particularly when the available records in the Bible can be understood so as to constitute no problem.

A second difficulty concerns the quail: when the Lord sent the quail to the Israelites in the wilderness, he let them fall "round about the camp, and as it were two cubits high *upon* the face of the earth" (Num. 11:31 KJV). Agnostics who have read this have hastily assumed that the quail were piled up two cubits (three feet) deep, giving each Israelite 2,888,463 bushels of quail for the month, or 69,620 bushels each meal! They have overlooked the fact that the Hebrew word translated "upon" in this verse is the word 'al, one of the regular meanings of which is "above," as in the NIV (BDB, 752, sec. 2). Inasmuch as this Hebrew word can mean either "upon" or "above," I take it as "above,"

since it fits the context better.[8] The quail, then, flew down *above* the earth about three feet, in other words, within easy reach of the Israelites so that they might take them for food. All of the ridiculous figures indicating that there were supposedly 69,620 bushels of quail for each Israelite for each meal are based on a false and deliberately misleading presupposition. A reasonable analysis of the other supposed difficulties and contradictions in Numbers shows no necessary improbability.

From Kadesh to the Plains of Moab (Numbers 13–36)

After the spies had been sent out from Kadesh to survey Canaan (Num. 13:1–2, 17ff.) and had returned with a report of the giants and the walled cities, the Israelites complained about going into the land (14:1–3). Only two of the twelve spies, Joshua and Caleb, wished to go on into the land, but the people refused their counsel (14:6–10). Because of the unbelief of the people and their lack of trust, the LORD said that they would remain in the wilderness for forty years (Num. 14:33). Some scholars believe that Israel was in the vicinity of Kadesh for most of this period, about thirty-eight years.[9]

When the Israelites finally left Kadesh, the Edomites refused them permission to go through the land of Edom (Num. 21:14, 21). So Israel went to the south, around the land of Edom (21:4), then north to the plains of Moab, where they encountered the prophet Balaam (ch. 22). After Balaam's dealings with Israel (chs. 22–24), God gave instructions through Moses to the people concerning the law of inheritance (ch. 27), the law of offerings (ch. 28), the preparation to enter the land of Canaan (ch. 34), and the provisions for

---

[7]T. Whitelaw, "Numbers," ISBE, 1929 ed., 2168.

[8]When a word has more than one meaning, what right has anyone to choose the reading that would constitute a problem?

[9]C.M. Cobern, *Recent Explorations in Palestine*, 98ff. [CREP].

cities of refuge (ch. 35). These closing events of the book of Numbers took place while Israel was at the plains of Moab,[10] near the north end of the Dead Sea. There they remained during the time that Moses spoke to them the words recorded in Deuteronomy (Deut. 1:5ff.).

The Book of Deuteronomy

Deuteronomy is made up principally of four main addresses of Moses to the people of Israel as they were encamped on the plains of Moab a few miles east of the Jordan River, somewhat north of the north end of the Dead Sea. These addresses begin successively at 1:5; 5:1; 27:1; and 29:1. The word "Deuteronomy" comes from two Greek words meaning "second law," and the term is used in the sense of a repetition of the law previously given in the Pentateuch. The purpose of Deuteronomy is to prevent a resumé of the law already given in Exodus and Leviticus for the benefit of the generation which had grown up in the wilderness, in order that they might be prepared for entering the land of Canaan. The subjects treated include:

1. Israel's journeys in the wilderness reviewed (chs. 1–3).
2. The Ten Commandments repeated (ch. 5).
3. Dietary laws (ch. 14), feasts such as Passover (ch. 16) reviewed.

4. Conditions of blessing in the Promised Land (ch. 28).
5. Moses' final instructions, his blessing of the tribes, and his death (chs. 31–34).

Critical View of the Date of Deuteronomy; Record of Moses' Death

The critical view holds that Deuteronomy was not written by Moses,[11] but was composed much later than his day. This position invaded many of the seminary faculties of mainline denominations in the United States during the first half of this century. For example, Otto Piper, professor at Princeton Theological Seminary, indicated his acceptance of the higher critical view when he stated that Deuteronomy was not written by Moses, but "by prophetic writers after his death."[12] S.A. Cartledge of Columbia Seminary (Decatur, Georgia), casually set aside the Mosaic authorship of many parts of the Pentateuch when he said, "Moses was considered the law giver par excellence, and so the priestly writers did not hesitate to ascribe new laws to Moses so long as they felt that they were in keeping with the spirit of Moses and the laws they did have from Moses."[13]

There are several reasons why liberals date the book of Deuteronomy late, usually in the seventh century B.C., and thereby deny the Mosaic authorship. Let us examine one of these reasons.[14] The last

---

[10]Numbers 36:13, last verse in the book.

[11]Cf. Pfeiffer (PIOT, 211), who concluded that the codes of the Pentateuch, which would include much of Deuteronomy, "could not have been promulgated by Moses."

[12]Otto Piper, *God in History*, 79 [PGH].

[13]Samuel A. Cartledge, *A Conservative Introduction to the Old Testament*, (Grand Rapids: Zondervan, 1943), 70 [CCIO]. This book was misnamed when it was titled *A Conservative Introduction*. It presented many liberal views with apparent approval. When Zondervan realized the implications of numerous statements in the book, they discontinued its publication. But the book was reissued by the University of Georgia Press.

[14]If this were a text in Old Testament Introduction (i.e., Old Testament Criticism), several other reasons and the answers would be developed. (For some material on the critical view of Deuteronomy in a book that is helpful, see ASOTI, 253–57). In summary, it could be said that another reason given by liberals for the late dating of Deuteronomy, often repeated in recent

chapter of Deuteronomy records the death of Moses (34:5ff.). Critics point out that since a man cannot write of his own death, Moses could not be the author of the book. This is not a new argument. Three hundred years ago, a Dutch philosopher named Spinoza (1632–1677) remarked about the record of the death of Moses, "Such testimony cannot have been given of Moses by himself . . . but it must have come from someone who lived centuries afterwards."[15] This argument has been repeated down to the present generation.

There are at least two possible explanations of this seeming discrepancy: (1) Moses was a prophet (Deut. 34:10) and consequently could have written of his death before it occurred, but that is highly unlikely. (2) Because Joshua was the assistant, the "minister" of Moses, what would be more natural than for him, as the successor to Moses, to add a few words telling of the death of his predecessor?

We may cite a modern illustration to show that the mention of an author's death within the confines of a book does not necessarily mean that the author could not have written the book in question. In 1938, the University of Chicago Press published a book called *They Wrote on Clay: The Babylonian Tablets Speak Today*, written by Edward Chiera, Professor of Assyriology at the University of Chicago. Professor Chiera was the author

of the book, yet on page vi we read of his "untimely death." Does this mean that Chiera could not and did not write the book, just as the reference to Moses' death in Deuteronomy 34:5 supposedly indicates that Moses could not and did not write Deuteronomy? A fuller knowledge of the facts gives the answer "No."

We find that Chiera did write the book, but he died before it was finished for publication, and a younger Assyriologist and associate of Chiera, George G. Cameron,[16] prepared the book for publication and wrote the preface, which tells of Chiera's death. The reference to Chiera's death was added at the beginning of his book, whereas in Deuteronomy the eight verses that tell of Moses' death were added at the end. If in the days of Moses books had been provided with full title pages, might we not read something like this: "*Deuteronomy*, by Moses, the servant of the Lord, with biographical note by Joshua, the minister of Moses"?

If the book of Deuteronomy only appears to have been written by Moses but actually was not, then we have a case of fraud; the critics of the past generation called it "pious fraud." Albright's examination of the ancient materials convinced him that the old critical theory of "pious fraud" is not sustained. He says, regarding the assumptions of the Wellhausen school, "A third assumption, that pious fraud and pseudepigraphy were common in Israel, is without parallel in the pre-

---

decades, is that its codes "reflect Palestinian conditions" (PIOT, 211). The liberal overlooks the obvious answer. In Deuteronomy Moses was giving instructions to Israel in advance concerning procedure in the agricultural economy in which they would find themselves after the conquest. The liberal erroneously assumes that the laws in Deuteronomy concerning an agricultural economy must indicate that they had already settled down in the land (e.g., laws prohibiting the removal of an ancient landmark or boundary stone, Deuteronomy 19:14). The Bible believer, on the other hand, acknowledges that God could and did give many of the provisions in Deuteronomy in order to prepare Israel for the conditions that would obtain in Canaan.

The objection to Deuteronomy on the ground that it contains laws too advanced for the time of Moses is dealt with in the next section entitled "Critical View of the Legislation of Deuteronomy."

[15]Benedict de Spinoza, *Tractatus Theologico-Politicus*, in *The Chief Works of Benedict de Spinoza*, 1670, trans. R.H.M. Elwes (London: George Bell, 1883), 124 [STTP].

[16]Subsequently head of the department of Near Eastern Studies at the University of Michigan.

Hellenistic Orient. . . there is hardly a single known case of *pia fraus*."[17]

Critical View of the Legislation of Deuteronomy; Bearing of Archaeology on the Problem

The critical theory has held that the social and moral level of the laws of Deuteronomy (as well as those of Exodus and Leviticus) were too advanced for the time of Moses and must be dated later in the history of Israel. This critical theory seemed to integrate with other reasons that were given for denying the Mosaic authorship of Deuteronomy and other books of the Pentateuch (see material in the preceding section).

Archaeological discoveries, however, have shown that the advanced laws of Deuteronomy and the rest of the Pentateuch do not have to be dated late in accordance with the supposition of the critical school. The Code of Hammurabi (written probably during the eighteenth century B.C.)[18] was found by a French archaeological expedition under the direction of M. Jacques de Morgan in 1901–1902 at the site of ancient Susa in what is now Iran, about 150 miles north of the head of the Persian Gulf. The code was written on a piece of black diorite, nearly eight feet high, and contained 282 sections or paragraphs. (See picture on page 55; also see PANET, 163–80.)

The Code of Hammurabi was written several hundred years before the time of Moses (c. 1500–1400 B.C.), and yet it contains some laws similar to those recorded by Moses. As noted in chapter 4, the Code of Hammurabi is actually late. It is similar in some respects to other ancient codes dating hundreds of years earlier. We now have traced the history of Mesopotamian

law codes back to the days of Abraham. In the light of this, the liberal has no right to say that the laws of Moses are too advanced for his time and could not have been written by him. This is acknowledged by Burrows, who says:

> Scholars have sometimes supposed that the social and moral level of the laws attributed to Moses was too high for such an early age. The standards represented by the ancient law codes of the Babylonians, Assyrians, and Hittites, as well as the high ideals found in the Egyptian Book of the Dead, and the early Wisdom Literature of the Egyptians, *have effectively refuted this assumption.*[19]

Some liberals have suggested in past years that perhaps Moses got his laws from the Code of Hammurabi. An examination of the Code during the earlier decades of this century has convinced most liberals, however, that there was no real connection between the Mosaic laws and the Code of Hammurabi. Such an acknowledgment was made by G.A. Barton, liberal professor at the University of Pennsylvania, who said, on the eve of World War II, "A comparison of the Code of Hammurabi as a whole with the Pentateuchal laws as a whole, while it reveals certain similarities, convinces the student that the laws of the Old Testament are in no essential way dependent upon the Babylonian laws" (BAB, 406). The Hammurabi Code contains many laws peculiar to itself, including those relating to soldiers, tax collectors, and wine merchants.

Why Were the Canaanites to Be Destroyed?

When Moses was giving his second address to Israel, he made it clear that the Israelites were not to compromise with

---

[17]W.F. Albright, "Archaeology Confronts Biblical Criticism," *American Scholar* 7, 2 (Spring 1938): 183 [AS].

[18]Note that the minimal chronology now dates Hammurabi 1728–1686 B.C. See W.F. Albright, "A Third Revision of the Early Chronology of Western Asia," BASOR 88 (December, 1942) and BASOR 106 (April, 1947), 19.

[19]BWMS, 56.

the natives of Canaan when the time of the conquest should come, but that they should drive out the Canaanites or destroy them (Deut. 7:1–5). The question has been raised as to how a good and loving God could order the driving out or destruction of great numbers of his creatures by their fellow creatures. The archaeological discoveries have given at least a partial answer, for they have shown that the Canaanites sacrificed their children, that their temples were places of vice, and that their morals were so low that they would inevitably corrupt the people of God if they remained in the land.

In fact, it may be argued that Canaanite morals and religious practices were so bad that they bred seeds of self-destruction. We should also observe that popular views of God today are far different from biblical views. To be sure, God is good and loving, but he is also just and holy and intolerant of sin, and he constantly reminds humankind of the ultimate judgment of sin. Also, there is a remarkable, blood-chilling verse tucked away in Genesis 15:16. In the context, God is talking with Abraham and is promising him and his descendants the land of Canaan as a permanent possession. But in the process God observes that the Hebrews will be out of the land for four hundred years and then will return once more, because "the sin of the Amorites has not yet reached its full measure," or quota. The intimation is that four hundred years later moral conditions among Amorites would be so bad that they would have reached divine limits, or their quota. Afterward, when the Israelites returned to the land, they were ordered to exterminate these foul people. Does God have quotas for all the peoples of the earth? If so, how near is contemporary society to the awful day of doom?

Copper out of the Hills
(Deuteronomy 8:9)

When Moses was giving the people the directions of the LORD concerning the conquest of Canaan, he said that Canaan was a land "where the rocks are iron and you can dig copper out of the hills" (Deut. 8:9). One day in Jerusalem, Nelson Glueck told me that many had thought the idea that copper might be found in Canaan was merely a "pious hope." It was Glueck who actually found the evidence of copper in the region to the south of the Dead Sea, showing the accuracy of this statement in Deuteronomy. In his explorations in southern Palestine, he found a large mining site at Khirbet en-Nahas, some twenty miles south of the Dead Sea. The surrounding hills were dotted with small ruined furnaces, and the whole area was black with heaps of copper slag. The rich copper veins that still protrude above the surface made mining a simple operation. Within a three-mile radius Glueck found three other large copper mining and smelting sites of which nothing had been recorded previously.[20] Referring to these copper and iron deposits, Glueck makes the interesting comment, "How accurate were the words of Scripture which spoke of 'a land whose stones are iron and out of whose hills you can dig copper' (Deut. 8:9)!" (GRJ, 146).

These ancient mines and mining camps are spread over an area of approximately four square miles in the western part of the Timna Valley, about thirteen to nineteen miles north of Eilat (Israel's port on the Red Sea). Earlier discoveries led to systematic Israeli exploration of the Timna Valley in 1959, to be followed by excavations in the area from 1964 to 1970 under the direction of Beno Rothenberg. Rothenberg showed that there were four periods of copper mining and smelting in this area. The first dated back to Chalcol-

[20]Nelson Glueck, "Explorations in Eastern Palestine and the Negeb," BASOR 55 (September 1934): 3–21, esp. 7–8. A photograph of a smelting furnace, made of stones, appears in GOSJ, 59.

ithic times in the fourth millennium B.C. The second occurred during the fourteenth through the twelfth centuries B.C., when the mining expeditions were royal projects of the Egyptian Nineteenth and Twentieth Dynasty pharaohs. This Egyptian activity came to an end by 1150 B.C. The mines were not operated again until the Roman period (1st–2nd centuries A.D.). During the Byzantine and Arab times a few minor sites were exploited.[21]

A Young Goat in Milk (Deuteronomy 14:21); Archaeological Light on This Rite

When Moses was giving certain restrictions and dietary laws, he repeated a command that appeared two times earlier in the Pentateuch, "Do not cook a young goat in its mother's milk" (Exod. 23:19; 34:26; Deut. 14:21). Though commentators have sought the explanation of this rather strange command, it was not until the discovery of the Ras Shamra tablets that a plausible explanation was forthcoming. A similar rite is recorded on the Ras Shamra tablets, which indicates that if one wishes to gain favor with a deity, he should slay a young goat in milk and present it to the deity. The discovery of this Ras Shamra text suggests why the LORD prohibited this rite before the children of Israel entered Canaan. He was forewarning Israel of the pagan rites they would be tempted to practice in imitation of their pagan neighbors in Canaan.

Although a large number of scholars have followed this interpretation proposed by Harold L. Ginsberg in 1935, and it is commonly held today, Peter Craigie observes that more recent scholarship translates the Ugaritic text in question in a very different way and that it provides no background for Deuteronomy 14:21. He concludes, however, "It remains highly likely that the biblical text prohibits something central to the religion of Canaan and Ugarit."[22]

The Death of Moses (Deuteronomy 34)

After Moses had completed his fourth address and had pronounced his blessing on the tribes (Deut. 33), he died and the LORD buried him, "but to this day no one knows where his grave is" (Deut. 34:6). The fact that Moses' death is recorded at the end of Deuteronomy in no way proves that he could not or did not write the book itself (See the section entitled "Critical View of the Date of Deuteronomy," pages 101–2).

---

[21]See Beno Rothenberg, *Were These King Solomon's Mines?* (New York: Stein and Day, 1972).
[22]Peter Craigie, *Ugarit and the Old Testament* (Grand Rapids: Eerdmans, 1983), 76.

Chapter 10

The Conquest of Canaan

(Joshua)

The New Leader—Joshua (Joshua 1); Summary of Joshua's Earlier Life

After the death of Moses, God commissioned Joshua to be the new leader of the people of Israel. Joshua first appeared in the history of Israel when the people were approaching the region of Mount Sinai and were attacked by the Amalekites at Rephidim (Exod. 17:8). Under Joshua's leadership the Israelites won a complete victory over the Amalekites (vv. 9–13). Later, Joshua is referred to as the aide of Moses, when he accompanied Moses to the foot of Mount Sinai, along with the other leaders. When Moses reached a certain point on the mountain, he told the other elders, "wait here for us until we come back to you" (Exod. 24:13–14). This seems to indicate that Joshua went on with Moses, being included in the "we." Blaikie believes that Joshua was with Moses during the six days when the glory of God remained on Mount Sinai and a cloud covered the mountain (vv. 15–16), but that when God called Moses to ascend still higher (vv. 16, 18), Joshua remained behind, being in a place of rest halfway between the spot where the elders saw God's glory and the summit where God talked with Moses.[1]

Joshua was one of the twelve spies sent out from Kadesh to discover the condition of the land of Canaan and the people (Num. 13:1–3, 16–17); and of the twelve, Joshua and Caleb were the only ones who wanted to go right in and possess the land (Num. 13:30; 14:6, 8). Because of the unbelief of the people and because of their unwillingness to enter Canaan, God said that they should not see the land but would spend forty years in the wilderness, a year for each of the forty days that the spies had engaged in their surveillance mission (Num. 14:23, 33–34). In the account of the years of wandering, Joshua is not particularly referred to. It seems likely, however, that he continued to serve as Moses' aide, as he was doing at the time of the giving of the law on Sinai (Exod. 24:13). Now at the close of the forty years in the Sinai region and the wilderness, Joshua was appointed to succeed Moses as the new leader and received

[1]William Garden Blaikie, *The Book of Joshua*, The Expositor's Bible (New York: Funk & Wagnalls, 1900), 28 [BJ].

The Lion Gate at the entrance of the ancient Hittite capital at Boghaz-kale, east of Ankara

God's promise that "as I was with Moses, so I will be with you; I will never leave you or forsake you" (Josh. 1:5).

Archaeological Confirmation Concerning the Hittites (Joshua 1:4)

In describing the extent of the Promised Land to Joshua, God referred to "the Hittite Country" (Josh. 1:4). This is just one of almost fifty passages in the Bible that mention the Hittites. Even though they are referred to as often as this, some scholars in the nineteenth century expressed doubts as to the existence or at least the importance of such an ancient people. At the end of the nineteenth century, A.H. Sayce, a British Assyriologist, identified the Hittites of the Bible with the mysterious Hatti of the monuments (CBS, 98) and published his *Story of a Forgotten Empire* (1892), but E.A.W. Budge of the British Museum, writing in 1902, still expressed doubt concerning this iden-

tification, and said that it had been made "on insufficient grounds."[2]

Discoveries during the twentieth century, however, left no doubts concerning the Hittites. In 1906, Hugo Winckler of Berlin launched a German Oriental Society dig at Bogazköy (now officially Bogaz-kale, Hittite Hattusha), about 125 miles east of Ankara, Turkey, by modern road. The massive site of more than four hundred acres (compare the eight and one-half acres of biblical Jericho) proved to be the capital of the Hittite Empire. Within a year Winckler uncovered a large Hittite royal archive of over ten thousand clay tablets in the citadel area. This archive included a treaty between the Hittites and Ramses II (PANET, 201), dating to the thirteenth century B.C. The Germans continue almost annual excavations at Bogaz-kale, and excavations have proceeded at numerous other Hittite sites, including Sinjerli, Carchemish, Alishar, Malatya, Hama (Hamath), Tell Tainat, and Tell

---

[2]E.A. Wallis Budge, *Egypt and Her Asiatic Empire* (New York: 1902), 136.

Atchana. Of course efforts to translate Hittite have gone forward as well, and scholars at the University of Chicago are now preparing a Hittite dictionary. No longer is the existence of the Hittites questioned nor their importance doubted. One can earn a Ph.D. in Hittite studies at select universities in the United States and abroad.[3]

Sending the Spies to Jericho (Joshua 2); Location of Shittim

When Joshua prepared to send the spies to Jericho, Israel was encamped at Shittim (Josh. 2:1), the more complete name of which was Abel Shittim (Num. 33:49). The name apparently survived in Josephus' time (Josephus was a Jewish historian of the first century, A.D.) in the name Abila, a site that, according to Josephus, lay seven miles east of the Jordan River.[4] In this region potsherds have been found from the Late Bronze Age (1600–1200 B.C.), testifying to the occupation of this region in the period of Joshua (c. 1400). The area is bounded by two watercourses, giving evidence of availability of water even today. Garstang thinks this would have been a favored camping spot and that it seems to conform to the indications of the site of Shittim where the Israelites had their camp (GJJ, 127).

The spies, leaving Shittim, would have traveled six or seven miles west, crossed the Jordan, and then journeyed another six miles west to Jericho.

Archaeological Light on Rahab's House

At Jericho, the spies were given lodging in the house of Rahab (Josh. 2:1). She concealed them on the roof of her house when the king of Jericho ordered a search

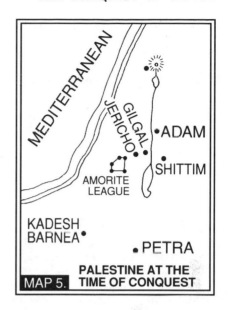

MAP 5. PALESTINE AT THE TIME OF CONQUEST

for these men, who were rumored to be in his city (vv. 2, 6). Rahab later let the men down from a window in her house, which was built on the town wall (v. 15). Excavations at Jericho now give an understanding of where Rahab's house may have stood. An outer stone revetment wall surrounded the mound on which the town was built. The revetment was in turn surmounted by a mud-brick wall. The revetment held in place a flat rampart, above which (higher up the slope) stood a second mud-brick wall that constituted Jericho's city wall proper. There were then two concentric walls with a flat area in between. When Ernst Sellin and Carl Watzinger excavated at Jericho before World War I, they found a number of houses just inside the revetment wall on the north side of the tell, and it is possible that one of these (the house of Rahab),

---

[3]For further information, see O.R. Gurney, *The Hittites*, rev. ed. (Baltimore: Penguin Books, 1961); J.G. Macqueen, *The Hittites*, rev. ed. (London: Thames & Hudson, 1986); C.W. Ceram, *The Secret of the Hittites* (New York: Knopf, 1956); Kurt Bittel, *Hattusha* (New York: Oxford University Press, 1970).

[4]Josephus, *Antiquities*, IV.8.1; V.1.1.

abutting the wall, had a window through the brick wall that stood on the revetment.[5] From such a window it would have been possible to lower the Israelite spies to the ground outside the city.

The Mountain to Which the Spies Went (Joshua 2:16)

When Rahab let the Israelite spies down from her house on the walls, she directed them to go to the hills to hide until their pursuers would return from their search (Josh. 2:16). A visit to Jericho makes it quite evident what Rahab was talking about when she mentioned the hills. Jericho lies in the plain of the Jordan, which at this point is about fourteen miles wide, with the Jordan flowing in the middle of the valley. Jericho is near the western edge of the valley. As one looks north, south, or east, no nearby hill meets the eye, only the flat plain of the Jordan. But just about a mile to the west lies the edge of a rugged plateau ridge, which is the beginning of the hills forming a part of the Judean Wilderness. Farther west these hills merge into the central mountain ridge of Palestine. The beginning of this mountain ridge, a mile west of Jericho, is so high that its shadow enfolds the city in the early afternoon. The cliff actually rises about fifteen hundred feet above the plain and presents numerous hiding places in the soft friable rock (GJJ, 133–34). It would have been to these hills that the spies hastened to conceal themselves for three days (v. 22), after which they would have traveled east across the plain, crossing the Jordan and continuing on to the camp at Shittim, where they reported to Joshua the things they had seen (vv. 23–24).

Israel Crossing the Jordan; Room for Israel to Cross; Possibility of an Earthquake

Joshua led the children of Israel from the place where they encamped at Shittim across the plain some seven miles to the Jordan. At this point, the Jordan was ordinarily about one hundred feet wide, although at harvest time it was wider and measured about ten or twelve feet in depth.[6] God caused the Jordan to stop flowing so Israel could cross the river bed on dry ground. One might wonder how some two or three million Israelites would have room to cross the Jordan in a reasonable length of time. An examination of Scripture shows that the waters of the Jordan were stopped in the vicinity of the cities of Adam and Zaretan (Josh. 3:16). The location of Adam is marked by the present site of Damieh, some sixteen miles north of Jericho (GJJ, 136). Inasmuch as Jericho is a few miles north of the Dead Sea, this would give a stretch of at least twenty miles of dry river bed[7] over which Israel could cross. They would not have been restricted to a narrow passageway but could have crossed several hundred or even several thousand abreast. Even two or three million people could have crossed in a reasonable time.

I see no reason for accepting Garstang's idea that instead of six hundred thousand Israelite men there were only six hundred families, based on the idea that the Hebrew word *Alif* may mean "thousand" and also "family group" (GJJ, 120). By way of answer it may be said with

---

[5]Bryant G. Wood, "Did the Israelites Couquer Jericho?" *Biblical Archaeology Review* (March/April 1990), 46, 56 [WDICJ].

[6]It is difficult today to visualize what the Jordan was like in Joshua's day because Syrian, Jordanian, and Israeli use of water from the Jordan River system for irrigation and other purposes has reduced the river to an insignificant stream. This water use has also resulted in a continued shrinkage of the Dead Sea.

[7]This would include the sixteen miles north to Adam and the three or four miles from Jericho south to the Dead Sea.

Conder that the word Aleph (*Alif*) is used in the singular in Exodus 12:37, and so could not be rendered in the plural, "families." Furthermore, Keil and Delitzsch point out that the normal birthrate would produce six hundred thousand men after the four-hundred-year sojourn in Egypt (KD, 2:29).

It has been suggested that God may have used an earthquake to cause a landslide to stop the Jordan River. Scripture gives possible evidence of an earthquake at the time of Israel's entrance into Canaan. Referring to that time, Judges 5:4, says, "The earth trembled," and Psalm 114:3–4 says, "Jordan turned back; the mountains skipped like rams," which quite likely could be a poetic description of an earthquake.

At Damieh, the site of Adam, there are high banks that, when broken loose in a landslide, block the water. Such a blocking of the Jordan occurred in the year 1267 A.D., when a lofty mound overlooking the river on the west fell into it and dammed it up for sixteen hours (GJJ, 136–37). There was a similar occurrence in 1927, when a section of the cliff 150 feet high fell into the Jordan and blocked the water for twenty-one and a half hours (GJJ, 137). Whether God used an earthquake to effect a landslide to block the Jordan cannot be proved. It is certain, however, that at precisely the right time he caused the Jordan to cease flowing so that Israel could cross the river. The miracle would then be in the timing rather than in the means of accomplishing God's purposes.

Archaeological Light on the Walls of Jericho (Joshua 6)

God directed the Israelites to march around the walls of Jericho once each day for six days, and seven times on the seventh day (Josh. 6:3–4). They did so, and after the completion of the seventh circuit on the seventh day, the wall collapsed (v. 20).

When Garstang excavated Jericho (1930–1936) he found what he identified as the very walls of the ancient city. The discovery was so striking that a statement as to what was actually discovered was prepared and signed by Garstang; Père Vincent, a Catholic archaeologist; and by Clarence Fisher, a pottery and architectural expert. A part of this signed statement reads as follows:

> The outer wall suffered most, its remains falling down the slope. The inner wall is preserved only where it abuts upon the citadel, or tower, to a height of eighteen feet; elsewhere it is found largely to have fallen, together with the remains of buildings upon it, into the space between the walls which was filled with ruins and debris. Traces of intense fire are plain to see, including reddened masses of brick, cracked stones, charred timbers and ashes. Houses alongside the wall are found burned to the ground, their roofs fallen upon the domestic pottery within. (GJJ, 145–46)

Garstang summarized the evidence concerning the falling of the walls as follows: "As to the main fact, then, there remains no doubt: the walls fell outwards so completely that the attackers would be able to clamber up and over their ruins into the city" (GJJ, 146).

Excavations of Kathleen Kenyon at Jericho (1952–1958) demonstrated that the wall on top of the mound that Garstang dated to Joshua's day actually belonged to the period 3000–2000 B.C. and could have no connection with Joshua (WDICJ, 50). That fact does not alter Garstang's conclusions concerning the fall of the city, however. Kenyon herself discovered piles of bricks that had fallen down from the revetment wall surrounding the city (see "Archaeological Light on Rahab's House," page 109) and that would have enabled attackers to climb up into the city (WDICJ, 54). Moreover, in line with God's commands not to take from the city goods from which Israelites might benefit, abundant and valuable supplies of grain turned up in the excavation (WDICJ, 56).

Date of the Fall of Jericho

Garstang's findings in the excavations at Jericho (1930–1936) indicated that the city fell about 1400 B.C., shown in part by the fact that Mycenean ware did not appear in any quantity (GJJ, 146; cf. this book, chapter 7). This date also fits in with the biblical indication concerning the date of the Exodus,[8] which, on the basis of Garstang's interpretation of the Jericho material and on the basis of the biblical indications of chronology, would have been about 1446 B.C.

Some scholars, however, felt that the Jericho evidence pointed to a date later than 1400 for the fall of the city. Vincent dated the fall of Jericho between 1250 and 1200,[9] but G.E. Wright pointed out that the characteristic painted pottery of the period 1300–1200, with its scenes of animals, birds, and trees, is entirely absent at Jericho, and therefore the fall of Jericho must be earlier than 1300.[10] While Wright concluded that Jericho must have fallen before 1300, he saw no way to date it more closely than to put it within the period between 1475 and 1300.[11] Albright was reported (1942) to favor a date between 1375 and 1300,[12] and in a treatise published in 1948 (AOTA, 144), though undoubtedly written somewhat earlier, Albright concluded that Jericho fell "somewhere between 1400 and 1250."

Garstang, however, published a revision of his book *The Story of Jericho* in 1948 (GSJ). In this revision he sought to deal with opinions that conflicted with his conclusion that Jericho fell in 1400 B.C. (p. xiv). Garstang observed that few of these opinions were based on first-hand knowledge of the results of his excavation at Jericho and that many were lacking in logical reasoning or were based on preconceptions concerning the date of the Exodus. He stated that no commentator had as yet produced from the results of his excavation any evidence that City IV remained in being after the reign of the Egyptian king Amenhotep III (1413–1377 B.C.); the archaeological criteria of the age of the next Egyptian king, Akhenaton[13] (1377–1361), were "distinctive, plentiful, and well established," but the Jericho evidence did not include one fragment characteristic of the reign of this king. Garstang pointed out, furthermore, that Jericho was not mentioned in the Amarna Letters, which mentioned the other great cities of southern Canaan.[14] He saw no need to discuss the date of the fall of Jericho "as though it were a matter of debate," and said that if there had not been a controversy concerning the date of the Exodus, there probably never would have been any question of the date of Jericho's fall. He concluded that the date of 1400 B.C. was plainly indicated by the evidence, which the reader "may examine for himself" (p. xiv).

In regard to the absence of any quantity of Mycenean pottery, Garstang pointed out that it began to be imported from the Aegean area about 1400 B.C., and yet only one small fragment of this pottery was found inside the city, where excavators examined more than 150,000 pieces of other types of pottery. Elsewhere, outside the city and in the tombs,

---

[8]See the sections entitled "The Pharaoh of the Exodus" (page 81) and "Date of the Exodus" (pages 86–89).

[9]Cf. H.H. Rowley, "The Exodus and the Settlement in Canaan," BASOR, 85 (February 1942): 31.

[10]G.E. Wright, "Two Misunderstood Items in the Exodus-Conquest Cycle," BASOR, 86 (April 1942): 33–34.

[11]Ibid., 34.

[12]Rowley, "Exodus," 31.

[13]Also spelled Ikhnaton.

[14]GSJ, 1948 ed., xiv, 126–27.

such specimens as were found were imitations of a later period and were not represented within the city's walls (p. 122).

Scholars generally were not prepared to accept Garstang's date for the fall of Jericho to the Hebrews. The debate about the matter contributed in part to Kathleen Kenyon's excavations at Jericho for the British School of Archaeology in Jerusalem (1952–1958). Although she concentrated on the neolithic levels at Jericho, she concluded that the city fell to Joshua somewhere between 1350 and 1325 B.C.[15] Kenyon's conclusion about various aspects of the Jericho dig led to a new round of debate that has continued to the present time. Kenyon herself died before the results of her fieldwork were published. These came in three separate volumes, which appeared in 1981, 1982, and 1983. Bryant Wood's independent assessment of this material concludes that Garstang was indeed right; Jericho fell about 1400 to the Israelites (WDICJ, 49–57).

The Capture of Ai (Joshua 7–8)

After the capture of Jericho, Joshua sent a detachment of men to capture the town of Ai, some fourteen miles to the northwest of Jericho. The three thousand Israelites were routed by the men of Ai (Josh. 4:4–5). The Lord permitted this defeat because one of the Israelites, Achan, had taken some plunder from Jericho at the time of its capture, contrary to God's command (Josh. 7:1, 20–21; cf. 6:18). After the sin of Achan had been judged, God told Joshua that Israel now would be able to take the city of Ai (Josh. 8:1). Joshua put an ambush of thirty thousand men between Bethel and Ai (vv. 3, 7), to which he added another ambush of five thousand (v. 12). The main body of the army under Joshua drew up on the

north side of Ai, so that the people of Ai would see them and come out to attack (GJJ, 157). When the people of Ai attacked the main body of Israelites, the invaders fled, drawing their pursuers out toward the Jordan Valley, to the northeast (GJJ, 158). At this point, the ambush set fire to Ai (v. 19), and Joshua and his forces stopped their retreat and attacked the army of Ai (v. 21). The men of the ambush then came out of Ai, and the men of Ai found themselves in a pincers movement between the men of the ambush and the main army (v. 22). The pincers movement, used to so much advantage by Adolph Hitler during the early days of World War II, is not new; the Israelites used it against the men of Ai nearly 3,400 years ago. Following Israel's victory, Ai was burned (v. 28).

The site identified as Ai, now called Et-Tell, was excavated in 1934–1935 by Judith Marquet-Krause. She found that apparently the mound had not been inhabited between 2400 and 1200 B.C. (EAEHL, 1, 49). This constitutes a problem, since the Bible indicates that Ai was captured by Joshua and the Israelites, the probable date of which would be about 1400. It could not be as late as 1200 or as early as 2400. This does not mean that the Bible is wrong, but merely that we do not have the full light on the situation. Critics often use a case like this to demonstrate what they call the "inaccuracy of the Bible," when what is involved is incomplete knowledge. Years ago the biblical statements about Jericho, the ivory palace at Samaria, the tabernacle (see chapter 1), the Hittites, and many other items constituted problems and even supposed inaccuracies. One archaeological discovery after another has shown the accuracy of these biblical indications and a multitude of others. In the light of such discoveries even one who did not label himself as

---

[15]Kathleen Kenyon, *Digging Up Jericho* (New York: Praeger, 1957), 262; idem, *Archaeology in the Holy Land*, 3rd ed. (London: Ernest Benn, 1970), 211.

conservative[16] acknowledged, "Archaeological and inscriptional data have established the historicity of innumerable passages and statements of the Old Testament; the number of such cases is many times greater than those where the reverse has been proved or has been made probable" (W.F. Albright, AS, 181). I believe that further archaeological research will make it necessary to modify even the last part of this statement. I do not know of any cases where the Bible has been proved wrong. There are instances where we do not have full light, as in the case of the Philistines (see chapter 5) and the above-noted problem of Ai, but these do not prove error in the Scriptures.

A possible explanation of the problem concerning Ai was offered by the French Catholic archaeologist Père Vincent. He suggested that when the Israelites attacked Ai, the Canaanites of Bethel were merely using the site of the Early Bronze Age city as a fort or an outpost against the invaders.[17] This would mean that the outpost at Ai was of such modest proportions and temporary nature that it left no remains to betray its existence to the excavator. Other possible explanations have been offered, though none have been so widely received as that of Père Vincent (BWMS, 272–73).[18]

Perhaps the real solution lies in the suggestion of J. Simons[19] that Et-Tell is not to be identified with biblical Ai. He offered four objections to this identification: (1) Et-Tell is not particularly near Beitin (Bethel), whereas Joshua 12:9 indicates that Ai is "beside Bethel." (2) Et-Tell is a large site, whereas Joshua 7:3 describes the people as "few." (3) Et-Tell was not a ruin in the postconquest period, whereas Joshua indicates that Ai was destroyed (8:28). (4) There is no broad valley to the north of Et-Tell, whereas Joshua 8:11 indicates the existence of a valley near Ai.

When Professor Joseph A. Callaway of Southern Baptist Theological Seminary led a new expedition to Et-Tell in 1964, he concluded, "Nothing in the present evidence warrants an identification of the

---

[16]W.F. Albright well described his theological position in his "Memoriam" article on Melvin Grove Kyle. There he said, speaking of their association prior to 1919, "In those days, the fact that we were apparently at antipodes with regard to most crucial Biblical and oriental problems seemed to preclude all real friendship." Then he told of his association with Kyle in archaeological work in Palestine over a period of years (1921ff.) and added, "We seldom or never debated Biblical questions, but there can be no doubt that our constant association with the ever-recurring opportunity for comparing Biblical and archaeological data has led to increasing convergence between our views, once so far apart. To the last, however, Dr. Kyle remained staunchly conservative on most of his basic positions, while the writer has gradually changed from the extreme radicalism of 1919 to a standpoint which can neither be called conservative nor radical in the usual sense of the terms" (BASOR, 51 [September 1933], 5–6). By 1933, then, his position had come to be "neither conservative nor radical."

Writing in 1938, Albright described his position in similar terms. After pointing out the triumph of criticism in certain areas and institutions, he stated, "By now the reader doubtless considers the writer an extreme liberal, full of enthusiasm for the triumph of scholarship, as represented by Wellhausenism, over obscurantist orthodoxy. Actually, this is not true, and the writer's position is as far removed from the former as it is from the latter, as will become clear in the coming pages" ("Archaeology Confronts Biblical Criticism," *American Scholar* 7, 2 (Spring 1938), 179 [AS]).

In an oral communication to me in 1946, Albright indicated that he held essentially the same views as those expressed in the article in the *American Scholar* (1938).

[17]*Revue Biblique* (1937), 231–66 [RB], cited in BWMS, 76, 273.

[18]The explanation that it was Bethel that was captured and that the story was later transferred to Ai is hardly acceptable. This view is presented in G.E. Wright and F.V. Filson, *The Westminster Historical Atlas to the Bible*, rev. ed. (Philadelphia: Westminster, 1956), 116.

[19]Summarized in "Archaeological Digest" of the *American Journal of Archaeology* (July–September 1947), 311.

village with the city of 'Ai captured by Joshua as described in Joshua 8:1–29."[20] Apparently Callaway never quite gave up on the idea that Et-Tell was Ai, however. In a 1975 publication (after seven seasons of excavation at Et-Tell, 1964–1972) he seemed to accept the identification (EAEHL, 1:36). Presumably his chief problem was that no other more likely candidate for the site of Ai had yet turned up. More recently, John Bimson and David Livingston have proposed Khirbet Nisya, eleven miles north of Jerusalem, as the site of Ai, and they have excavated there for six seasons (1979–1986).[21] The jury is still out on this proposal, however.

If Et-Tell is not to be identified with Ai, then the indication that Et-Tell was not in existence in 1400 or 1250 B.C. has no bearing on the biblical indication concerning Ai. Or if Père Vincent's suggestion that Ai was a fortress, which would leave little or nothing in remains, is correct, again the biblical narrative offers no difficulty. Of course, if Khirbet Nisya or some other site should be identified as Ai, the problem would also be eliminated. In view of such possible solutions, it is inadvisable to *insist* that the Bible must be wrong.

The Southern Campaign (Joshua 9–10)

After the defeat of the people of Ai, a group of the native dwellers of Canaan, called the Hivites, came to Joshua and asked to make a league with him and the Israelites (Josh. 9:6). The Hivites pretended to have come from a great distance, and to carry out the deception, they wore old shoes and old garments and carried dry and moldy bread with them (vv. 12–13). Joshua made a league with them (v. 15) and thus obligated himself to come to the aid of the Hivites, who came from the four cities of Gibeon, Chephirah,

Beeroth, and Kirjath-jearim, all of them just a few miles to the northwest of Jerusalem. (For excavation at Gibeon, see chapter 13, "Establishment of David as King," page 133.)

When another group of native dwellers of Canaan, called the Amorite league, heard that the Hivites, headed by the town of Gibeon, had made a league with Joshua, they determined to make war with the Hivite league (Josh. 10:1–5). The men of Gibeon sent word to Joshua at Gilgal, where the Israelites were encamped, and Joshua made a night march from Gilgal to Gibeon, a distance of about twenty-four miles. Joshua and the Israelites fought against the Amorite league and defeated it (v. 10). It was during this battle that the miracle of the sun's standing still took place (vv. 12–14). The Amorite league was made up of five cities— Jerusalem, Hebron, Eglon, Lachish, and Jarmuth (vv. 5, 23), all in the south of Palestine (see map on page 109). With the conquest of these southern cities, the southern campaign was finished and the Israelites were ready for the northern campaign.

The Northern Campaign; Division of the Land

The northern Canaanites were gathered in a confederacy under the leadership of Jabin, king of the city of Hazor (Josh. 11:1). The Israelites defeated this coalition and burned the city of Hazor (vv. 11, 13). The site of Hazor, examined by Garstang, gave evidence of being burned about 1400 B.C. (GJJ, 197, 383).

Yigael Yadin, in his subsequent Hebrew University excavation at Hazor (1955– 1958, 1968), claimed that Hazor did not fall to the Israelites until the second third of the thirteenth century B.C. (EAEHL, 2:494). But Scripture indicates that Hazor

[20]Joseph A. Callaway, "The 1964 'Ai (et Tell) Excavations," BASOR (April 1965), 27–28.
[21]John J. Bimson and David Livingston, "Redating the Exodus," *Biblical Archaeology Review* (September/October 1987), 48.

fell to the Israelites twice: in the days of Joshua (Josh. 11:10–11), when Jabin I ruled, and in the days of Deborah and Barak (Judg. 4:2, 23–24), when another Jabin ruled. Yadin assumed that Joshua's conquest was to be related to the destruction in the thirteenth century of the lower city of Hazor. There was, however, evidence of destruction at the site around 1400 B.C. or a little later in Yadin's Areas H and K of the lower city (EAEHL, 2:481–82). What is more natural than to conclude that the 1400 B.C. destruction dates to Joshua's day and the thirteenth-century destruction dates to the period of the judges?

Most of the remainder of the book of Joshua concerns the division of the land of Canaan among the twelve tribes of Israel.

Archaeological Light on the Period of the Conquest from the Amarna Tablets

The Amarna Tablets comprise a group of letters written by the kings of various Palestinian and Syrian cities to the two kings of Egypt who lived about 1400 B.C.[22] The tablets illuminate and confirm the picture the Bible gives of Palestine at that time. Canaan in the period of the conquest was subject to many local kings who ruled over individual cities with perhaps their surrounding territory. The book of Joshua (12:9–24) lists some thirty-one such kings with whom Joshua and Israel came in contact during the military campaigns in Canaan. At times some of these little city-states banded together for mutual aid against Joshua, as in the case of the king of Gezer who came to help the city of Lachish (Josh. 10:33). Sometimes they sought an alliance with Joshua, notably in the instance of the Hivites (Gibeonites), who forsook the group of Amorite cities banded together against Joshua, and asked that Joshua make a league with them (Josh. 9:11). As noted above, for their betrayal of the Canaanite-Amorite cause, the Hivite group was attacked by a coalition of five Amorite kings (Josh. 10:5). The Amarna Tablets confirm this picture of Canaan, for they were actually written by such kinglets who ruled over various cities. Seven of the letters were written by the king of Jerusalem, and others were from the kings of such places as Tyre and Sidon (BAHE, 383). They reflect the same general lack of unity among the city-states of Canaan as indicated in the biblical record.

Several of the Amarna Tablets tell of the invasion by a group called the Habiru. Some scholars believe that the Habiru are to be identified with the Hebrews under Joshua (BWMS, 271); it is at least possible that the Amarna Tablets reflect the conquest from the standpoint of the native dwellers of Canaan.

---

[22]See PANET, 483–90; Charles F. Pfeiffer, *Tell El Amarna and the Bible* (Grand Rapids: Baker, 1963); F.F. Bruce, "Tell el-Amarna," in *Archaeology and Old Testament Study*, ed. D. Winton Thomas (Oxford: Clarendon, 1967), 3–20.

Chapter 11

The Period of the Judges

(Judges)

The Book of Judges; Causes of Failure; Outline of the Book

The book of Judges recounts the history of Israel during the three and one-half centuries following the conquest of Canaan and the settlement of the land. According to Garstang's computation, the main part of the period of the judges falls between the oppression of Cushan[1] in 1367 B.C. and the beginning of the reign of Saul about 1025, giving a span of 342 years (GJJ, 62–65). The last part of this era, concerning Eli and Samuel, is described in the early chapters of 1 Samuel.

The book of Judges records the failure of Israel and their turning aside from the Lord. Their moral and spiritual decline was due to at least three factors: (1) failure to drive out the pagans (Judg. 1:21, 27, 29, 33), (2) idolatry (2:12–13), and (3) intermarriage with the pagans (3:5–6). The Lord had given specific instructions that the people of the land should be driven out or destroyed, but this command had not been carried out completely, and the people remained to corrupt the Israelites. In the era of the judges, Israel reaped the result of their disobedience in not driving out the degraded pagan peoples.

The book of Judges is often called "The Book of Failure," and as such, it may be conveniently outlined as follows: I. Cause of the Failure: presence of the pagans, idolatry, intermarriage with the pagans (1:1–3:6); II. Course of the Failure: apostasies, servitudes, and deliverances (3:7–16:31); III. Conditions Growing out of the Failure: apostasy, idolatry, civil war (chs. 17–21).

Authorship of the Book of Judges

Rabbinic tradition makes Samuel the author of the book of Judges, and the internal evidence confines it to Samuel's period. The expression "In those days Israel had no king" (Judg. 17:6 et al.) shows that the writer was familiar, as Samuel was, with the era when kings were ruling in Israel; and the indication that Jerusalem had not yet been taken by Israel shows that it was written before the time of David, for it was David who took the city (Judg. 1:21; cf. 2 Sam. 5:6–8).

[1]Rendered Cushan-rishathaim in Judges 3:8.

OPPRESSING NATION	TIME	DELIVERING JUDGE
1. Mesopotamia, under Cushan-Rishathaim	8 years	Othniel
2. Moab, under King Eglon	18 years (3:14)	Ehud
3. Canaanites, under Jabin of Hazor (4:2)		Deborah, Barak
4. Midian	7 years	Gideon
5. Abimelech (8:33–35 shows this fifth apostasy)		
6. Ammonites (10:9)	18 years (10:8)	Jephthah
7. Philistines (13:1)	40 years (13:1)	Samson

The Nature of the Office of the Judges; the Number of Judges

The office of the judge in Israel was unlike that of a judge today. The judges were primarily military leaders, raised up for particular national crises, but they also exercised an executive function.

By most commentators, the number of judges is computed as either twelve or thirteen. Some omit Barak, considering him the helper of Deborah; some omit Abimelech, considering him a petty king rather than a judge; Eli and Samuel are ordinarily omitted from the list of those strictly considered judges. In the following list, those who are usually considered judges are numbered. The most significant judges are italicized:

1. *Othniel*, of the tribe of Judah (3:9)
2. *Ehud*, a Benjamite (3:15)
   Shamgar (omitted in BBHM, 141)
3. Deborah, a prophetess (4:2) Barak (included with Deborah, BBHM, 141)
4. *Gideon*, of Manasseh (6–8)
5. Abimelech, son of Gideon (9:1; cf. 7:1. Raven makes him a king, ROTI, 161; BBHM, 141, includes him as a judge)
6. Tola, of Issachar (10:1, 2)
7. Jair, of Gilead (10:3)
8. *Jephthah*, of Gilead (11:1)
9. Ibzan, of Bethlehem (12:8)
10. Elon, of Zebulun (12:11)
11. Abdon, a Pirathonite (12:13; Pirathon, possibly six miles southwest of Nablus)
12. *Samson*, of Dan (13:2)

The Seven Cycles of Apostasy, Servitude, and Deliverance in the Book of Judges

Each time Israel went into apostasy and spiritual decline, God used one of the surrounding nations to punish the people and bring them to repentance. When the people cried for help, God sent a deliverer in the person of a judge, who, as military leader, delivered Israel from the oppressor nation.

This sequence of apostasy, servitude, and deliverance occurred seven times, and may be outlined in the chart (above).

Critical View of Judges: "Good Stories"; Garstang's Statement; Archaeological Confirmation

The critical view holds that Judges is made up of stories about Israel that were handed down and finally committed to writing in a late period, about 550 B.C. according to Pfeiffer (PIOT, 315). The beginning and end of the book (1:1–2:5) and chs. 17–21) were supposedly added even later, probably in the third century B.C. (PIOT, 337).

I took a course a few years ago in the Hebrew text of the book of Judges. Quite often the professor would remark, "These are *good stories* and I like them; they're just like the stories the Arabs tell around the campfire today over in the Near East." The Bible believer, however, wants to know whether these are just "good stories," containing a mixture of myth, legend, and fact, or are really the Word of God, recording actual events in this period of Israel's history.

Garstang's statement in regard to the historicity of Judges is significant, particularly so because he held to the documentary theory.[2] Garstang wrote:

> We find no reason to doubt that the historical narrative contained in the Books of Joshua and Judges, so far as it was derived from the old sources J and E, was founded upon fact. Further, in view of the remarkable accuracy and fullness of topographical detail. . . it is difficult to believe that these records were not written down in any form until the ninth or eighth century B.C. (GJJ, 341)

Archaeological discoveries have confirmed one item after another in the book of Judges, showing its accuracy and validity. We will now consider some of these confirmations.

Canaanite Leaders (Judges 1:10); Archaeological Evidence of These Names

The first chapter of Judges states that two Canaanites, apparently leaders of Hebron, were named Ahiman and Talmai. These names also appear as Canaanite names in the Ras Shamra Tablets (AOTA, 145), showing that they fit in the same general period as the time of the judges.

Jerusalem Not Captured (Judges 1:21); Archaeological Indications Concerning Other Cities

We find the indication in Judges 1:21 that at the time of the Israelite conquest of Canaan, they did not drive out the inhabitants of Jerusalem. The fact that Israel did not take Jerusalem is confirmed by the Amarna Tablets, which show that the king of Jerusalem remained loyal to the pharaoh of Egypt.[3]

According to the Bible, Bethel was destroyed during the early period of the judges (1:23–25), and excavations there in 1924 showed that the town was completely destroyed during that period (AOTA, 145). The Bible indicates, on the other hand, that during this same period Bethshan, Megiddo, and Gezer were thriving towns (1:27, 29), but not subject to the Israelites. The excavations at these latter sites show the correctness of this indication that they were not held by Israel at the time of the judges (AOTA, 145).

Archaeological Evidence of the Early Existence of Hazor (Judges 4:2)

The third group that oppressed the Israelites during the period of the judges were the Canaanites, under King Jabin of Hazor (Judg. 4:2). If these stories in Judges are a late creation, reflecting both myth and legend, how would the writers of the stories know that such places as they mention really existed in the days of the judges (1350–1050)? As an example, consider the city of Hazor. The archaeological work there showed that it was in existence in the days of the judges and, in fact, was destroyed during the second half of the thirteenth century. The excavator, Yigael Yadin, attributed this destruction to the forces of Joshua, though I have

---

[2]The JEDP analysis. See chapter 2, the section entitled " Critical View of Genesis 1 and 2," pages 22–23. See also chapter 2, footnotes 2–7.

[3]For details, see GJJ, 218. The Amarna Tablets apply to this situation in the conquest and the time of the judges if one accepts the early date of the Exodus (1446 B.C.). See chapter 8, section entitled "Date of the Exodus," pages 86–89.

The temple of the house of Berith, Shechem

argued earlier that it occurred during the days of the judges.[4] Likewise, destruction at Debir (Judg. 1:11) and Bethel (v. 22) took place during the thirteenth century, as shown in the excavations.[5] Thus the book of Judges again commends itself as trustworthy, as excavations at sites referred to in the book have shown these places to have been in existence and to have suffered destruction during the thirteenth century B.C.

Writing in the Days of Gideon (Judges 8:14); Archaeological Evidence

The fourth oppression of the Israelites was imposed on them by the Midianites for a period of seven years (Judg. 6:1). In this instance the LORD raised up Gideon to deliver Israel. Gideon did so with his hand-picked commando group of three hundred men (7:7–25). Following the expulsion of the Midianites, Gideon, wishing to learn the names of the chief men of Succoth, caught a young man

from this place and had him write down the names of the principal men of the town (8:14). According to the older critical view, that writing was not well developed until about 800 B.C., Gideon's young man would likely have been unable to write the list of names. Archaeological discoveries have abundantly answered this older view concerning writing, by revealing well-developed writing before the days of Gideon, not only in the other Bible lands but in Palestine as well. Albright pointed out that archaeological evidence from the Palestinian sites of Lachish, Bethshemesh, and Megiddo indicates the use of the Hebrew alphabet written in ink in the fourteenth and thirteenth centuries B.C. (ASAC, 193). Moreover, Albright reported that the earliest known alphabetic inscriptions, dating between 1800 and 1500 B.C., were found at Gezer, Shechem, and Lachish in Palestine.[6] Burrows acknowledges that "the fact that Gideon could find a young man who was able to write

---

[4]EAEHL, 2:494. See discussion under "The Northern Campaign," in the preceding chapter, pages 115–16. Yadin led an excavation at Hazor for five seasons from 1955 to 1958 and in 1968.
[5]See discussion under "Date of the Exodus," in chapter 8, pages 86–89.
[6]Noted in correspondence with the reviser, Howard F. Vos.

indicates a high degree of literacy in the Early Iron Age population of Transjordan (Judg. 8:14)" (BWMS, 183).

The House of Berith (Judges 9); Archaeological Evidence of Burning

The son of Gideon, Abimelech, sought to gain power in Israel but soon found himself opposed by the men of Shechem. When Abimelech and his followers attacked the town of Shechem, the Shechemites shut themselves in an inner fortress called the "stronghold of the temple of El-Berith" (Judg. 9:45–46). In order to gain this stronghold, Abimelech and his men gathered wood, piled it about the structure, and set fire to the wood pile (v. 49). Archaeological confirmation of such a burning was found in 1926 in the excavations of the German archaeologist Sellin. He found a building from this period that he identified with the "House of Berith." The pottery evidence showed that it had been built about 1300 B.C. and was finally destroyed by burning about 1150 (BAB, 113–14). The event therefore falls within the period of the judges in which Abimelech lived. This correlation between the destruction recorded in Judges 9 and archaeological investigation was confirmed by the Drew-McCormick excavation at Shechem (1956–1966) under the direction of G.E. Wright (See EAEHL, 4:1092).

Archaeological Light on the Philistines in the Days of Samson (Judges 13–16)

God raised up Samson to deal with the Philistines. The Bible clearly shows that the Philistines not only existed but also exercised extensive power at this time. Much of the biblical indication concerning the Philistines, however, used to be doubted by the critics. Pfeiffer, speaking of the time of Samson, referred to the "legendary and fabulous beginnings of

the conflict with the Philistines" (PIOT, 342). Archaeology, on the contrary, has given factual evidence concerning the power of the Philistines. It is probably this evidence that caused Pfeiffer himself to admit that in the days of Eli and Samuel (1 Sam. 4) "the author continues the story of the same conflict on solid historical ground" (PIOT, 342).

Philistine archaeology is just beginning to come into its own. An introduction to Philistine study (now somewhat dated) is Edward E. Hindson, *The Philistines and the Old Testament* (Grand Rapids: Baker, 1971). The most definitive treatment of the Philistines and the various Philistine sites is Trude Dothan, *The Philistines and Their Material Culture* (New Haven: Yale University Press, 1982). This book describes Philistine remains at twenty-eight sites in Palestine. Dothan continues to excavate at Ekron (Tel Mikne), one of the five major centers of the Philistines (Gaza, Ashdod, Ashkelon, Gath, and Ekron). The only Philistine cultic center excavated to date has appeared at Tel Qasile (on the northern outskirts of Tel Aviv), as a result of the work of Amihai Mazar.[7] With every passing year we experience an increase in our knowledge of the Philistines during the days of the judges. There is no longer any doubt about the significance of this ancient people.

The Dark Days at the Close of the Period of the Judges (17–21); the Crime at Gibeah; Civil War; Archaeological Confirmation of the Burning of Gibeah

The last chapters of the book of Judges (17–21) give us the picture of apostate priests (17:1ff.), idolatry (v. 3), sexual crimes (19:25), civil war (20:14), and almost every other type of sin. The mistreatment of the Levite's concubine by the wicked men of Gibeah (19:25) caused her death.

---

[7]See Amihai Mazar, *Archaeology of the Land of the Bible* (New York: Doubleday, 1990 [MALB]), 300–328, for a discussion of the Philistines in general and Qasile in particular.

The holy of holies of the Philistine temple at Tel Qasile

The Levite then cut her body in pieces and sent a piece to each of the districts of Israel as a horrible reminder of the event (vv. 23–30). Since the crime had occurred at the town of Gibeah, in the territory of Benjamin, the rest of Israel determined to fight against the Benjamites and particularly against the town of Gibeah (20:8–9). The men of Benjamin mustered their troops, twenty-six thousand strong (20:13), including their slinger division of seven hundred left-handed slingers (v. 16). The civil war culminated in the defeat of the Benjamites (v. 35) and the burning of Gibeah (vv. 37, 40). The historicity of these events that culminated in the burning of Gibeah has often been doubted. Confirmation of the burning of the town, however, was found in Albright's excavation of that site.[8] The first stratum of remains in the fortress, dating from the time of the judges, had been burned as described in the Bible (v. 40). The sin and confusion in the period of the judges is well summed up in the last verse of the book: "Everyone did as he saw fit" (Judg. 21:25).

As we have examined the events of the book of Judges, we have found that archaeological discovery has helped to confirm the validity of the records. The book cannot be set aside as a collection of "good stories such as are told about the campfire in the Near East."

[8]AAPB, 47; AOTA, 147; BWMS, 281.

Chapter 12

The Beginning of the Monarchy

(1 Samuel: Eli, Samuel, Saul, David)

The Book of First Samuel; Contents

The two books of Samuel were originally a single volume in the Hebrew Bible, as shown by the Talmud. When the Greek translation of the Old Testament (Septuagint) was made, it required more space because the vowels were not written in the ancient Hebrew language; hence the book of Samuel was divided into two books when it was translated into Greek (probably in the second or third century B.C.). The Hebrew text was divided into two books for the first time in 1516 A.D. in the edition of Daniel Bomberg, and thereafter this division became current. In the Greek and Latin Bibles, the books of 1 and 2 Samuel and 1 and 2 Kings are called I, II, III, and IV Kingdoms (PIOT, 338; ASOTI, 282).

The contents of 1 Samuel deal with two main subjects—the judgeship of Samuel (1–7) and the reign of Saul (8–31). The book may be analyzed by chapters as follows:

1. Birth of Samuel
2. Childhood of Samuel
3. Vision of Samuel
4. Eli's death
5. Ark a curse to the Philistines
6. Ark returned
7. Revival and victory over Philistines
8. Israel's demand for a king
9. Saul chosen
10. Saul anointed (privately, v. 1; publicly, vv. 17, 25)
11. Saul's conquest of the Ammonites
12. Samuel's proclamation of the kingdom (v. 13)
13–15. Wars of Saul and his rejection
16. David chosen
17. Goliath killed
18. David's marriage to Michal
19–23. Enmity of Saul toward David
24–26. David's sparing of Saul's life
27–30. David in Philistia
31. Saul's death

The Character and Work of Samuel

Samuel is called a judge[1] and also a prophet (1 Sam. 3:20), and as such he is sometimes characterized as the last of the judges and the first of the prophets. Samuel established the schools of the

---

[1]Samuel's work as judge is recorded in 1 Samuel 7:6, 15, 17.

prophets at Rama (about five miles north of Jerusalem); he also served as the leader who anointed Saul (10:1, 24) and David (16:1, 13) as kings of Israel.

Childhood of Samuel; Last Days of Eli; Power of the Philistines
(1 Samuel 1–4)

During the time that Samuel was growing up under the guardianship of Eli at the tabernacle (1 Sam. 2:18ff.), Israel was having difficulties with the Philistines. Finally the elders of Israel thought that if they took the ark of the covenant with them to battle, they might overcome the powerful Philistines (1 Sam. 4:3–4). The presence of the Philistines in Canaan at this time is specifically illuminated by archaeological discoveries (see the preceding chapter).

At the bidding of the elders, the people of Israel brought the ark of the covenant from Shiloh in order to take it with them as they went out to meet the enemy Philistines (1 Sam. 4:4–5). During the battle that ensued, the Philistines took the ark, and the sons of Eli were slain (4:11). When Eli received the report of these events, the shock was so great that he fell over backward and broke his neck (4:17–18).

The Ark in the Temple of Dagon
(1 Samuel 5); Archaeological Light on Dagon

After the Philistines had captured the ark of the covenant, they brought it to Ashdod to the temple of their god, Dagon (1 Sam. 5:1–2). The next morning they found Dagon fallen on his face before the ark. They set him in his place, but the following morning they found the god not only fallen again, but with his hands broken off (vv. 3–4). When other calamities came upon the Philistines, they finally sent the ark back to the Israelites (1 Sam. 6–7).

Archaeological light and confirmation concerning the god Dagon have been brought out by excavations. A temple of Dagon, identified by the inscriptions, has been found at Ugarit (the ancient name of Ras Shamra), as well as two steles erected to the same god.[2] The Ras Shamra tablets also mention Dagon, the grain-god, whose son was Baal (AARI, 74). Albright points out that actually Dagan[3] was one of the oldest Accadian deities and was worshiped all through the Euphrates region as early as the twenty-fifth century B.C.; he believed that Dagan was undoubtedly a vegetation deity, though the original meaning of the name is as yet unknown (AARI, 74). Interestingly, there is a town called Bet or Beit Dagan in Israel today, located about halfway between the airport at Lod and the city limits of Tel Aviv. The name, meaning "house of Dagon," preserves the name of the ancient deity Dagon, the god of the Philistines.

Why Was the Ark Brought to Kiriath Jearim? (1 Samuel 6–7): Archaeological Confirmation Concerning Shiloh

In order to send the ark back to the Israelites, the Philistines put it on a cart drawn by two cows, which took it to the town of Beth Shemesh, a few miles to the southwest of Jerusalem (1 Sam. 6:7–8, 10, 12). Word was sent ahead to the men of the town of Kiriath Jearim, a few miles nearer to Jerusalem, who brought the ark to their town, where it remained (1 Sam. 7:1).

The question arises, "Why was the ark brought to Kiriath Jearim, to remain there, rather than to Shiloh (nineteen miles north of Jerusalem), where it had been taken earlier by the Israelites?" It is likely that Shiloh had been destroyed by

---

[2]W.F. Albright, *Archaeology and the Religion of Israel* (Baltimore: Johns Hopkins Press, 1942), 42, 106 [AARI].

[3]An early Semitic form DAGAN, could easily give, as a later form, DAGON.

the Philistines either after the battle of Ebenezer (1 Sam. 7:11–12), or a little later (AARI, 104). Jeremiah definitely indicates that the Shiloh sanctuary was desolate in his day (Jer. 7:12, 14; 26:6, 9), about 600 B.C., and it is quite likely that this desolation dated from its probable destruction by the Philistines about 1050 (PIOT, 343; AARI, 104).

Confirmation of the biblical indication of the desolation of Shiloh was found in the excavation by the Danes, under Aage Schmidt, 1922–1931 (BAB, 127–128). This excavation showed that Shiloh was occupied from the thirteenth to the eleventh centuries B.C., but not for some centuries after about 1050. This is exactly what one would expect, for the Israelites established the ark at Shiloh in the fourteenth or thirteenth century (Josh. 18:1), and later the site became desolate, probably about 1050, and at least the area of the sanctuary was still desolate in the days of Jeremiah, as this prophet tells us. Robinson comments, "Indeed, all that has been found by the Danes at Shiloh agrees exactly with what is implied in the Old Testament" (RBA, 172). Although Pfeiffer is very weak in his inclusion of material on archaeology in his book on Old Testament introduction,[4] he does acknowledge this archaeological discovery at Shiloh in a two-line footnote (PIOT, 343).

Since 1981, I. Finkelstein of Bar-Ilan University in Tel Aviv has been excavating at Shiloh. The expedition confirmed that the town was destroyed by an intense fire in the mid-eleventh century B.C. and that it remained desolate until a small settlement was established there during the Iron II period (900–600).[5]

The archaeological discoveries at Shiloh are all the more significant because scholars holding the critical view frequently asserted in the past that the story of the tabernacle at Shiloh was a late fiction (AOTA, 147). This view was based, in large part, on the theory that the part of Exodus telling of the tabernacle was a late document (see chapter 2, section entitled "Documentary Theory," pages 22–23), dating from the sixth century B.C. However, when the Danish excavation showed that Shiloh was at the height of its prosperity in the period of the judges, as indicated in the Bible, and that it was destroyed by a fire in the days of Eli and Samuel (c. 1050), it was evident that the skeptical attitude toward the historicity of these events was "sheer nonsense" (AOTA, 147).

The Beginning of the Monarchy; Saul as King (1 Samuel 8–15)

The chronology of the events and characters involved in the establishing of the monarchy is outlined by Garstang (GJJ, 65) as follows:

(1) Eli	1065–1045 B.C.	20 years as leader
(2) Samuel	1045–1025 B.C.	20 years as leader
(3) Saul	1025–1010 B.C.	15 years as king
(4) David	1010–971 B.C.	40 years as king

During the later days of Samuel, Israel asked for a king. Samuel was displeased at this request, but the Lord pointed out that Israel had not rejected Samuel but in reality had rejected the Lord as their ruler (1 Sam. 8:7). Saul was then chosen to be king, and Samuel anointed him (1 Sam. 10:1) in a private ceremony, and later in a public ceremony before all of Israel (vv. 17, 25). Saul engaged in war against the Ammonites (1 Sam. 11:11ff.), against the Philistines (13:1ff.), and against the other enemies of Israel (14:47).

During the time of strife with the Philistines, Saul intruded into the office of

---

[4]Albright criticized him for this in his review of Pfeiffer's book (JBL [June 1942], 112).

[5]*Excavations and Surveys in Israel* (Jerusalem: Israel Department of Antiquities and Museums, 1984), 2, 100.

The sanctuary area at Shiloh

the priesthood, offering a sacrifice himself (1 Sam. 13:9–10). Samuel told Saul that he had disobeyed the commandment of the LORD, and he announced that Saul's kingship would not continue indefinitely (v. 14). Saul's line did not continue on the throne of Israel after his death, but was supplanted by David and his descendants. Even during this period of Saul's life, the LORD indicated that David would be the next king (1 Sam. 16:1ff.).

Davidic Music (1 Samuel 16ff.); Critical View; Archaeological Light

David's musical ability was evident from the time he was a young man, for when Saul requested a man who could play well, David was brought to play for him (1 Sam. 16:17, 21, 23). David's interest in music is also shown by the fact that the author of Chronicles attributes to David the organization of the guilds of temple musicians (1 Chron. 23:5–6).

As Albright points out, the critical theory holds that the formal establishment of classes of temple musicians and musical guilds is strictly postexilic (after c. 538 B.C.), and that the attribution of their

founding to David is aetiological in origin (AARI, 125). An aetiological story is one that is invented to explain a known fact, like the story, for example, that the robin got its red breast by getting too close to the fire. According to the critical view, some late writer tried to explain the existence of the temple choirs and classes of musicians in Israel, supposedly a late development, by attributing their founding to David. Albright pointed out in 1942 that "until the past year or two this position was difficult to refute, since external evidence was totally lacking" (AARI, 125).

Archaeological discoveries show, however, that the critic has no right to say that David could not have developed the temple music, for the excavations show a definite development of music and musical instruments not only in David's time (c. 1000 B.C.), but also very much earlier (see chapter 3). The tombs at Beni-Hassan in Egypt, about 170 miles south of Cairo, dated about 1900 B.C., show Asiatic Semites coming into Egypt with musical instruments; one of them carries a lyre, which antedates David's time by nearly a thousand years.[6] Tomb No. 38 at Thebes in Egypt (c. 1420) portrays a girl with a lyre and another girl with a double oboe.[7] A vase from Megiddo (c. 1025) pictures a lyre that came from the time of David.[8] Pictorial representations and material remains from Egypt, Mesopotamia,[9] and Palestine show a high development of musical instruments from an early period (before 2000) down to the time of David and later.

For example, from the Royal Cemetery at Ur, dating to about 2500 B.C. have come the remains of nine richly ornamented lyres, a harp, and a set of pipes (see, e.g., PANEP, 61 and index). The so-called Standard of Ur, picturing a banquet scene with entertainment provided by a male lyre player and a singer dates from the same period. And from the Ur III period (twenty-first century B.C., the time of Abraham) come numerous hymns replete with musical terminology.[10] Unfortunately, most of the critical views concerning the Bible were spun out in the days before Near Eastern studies began to come into their own. Many of these positions no longer seem to have much validity as archaeological discoveries throw increasing light on the civilizations that provided the cultural context for the ancient Israelites.

Albright believes that evidence for the antiquity of the musical guilds is to be seen in the Canaanite character of some of the names of these guild musicians. The name Chalcol (Calcol) appears in 1 Chronicles 2:6, and the same name appears on the Megiddo ivories, dating from the thirteenth century B.C. Two other of these musicians, Ethan and Heman (1 Chron. 2:6) are closely paralleled by scores of abbreviated names found at Ras Shamra (Ugarit) and elsewhere in the late second millennium B.C. (AARI, 127). Albright says that these names, thanks to archaeological discoveries (AARI, 127), prove the correctness of the biblical indication concerning early musical guilds. Although I do not agree with every implication of Albright's development of this idea, it is certainly true that the evidence supports the conservative view of the Bible in a very definite way.

The Later Life of Saul and His Death (1 Samuel 17–31); Archaeological Light on Ashtaroth and Beth Shan

After David killed Goliath (1 Sam. 17), Saul's hostility toward David increased. On more than one occasion Saul tried to kill David, but David was spared. Twice when David came upon Saul, he had opportunity to harm him, but with generosity of spirit he did not take advantage of the king (1 Sam. 24, 26). For some time it was necessary for David to take refuge with the Philistine people (1 Sam. 27–30). Happily he was spared the bitterness of having to fight with the Philistines against his own people, since some of the Philistines, fearing treachery on David's part (1 Sam. 29:4, 9), did not wish to have him with them. Finally Saul engaged in battle with the Philistines at Mount Gilboa in northern Palestine (1 Sam. 31:1ff.). Saul was wounded and, in order to avoid being taken by the Philistines, fell on his own sword (1 Sam. 31:3–4). When the Philistines found the body of Saul, they took it to the city of Beth Shan, fastened it to the wall of the city and put Saul's armor in the temple of Ashtaroth, referred to in the Bible as "the house of Ashtaroth" (v. 10). Our archaeological and historical

---

[6]For picture of this tomb painting, see PANEP; also see article by O.R. Sellers, *Biblical Archaeologist* (September 1941), 37. Also, BAB, figure 1; POTH, 80; PMOT, 170.

[7]Sellers, *Biblical Archaeologist*, 39.

[8]Ibid., 33.

[9]Evidence of early musical instruments in Mesopotamia is noted in chapter 3 under "Early Civilization," 36–37.

[10]See D.A. Foxvog and A.D. Kilmer, "Music," ISBE, 1986 ed., 3:436–49.

The mound of Beth Shan

sources show that Ashtaroth was one of the best known fertility goddesses. She was known in certain areas in the Near East under the names Ashtart and Astarte, and to the Babylonians as Ishtar. She is pictured on a seal found at Bethel (BWMS, 230).

The excavations at Beth Shan, where Saul's body was placed, showed that the city was destroyed between 1050 and 1000 B.C., the approximate period of David and Saul. It is likely that the destruction of the town was due to military action on the part of David after the death of Saul (AAPB, 40; BWMS, 251).

Archaeological Light on the Temples of Ashtaroth and Dagon at Beth Shan (1 Samuel 31:10; 1 Chronicles 10:10)

The University of Pennsylvania expedition at Beth Shan (1921–1933) unearthed a temple the excavators identified with the temple of Ashtaroth, in which Saul's armor had been placed (1 Sam. 31:10). This temple was found on the extreme south side of the tall summit and had been built, as shown by the excavation, before the time of Saul, and therefore would have dated back to his time. It was about twenty-four meters long (c. 80 feet) and nineteen meters broad (c. 62 feet), with its axis running west to east, and contained a long central hall with three circular stone bases on either side. It was assumed that wooden columns must have been set on these bases. At the center column base on the south side of the wall was discovered a foundation deposit, consisting of a container filled with ingots, rings, and earrings of gold and silver.[11]

Within the temple, a monument of basalt was found. It bore a figure of the goddess Ashtaroth, depicted as wearing a long dress and the conical crown customary for all Syrian goddesses, with two feathers attached. She held a sceptre in her left hand and the sign of life in her right hand. She is referred to as "Anaitas" (Antit), which Rowe, the excavator, says is

[11]Alan Rowe, "Discovery of the Temple of Ashtaroth: Report of the Expedition to Palestine," *Museum Journal* 16, 4 (December 1925): 311.

a variant form of the name Ashtaroth.[12] Rowe concludes that all the available evidence shows that the temple was constructed by the Egyptian dwellers in Beth Shan in honor of the goddess Ashtaroth.

As indicated in 1 Chronicles 10:10, there was a second temple at Beth Shan, namely, the house of Dagon, where Saul's head was placed. The excavations revealed a temple to the south of the house of Ashtaroth, which Rowe identified with this second temple mentioned in the Bible. He asserted, in conclusion, that the Chronicles reference indicates two temples at Beth Shan during the Philistine regime, and the excavations have certainly "proved that such was the case."[13]

[12]Ibid., 310.

[13]Alan Rowe, "The Temples of Dagon and Ashtoreth at Beth-shan," *Museum Journal* 17, 3 (September 1926): 298.

Chapter 13

David's Reign

(2 Samuel; 1 Chronicles 11–29)

The Report of the Amalekite Concerning Saul's Death; Explanation (2 Samuel 1)

The report of Saul's death was brought to David by an Amalekite who escaped from the camp of the Israelites after the Philistines defeated Israel (2 Sam. 1:2–3). According to the Amalekite, he came upon Saul and slew him at his request (2 Sam. 1:9–10). On the other hand, the record at the end of 1 Samuel indicates that Saul fell on his own sword and died (31:4–5). These accounts are not necessarily contradictory, for there are at least two possible explanations of the facts as we have them: (1) The Amalekite was lying. Many commentators hold this view, explaining that possibly the Amalekite saw Saul's act of suicide and then thought of turning it to his own advantage by fabricating the story that he had acceded to Saul's request to kill him (JFB, 195; Lange [LC], 363). (2) Saul's armorbearer merely thought that Saul was dead (1 Sam. 31:5), but Saul was not actually dead, only wounded; he later raised himself on his spear and begged the Amalek-

ite to kill him. In this case the Amalekite was telling the truth![1]

Pfeiffer says critics have generally concluded that the same author could not have written both accounts of the death of Saul. But Pfeiffer, in this case, does not follow the critical view, for he says, "After giving the true version of Saul's death in I Samuel 31, the author has a right to assume that the reader will recognize the falsehood of the Amalekite's report in II Samuel 1" (PIOT, 350–51). As noted above, the facts may harmonize very easily in at least two different ways.

David's Elegy Over the Death of Saul (2 Samuel 1:17–27)

In the Hebrew text of the Bible David's elegy over the death of Saul is entitled "the bow" (2 Sam. 1:18), and the KJV supplies the words "The use of," thus giving us the reconstructed full title, "The use of the bow." The ASV suggests a better phrase, perhaps, to fill out the sense, "The song of the bow." The NIV calls it the "lament of the bow."

In regard to authorship, even one as liberal as Pfeiffer acknowledges the rela-

---

[1]Note on 1 Samuel 31:3 in Scofield Reference Bible.

tionship of this passage to David: "His authorship of the poem is unquestionable. The deep pervading emotion shows that it was composed immediately after the battle of Gilboa, under the first shocking impression of the calamity. . . . The poet's grief is intense and sincere but nevertheless virile" (PIOT, 351).

Blaikie fittingly says of the song, "The song embalms very tenderly the love of Jonathan for David," and he likewise points out the implied patriotism: "The thought of personal gain from the death of Saul and Jonathan is entirely swallowed up by grief for the public loss" (BBS, 9). David shows a true love for his enemies, mourning the death of Saul as that of a friend. Some of the thoughts of the poem have become a part of our everyday language, particularly the phrase "How are the mighty fallen" (vv. 25, 27 KJV).

Possible Archaeological Light on the Text of David's Elegy (2 Samuel 1:21)

The remarkable agreement among the various manuscripts of the Bible has long been recognized by scholars. Regarding the New Testament, Hort pointed out that only one word in a thousand appears with sufficient variation in different manuscripts to make necessary the services of a scholar in deciding between the readings. The Hebrew manuscripts of the Old Testament that have survived also show very little variation, as pointed out by William Henry Green (see this book, chapter 1, section entitled "Accuracy of the Text of the Bible," pages 14–15).

Sometimes, however, scribes have made "slips of the pen" in copying the ancient manuscripts of the Bible, and occasionally ancient documents recovered by excavation have enabled us to correct such readings. An interesting possibility of a case of this type has been suggested by H.L. Ginsberg (JBL, 1938,

209–13) and is summarized by Burrows (BWMS, 39). It concerns the verse in David's lament over Saul and Jonathan which reads, "Ye mountains of Gilboa, let there be no dew, neither let there be rain, upon you, nor fields of offerings" (2 Sam. 1:21 KJV). The expression "fields of offerings" seems somewhat strange, for in this context one would expect, as parallel to dew and rain, some reference to water, rather than to "fields of offerings." Commentators have never found a completely satisfying explanation of this awkward expression.

In one of the Ras Shamra tablets that records the poem of "Dan'el," Ginsberg pointed out a passage that curses the land in words similar to those of David: "Seven years may Baal fail, even eight the Rider of the Clouds; *nor dew, nor rain, nor upsurging of the deep,* nor sweetness of the voice of Baal!" The word in the Ras Shamra tablets rendered "deep" is related to the Hebrew word translated "deep" in Genesis 1:2 (*tehom*), which is similar in appearance to the word for "offerings" in 2 Samuel 1:21. The Hebrew word for "fields" also looks like the Ras Shamra word rendered "upsurging" if both are written in Hebrew characters.[2] On this evidence, Ginsberg has suggested that the original text of David's poem read, instead of "fields of offerings," the similar looking words "upsurging of the deep," referring to the mountain springs that were fed by the fountains of the deep. According to this explanation, the present text would be due to the error of a copyist who was misled by the resemblance of the words, and the original text would have read, "Ye mountains of Gilboa, let there be no dew, neither let there be rain upon you, nor upsurging of the deep." Burrows acknowledges that one cannot say this explanation is certain but feels that it does offer an interesting and possible explanation of a difficult passage (BWMS, 39).

[2]Also cf. H.L. Ginsberg, "Ugaritic Studies and the Bible," BA (May 1945), 56.

In regard to the discoveries that concern the actual text of the Bible, Burrows acknowledges that

> on the whole such evidence as archaeology has afforded thus far, especially by providing additional and older manuscripts of the books of the Bible, strengthens our confidence in the accuracy with which the text has been transmitted through the centuries. . . they have also shown that not only the main substance of what has been written but even the words, aside from minor variations, have been transmitted with remarkable fidelity, so that there need be no doubt whatever regarding the teaching conveyed by them. Regarding what Amos, Isaiah, Jesus, or Paul thought and taught, our knowledge is neither increased nor altered by any of the manuscripts discovered" (BWMS, 42).

The Establishment of David as King; Fall of Ishbosheth (2 Samuel 2–5)

Following the death of Saul, there were actually two kings reigning in Israel. David was anointed to be king by the men of Judah at the town of Hebron (2 Sam. 2:3–4), some twenty miles south of Jerusalem, and Ishbosheth, the fourth son of Saul, was established as king by Saul's military commander at the town of Mahanaim (v. 8), in the territory of Transjordania, east of the Jordan River.

At one point in the struggle between the two kings, a meeting of the followers of Ishbosheth and the followers of David took place by the pool of Gibeon (2 Sam. 2:12–13). When negotiations apparently broke down, the two groups fell upon each other with the sword. The site of Gibeon, identified with present-day El Jib, a few miles north of Jerusalem, was excavated from 1956 to 1962 by Professor James Pritchard of the Church Divinity School of the Pacific. He discovered a large rock-cut pool nearly thirty-eight feet in diameter which he identified with the pool where the followers of Saul's son and of David fought. (EAEHL, 2, 447).

A series of events led to the downfall of Ishbosheth. Abner, the military commander of Saul and Ishbosheth, took a concubine of Saul as his wife, and Ishbosheth rebuked him for doing so (2 Sam. 3:7). Abner, angered by the rebuke, proposed to turn the kingdom over to David (v. 12), but during the negotiations, Joab, the military commander of David, slew Abner at the gate in Hebron (2 Sam. 3:27). A short time later, two of Ishbosheth's captains murdered Ishbosheth (2 Sam. 4:2, 5–6), and the northern tribes of Israel then acknowledged David as their king (5:3).

The Capture of Jerusalem; Method of Conquest (2 Samuel 5:6–9; 1 Chronicles 11:4–8)

The conquest of Jerusalem is described briefly in 2 Samuel 5:6–9 and 1 Chronicles 11:4–8. From these verses the general situation is clear. The Jebusites felt secure behind virtually impregnable fortifications—so much so that they said the blind and lame could ward off the attacks of David. David was determined, however, and offered the captaincy of the armed forces to the one who would lead a successful attack against the Jebusite defenders. Joab earned the reward promised by David.

A problem arises, however, in interpreting the method Joab used to accomplish this military feat. Second Samuel 5:8 speaks of ascending the "gutter" in the KJV, the "watercourse" in the ASV, and the "water shaft" in the RSV and NIV. In recent decades, the common opinion has been that the city water supply was in view here and that the "watercourse" was to be identified with a discovery of Sir Charles Warren at Jerusalem. He found that since there was no natural water supply within the walls of the ancient city, a water channel had been cut leading from a point inside the walls to the Spring Gihon, or the Virgin's Fountain, on the outside. More specifically, a horizontal tunnel leading from the spring had been dug into the hill on which the city was located; this ended in a cave that served as a cistern. Above the cave rose a 52-foot vertical shaft, which connected with a sloping passageway 127 feet long. The entrance to this passageway was inside the city wall. Women could then descend the sloping passage to the vertical shaft and lower their waterskins into the cave to procure a water supply, in spite of military forces that might be encamped outside the walls. Joab supposedly discovered this water system, ascended the passageway, and entered the city at night, delivering it into the hands of David.

J. Garrow Duncan took issue with this suggestion, asserting that it is almost humanly impossible to scale the shaft, which is very steep. Furthermore, the sides of it have been worn almost smooth by the constant rubbing of waterskins, to say nothing of the fact that it is so narrow at one point that a large man could not even get through.[3] A. Rendle Short claimed, however, that some British army officers were able to accomplish this feat in 1910.[4] The water system was finally cleared in 1980, and two young Americans subsequently did manage to ascend the shaft.

Duncan also argued that Warren's Shaft led into the lower part of the Jebusite city only, and thus still would not have given David access to the fortress area. In reporting his excavations at Jerusalem, he claimed that part of the eastern wall of the lower city was battered in during Davidic times and that David therefore forced his way into the lower city.[5]

Duncan, puzzled with the meaning of tsinnor, translated "watercourse" in the ASV, pointed out that in Aramaic and Arabic its connotation is "hook."[6] Albright believed that was the real solution to the matter and identified it as a hook used in scaling ramparts.[7] The resultant translation, then, would be "whoever gets up by means of the hook and smites the Jebusites." The NEB follows Duncan and Albright by translating tsinnor with the word "grappling-iron."

Kathleen Kenyon, in her 1961–1967 excavations at Jebusite Jerusalem, discovered that the city wall was not located as far up the slope of the hill as Duncan, Macalister, and others would have put it. Therefore if Joab and his men had ascended the channel of the city water supply in their conquest of Jerusalem, they would have been able to enter the strategically important parts of the town. And she concluded that David's men did indeed capture the city in this way when they made it the capital of Israel about 1000 B.C.[8]

In his new 1990 study, Amihai Mazar of the Hebrew University in Jerusalem concludes that Warren's Shaft should probably be dated to the period of the divided monarchy (after the division at Solomon's death in 931 B.C.) and before the days of Hezekiah (716–687) (MALB, 480–81) and that it definitely was not the "Sinnor" of the Jebusites (MALB, 31).

To complicate the discussion further, the Revised English Bible, published in 1989, reversed itself on the translation of 2 Samuel 5:8 and now phrases the passage as follows: "Everyone who is eager to attack the Jebusites, let him get up the water-shaft to reach the lame and the blind." At least two issues currently face the biblical interpreter: (1) What is the meaning of the Hebrew word tsinnor?

[3]J. Garrow Duncan, The Accuracy of the Old Testament (London: SPCK, 1930), 136–38.
[4]A. Rendle Short, Modern Discovery and the Bible, 3rd ed. (London: InterVarsity, 1952), 182.
[5]Duncan, Accuracy of the Old Testament, 138–41.
[6]Ibid., 141.
[7]William F. Albright, "The Old Testament and Archaeology," in Old Testament Commentary, ed. Herbert C. Alleman and Elmer E. Flack (Philadelphia: Muhlenberg, 1948), 149.
[8]Kathleen Kenyon, Royal Cities of the Old Testament (New York: Shocken, 1971), 24–27.

(2) When should Warren's Shaft be dated? At the present time a final answer to either question does not seem to be forthcoming.

The Capture of Jerusalem; Archaeological Light on Millo (2 Samuel 5:6–9; 1 Chronicles 11:4–9)

The city of Jerusalem had not been taken over by the Israelites in the days of Joshua and the judges.[9] But now David, after a rule of seven and a half years in Hebron (2 Sam. 5:5), went against Jerusalem and captured it through the strategy of his military commander, Joab (vv. 7–8; 1 Chron. 11:5–6).

In connection with David's building activities after taking Jerusalem, the Bible says that he "built the city round about, even from Millo" (2 Sam. 5:9; 1 Chron. 11:8 KJV). Commentators have not been sure just what the word "Millo" referred to; some have suggested that it was "perhaps a corner tower" (JFB). The Hebrew word means "filling," being a form of the word used in Genesis 1:28, where the Lord told Adam and Eve to "fill the earth" (the KJV reads "replenish"; it is really the word "fill"). Possible archaeological light on the identity of this Millo or "filling" was found by Macalister in his excavation at the northern end of the ancient Jebusite city of Jersalem. He found a breach or opening in the north wall and the remains of a fortress that had apparently been constructed to fill the gap in the wall. Macalister identified this fortress as the Millo, or filling (MCEP, 106). Duncan, who was associated with Macalister in this excavation, also believed that Millo was at the north end of the early city of Jerusalem.[10] Thus archaeology illuminates the "Millo," which otherwise would be merely a word to us. The NIV has "supporting terraces."

Jerusalem the Political and Religious Capital of Israel (2 Samuel 5–6)

In making Jerusalem the political and religious capital of Israel David took three important steps: (1) he captured the city (2 Sam. 5:8) and thus made it the possession of Israel; (2) he had a palace built for himself there (2 Sam. 5:11); and (3) he brought the ark from the house of Abinadab (Obed-Edom), where it had remained after it was returned by the Philistines (1 Sam. 7:1–2), and placed it in the tent he had erected for it in Jerusalem (2 Sam. 6:12, 17). Thus with the establishment of the palace and the worship at Jerusalem, this city effectively became the political and religious center for Israel. The significance of Jerusalem for Israel (and eventually for the church and the world) down through the centuries may be traced back to the days of David (c. 1000 B.C.).

King Hiram of Tyre (2 Samuel 5:11); Archaeological Light

David was aided in the construction of his palace at Jerusalem by Hiram, the king of Tyre (2 Sam. 5:11; 1 Chron. 14:1). Possible archaeological light on King Hiram was found when a French excavation of Jebeil or Byblos[11] in 1923–1924 uncovered a sarcophagus[12] on which was inscribed in Phoenician writing the name Ahiram, equivalent to the biblical Hiram (BAB, 128). This may possibly be a reference to the biblical King Hiram, or one of his line, inasmuch as the inscription dates no earlier than the eleventh or twelfth

---

[9]Judges 1:21. Also see this book, chapter 11, section entitled "Jerusalem Not Captured."
[10]J. Garrow Duncan, *Digging up Biblical History* (New York: Macmillan, 1931), 115 [DDBH].
[11]Called Gebal in Bible times. See Ezekiel 27:9.
[12]Montet, *Syria*, vols. 3 and following, cited BAB, 128.

century b.c. (ARDBL, 18; AARI, 40), and may be dated as late as 975 b.c.[13]

One should be cautious here, however, for the sarcophagus was found at Byblos, and the biblical Hiram was king of Tyre. Of course the inscription does show that someone by the name of Hiram was important in Phoenicia about 1000 b.c., about the time of David, and it gives a greater ring of authenticity to the biblical narrative.

The Davidic Covenant (2 Samuel 7)

The realization that the ark of the covenant resided in a tent caused David to propose that he build a house or temple for the LORD (2 Sam. 7:2). The Lord showed David that one of his family or "seed" would build the house for the Lord instead (7:12–13), and at the same time God made several other promises to David, which are usually known as the Davidic covenant. According to 7:16, this covenant provided that David should have (1) a "house," that is, a posterity; (2) a "throne," that is, royal authority; (3) a "kingdom," that is, a successor on the throne; and (4) perpetuity of the kingdom, that is, a throne that should last "forever." This last provision is to be fulfilled in the reign of Christ, for as the angel announced to Mary, "the Lord God will give him the throne of his father David." Christ "will reign over the house of Jacob forever," as the rightful heir of David (Luke 1:32–33).

David's Victories (2 Samuel 8–10)

David smote the Philistines (2 Sam. 8:1), Moabites (8:2), and the Syrians of Damascus (8:5) and extended his control to the south, over the area of Edom (8:14). When the emissaries of David went over into the Ammonite region to the east of the Jordan, the Ammonites shaved off the beards and cut off half the clothes of David's men and then sent them back. When David heard how the Ammonites had insulted his emissaries, he went out against the Ammonites, who were joined by the Syrians in battle against David (2 Sam. 10:7–8).

Archaeological Light on the Extent of the Davidic Empire (2 Samuel 8:1ff.)

Albright pointed out a tendency, inaugurated by scholars such as Hugo Winckler and developed by men like Hermann Guthe, to reduce the extent of the Davidic empire. The Bible indicates that David's empire included Damascus and the area of Zobah (2 Sam. 8:3, 6; 1 Chron. 18:3, 6). But liberal scholars have excluded Damascus from the empire of David and have located Zobah, the land of King Hadad-ezer (whom David conquered), in the Hauran, the area to the east of the Sea of Galilee. Archaeological discoveries, however, have given us much light on the Assyrian provincial organization and have demonstrated conclusively that Zobah, which the Assyrians called Subatu, lay north of Damascus and not south of it.[14] Thus the biblical indication that David's empire extended up to the north of Damascus in the area of the city of Homs (Hums) is confirmed by these archaeological discoveries. Albright concluded, "It follows that the biblical narrative is perfectly reasonable geographically. . . . David's empire then extended from the Gulf of Aqabah in the south to the region of Hums in the north, and it remained, at least nominally, in Solomon's hands until his death or shortly before" (AARI, 131).

---

[13]As indicated by the sherds found by Dunand in the tomb of Ahiram. This has been pointed out by Albright in his *Archaeology of Palestine* (Harmondsworth-Middlesex, Penguin Books, 1949), 191 [AAP].

[14]E. Forrer, *Die Provinzeinteilung des assyrischen Reiches* (1921), 62, 69, cited in AARI, 131; AOTA, 149.

David's Sin; God's Punishment
(2 Samuel 11–12)

During the war between Israel and the Ammonite-Syrian coalition, Israel was able to overcome the Syrians (2 Sam. 10:18–19), but it was necessary to continue the battle against the Ammonites and to besiege their city of Rabbah (2 Sam. 11:1ff.). At this time David made the acquaintance of Bathsheba and committed adultery with her (11:3–4) while her husband, Uriah, was fighting in the armies of Israel against Rabbah. David tried to cover up his sin, but when this failed (vv. 5–9), he had Uriah assigned to a front-line battle position so that he would be killed (vv. 14–17). After the death of Uriah, David took Bathsheba as his wife (v. 27).

God's punishment of David for his sin was threefold. The Lord told David that (1) the sword would never depart from his house (12:10); that is, he would have wars and rebellions; (2) others would commit sin with his wives (v. 11); and (3) the child that would be born to him by Bathsheba would die (v. 14).

Several lessons are connected with the sin of David: (1) David was a great man, yet he sinned; how foolish are those who trust their own hearts rather than in the Lord to direct their ways. (2) David's sin is not excused, but condemned. It was a wicked act, and God so labels it. (3) David repented deeply (Ps. 51) and confessed his sin; but because he had given the enemies of the Lord occasion to blaspheme, the threefold punishment was not removed (2 Sam. 12:13–14).

David's Later Days (2 Samuel 13–24)

David's later days were beclouded by the rebellion of his son Absalom (2 Sam. 13–19), by the rebellion fostered by Sheba (2 Sam. 20:1ff.), by the three-years' famine (2 Sam. 21), and by David's sin of numbering the people (2 Sam. 24).

Chapter 14

Solomon's Reign

(1 Kings 1–11; 2 Chronicles 1–9)

The Book of 1 Kings;
Contents; Outline

In the Hebrew Bible, 1 and 2 Kings were originally one book, and, as in the case of 1 and 2 Samuel, when the Hebrew text was translated into Greek, it was divided into two books. In modern Hebrew Bibles, the material has been divided into two books ever since the publication of the Rabbinic Bible of Daniel Bomberg at Venice in 1516 (ASOTI, 282).

The contents of 1 Kings deal with three main subjects: (1) The last events of the life of David (1:1–2:11); (2) the reign of Solomon (2:12–11:43); and (3) the events of the first seventy-five years of the divided kingdom (12–22), running from about 931 B.C. (the death of Solomon) through the reign of Ahab (874–853), and into part of the reign of Ahab's son Ahaziah (853–852).

The contents of 1 Kings may be outlined by chapters as follows:

1. Anointing of Solomon
2. Death of David
3. Wisdom chosen by Solomon
4–5. Alliance with Hiram
6–8. Temple built and dedicated

9–11. Greatness of Solomon and his reign
12–22. Divided kingdom

David's Last Years; Adonijah's Rebellion
(1 Kings 1)

David was approaching the age of seventy as he came to the end of his forty-year reign (2 Sam. 5:4). At this time, David's fourth son, Adonijah, the oldest one living, laid plans to seize the throne (1 Kings 1:5). It is evident that Adonijah was a good example of a spoiled child, for we are told that "his father had not displeased him at any time" (v. 6). As Lange well comments, "A perverted parent love is self-punished" (LC, 27), for if the father does not "trouble" the son, the son will "trouble" the father.

Adonijah secured the help of the military leader, Joab, and the aid of the priest, Abiathar (1 Kings 1:7). Abiathar's willingness to help in the rebellion may have been due to fear that Zadok, another priest, might replace him. Adonijah now felt that he had the "church and the army" behind him; but his plans were upset when Nathan the prophet and Bathsheba, the mother of Solomon, advised David of the situation (vv. 11, 15, 24).

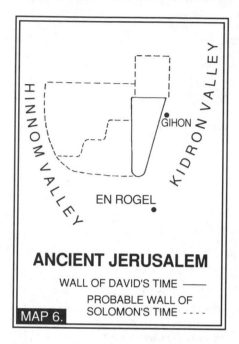

ANCIENT JERUSALEM

WALL OF DAVID'S TIME ———

PROBABLE WALL OF
SOLOMON'S TIME - - - -

MAP 6.

mon was here at Gihon, while Adonijah and his friends were at the spring En Rogel, some seven hundred yards farther south in the Kidron Valley. A knowledge of the relative positions of Gihon and En Rogel permits a vivid reconstruction of this event. Solomon and Adonijah were out of sight of each other due to the terrain of the Kidron Valley, yet they were close enough that the shout of the multitude at Gihon could have been heard by the followers of Adonijah at En Rogel (v. 9 shows that Adonijah was at En Rogel). See map 6.

When Adonijah's friends heard that Solomon had been anointed king (1 Kings 1:43), the meeting broke up very quickly and they dispersed (v. 49). Then Adonijah became afraid of Solomon (v. 50), his ostentation and boasting ending in cowardice and cringing.

David settled the matter of succession by ordering that his son Solomon be anointed by Zadok the priest at the spring Gihon (vv. 33–34). Solomon was duly anointed, and when the assembled people shouted, "God save the king," the shout reached the ears of Adonijah and his guests, who were gathered near En Rogel (vv. 39–41; cf. v. 9), some distance away.

Topographical Light on Solomon's Anointing Ceremony as Heard by Adonijah

How could Adonijah have heard so readily the shout of the people at the anointing ceremony of Solomon (1 Kings 1:41)? The older commentaries are wrong in locating the spring Gihon on the west side of Jerusalem (LC, 24). Gihon is to be identified with the source of water that today is called the Virgin's Fountain, located just under the brow of the southeastern hill, some four hundred yards north of the south end of the hill. Solo-

David's Charge to Solomon; Death of David (1 Kings 2)

As David came to his closing days, he charged his son Solomon to walk in the ways of the Lord. The play on words in David's injunction "Observe what the LORD your God requires" (2:3) is best appreciated in the original language, which may be rendered, "Observe the observances," since the two words are from the same verbal root.

David's charge concerning Joab indicated that he was not to be allowed to live (1 Kings 2:5–6), and an examination of the situation shows the reason. Joab was guilty of the following offenses: (1) the murder of Abner (2 Sam. 2:27ff.), (2) the murder of Amasa (2 Sam. 20:8ff.), and (3) active conspiracy against Solomon on behalf of Adonijah (1 Kings 1:7).

David died at the age of seventy, having begun his reign at the age of thirty. He ruled for seven years at Hebron and thirty-three years at Jerusalem, following the capture of that city. The dates of his reign are probably 1010–971 B.C.

Solomon the King; Alliance with Pharaoh; Choice of Wisdom
(1 Kings 3)

After the death of David, Solomon began his reign of forty years (971–931 B.C.).[1] Solomon soon made himself a relative of the pharaoh of Egypt by marrying his daughter (1 Kings 3:1). The identity of this pharaoh has always been a matter of interest to Bible students. Barton believes that it was either Siamon (976–958) or Pesibkhenno II (958–945) (BAB, 20). Knight also indicates Pesibkhenno II as the pharaoh with whom Solomon made an alliance.[2] The tomb of this king was found in excavations in the delta of Egypt and was opened in March, 1939. The royal sarcophagus was opened about February, 1940.[3] Breasted, however, feels that the pharaoh with whom Solomon had to deal was the next king of Egypt, Sheshonk I (945–924),[4] because the biblical description fits an energetic king such as Sheshonk I, and not the degenerate kings at the end of the twenty-first dynasty, such as Siamon or Pesibkhenno II (BAHE, 529). Future discoveries may enable us to determine with certainty which of these pharaohs was the father-in-law of Solomon.

The Lord appeared to Solomon in a dream and said, "Ask for whatever you want me to give you" (1 Kings 3:5). Solomon asked for an understanding heart, and in response God said that he would give him (1) a wise and understanding heart (v. 12), (2) riches and honor (v. 13), and (3) length of days if he would walk in God's ways and keep his statutes (v. 14). The first two were unconditional, and the last one was conditional. Solomon asked only for an understanding heart, but the Lord gave him much more, showing that

if one asks for the right thing, God will also give many other things. "Seek first his kingdom and his righteousness, and all these things will be given to you as well" (Matt. 6:33).

The Greatness of Solomon's Empire
(1 Kings 4:21; 2 Chronicles 9:26)

The greatness of Solomon's empire is definitely indicated in Scripture (1 Kings 4:21; 2 Chron. 9:26), yet because of the great empires of Assyria on the Euphrates and Egypt on the Nile, it might seem unlikely that such a kingdom as Solomon's could have existed. Archaeological discoveries show us, however, that precisely during the period 1100–900, when the kingdom of Israel was being built up, the "weak and inglorious twenty-first dynasty" was ruling in Egypt, Assyria had gone into a period of decline, and the Hittite Empire in Asia Minor had come to an end, and the glory of the Myceneans had disappeared in Greece. There was a power vacuum in the Mediterranean world and the Near East. Thus God in his providence overruled so that "Solomon ruled over all kingdoms from the River to the land of the Philistines, as far as the border of Egypt" (1 Kings 4:21).

Solomon's Phoenician Friends (1 Kings 5:1; 2 Chronicles 2:3); Archaeological Light on Phoenician Activity

When Solomon prepared to build the temple, he received aid from King Hiram of Tyre. We have already seen that the name Hiram, in the form Ahiram, was found on a sarcophagus excavated at Jebeil in Syria (see chapter 13). The biblical references to the Phoenician king Hiram and to his subjects indicate that the Phoenicians were a people of some

---

[1]The factors involved in the chronology of the period of the kings are dealt with at the beginning of chapter 15.

[2]KNJ, 270. He spells the name Pasebkhanut; it is rendered Psou Sen Nef by others.

[3]See *Illustrated London News* (March 9, 1940) [ILN].

[4]Spelled Shishak in the Bible (1 Kings 14:25).

importance (1 Kings 5:8–9, 18; 9:27), yet earlier in the twentieth century, writers such as Salomon Reinach and Julius Beloch denied the validity of such references to important Phoenician activity as early as this period.[5] Archaeological inscriptions, however, in the Cyprus Museum and on the Island of Sardinia, dating back to the ninth century B.C., reveal early Phoenician activity in the Mediterranean, as implied in the biblical references to Solomon's relations with the Phoenicians. Albright comments on the significance of these inscriptions in this way: "Once more we find that the radical criticism of the past half century must be corrected drastically. . . . Incidentally the Biblical account of Solomon's reign is again proved to be historically reasonable."[6]

Solomon's Temple; Its Size and Appearance (1 Kings 6ff.; 2 Chronicles 3:1)

The temple proper was sixty cubits long and twenty cubits wide (1 Kings 6:2), just twice the size of the tabernacle (Exod. 26:16, 18). If the cubit is taken as a foot and a half, as shown by the Siloam tunnel and inscription,[7] then the floor plan of the temple would have been ninety by thirty feet. It was divided into two rooms. The inner one, the Most Holy Place or the oracle, was a cube, twenty by twenty cubits (1 Kings 6:16, 20); the outer chamber, or Holy Place, was forty by twenty cubits.

The floor and walls were of stone, covered with cedar, and in turn overlaid with gold (1 Kings 6:16, 21–22). Around the temple on the two sides and back, chambers were constructed (vv. 5–6), and across the front there was a porch twenty cubits long and ten cubits wide (v. 3), decorated with two large pillars (1 Kings 7:15, 21).

Archaeological Light on the Temple

Wright[8] points out that with the information given in the Bible and

with the aid of a wealth of archaeological data it is possible to reconstruct it in a general way, even though no remains of it have ever been found in Jerusalem. . . . It was a comparatively small building standing on a platform in a walled-in courtyard. . . . The over-all interior length, including the width of the dividing walls, would thus have been c. 135 feet, and the interior width c. 35 feet. . . . The structure was probably built entirely of the type of hewn and carefully bonded stone which we have previously noted in Solomonic construction at Megiddo, but the interior was lined with cedar and was highly decorated with Phoenician motifs. . . . In the rear room (Holy of Holies) were two olivewood cherubim, standing c. 17 feet high and overlaid with gold leaf, under whose outstretched wings the Ark was placed. . . . In the exterior court were the large altar of burnt offering, the lavers, and the bronze "sea." The latter was a tremendous bowl, c. 17 feet in diameter, c. 8 feet high, and holding c. 10,000 gallons of water. It was cast in the clay beds of the Jordan Valley at Adamah. The "sea" and the bronze pillars placed in front of the Temple (1 Kings 7:15ff.) were so large that we marvel

---

[5]W.F. Albright, "New Light on the Early History of Phoenician Colonization," BASOR, no. 83 (October 1941): 14–15.

[6]Ibid., 22. In a lecture at the Archaeology Conference at Wheaton College, October 16, 1961, Albright reported on Phoenician materials dating to the tenth–ninth centuries B.C. that were discovered in Spain during the late 1950s.

[7]See chapter 3, the article entitled "The Flood; the Size of the Ark," pages 38–39.

[8]G. Ernest Wright of McCormick Theological Seminary, Chicago, and Harvard. His field was archaeology and Old Testament studies.

at the genius of the artisan Hiram who cast them.[9]

Archaeological Light on Solomon's Use of "Dressed Stone and Trimmed Cedar Beams" (1 Kings 7:12)

The record in 1 Kings tells us that the courts of Solomon's palaces were constructed of "three courses of dressed stone and one couse of trimmed cedar beams" (1 Kings 7:12). Archaeological light on this type of construction was found in the University of Chicago excavation at Megiddo. There the remains of a large building consisted of well-cut stone foundations, the upper surfaces of which were burned black. Fragments of mud brick and ashes from the superstructure lay scattered about. From these ashes was taken a piece of charred wood, which was shown by chemical analysis to be cedar, indicating that the superstructure was built with a "half timber" type of construction similar to the courts of Solomon, which were made with rows of hewn stone and cedar beams. Guy, the excavator, was inclined to see Hittite influence in this type of construction, though it may be indirect influence.[10]

Solomon's Stables (1 Kings 9:19; 2 Chronicles 8:6); Archaeological Confirmation

The Bible indicates that Solomon had whole cities given over to the stabling of his horses (1 Kings 9:19), yet such features of the glorious reign of Solomon were once thought to be late legendary additions to Scripture, and it was easy to suggest that "Solomon was really a very insignificant ruler" (AAPB, 46). The University of Chicago excavation at Megiddo

(1925–1939) identified the fourth stratum as Solomonic and discovered there two stable compounds capable of housing about 450 horses (EAEHL, 3: 830–55; for a picture of a stable and reconstruction, see PANEP, 232). J.W. Crowfoot subsequently sought to date these stables a little later than Solomon's time and to assign them to the days of Omri and Ahab,[11] and when Yigael Yadin excavated at Megiddo (1960–1970), he came to the same conclusion.[12] Yohanan Aharoni of Tel Aviv University defended the University of Chicago dating of the stables as Solomonic, and W.F. Albright concluded that they were built in Solomon's time and used down through the period of Omri and Ahab (AAP, 124, and oral communication to me). Albright's position seems to take into account all the facts in the case. Such discoveries confirm the biblical indication concerning this phase of Solomon's building activity and show that the splendor of his reign can no longer be doubted.

Solomon's Seaport (1 Kings 9:26; 2 Chronicles 8:17–18); Archaeological Light

The Bible records that Solomon had a seaport named Ezion Geber, located on the eastern arm of the Red Sea. The site has been identified with Tell el-Kheleifeh, midway between Jordanian Aqabah and Israeli Eilat in no-man's-land about five hundred yards from the shore of the Gulf of Aqaba. Nelson Glueck led a Smithsonian-American Schools of Oriental Research dig there during the spring seasons of 1938 to 1940. He found a wall two and a half to three yards thick, originally easily twenty-five feet high, surrounding a site of an acre and a half. Near the

[9]G.E. Wright and F.V. Filson, *The Westminster Historical Atlas to the Bible*, rev. ed. (Philadelphia: Westminster, 1956), 49 [WFWA].

[10]*Oriental Institute Communications*, 9:35 cited in BWMS, 127.

[11]See J.P. Free, "Oriental Institute Archaeological Report on the Near East, 1941," *American Journal of Semitic Languages* 58, 4 (October 1941): 410 [AJSL].

[12]Yigael Yadin, "New Light on Solomon's Megiddo," BA (1960), 62–68; see also Yadin, EAEHL, 3:853–56.

The foundations of Solomon's stables at Megiddo.   Courtesy of Oriental Institute of the University of Chicago

A model of Solomon's stables, reconstructed on the basis of the excavations.   Courtesy of Oriental Institute of the University of Chicago

southwest corner of the town and facing the sea stood a triple gate. In the northwest corner of the site he found an installation that he identified as a smelting and refining plant used for finishing ore that had been partially smelted in the Arabah to the north. Glueck found five periods of occupation from Solomon's day to the fourth century B.C.

In recent years there have been numerous modifications to the dramatic story spun around Solomon's having built a fleet and established a mining industry. In the first place, doubt arose as to the nature of the "smeltery" Glueck found, and he himself decided it was a citadel also used as a storehouse or granary.[13] Then he concluded that Tell el-Kheleifeh may have been only a satellite of Ezion Geber instead of the port itself. There is no evidence of port facilities at the tell, and it is not on the seacoast.

Moreover, Rothenberg and others have suggested the possibility that the island of Jezira Fara'un, about three hundred yards from the shore at Eilat, may have been the site of Ezion Geber. Rothenberg has observed further that no great fortress and port installation would have been necessary for the occasional use that Egyptian miners, Solomon, and Jehoshaphat of Judah required in the area.[14] So, evidently archaeologists have not yet found Solomon's seaport, but that fact has not thrown any doubt on its existence at the head of the Gulf of Aqaba.

Rothenberg has also shown that what used to be called Solomon's copper mining industry in the area south of the Dead Sea was incorrectly dated. Instead, the Egyptians operated the mines there during the fourteenth to the twelfth centuries B.C., and Egyptian mining activity there came to an end by 1150. The mines were not operated again until the Roman period.[15]

The Visit of the Queen of Sheba (1 Kings 10:1ff.); Archaeological Light on Camels and Sheba

When the Queen of Sheba heard of Solomon's fame, she came to visit him at Jerusalem, bringing with her a great caravan that included camels bearing gold, spices, and precious stones (1 Kings 10:1–2). This casual mention of a camel caravan is significant in view of the doubt that has been expressed in past years concerning the early use of the camel.[16] Archaeological discoveries show, however, that the effective domestication of the camel came at least as early as the period 1200–1000 B.C. It is during this period that the camel appears in cuneiform inscriptions, on the monument known as the Black Obelisk of Shalmaneser (FSAC, 120; for a picture see PANEP, 120), and on a sculptured stone relief from Halaf showing a one-humped dromedary with a rider sitting on the saddle.[17] Thus the archaeological evidence shows the effective domestication of the camel even before the time of the Queen of Sheba (c. 950 B.C.). Actually some knowledge of the camel, even in Egypt, goes back to at least 3000, as I have shown.[18] To set aside the reference to Abraham's having camels in Egypt (Gen. 12:16) is presumptuous in the light of such evidence as camel statuettes, bones, and other evidences that appear in archaeo-

---

[13] Nelson Glueck, "Ezion-geber," BA, 28 (September 1965), 75.
[14] Beno Rothenberg, *Were These King Solomon's Mines?* (New York: Stein & Day, 1972), 206–7.
[15] Ibid.
[16] As done by T.E. Peet (PEOT, 60), R.H. Pfeiffer (PIOT, 154), and others.
[17] Max Freiherr von Oppenheim, *Der Tell Halaf* (1931), Pl. XXIa (facing p. 136) and p. 140; cf. FLAP, 55 and figure 25.
[18] J.P. Free, "Abraham's Camels," *Journal of Near Eastern Studies*, University of Chicago (July 1944), 187–93.

logical materials beginning before 3000.[19] Albright came to acknowledge that "partial sporadic domestication may go back" several centuries before 1100 B.C. (FSAC, 120), and that "it is by no means impossible that successful efforts to domesticate this animal" were made in the Patriarchal Age (AOTA, 146).

The Queen of Sheba lived in southern Arabia and probably controlled the southern caravan routes and possibly the sea commerce that passed through the straits called Bab-el-Mandeb, the southern entrance into the Red Sea. It is possible that she discussed commercial interests when she visited Solomon, inasmuch as Solomon's merchant ships sailed down the Red Sea and probably came within the "sphere of interest" of the Queen of Sheba's enterprises.

James A. Montgomery[20] has pointed out that some scholars have dismissed the record of the visit of the Queen of Sheba to Solomon as "a romantic tale." It was objected that no such cultured Sheba existed at that early time, since any culture that appeared to exist in that area apparently belonged rather to the Minaeans (another people of Arabia). The archaeological discoveries, however, have produced historical inscriptions of several Assyrian kings[21] showing that the Sabaeans (people of the country of Sheba), though appearing to some extent in northwest Arabia, were purveyors of the South-Arabian trade. Professor Montgomery points out that this is a parallel to the Queen of Sheba's activity involved in bringing the precious gifts of the South to Solomon, and in this connection he observes that the biblical setting is "quite correct."[22]

Further evidence of relations between Palestine and South Arabia (Sheba area) came in the discovery of an inscribed South Arabian clay stamp in the third season of excavation at Bethel (1957). Partly broken, it was originally about three by four inches and evidently used to seal bags of cargo such as frankincense and myrrh.[23]

The stamp is significant because it is the earliest and possibly the first South Arabian object found in Palestine, and it proves that contact had already been set up between Israel and South Arabia early in the first millennium B.C., near the time of the visit of the Queen of Sheba to Solomon. Van Beek concludes, "While the substantial historicity of this event has been increasingly accepted in recent years, this object carries us closer to that period than most scholars had dared hope."[24]

Archaeological Light on Tarshish
(1 Kings 10:22)

A part of Solomon's commercial activity included the operation of a "fleet of trading ships" at Tarshish, which brought gold, silver, ivory, and apes from far away places (1 Kings 10:22). The word *tarshish* is explained by Albright as a loan word from Akkadian (Babylonian) meaning "smelting plant" or "refinery."[25] The location of the site referred to in the Bible as Tarshish has usually been assumed to be

---

[19]Cf. chapter 4, the section entitled "Abraham in Egypt," pages 50–51.

[20]Professor of Hebrew and Aramaic at the University of Pennsylvania; deceased 1949. For "Memoriam" article on Professor Montgomery, see BASOR, no. 115 (October 1949): 4–8.

[21]Tiglath-Pileser, Sennacherib, and others.

[22]James A. Montgomery, *Arabia and the Bible* (Philadelphia: University of Pennsylvania Press, 1934), 180.

[23]G.W. Van Beek, BASOR (October 1958).

[24]A similar stamp, found earlier, was reported in BASOR (October 1961).

[25]W.F. Albright, "New Light on the Early History of Phoenician Colonization" BASOR, no. 83 (October 1941): 21.

Tartessus in Spain,[26] but one of the Phoenician inscriptions found at Nora on the Island of Sardinia gives the name Tarshish immediately before the name Sardinia, which indicates that Tarshish was likely the Phoenician name for Nora.[27] The name Tarshish has also been found in an inscription of Esarhaddon,[28] referring to a Phoenician land at the opposite end of the Mediterranean from the Island of Cyprus (AOTA, 151). In light of the archaeological evidence available up to the present, Tarshish was in the western Mediterranean, and likely was the Phoenician name for Nora on the Island of Sardina.

But perhaps the foregoing discussion does not tell the whole story. First Kings 10:22 mentions "apes" and "ivory"; these would not have come from the western Mediterranean. "Ships of Tarshish" were not necessarily ships connected with a specific locale, but were ships constructed for transporting ore and other heavy cargoes, as Unger has pointed out.[29] As such, they would compare with large ships the Egyptians built in the third millennium B.C. for long-range shipping. These were called "Byblos travelers" and were used especially but not exclusively in trade with Byblos in Lebanon.[30]

Solomon's Spiritual Decline
(1 Kings 11)

Solomon married many foreign women (1 Kings 11:1), even though the Lord had warned against such a practice (v. 2; Deut. 7:3). These foreign wives turned Solomon's heart away after other gods, and he turned his attention to such pagan deities as Ashtoreth (vv. 4–5). From the archaeological discoveries we actually have a seal impression, found at Bethel, which pictures this goddess.[31] She was one of the best known of the fertility goddesses; she was known in Greek as Astarte and was worshiped in Babylonia under a slightly different form of the name—Ishtar (BWMS, 230–31).

Solomon finally came to build a high place of worship for the pagan god Chemosh on the "hill that is before Jerusalem" (1 Kings 11:7), probably the Mount of Olives.

Because of these sins of Solomon, God said that he would rend the kingdom from him, but because of David, his father, he would not do this until the time of Solomon's son. One tribe would remain to the descendants of Solomon (1 Kings 11:11–13).

During the reign of Solomon there came to prominence a young man named Jeroboam, who later was to be the king of the northern tribes after the division of the kingdom. The prophet Ahijah had predicted this as he tore Jeroboam's garment into twelve pieces, symbolic of the rending of Solomon's kingdom at the time of Solomon's death (1 Kings 11:30–31). Solomon seems to have become suspicious of Jeroboam, and Jeroboam found it advisable to flee to Egypt and to remain there until Solomon finished his reign of forty years and rested with his father (vv. 42–43).

---

[26]Brown, Driver, Briggs, *A Hebrew and English Lexicon of the Old Testament* (New York: Houghton Mifflin, 1906), 1076. For a discussion see Paul MacKendrick, *The Iberian Stones Speak* (New York: Funk & Wagnalls, 1969), chapter 2.

[27]Albright, "New Light," 21, AOTA, 151.

[28]King of Assyria from 681–668 B.C.

[29]Merrill F. Unger, *Archaeology and the Old Testament* (Grand Rapids: Zondervan, 1954), 226.

[30]See Charles F. Pfeiffer and Howard F. Vos, *The Wycliffe Historical Geography of Bible Lands* (Chicago: Moody Press, 1967), 190.

[31]BWMS, 230. See chapter 12, section entitled "The Later Life of Saul and His Death," pages 127–28.

Chapter 15

The Divided Kingdom

(1 Kings 12–22; 2 Chronicles 10–20; Jeroboam Through Ahab, 931–853 B.C.)

Division of the Kingdom; Rehoboam's Policy (1 Kings 12; 2 Chronicles 10)

After the death of Solomon (931 B.C.), Rehoboam, his son, prepared to ascend the throne (1 Kings 12:1ff). The people of the northern tribes, Israel, asked Rehoboam to make their lot easier (vv. 3–4). Rehoboam consulted with the older men, who counseled him to accede to the request of the people; but later he counseled with the young men who were his associates, and they advised him to add to the yoke of the people. Rehoboam foolishly followed the advice of the young men (vv. 13–14), telling the people of Israel that he would add to their yoke, whereupon the northern tribes rallied around Jeroboam, making him the new king of the ten northern tribes (v. 21). Rehoboam prepared to fight against the secessionist tribes, but the Lord sent a message through his prophet Shemaiah telling him not to subdue the rebellious tribes, explaining, "This is my doing" (v. 24). It evidently was not God's original

plan[1] to have a division, but the situation that had come to exist made the division necessary. If the north and south had remained together, it is possible that the idolatry of the north would have penetrated deeply into the southern kingdom of Judah and brought corruption there all the sooner.

Data for Determining the Dates of the Kings of Israel and Judah; Chronology

The reader will notice that the date of 931 B.C. has been indicated for the death of Solomon and the division of the kingdom. However, in older books a date forty or fifty years earlier was usually given for the death of Solomon; Raven, for example, gave this date as 979 B.C. (ROTI, 175). All books written in the light of recent discoveries date Solomon's death in the 930s B.C.

How is it possible to fix a date of 931 B.C. or thereabouts for the death of Solomon and the division of the kingdom? A partial answer will prove helpful. Fortunately the

---

[1]This does not mean that God changes his mind in human fashion and that therefore his character is changeable. It means, rather, that when humans change or fail, God alters his dealing with them in accordance with the situation. His character never changes.

Assyrians kept lists of years, noting their principal events and ruling officials. These we call Eponym Lists; an eponym was a year named for a person who held office during that year. Archaeological excavations have produced tablets that give specific lists from 893 to 666 B.C. (BAB, 57). One of these lists mentions an eclipse that occurred at Nineveh in May–June, 763 B.C. Astronomers have checked this eclipse, and thus we have a fixed date in the eponym lists, from which we can calculate other dates in the period 900–600.

From these Assyrian records, we know that the great battle of Qarqar was fought in the year 853 B.C. The archaeological records of King Shalmaneser III (858–824) tell us that he was opposed in the battle of Qarqar by a coalition of twelve allies, one of whom was King Ahab of Israel.[2]

Since Ahab fought in the battle of Qarqar in 853, the dates of Ahab must include this year. Apparently the battle came near the end of Ahab's reign (ORHI, 291), and so Ahab's rule is to be dated 874–853. Since the Bible gives us the length of reign for each of the kings of Israel and Judah, we can figure back from Ahab to the death of Solomon and arrive at the date of approximately 931. The preceding development provides an example of some of the processes employed in working out the chronology of the period of the Hebrew kings.

Problems in Connection With the Chronology of the Period of the Kings; Pfeiffer's Acknowledgment

Why is it that the date given by an assortment of scholars for the death of Solomon and the division of the kingdom varies by several years? The answer is that there are problems in connection with the chronology of the kings of the Bible concerning which we did not have full light in the past. For example, we find that the length of time from Jeroboam I to Jehoram in Israel should be the same as the time from Rehoboam to Ahaziah in the southern kingdom of Judah. This is true because Jehoram and Ahaziah met their death simultaneously at the hands of Jehu. However, when we add up the reigns of the kings in each line, we arrive at the following result:

ISRAEL

Jeroboam I	22 years
Nadab	2 years
Baasha	24 years
Elah	2 years
Zimri	7 days
Omri	12 years
Ahab	22 years
Ahaziah	2 years
Jehoram	12 years
Total	98 years, 7 days

JUDAH

Rehoboam	17 years
Abijam	3 years
Asa	41 years
Jehoshaphat	25 years
Jehoram	8 years
Ahaziah	1 year
Total	95 years

Thus we see that the same period of time adds up to ninety-eight years and seven days for Israel, and only ninety-five years for Judah. Such problems have caused some scholars to feel that the chronological data from the Old Testament is of such a nature that a valid chronology cannot be constructed.

Archaeological discoveries, however, have led writers as liberal as Pfeiffer to acknowledge the value of the Old Testament chronological indications. He says,

---

[2]D.D. Luckenbill, *Ancient Records of Assyria and Babylonia* (Chicago: University of Chicago Press, 1926), 223 [LARA]; PANET, 278–79.

"The chronology of the histories of the kings of Judah and Israel—the synchronisms—are genuine, though not errorless" (PIOT, 394). He adds on the next page, "In spite of these discrepancies, inaccuracies, and errors, the chronology of Kings is not fantastic. . ." (PIOT, 395). But what about the apparent discrepancies such as appear in the above chart?

Thiele's Work on Chronology; Significance of the Work

E.R. Thiele[3] wrote his doctoral dissertation at the Oriental Institute of the University of Chicago on the chronology of the period 900–600 B.C. It was published in substance in the *Journal of Near Eastern Studies* under the title "The Chronology of the Kings of Judah and Israel" [JNES],[4] and in book form by the University of Chicago Press under the title, *Mysterious Numbers of the Hebrew Kings* (1951). In a revised edition, it has now been published by Zondervan (1983). A spokesman at Paternoster Press in Britain has called Professor Thiele's work "the basis of all subsequent investigation in this field, and the standard authority on the subject."

Thiele discovered that the chronological data in the period of kings in the Old Testament harmonize in a most wonderful way. He utilized several factors that many scholars have only partially taken into consideration and in this way was able to solve many apparent problems and contradictions in the length of reigns. Of these, the principle factors are as follows:

1. In Israel the regnal year began with the month Nisan, while in Judah it began with the month Tishri.

2. At the time of the division of the kingdom, Judah reckoned the years of its kings according to the accession-year system. In this system, the fraction of the year the king ruled when he first came to

the throne was regarded as his accession year, and not as his first year. His first year was reckoned as beginning with the month Tishri following his accession to the throne. Judah continued to follow this system until the fall of the kingdom, except for the period from Jehoram to Joash, when they employed the nonaccession-year system. Israel, on the contrary, during her early history employed the nonaccession-year system, whereby the part of the year during which the king first reigned was counted as his first year, and his second year began with the first of Nisan following his accession. Israel followed this system until the reign of Jehoash in 798, when they shifted to the accession-year system. Thus, during the later history of the two kingdoms, they were using the same system.

3. Both Judah and Israel, when computing the years of each other's kings, did so according to the method of reckoning in force in their own countries and not according to the system used by their neighbors.

4. Both Israel and Judah made use of co-regencies, but in neither nation did interregna occur.

5. When there were co-regencies, the years of the king were usually counted from the beginning of the co-regency.

The Dates of the Kings of Israel and Judah

A serviceable list of the kings of Israel and Judah, with dates of their reigns, is given by Pfeiffer (PIOT, 375–76), by Robinson (ORHI, 463–64), and in recent encyclopedias. Generally these place the division of the kingdom between 936 and 931 B.C. and are quite usable. However, because of Thiele's use of factors that harmonize the data, we are presenting an adaptation of his results below. (Many of

---

[3]Then professor in the field of Biblical Studies at Andrews University, Berrien Springs, Michigan.
[4]3,3 (July 1944): 137–86.

ISRAEL	Reign	Co-regency	JUDAH	Reign	Co-regency
1. Jeroboam	931–910		1. Rehoboam	931–913	
2. Nadab	910–909		2. Abijam	913–911	
3. Baasha	909–886		3. Asa	911–870	
4. Elah	886–885		4. Jehoshaphat	870–848	873–870
5. Zimri	885		5. Jehoram	848–841	853–848
Tibni	885–880	885–880			
6. Omri	880–874	885–880	6. Ahaziah	841	
			Athaliah	841–835	
7. Ahab	874–853		7. Joash	835–796	
8. Ahaziah	853–852		8. Amaziah	796–767	
9. Jehoram	852–841		9. Azariah	767–740	791–767
10. Jehu	841–814		10. Jotham	740–736	750–740
11. Jehoahaz	814–798		11. Ahaz	736–716	
12. Jehoash	798–782		12. Hezekiah	716–687	
13. Jeroboam II	782–753	793–782	13. Manasseh	687–642	696–687
14. Zechariah	753–752		14. Amon	642–640	
15. Shallum	752		15. Josiah	640–609	
16. Menahem	752–742		16. Jehoahaz	609	
17. Pekahiah	742–740		17. Jehoiakim	609–597	
18. Pekah	740–732	752–740	18. Jehoiachin	597	
19. Hoshea	732–723, 722		19. Zedekiah	597–586	

these dates will approximate and others will equate with the chronologies mentioned above.)

Jeroboam, the First King of Israel (1 Kings 12); Archaeological Light on His Name

Jeroboam was chosen to be the first king of the northern tribes after their secession from Rehoboam (1 Kings 12:20). Archaeological confirmation of the name Jeroboam was found in the excavation by the German expedition at Megiddo (1903–1905) directed by Gottlieb Schumacher. In the fifth stratum from the bottom, in a palace of the Hebrew period, they found a seal bearing an inscription that read, "Belonging to Shema, servant of Jeroboam."[5] We do not know whether this Shema was the servant of Jeroboam I (931–910 B.C.) or Jeroboam II (782–753),

but in any event the seal does reveal the presence of this personal name in the time of the monarchy of Israel.

Jeroboam's Calf Worship; Critical View; Light From Archaeology

Shortly after Jeroboam became king of Israel, he established calf worship by setting up a calf at Dan far in the north and another one at Bethel in the southernmost part of the northern kingdom. His purpose in doing this was to prevent the people of his kingdom from going to the temple at Jerusalem, where they might be influenced to return to the allegiance of Rehoboam (1 Kings 12:27). A. Biran in his excavations at Tel Dan has uncovered the high place of the town (an almost square platform about fifty-nine by sixty feet), which he thought was erected

[5]BAB, 110, 456.

Ruins of the high place at Dan, built by Jeroboam I

by Jeroboam I and enlarged during the reigns of Ahab and Jeroboam II.[6]

Critics have often held that Jeroboam was merely continuing an older form of worship in which the Lord was represented as a bull. The archaeological discoveries in Egypt, however, show the presence of bovine worship there. The sacred bull was an object of worship in Egypt, its tomb being found at Memphis during the last century. The sacred cow was the symbol of the goddess Hathor. In the light of this evidence, it is more likely that Jeroboam became acquainted with bovine worship when he fled to Egypt while Solomon was yet alive (1 Kings 11:40; 12:2) and upon his return to Palestine introduced the worship he had observed in Egypt. The German Egyptologist Steindorff and the American Old Testament scholar George L. Robinson both reflect this view (RBA, 66). The question is sometimes raised as to how Jeroboam could get the Israelites to switch from worship of an invisible God to calf worship. A possible explanation is seen in the artistic illustrations of several ancient Near Eastern peoples that pictured their gods as standing or sitting on the back of an animal, such as a bull or lion, with the animal sometimes thought of as being there invisibly.[7]

---

[6]These excavations, under the auspices of the Israel Department of Antiquities and Museums, have been in progress since 1966. See EAEHL, 1:320.

[7]For example, for the Hittites see O.R. Gurney, *The Hittites*, rev. ed. (Baltimore: Penguin Books, 1961), 143; for the Assyrians, see PANEP, 180–81.

Rehoboam, the First King of Judah (1 Kings 12, 14); Archaeological Confirmation of Shishak's Invasion

During the reign of Rehoboam, Sheshonk I (spelled "Shishak" in the Bible) came from Egypt to Palestine and took the treasures of the temple at Jerusalem (1 Kings 14:24ff.). Archaeological confirmation of this campaign of Shishak is found in his inscription on the wall of the great temple of Karnak in Egypt. The inscription shows his god Amon leading by cords rows of Asiatic captives, undoubtedly Israelites. On the relief 156 captives are represented and on the bodies of these people are inscribed names of many Palestinian towns, such as Taanach, Gibeon, Ajalon, and Beth Shan (see PANEP, 118, and ANET, 242–43). The archaeological material adds further light to what is revealed in the Bible, showing that Shishak went to other towns in addition to Jerusalem and even invaded the northern kingdom.

Omri, the Sixth King of Israel; Archaeological Light on Samaria, His Capital

For six years (885–880 B.C.) Omri ruled in opposition to the usurper Tibni. But finally the followers of Omri prevailed over the people who followed Tibni, and Omri gained sole rule over Israel (880–874; 1 Kings 16:21–22). He established the capital at Samaria (v. 24), confirmation of this being found when Harvard University excavated the site (1908–1910) under the direction of G.A. Reisner. On the native rock a large palace was found, identified as that of Omri (BAB, 120; EAEHL, 4:1041–42). Thus the biblical indication that Samaria was founded by Omri is confirmed. Burrows acknowledges this in his statement that "Samaria was built at a time corresponding to the statement that Omri established it as the capital of the northern kingdom. The examples of such confirmation which might be given are almost innumerable" (BWMS, 281).

The Progress of Idolatry in the Northern Kingdom

The progress of idolatry in the northern kingdom is well outlined by William G. Blaikie in his *Manual of Bible History*. This outline is retained in the revision (though the revision, having been done by a liberal, has suffered in many other respects—cf. BBHM). Blaikie's outline is as follows:

1. Idolatry taking root (under Jeroboam: calf worship, etc.)
2. Idolatry rampant (under Omri, Ahab, Jezebel; Elijah and Elisha raised up to combat the progress of idolatry and Baal worship)
3. Idolatry slightly checked (Jehu, Jeroboam II; Elisha)
4. Idolatry terminating in destruction (the northern kingdom finally ended in a series of murders in the palace.) (BBHM, 207, 211, 227, 229).

Ahab's Reign; His Marriage; Elijah and Elisha (1 Kings 16:30ff.)

Ahab (874–853 B.C.), the seventh king of Israel, married Jezebel, the daughter of the king of the Sidonians (1 Kings 16:31). Jezebel brought in the worship of Baal from her home in Phoenicia. When this new curse was about to engulf the kingdom, God raised up Elijah, and later Elisha, to sustain the true believers in Israel. We might wonder why Elijah and Elisha did not cry out against the calf worship (see earlier section in this chapter entitled "Jeroboam's Calf Worship," pages 152–53), but as Albright points out, the Baal worship was so much worse that Elijah and Elisha spent their energies on the most serious problem in this hour of crisis (AARI, 156).

Archaeological Light on Baal Worship in the Northern Kingdom

Archaeological discoveries show that the name "Baal" appears in the personal names of people who lived in the northern kingdom, being evidenced in the seals and inscriptions that have been found. On the other hand, it is very significant that the seals and inscriptions from Judah, which become more common in the eighth century and are very numerous in the seventh and early sixth, never seem to contain any names of Baal (AARI, 160).

In the Harvard excavation at Samaria, a number of inscribed potsherds (called ostraca) were found,[8] sixty-three of which contained writing in ancient Hebrew, which was fairly legible.[9] These inscribed ostraca served as notations concerning payments of oil and wine that had been sent in by individuals as revenue or taxes to the storerooms of the royal palace.[10] Ostracon No. Two tells that in the tenth year of the king, there was sent to Gaddiyau, the royal steward (or tax collector), from the town of Azah, two jars to be credited to Abibaal, two to be credited to Ahaz, one to Sheba, and one to Meribaal. It reads literally, "In the tenth year, to Gaddiyau, from Azah, Abibaal 2, Ahaz 2, Sheba 1, Meribaal 1."[11] It is significant that these ostraca, dating from about 775 B.C.,[12] contain many names formed with Baal,[13]

showing what a great impact the Baal worship introduced by Jezebel had on the land of Israel. (See also EAEHL, 4: 1044.)

Archaeological Light on Ahab's Ivory House (1 Kings 22:39)

The biblical summary of Ahab's life refers to "the palace he built and inlaid with ivory" (1 Kings 22:39). The excavations at Samaria revealed a palace platform 315 feet from north to south.[14] The remains of the palace structure found on this site dating from Ahab's period gave evidence of walls faced with high-quality white limestone, which would, in itself, give the appearance of an "ivory" palace as it stood there gleaming in the Palestinian sun. But, more than that, numerous ivory decorations were found, in the form of plaques and panels for decorating furniture and wall paneling (FLAP, 187–88).[15] As Clarence Fisher, one of the excavators of Samaria, remarked to me, there was a double reason for calling Ahab's palace an "ivory house"—the gleaming white walls and also the ivory decorations.

---

[8]BAB, 120–21.

[9]J.W. Jack, *Samaria in Ahab's Time; Harvard Excavations and Their Results* (Edinburgh: T. & T. Clark, 1929), 37 [JSAT].

[10]Ibid., 97–98.

[11]Hand copies of these ostraca are published in George Andrew Reisner, *Israelite Ostraca from Samaria*, Harvard University. Three are reproduced in Albright's *Archaeology of Palestine* (AAP, 135, figure 40).

[12]The Samaria Ostraca were formerly dated in the reign of Ahab (874–853 B.C.), but on the basis of the forms of the letters and the contents, Albright later dated them in the reign of Jeroboam II (782–753, according to Thiele's chronology. Albright's dates for Jeroboam are 774–766 in AARI, 41; and 782–742 in AOTA, 152).

[13]Note the two names Abibaal and Meribaal in the inscription given above; cf. AARI, 160; BWMS, 252.

[14]A.T. Olmstead, *History of Palestine and Syria* (New York: Scribner, 1931), 372 [OHPS].

[15]For another significance of the ivory decoration, see chapter 17, the section entitled "Archaeological Light on Amos' Condemnation of the Idle Luxury of Samaria," 166–67. On the Samaria ivories, cf. also AAP, 137, and AOTA, 152.

A public building at Hazor from the time of King Ahab

Steps leading to the temple to Augustus at Samaria, constructed by Herod the Great in New Testament times

The Greco-Roman theater at Samaria, also constructed by Herod the Great

Chapter 16

The Northern and Southern Kingdoms, Israel and Judah, c. 850–750 B.C.

(2 Kings 1–14; 2 Chronicles 21–25. Israel: Ahaziah Through Jeroboam II, 853–753 B.C. Judah: Jehoram to Azariah (Uzziah), 848–767 B.C.)

Ahaziah's Illness and Elijah's Message (2 Kings 1)

In dealing with the kings of Israel and Judah, it will be helpful for the reader to refer constantly to the chart of kings on page 152, in order to keep in mind the relative relationship of the various kings and their approximate dates of rule.

After the death of Ahab (874–853 B.C.), the seventh king of Israel, his son Ahaziah (853–852) came to the throne and continued the wicked practices of his father by worshiping Baal (1 Kings 22:51–53). When Ahaziah became sick, he sent messengers to inquire of the god of Ekron, in the Philistine territory, whether he would recover from his disease (2 Kings 1:2). The messengers were met on their way by Elijah, who first asked why they should go to Ekron when there was a God in Israel and then told them that the king would not recover from his illness but would surely die (2 Kings 1:3–4). In accordance with Elijah's prophecy, Ahaziah died; he was succeeded by his brother Jehoram (852–841), another son of Ahab.

Elijah's Translation; Elisha's Ministry, c. 850 B.C. (2 Kings 2–8)

Elijah had been raised up to cry out against the introduction and spread of Baal worship, which was fostered and spread by the Phoenician wife of Ahab, Jezebel, in the period c. 875–850 B.C. (see chapter 15). Elijah's ministry came to an end about 850, when the great prophet was taken to heaven by the Lord without suffering death (2 Kings 2:11).

Elijah's successor, Elisha, had asked that he might inherit a double portion of Elijah's spirit (2 Kings 2:9b). It is often assumed that Elisha was asking to excel his master in spiritual power and that the granting of his request is seen in Elisha's performing fourteen recorded miracles in comparison to Elijah's seven. But on the face of it, that is not a very "spiritual" or kind request, and it does not fit Hebrew thought patterns or customs. Apparently what Elisha was asking for was not to excel his master but to receive the double portion of the eldest son as inheritance rights under Hebrew law (Deut. 21:17). That is, he was asking to be the true heir and successor of Elijah. It is true, however, that Elisha did perform fourteen miracles, and they are summarized as follows: (1) He made the bad water of a spring wholesome (2:19–22). (2) He cursed children who mocked him (2:23, 24; the Hebrew word does not indicate little children, but rather "young men"; they may have been participants in the idolatrous Baal practices). (3) He provided water for the armies (3:11–20); the armies of Israel and Judah were fighting against the Moabites, and were about to succumb because of lack of water; God showed Elisha that water would be provided; at Elisha's direction, ditches were dug and were found to be filled with water the next day. (4) He multiplied a widow's oil (4:1–7). (5) He raised the Shunamite woman's son (vv. 8–37). (6) He healed the deadly pot of stew (vv. 38–41). (7) He miraculously fed one hundred men (vv. 42–44). (8) He cleansed the leper Naaman by having him bathe in the Jordan River (5:1–19). (9) He smote Gehazi with leprosy when Gehazi accepted gifts from Naaman without Elisha's permission (vv. 20–27). (10) He caused the iron ax head to swim (6:1–7). (11) He revealed the movements of the Syrian army (vv. 8–13). (12) He struck the Syrians with blindness (vv. 14–19). (13) He healed the blindness of the Syrians (vv. 20–23). (14) He raised a dead man (13:20–21).

Intimate Relations Between Israel and Judah, c. 850 B.C.

King Jehoshaphat (870–848 B.C.), the fourth king of Judah, had introduced a period of intimate interrelationships between Israel and Judah, with the royal families intermarrying (2 Kings 8:18, 26), adopting the same names for their children (2 Kings 3:1; 8:16), and visiting each other (2 Kings 8:29; 2 Chron. 18:1–2). They made joint ventures in foreign trade, establishing a merchant marine at Ezion Geber (2 Chron. 20:35–36), where Solomon had established his seaport about a century earlier (see chapter 14); and at various times Israel and Judah made a joint disposition of their military forces, as in the case of the battle at Ramoth Gilead (1 Kings 22:29ff.), and the alliance

between Jehoram of Israel and Jehoshaphat of Judah to put down the rebellion of the Moabites (2 Kings 3:6–7). These entangling alliances brought no real gain to Judah but merely served to yoke her unequally with the kings of idolatrous Israel and to undermine her own spiritual progress. Elisha specifically spoke a word of rebuke concerning this last mentioned alliance of Israel and Judah against the Moabites (2 Kings 3:13–14).

Archaeological Light on the Moabite Rebellion (2 Kings 3:4–27; c. 850–840 B.C.); the Moabite Stone

During the days of Ahab, seventh king of Israel (874–853 B.C.), the king of Moab, Mesha, had been subject to Israel. After the death of Ahab, Mesha rebelled, and the ninth king of Israel, Jehoram (852–841), proceeded to ally himself with Jehoshaphat (870–848), the fourth king of Judah, for the purpose of subjugating Mesha again (2 Kings 3:5–7).

Interesting light and confirmation on Mesha is found on the Moabite Stone, a monument that was seen in Dibon in Transjordan in 1868 by a German clergyman, F.A. Klein. The Germans and the French both tried to obtain the stone, and during the negotiations some Arabs heated it and poured cold water on it, causing it to break in many pieces. According to one theory, this was done in the hope of making more profit out of the fragments. Fortunately, much of the stone was recovered, and with the aid of a "squeeze"[1] made previously, it could be read. (For a picture of the reconstructed Moabite Stone, now in the Louvre in Paris, see PANEP, 85.)

The inscription on the Moabite Stone confirms the fact of Mesha's rebellion and also the fact that he had been subject to Israel. On the stone, Mesha says, concerning his subjection to Israel, "Omri, king of Israel—he oppressed Moab many days

[1]A type of impression or cast.

... and his son succeeded him, and he also said I will oppress Moab" (PANET, 320–21).

Some scholars have thought that there is not complete harmony between the statements of the Moabite Stone and the Scriptures. Barton, for example, says, "There are some differences of statement which are perplexing" (BAB, 462). Significant work, however, was done on this problem by John D. Davis, formerly of Princeton Seminary, who showed how the two accounts may be harmonized.[2] Davis correctly observes, "Mesha is in no wise contradicting, but only unintentionally supplementing the Hebrew account" (RBA, 167). For a summary of Davis' analysis, see Robinson (RBA, 167–69); Caiger also briefly shows the harmonization of the Moabite Stone and the scriptural records (CBS, 135–38).

Excavations at Dibon, forty miles south of Amman, were carried out by the American School of Oriental Research in Jerusalem, 1950–1955. A fragment bearing the same script as that of the Moabite Stone was discovered.[3] The walls of the old Moabite city, destroyed by Nebuchadnezzar in 582 B.C., were explored, Unfortunately, a Nabatean temple was built on the apparent site of Mesha's palace, thus destroying much of the evidence of the earlier period (see EAEHL, 1: 330–33).

Ben-Hadad's Advance Against Israel in the Days of Jehoram (852–841 B.C.) (2 Kings 6–7)

During the days of Jehoram, the ninth king of Israel, the Syrian king Ben-Hadad came up against Israel and besieged the city of Samaria, capital city of Israel (2 Kings 6:24ff.). Elisha promised that the Syrian siege would be lifted (2 Kings 7:1ff.), and this occurred when the Syrians wrongly assumed that the Hittites and Egyptians were coming to the aid of the

Israelites (2 Kings 7:6–7). This false assumption caused the Syrians to flee, and Elisha's promise was fulfilled.

The Bible indicates that Elisha sojourned at Dothan in the period 850–800 B.C. (2 Kings 6:12–13). Certain critics have been skeptical of the scriptural record of Elisha, and some have even doubted his existence. In view of these doubts, it is significant that my excavations at Dothan (1953–1962) have uncovered areas of the city of Elisha's day in the upper stratification of the ancient mound. Dothan was a thriving city in the days of that prophet, as implied in the biblical record and confirmed by our excavations (see BASOR, Nos. 131, 135, 139).

Archaeological Light on Hadad; Connection with Ben-Hadad (2 Kings 6:24ff.)

The significance of a name is often illuminated by archaeological discoveries. The name Ben-Hadad, meaning "son of Hadad," is intelligible when we know that Hadad was one of the most prominent of Near Eastern deities, being the Aramean storm god. An archaeological reference to this god was found on a stone statue of about 800 B.C. at Zinjirli in northern Syria; it bears an Aramaic inscription stating that King Panammu had dedicated the statue to Hadad. The Amarna Tablets also show that Hadad was already a prominent figure in the religion of Palestine in the Bronze Age, i.e., before 1200 B.C. (BWMS, 228).

Archaeological Confirmation of Hazael the Usurper (2 Kings 8:7–15)

Ben-Hadad, the Syrian king, came to a sudden end when Hazael suffocated him with a cloth and usurped the throne (2 Kings 8:15). Archaeological confirmation of the fact that Hazael succeeded Ben-Hadad and gained the throne but

---

[2]"The Moabite Stone and the Hebrew Records," *Hebraica* 7 (1891): 178–82, cited in RBA, 167.
[3]BASOR 125 (February 1952): 20–23.

was not of royal blood or in the royal line of succession was found in an inscription of Shalmaneser III of Assyria (860–825 B.C.), which reads, "Hazael, son of nobody, seized the throne" (PANET, 280–81).

Further confirmation of Hazael was found on some ivory decorations discovered at Khadatu in northwestern Mesopotamia. One of these ivory objects bears the name of Hazael, king of Damascus (ARDBL, 34).

Climax of Elisha's Fight Against Baalism—the Anointing of Jehu as King (2 Kings 9:1–13)

Ahab and his wife, Jezebel, had fostered the introduction and growth of Baal worship in Israel. The successor of Ahab, his son Ahaziah (853–852 B.C.), had continued the worship of Baal (1 Kings 22:53), and the next king, another son of Ahab, Jehoram (852–841), still continued in the sins of Jeroboam, although he did "put away the image of Baal that his father had made" (2 Kings 3:2–3). The house of Ahab was still on the throne, and Baalism could again flourish in all its power at any moment. God used Elisha to initiate the train of events that would preclude the fostering of any further Baal worship by the family of Ahab. Elisha had Jehu anointed to become the next king of Israel and to bring to an end the house of Ahab (2 Kings 9:7–8), thus avenging the crimes perpetrated by the followers of the Baal cult.

The Activity of Jehu, the Tenth King of Israel, 841–814 B.C. (2 Kings 9–10)

After Elisha directed one of the prophets to anoint Jehu as king over Israel (2 Kings 9:1–3), the prophet carried out the instructions, and in addition told Jehu that he would smite the house of Ahab (v. 7), and the house of Ahab would perish (v. 8). The army subsequently acknowledged Jehu as king of Israel (v. 13).

Jehu set out for the town of Jezreel in north central Palestine, where Jehoram,[4] the ninth king of Israel (852–841 B.C.) had returned after being wounded in battle with the Syrians (2 Kings 8:28–29). Ahaziah, the sixth king of Judah (841), had already come to see Jehoram at Jezreel, because he was sick (8:29; 9:16). The watchman on the tower in Jezreel saw Jehu's military company approaching and surmised that it was Jehu, for, as the watchman said, "the driving is like that of Jehu the son of Nimshi—he drives like a madman" (2 Kings 9:20).

Upon hearing the news that the approaching company was that of Jehu, Jehoram of Israel and Ahaziah of Judah went out to meet him (2 Kings 9:21). Both kings were slain (vv. 24, 27), and at the direction of Jehu, Jezebel was thrown down from an upper window and killed (v. 33). Jehu also had the sons of Ahab put to death (10:1ff.) and the prophets of Baal slain (vv. 19–25); he finally concluded his purge of Baal worship by burning the images of the house of Baal and breaking down the house of Baal (vv. 16–28).

Jehu's reforms brought in the third period in the progress of idolatry in Israel, a period in which idolatry was slightly checked (see Blaikie's outline, page 154). Jehu stopped short of a complete spiritual house-cleaning in Israel, for he allowed the worship of the golden calves at Bethel and Dan to continue (2 Kings 10:29), thus perpetuating the sins of Jeroboam I, the first king of divided Israel, who had had these calves erected (v. 31). Jehu's incomplete obedience shows that he went far enough in the reform to seat himself securely on the throne by killing Ahab and his family but did not completely serve the Lord by thoroughly destroying idolatry.

Hazael of Damascus attacked the borders of Israel on the north and east during the latter part of the reign of Jehu

---

[4]Often rendered in the shorter form, Joram.

(2 Kings 10:32–33). Jehu died after a reign of twenty-eight years (v. 36).

Archaeological Confirmation of Jehu: the Black Obelisk of Shalmaneser

A monument called the Black Obelisk of Shalmaneser was found by Layard at Nimrud (Calah), south of Nineveh, about the middle of the nineteenth century. The second register from the top pictures the tribute brought to Shalmaneser III of Assyria (860–825 B.C.) by the Hebrew caravan. One of the panels shows Jehu or his envoy bowing down before King Shalmaneser III. (For a picture of this, see PANEP, 120–22, 290–91.) The inscription of this panel reads, "Tribute of Jehu, son of Omri" (PANET, 281). In the Assyrian cuneiform the name Jehu was rendered by the syllables Ya-u-a; it was Hincks, an Irish clergyman and cuneiform scholar, who, in 1851, first recognized in these syllables the equivalent of the biblical name Jehu (CBS, 141). The Black Obelisk of Shalmaneser is in the British Museum in London. It is a specific confirmation of the reign of Jehu and supplements the Scriptures by telling us of the tribute he paid to Shalmaneser III.

Athaliah of Judah (2 Kings 11)

After Jehu had slain Ahaziah, king of Judah (841 B.C.), Ahaziah's mother, Athaliah, took the throne of Judah, slaying all those who might be heirs to the throne except Joash, who was concealed from the fury of Athaliah (2 Kings 11:1–2). After Athaliah had ruled for six years (841–835), a movement was instituted by Jehoiada the priest resulting in the overthrow of Athaliah and the elevation of Joash to the throne (vv. 4–18). Jehoiada the priest was able to break down the house of Baal (vv. 17–18) and to make repairs on the temple (vv. 9–16).

The Seventh and Eighth Southern Kings: Joash (835–796 B.C.) and Amaziah (796–767) (2 Kings 12–14)

After the six-year rule of Athaliah (2 Kings 11:3), Joash came to the throne of Judah at the age of seven (12:1). Jehoiada the priest probably guided the fortunes of Judah until Joash was old enough to reign. When Hazael of Damascus headed for Jerusalem, Joash sent him the sacred treasures of the temple (vv. 17–18). Joash died in a palace conspiracy (v. 19) and was succeeded by his son, Amaziah, who suffered an invasion from Jehoash, king of Israel (vv. 13–14).

The Eleventh, Twelfth, and Thirteenth Northern Kings: Jehoahaz (814–798 B.C.), Jehoash (798–782), and Jeroboam II (782–753) (2 Kings 13–14)

In Israel, Jehu was followed by his son, Jehoahaz (2 Kings 13:1), who made concessions to idolatry (v. 2), yet had some regard for the things of God (v. 4). Jehoahaz was followed by his son Jehoash (v. 9), who took the temple treasures from Jerusalem (14:13–14), and Jehoash was followed by his son Jeroboam II (v. 23), who was able to restore the eastern borders of Israel (v. 25), which had earlier been smitten by Hazael of Damascus in the days of Jehu (10:32–33).

A reconstruction of the palace of Sargon II of Assyria at Khorsabad   Courtesy of the Oriental Institute of the University of Chicago

A great stone winged bull from the palace of Sargon II, carved from a single block of stone and weighing forty tons   Courtesy of the Oriental Institute of the University of Chicago

Chapter 17

The End of the Northern Kingdom, c. 750–722 B.C.

(2 Kings 15–17; 2 Chronicles 26–28. Israel: Zechariah Through Hoshea, 753–722 B.C. Judah: Azariah [Uzziah] Through Ahaz, 767–716 B.C.)

ISRAEL			JUDAH	
13. Jeroboam II	782–753		9. Azariah	767–740
14. Zechariah	753–752			
15. Shallum	752			
16. Menahem	752–742		10. Jotham	740–736
17. Pekahiah	742–740			
18. Pekah	740–732		11. Ahaz	736–716
19. Hoshea	732–722			
End of Northern Kingdom	722		12. Hezekiah	716–687

The Last Kings of Israel; Their Contemporaries in Judah
(2 Kings 15–17)

For convenience in dealing with this period, the last kings of Israel and their contemporaries in Judah are listed above.

The Prophets of the Mid-Eighth Century: Amos and Hosea (c. 750 B.C.)

Amos prophesied during the reign of Jeroboam II of Israel and Azariah (Uzziah) of Judah. Scholars generally agree in dating him about 750 B.C., though some have placed him as early as 760. Amos did not belong to the regular schools of the prophets (1 Sam. 19:20) but was a herdsman and a gatherer of sycamore figs (Amos 1:1; 7:14), whom the Lord called to prophesy (7:15). Although Amos lived in the kingdom of Judah, at Tekoa, some ten miles south of Jerusalem (Amos 1:1), he took to task not only his own southern kingdom for her sins (Amos 2:4–5), but also the northern kingdom of Israel in particular (vv. 6ff.), singling out for rebuke the capital city of Samaria in the north (4:1) and the idolatry of Bethel, where Jeroboam's calf was erected (v. 4). Amos scored the decadent and luxury-loving people of Israel for their extortion from the poor (5:11), their crookedness and use of bribes (v. 12), and their use of sacrifice and offering to cover up their sins—a form of hypocrisy, which God hates (vv. 21–22). After portraying this sordid picture, Amos pointed forward to the time of the restoration of the Davidic kingdom (9:11), and the time of prosperity (vv. 13–

15) that will be brought in with the millennial reign of Christ.

The prophet Hosea, a contemporary of Amos, prophesied in the time of Jeroboam II (782–753 B.C.) against the sins of the northern kingdom of Israel. Hosea used his own family experience as a symbol of the situation in Israel. This prophet had taken an unchaste woman, who bore him children whose names were symbolic (Lo-ruhamah, "no mercy," Lo-ammi, "not my people"; Hosea 1:6, 9). Hosea's wife, it seems, forsook him for an adulterous life (2:1–2) but was restored to him after a time (3:1–3). Hosea used the fact of her adultery as a symbol of the apostasy (spiritual adultery) of Israel, and her restoration as an illustration of the fact that one day Israel will be restored in the future Davidic kingdom (v. 5). Hosea pointed out the many sins of Israel, their forgetting of the things of God (4:6), their idolatry (v. 13), their adultery (7:4), and all manner of other sins. It was a stern rebuke, but it was greatly needed in the days of low spirituality and low morality in the era of Jeroboam II.

Archaeological Light on Amos's Condemnation of the Idle Luxury of Samaria (Amos 6:4, 6)

Amos pointed out the dishonesty, extortion, and crookedness of the decadent luxury-loving people of Samaria, who took their ease "on beds inlaid with ivory," drank "wine by the bowlful," and anointed themselves with the "finest lotions [oils]" (Amos 6:4, 6). The excavation of Samaria begun in 1931 under the direction of J.W. Crowfoot uncovered from the citadel area of the city numerous fragments of ivory inlay, which illuminate Amos' reference to the "beds inlaid with

ivory." Most of these ivory pieces are in the form of plaques or panels bearing reliefs, and apparently formed part of the inlay decoration of the furniture. The subjects portrayed in the reliefs include lotus, lilies, papyrus, lions, bulls, deer, winged figures in human form, sphinxes, and figures of Egyptian gods, such as Isis and Horus (FLAP, 185–88).

Several of the Samaria ostraca,[1] which record the payment of taxes to the royal treasury at the capital or income from the royal estates, list such payments in wine and oil. A typical ostracon (No. 1) tells that in the tenth year contributions of wine were sent to Shemaryo, the royal steward from the town of Beeryam, by Raga son of Elisha, Uzza, Eliba, Baala son of Elisha, and Yedayo. The words on the potsherd read literally, "In the tenth year, to Shemaryo from Beeryam, jars of old (wine), Raga son of Elisha, Uzza," etc.[2] Another ostracon (No. 17) reads, "In the tenth year, from Azzah to Gaddiyo, a jar of fine oil,"[3] These ostraca show that the payment of taxes in wine and oil provided a source for the wine that the ease-loving people of Samaria were drinking, and also a source for the fine oil they used to anoint themselves (Amos 6:6). There is some debate over the date of the Samaria ostraca. When they were initially found, the excavators dated them to the reign of Ahab. Albright and others have since placed them during the general time of Amos' ministry, c. 785–750 B.C. (EAEHL, 4:1044).

Earlier in his message of rebuke, Amos referred to the statement that the Lord would "tear down the winter house along with the summer house" (3:15). Archaeological discoveries show that the winter and summer houses were characteristic of that period, being included among the

---

[1]See chapter 15, section entitled "Archaeological Light on Baal Worship. . . ," pages 154–55.

[2]Hand copies of these ostraca appear in George Andrew Reisner, Clarence Stanley Fisher, David Gordon Lyon, *Harvard Excavations at Samaria*, 1908–1910, vol. 1, Text (Cambridge: Harvard University Press, 1924), 239 [RHES]; cf. JSAT, 85–86; PANET, 321.

[3]RHES, 239; JSAT, 87; FLAP, 187.

buildings of Syrian royalty in the eighth century. In an inscription found at Shamal in Syria, dated about 740 B.C., the king, Bir-Rakeb, said that his royal predecessors had three palaces, including a winter house and a summer house (AOTA, 167).

Murder in the Palace of Israel: Zechariah, Shallum, Menahem (2 Kings 15)

The materially prosperous yet sinful era of Jeroboam II (782–753 B.C.), the thirteenth king of Israel, was followed by bad times in the northern kingdom. The wickedness of the nation caught up with it, and the last years were characterized by greater sin, with murder even in the royal palace.

Jeroboam II was succeeded by his son Zechariah, the fourteenth king of Israel. Zechariah ruled only six months (2 Kings 15:8), and was then slain by Shallum (v. 10). This brought to an end the dynasty of Jehu, with the death of his fourth descendant, who occupied the throne of Israel. God had promised Jehu that four generations of descendants would sit on the throne (2 Kings 10:13).

Shallum, the fifteenth king of Israel, usurping the throne after he had murdered Zechariah, ruled for only one month, during the year 752 B.C. and then was slain by Menahem (2 Kings 15:14), who became the sixteenth king of Israel (752–742).

The Kings of Assyria; Their Relationship with Israel

After 750 B.C., the kings of Assyria pushed down into Syria and Canaan from time to time and came in direct contact with the kings of Israel and Judah. In order to integrate these kings of Assyria with the biblical record, it will be helpful to list them:

Tiglath-Pileser III	745–727
Shalmaneser V	726–722
Sargon II	721–705

Tiglath-Pileser III was a usurper, apparently a general who put himself on the throne, took the name of the famous Tiglath-Pileser I (c. 1100 B.C.), and then boasted about the kings of his fathers (OHA, 175). Tiglath-Pileser III reorganized the army of Assyria and then made a drive for an empire. He annexed the area southeast of his own country, that is, Babylonia, and thereafter proceeded to extend control over Syria and Palestine. Menahem, the sixteenth king of Israel (752–742 B.C.), paid tribute to Tiglath-Pileser III, as recorded in 2 Kings 15:20, where Tiglath-Pileser is called Pul (for an explanation, see the next section).

Archaeological Light on the Problem of Tiglath-Pileser III and Pul

As noted above, it is recorded that Menahem, the sixteenth king of Israel (752–742 B.C.), paid tribute to Pul, the king of Assyria, when the Assyrian king came against the land of Israel (2 Kings 15:19–20). Another biblical reference refers to both Pul and Tiglath-Pileser as involved in the affairs of Israel at this time: "And the God of Israel stirred up the spirit of Pul king of Assyria, *and* the spirit of Tilgath-pilneser [Tiglath-Pileser] king of Assyria, and *he carried* them away. . ." (1 Chron. 5:26 KJV). In trying to harmonize the facts, some scholars argued in the past that Pul and Tiglath-Pileser III were two different individuals, and the above-mentioned reference in 1 Chronicles referring to "Pul *and* Tiglath-pileser" was cited to support this view. Horner pointed out, however, that the Hebrew word for "carried" is in the singular (therefore correctly rendered "he carried"), and that the word "and" in the middle of the section would in this context more properly be translated "even," as may be done in accordance with Hebrew usage. In view of these considerations, the verse should read, as in the NIV: "So the God of Israel stirred up the spirit of Pul king of Assyria (that is, Tiglath-Pileser king of Assyria). . . ." Thus this verse does not indicate that Pul and Tiglath-Pileser were different individuals, but is rather a definite piece of evidence that they were the same.[4] The newer Bible versions follow this approach to Hebrew usage. The NASB uses the word "even" to equate Pul with Tiglath-Pileser; the NKJV also equates the two kings.

In addition to the biblical indication that Tiglath-Pileser and Pul are the same, archaeological evidence of the identification has long since been established by Schrader (TCK, 155; TMN, 141). Specific evidence is found in two clay tablets that give similar material about this period of Assyrian history, with the name of Tiglath-Pileser in one tablet and Pul as the corresponding name in the other (translations of these records appear in TCK, 156; TMN, 140).

Furthermore, archaeological light as to why Tiglath-Pileser had these two names has surfaced in other inscriptional material. When Tiglath-Pileser III annexed Babylonia to the Assyrian Empire, he went through the ceremony used for assuming the kingship of Babylonia. And it seems that in order to spare the tender susceptibilities of the Babylonians, he even permitted them to use a separate name for him, Pul (Pulu), so that they would feel they had a king of their own. This explains why he is called Pul in the book of Kings (OHA, 181) and enables us also to understand why he is called Pulu from time to time in the cuneiform records (BWMS, 102).

Tiglath-Pileser and Menahem

When Tiglath-Pileser came with his army against Israel, Menahem paid him a thousand talents of silver, a considerable sum, to induce him to allow Menahem to remain securely on his throne (2 Kings 15:19). The usual date assigned for this

campaign of Tiglath-Pileser has been 738 B.C., but Thiele produced evidence to show that it could have been in the year 743 B.C. (TCK, 156–63, esp. 156, 161; TMN, 108, 121, 139–62). Thus it would have occurred during the dates of Menahem's reign, as now correctly understood (752–742).

Archaeological Light on Tiglath-Pileser and Azariah of Judah (767–740 B.C.)

The archaeologicl records of Tiglath-Pileser III (745–727 B.C.) reveal that he came in contact with Azariah of Judah in his campaign to the region of Syria and Canaan (the same one in which he received tribute from Menahem as noted above). The Bible does not tell us anything about the contact of Azariah with Tiglath-Pileser, and so this is a case of further illumination from the archaeological discoveries. As Thiele points out, there is no reason to doubt the identification of "Azriau of Yaudi" in the Assyrian inscription with Azariah of Judah (TCK, 156).

Archaeological Light on Tiglath-Pileser and Pekah of Israel (740–732 B.C.)

Menahem (752–742 B.C.), the sixteenth king of Israel, was followed by his son, Pekahiah (2 Kings 15:22–23), who reigned for two years (742–740). Pekahiah was murdered by one of his military officers, Pekah (v. 25), and Pekah became the eighteenth king of Israel (740–732).

The Bible records that in the time of Pekah, Tiglath-Pileser III came into the northern part of Israel, the region around Galilee and the land of Naphtali. From there he carried off some of the inhabitants and apparently subjugated the area (2 Kings 15:29). Archaeological evidence of the extension of Tiglath-Pileser III's sway over northern Palestine is indicated in his inscription, which reads in part,

---

[4]Joseph Horner, "Biblical Chronology," *Proceedings of the Society of Biblical Archaeology* (1898), 237 [PSBA], cited in TCK, 155; Edwin R. Thiele, *The Mysterious Numbers of the Hebrew Kings*, new rev. ed. (Grand Rapids: Zondervan, 1983), 189 [TMN].

"...the border of Bit-Humria [House of Omri, i.e., Israel] ... the wide land of Naphtali, in its entirety, I brought within the border of Assyria" (LARA, 1: 292, paragraph 815; CBS, 146).

Jotham, the Tenth King of Judah
(2 Kings 15:32-38; 740-736 B.C.)

When Azariah, the ninth king of Judah, was smitten with leprosy, his son Jotham ruled with him as co-regent (2 Kings 15:5), and after the death of Azariah, Jotham ruled for several years as king of Judah (740–736 B.C.). Jotham had some interest in the things of God, for we are told that "he walked steadfastly before the LORD his God" (2 Chron. 27:6), but all was not well in Judah, because the high places of pagan worship were not removed (2 Kings 15:35).

Ahaz, the Eleventh King of Judah
(2 Kings 16:1-20; 736-716 B.C.)

After the death of Jotham, Ahaz his son became the eleventh king of Judah (2 Kings 15:38). He proved to be a wicked king, aping the idolatrous "ways of the kings of Israel and [he] even sacrificed his son in the fire" (16:3). When Ahaz went up to Damascus to see Tiglath-Pileser III, he noticed a pagan altar there and sent the pattern back to Jerusalem to have a copy of this altar produced. Upon his return from Damascus, he used the new pagan altar (16:10, 12).

Ahaz and Tiglath-Pileser III
(2 Kings 16:7ff.)

The king of Syria (Rezin) and the king of Israel (Pekah) fought against Ahaz, apparently with plans to punish him for not coming into an alliance with them against Tiglath-Pileser. Ahaz sought help from Tiglath-Pileser, seeking to gain favor by the payment of the wealth of the temple and the palace to him (16:8).

Tiglath-Pileser went up against Damascus and gave the Syrians a thorough beating, killing the king, Rezin, and carrying the people into captivity (16:9). The archaeological records of Tiglath-Pileser tell of the attack on Damascus (LARA, 1:279, paragraph 777).

Hoshea, the Last King of Israel; the
End of the Northern Kingdom
(2 Kings 17)

Pekah, the eighteenth king of Israel, came to a sudden end when he was slain by Hoshea in a conspiracy (2 Kings 15:30). Hoshea became the nineteenth king of Israel (732–723, 722 B.C.) and was the reigning king when the northern kingdom was brought to an end with the siege of Samaria by the Assyrians.

The Siege of Samaria (2 Kings 17:3-6)

When Tiglath-Pileser died in 727 B.C., Hoshea apparently became tired of paying his huge annual tribute in gold and silver to Assyria, and looked to Egypt for help in resisting Assyria (POTH, 302). The new king of Assyria, Shalmaneser V (726–722), swept into Canaan and besieged the city of Samaria. After a three-year's assault, the city fell (2 Kings 17:5–6). The principal inhabitants of the northern kingdom were carried off into captivity by the Assyrians, bringing to an end the northern kingdom and beginning the captivity of Israel, in about 722.

The King Who Captured Samaria

Sargon, in his inscriptions claimed that he captured Samaria (PANET, 284–85). Most writers have accepted this assertion and have held that, although Shalmaneser initiated and carried on the siege of Samaria, it was Sargon who completed the capture of the city. According to this view, Sargon is to be identified with the "king of Assyria" in 2 Kings 17:6, who took the inhabitants of Samaria to Assyria. Olmstead pointed out, however, that Sargon was silent concerning the capture of Samaria in his own accounts inscribed at the beginning of his reign, and that a Babylonian chronicle seems to justify ascribing the capture to Shalmaneser V just at the end of his reign, in 723–722 B.C., rather than to Sargon during his first year of rule, 722–721. Thus it is likely that Shalmaneser V, and not Sargon II captured Samaria[5] and that, with the passing of the years, Sargon's "press corps" ascribed the siege to this latter king. It is only in the royal chronicles recorded in the later part of his reign that Sargon is credited with taking Samaria. Apparently what happened is that Samaria fell during the fighting season (spring or summer) of 722 B.C. Shalmaneser died late in December, and Sargon then took the reins of government. He finished mopping up in 721 and collected the prisoners and established a government for the defeated province. His claim to have carried off 27,290 inhabitants (PANET, 284–85) may well be accurate; the government probably tried to establish accurate records of booty and prisoners that could be sold into slavery or used for construction projects. Such a number was too large to have come from the town of Samaria alone and must represent captives from the whole province of Samaria. Presumably, at least some of these captives were used on the construction gangs when Sargon started to build his new capital and palace at Khorsabad, about twelve miles northeast of Nineveh. For pictures of the great stone winged bull at the entrance of Sargon's palace and an artist's reconstruction of the palace, see page 164.

Archaeological Confirmation Concerning Sargon's Existence

Though certain verses in the Bible that speak of "the king of Assyria" may refer to King Sargon, the name "Sargon" actually occurs only once in the Bible: "In the year that the supreme commander, sent by Sargon king of Assyria, came to Ashdod and captured it" (Isa. 20:1). Up to a century ago, no evidence of the existence of such a king had been found in other available historical records.[6] A.T. Olmstead[7] pointed out that scholars once argued that Sargon was the same as Shalmaneser.[8] Such an absence of Sargon's name from historical records made it easy for some critics and historians to doubt "his very existence."[9]

In 1843 the French consular agent at Mosul began digging at Khorsabad (FLAP, 174), some twelve miles north of the site of ancient Nineveh, and there found the great palace of Sargon. The palace area occupied some twenty-five acres, and the walls of the palace proper varied from nine and one half to sixteen feet in thickness (HEBL, 86). No longer was there doubt about the existence of Sargon. (A restoration of his palace based on the excavations appears in PANEP, 236; and a picture of Sargon in PANEP, 154.)

One of the large stonewinged bulls that stood at the entrance of Sargon's palace was found in later excavations made by Chiera (1929ff.) and was brought to the University of Chicago, where it may now be seen in the Oriental Institute Museum. This winged bull is sixteen feet long, sixteen feet high, and weighs forty tons. Fortunately for purposes of transporta-

---

[5]A.T. Olmstead, "The Fall of Samaria," *American Journal of Semitic Languages* [AJSL] 21 (1904–1905): 179–82; idem, *Western Asia in the Days of Sargon*, 45ff., n. 9; cited in TCK, 173. See also FLAP, 208–10.

[6]Finegan points out that "for a long time" the reference in Isaiah was the sole place in extant literature where Sargon's name appeared (FLAP, 209).

[7]Professor of Oriental History at the Oriental Institute of the University of Chicago until his death in 1945.

[8]A.T. Olmstead, *History of Assyria* (New York: Scribner, 1923), 282 [OHA].

[9]Noted by George L. Robinson, RBA, 96.

tion, this large monument was found broken in several pieces, the largest one weighing nineteen tons. Even this partial "fragment" constituted somewhat of a transportation difficulty when it began its land and sea journey. The various pieces, assembled into a unit, form "without doubt the most valuable ancient work in the Institute collection."[10] A marvelous collection of reliefs and stonewinged bulls from the palace of Sargon is on display at the Louvre Museum in Paris.

[10]James Henry Breasted, *The Oriental Institute* (Chicago: University of Chicago Press, 1933), 368 [BOI].

Chapter 18

Judah, 722–640 B.C.

(2 Kings 18–21; 2 Chronicles 29–33.
Hezekiah, Manasseh, Amon)

The Date of Hezekiah, the Twelfth King of Judah (2 Kings 18)

Most recent writers believe that Hezekiah began to reign sometime between 730 and 720 B.C. Their dates are based for the most part on the synchronism of 2 Kings 18:1, which indicates that in the third year of Hoshea, the last king of Israel, Hezekiah began to reign in Judah. Since most recent chronologies give about 730 or a little later for the beginning of Hoshea's reign, Hezekiah's reign is ordinarily indicated as beginning shortly after that.

Thiele, however, feels that the synchronisms of 2 Kings 18:1, 9–10 are "open to question" (TCK, 165; TMN, 134–38), and that therefore other criteria must be taken into consideration. The passage in 2 Kings 18:13 tells of Sennacherib's invasion of Judah when he came up against the cities of Hezekiah's land. This invasion is recorded as being in the fourteenth year of Hezekiah, and in turn the Assyrian records give reasonable indication that this was in the year 701 B.C.[1]

Fourteen years prior to 701 would give the year 716–715 as the inaugural year of the reign of Hezekiah (TCK, 174; TMN, 134–35). This would mean that the northern kingdom had come to an end with the capture of Samaria several years earlier, about 722.

Several details noted by Thiele seem to show that the northern kingdom was at an end in the days of Hezekiah. When Hezekiah sent out invitations to the Passover, held early in his reign, he included the northern tribes of Ephraim and Manasseh (2 Chron. 30:1) and even Zebulun (v. 10). These tribes inhabited areas that would more likely be open to the envoys of the southern kingdom after the northern kingdom had fallen (TCK, 174). Furthermore, after the Passover, when the people went out to break down the pagan images and groves, they extended their activity to Ephraim and Manasseh (2 Chron. 31:1)—another indication that the northern kingdom was at an end and that her territory was open to contact with Judah (TCK, 175). These are some of the considerations that led Thiele, in his

[1]D.D. Luckenbill, *The Annals of Sennacherib* (Chicago: University of Chicago Press, 1924), 10–14 [LAS].

chronology, to date the beginning of Hezekiah's reign in 716 B.C.

Future study may throw more light on the synchronisms of 2 Kings 18:1, 9–10, which Thiele holds are "open to question" (TCK, 165). Thiele correctly points out the competence of the Old Testament writers in keeping the biblical chronology and comments that in this complex procedure they were able to "keep their bearings" and pass on records to us which are so straight that we can unravel the seemingly tangled skein (TCK, 177).

Hezekiah's Reforms (2 Kings 18:3–7; 2 Chronicles 29–31)

Reacting sharply against the wickedness of his father, Ahaz, who had participated in the detestable ways of the nations (2 Kings 16:3–4), Hezekiah opened the doors of the house of the Lord and repaired them (2 Chron. 29:3) and then fostered the resumption of the normal worship with the keeping of the Passover (2 Chron. 30:15ff.). The resultant spiritual awakening caused the people to break down the images and the groves and destroy the high places of pagan worship, even in parts of the northern area (2 Chron. 31:1). Hezekiah's attitude in spiritual matters is well summarized by the writer of Kings: "He held fast to the LORD and did not cease to follow him; he kept the commands the LORD had given Moses" (2 Kings 18:6).

Isaiah and Hezekiah

The prophet Isaiah states that he carried on his ministry in the days of Uzziah (Azariah), Jotham, Ahaz, and Hezekiah (Isa. 1:1). His great transforming vision came in the year that King Uzziah died (Isa. 6:1), probably about 740 B.C. This means that Isaiah lived through the rule of Jotham (740–736) and the wicked reign of Ahaz (736–716), who sacrificed his own son in the fire (2 Kings 16:3) and who also copied the pagan altar at Damascus for the temple of God in Jerusalem. It ap-

pears that Isaiah's words of admonition concerning these ravages made upon the worship and the temple of the Lord were disdained, ignored, and scorned by Ahaz (POTH, 309). The period of Ahaz figures to some degree in much of the material in Isaiah 1–35. This part of the book of Isaiah falls into several sections and in most cases the events of a given section begin in the reign of Ahaz.

Isaiah's great opportunity for influence at the court came after the death of Ahaz, when Hezekiah came to the throne. It seems likely that Isaiah had had close contact with Hezekiah during his boyhood, and this influence now bore fruit, undoubtedly being largely responsible for the reforms that Hezekiah instituted in the breaking down of the pagan images, the destruction of the high places, and the fostering of the resumption of the normal worship in Jerusalem. Isaiah 36–39 describes events during the reign of Hezekiah, when Sennacherib came into Judah, besieged Jerusalem, and suffered defeat because the Lord delivered the city (Isa. 36:36). The last chapters of Isaiah (40–66) were probably written during the reign of Manasseh (687–642), the wicked king who succeeded Hezekiah; in these chapters the prophet turns from the sad condition in Judah and looks forward to the glorious redemption that the Lord promised would come after the Exile.

Archaeological Light on Isaiah's Words to the Vain Women of His Time (Isaiah 3:16–24)

When Isaiah pointed out the greed of the rich and their oppression of the poor (3:14–15), he went on to ridicule some of the women of his day for their "outstretched necks," their "flirting" eyes, their "mincing" walk, their elaborate hairdressing, their "sweet-smell," and their overindulgence in the use of cosmetics and other fineries (Isa. 3:16–23). M.G. Kyle, describing the excavations at Kiriath

Sepher,[2] remarked that while the women of that day had different names for their cosmetics than women have today, nevertheless their fashions in make-up most remarkably resembled the extremes of fashionable "make-up" that we are accustomed to see in modern times. Scarcely a day went by during their excavating, he said, that they did not find, in the city of the days of the late monarchy, a vanity pallette of one of these pampered ladies. As Kyle wrote in his report concerning the excavation at Kiriath Sepher, "It seems as if every Jewess in the town had one" (KEK, 199–200).

Discovery of an Ancient Isaiah Manuscript

One day in the spring of 1948, John C. Trever,[3] one of the Fellows at the American School of Oriental Research in Jerusalem, taking a phone call for the school, learned that Father Sowmy of the Syrian Orthodox Convent wished some information on five ancient Hebrew scrolls recently acquired by the convent from some Arabs.[4] After the scrolls were brought to the school, Trever examined and photographed one manuscript, which later proved to be a complete copy of the book of Isaiah. A photograph was

[2]Carried on from 1926 to 1932; KEK, 189ff.

[3]John Trever gave his account of the Jerusalem scrolls in *The Biblical Archaeologist* (September 1948). A preliminary report was presented in the same publication in May 1948 by G. Ernest Wright.

[4]In addition to Albright, also Burrows of Yale, Sukenik of the Hebrew University in Jerusalem, and Trever, who photographed the manuscript, were all convinced that it was ancient. Further studies showed that little value was to be attached to the suggestion that it dated from the Middle Ages (made by Solomon Zeitlin, Professor of Rabbinical Literature at Dropsie College in Philadelphia) (Report on Zeitlin's suggestion published in *New York Times*, summarized in *Presbyterian Guardian* [March 1949], 57; also see article by Zeitlin in *Jewish Quarterly Review* [January–March 1949]).

An Associated Press dispatch from Jerusalem dated March 18, 1949, reported that the cave where the Arabs found these scrolls had been examined by Lankester Harding, Director of Antiquities in Transjordan, and by Father De Vaux of the Dominican Bible School in Jerusalem. Regarding their finding, O.R. Sellers, director of the American School of Oriental Research in Jerusalem, reported that they found late Hellenic pottery in the cave, which would point to the first or second century B.C. (Article in *Philadelphia Inquirer* [March 1949]; substantially the same report was given in the *Biblical Archaeologist* 12, 2 [May 1949]: 32.) The pottery, then, also supports the date of 100 B.C. for the manuscript.

Writing in the February 1949 issue of the *Bulletin of the American Schools of Oriental Research*, John Trever reported that he had examined the individual letters used in the Isaiah manuscript, had made comparisons with other early manuscripts, and had concluded that the Isaiah manuscript should be dated about 125–100 B.C. In the same issue, Solomon Birnbaum, one of our ablest palaeographers, reported that he had made comparisons between the Isaiah manuscript and documents of Jewish colonists settled in Egypt in the third century, and also with the boundary stones of about 100 B.C. and several other inscriptions, and that on the basis of those studies, he had concluded that the first half of the second century B.C. suggested itself as the date of the writing of the Isaiah manuscript (Solomon A.Birnbaum, "The Date of the Isaiah Scroll," BASOR 113 [February 1949], 33).

In view of the pottery evidence from the cave and the studies of Albright, Burrows, Sukenik, Trever, and Birnbaum, there appears to be no reason to doubt the date of c. 100 B.C. that has been assigned to this Isaiah manuscript.

Reporting further in the October 1949 issue of BASOR, Albright pointed out that further study, including examination of a new infrared photograph of the Nash Papyrus (containing the Ten Commandments and the Shema passage and dated in the first or second century B.C. by Albright, Birnbaum, et al.) only adds additional evidence for the early date of the Isaiah manuscript (first or second century B.C.). Albright also observes that the rapid progress of discovery and publication of material concerning the Isaiah manuscript will soon render discussions like Zeitlin's "antiquated" (W.F. Albright, "On the Date of the Scrolls from Ain Feshkha and the Nash Papyrus," BASOR 115 [October 1949]: 10–19).

sent to W.F. Albright of Johns Hopkins University, who concluded that the form of the script would indicate a date of about 100 B.C. Such an early manuscript of Isaiah is of great significance, inasmuch as the oldest manuscript up to that time dated from about 900 A.D. Even more important was the close agreement between this newly found Jerusalem manuscript and the traditional Hebrew text, which was copied much later. Millar Burrows of Yale indicates that there is nothing in this manuscript that can be called "a major addition or omission" and that there is "no important dislocation or disarrangement of the text."[5] The substantial agreement between this ancient manuscript and those of a thousand years later shows the care with which biblical manuscripts were copied and adds to our assurance concerning the substantial accuracy of the later manuscripts from which our English translations were made.

This manuscript became available to the scholarly world at the time when the RSV translation committee was preparing the new version. They finally decided to adopt only thirteen readings for their translation based on the new manuscript. Millar Burrows, a member of the translation committee, later concluded that even some of these were unwarranted and that in five of the thirteen instances the Masoretic reading should have been retained.[6]

Burrows observed further, "It is a matter for wonder that through something like a thousand years the text underwent so little alteration. As I said in my first article on the scroll, 'Herein lies its chief importance, supporting the fidelity of the Masoretic tradition'" (BDSS, 304). In fact, he concluded that at many points the Isaiah manuscript had readings inferior to those in some of the medieval manuscripts already possessed (BDSS, 303).

In time a second Isaiah manuscript, from the same cave at Qumran and not complete, became available to biblical scholars. In commenting on this discovery, Gleason Archer noted that it "proved to be word for word identical with our standard Hebrew Bible in more than 95 percent of the text. The five percent of variation consisted chiefly of obvious slips of the pen and variations in spelling" (ASOTI, 25).

More Manuscript Discoveries

As the world generally knows now, the discovery of the Isaiah manuscripts in a cave at Qumran, adjacent to the Dead Sea, was only the tip of the iceberg. Eventually the State of Israel came into possession of a whole collection of scrolls from what is now called Cave 1 at Qumran. These include a complete scroll of Isaiah, a partial Isaiah, the Habakkuk Commentary (including two chapters of Habakkuk), the Manual of Discipline (rules for members of the religious community who lived nearby), Thanksgiving Hymns, a Genesis Apocryphon (apocryphal accounts of some of the patriarchs), and Wars of the Sons of Light Against the Sons of Darkness (an account of a real or spiritual war between some of the Hebrew tribes and the tribes east of the Jordan—Ammonites, Moabites, etc.).

The magnificent collection from Cave 1 raised the possibility of finding treasures in other caves of the Qumran area. A massive search of the region between 1949 and 1956 resulted in the discovery of biblical manuscripts in a total of eleven caves. Excavation of Cave 2 turned up about one hundred fragments of Exodus, Leviticus, Numbers, Deuteronomy, Jeremiah, Job, Psalms, and Ruth. In Cave 3, in addition to inscribed fragments of hide and papyrus, there was the curious cop-

---

[5]Article on "The Contents and Significance of the Manuscripts," *The Biblical Archaeologist* (September 1948), 60–61.

[6]Millar Burrows, *The Dead Sea Scrolls* (New York: Viking, 1955), 305 [BDSS].

Cave 4 at Qumran

A jar in which Dead Sea Scrolls were stored at Qumran   Courtesy of Palestine Archaeological Museum in Jerusalem

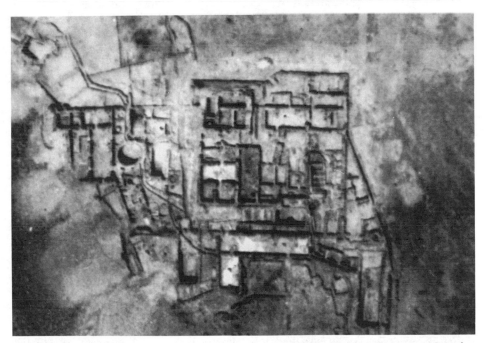

Aerial view of the excavations at Qumran   Courtesy of Palestine Archaeological Museum in Jerusalem

per scroll (about twelve inches high) with directions to over sixty sites containing hidden treasure. To date no treasure has been found, and there is a variety of speculations concerning this scroll. Cave 4 was in many ways the most exciting of all. It provided some forty thousand fragments of an unknown number of manuscripts, about four hundred of which have been identified. About one hundred were biblical scrolls and represent all Old Testament books except Esther. There were fragments from thirteen scrolls of Deuteronomy, twelve of Isaiah, ten of Psalms, six of Exodus, and five of Genesis. A fragment of Samuel, dating to the third century B.C., is thought to be the oldest known piece of biblical Hebrew. Caves 5 through 10 had a variety of scroll fragments too diverse to list here. Prize pieces from Cave 11 included very fine portions of Psalms and Leviticus. The former included forty-eight psalms—forty-one biblical and seven nonbiblical.

After Cave 1 was excavated, attention centered on Khirbet Qumran, a ruin on a plateau between Cave 4 and the Dead Sea. Excavated between 1951 and 1956, it turned out to be the center of a religious community. Presumably Caves 1–11 constituted the library of the community, and some of the manuscripts found there were no doubt produced in the writing room or scriptorium of the community.

It is not possible in a survey book of this sort to tell the story of the Dead Sea Scrolls and their significance.[7] Nevertheless, some of the significance of the scrolls can be briefly told. First, as noted,

the discovery of the scrolls pushed back the history of our Hebrew manuscript collection by a thousand years. Second, again as noted, during the long period of copying the Old Testament text by hand, there was a remarkable—can we say miraculous—degree of preservation of the text. What could be said for the Isaiah manuscripts was approximately true of the rest of the scrolls as well. Third, evidently the standardization of the Hebrew text as we now know it was taking place during the first Christian century. Fourth, the early date of some of the Dead Sea Scrolls has helped to answer critical views on the nature and date of composition of some Old Testament books—e.g., the unity of Isaiah and the second-century B.C. date of Daniel. Last, the discovery of this large body of literature, biblical and nonbiblical, has provided a means for a better understanding of the meaning of Old Testament words.

The Assyrian Kings of Hezekiah's Time and After

We have already noted the Assyrian kings of the middle of the eighth century (see chapter 17). The Assyrian kings contemporary with Hezekiah and following his time are as follows:

Sargon II	721–705 B.C.
Sennacherib	704–681 B.C.
Esarhaddon	680–669 B.C.
Ashurbanipal	668–627 B.C.

Either Sargon or probably his predecessor captured the city of Samaria and

---

[7]For a fuller study of the subject read one or more of the following books: F.F. Bruce, *Second Thoughts on the Dead Sea Scrolls*, 2nd ed. (Grand Rapids: Eerdmans, 1961); Millar Burrows, *Burrows on the Dead Sea Scrolls* (a combination of *The Dead Sea Scrolls* and *More Light on the Dead Sea Scrolls*) (Grand Rapids: Baker, 1978); Frank M. Cross, *The Ancient Library of Qumran and Modern Biblical Studies* (Grand Rapids: Baker, 1958); Philip R. Davies, *Qumran* (Grand Rapids: Eerdmans, 1982); William S. LaSor, *The Dead Sea Scrolls and the Christian Faith* (Chicago: Moody Press, 1962); idem, *The Dead Sea Scrolls and the New Testament* (Grand Rapids: Eerdmans, 1972); Charles F. Pfeiffer, *The Dead Sea Scrolls and the Bible* (Grand Rapids: Baker, 1969); R. de Vaux, *Archaeology and the Dead Sea Scrolls* (London: Oxford University Press, 1973); Geza Vermes, *The Dead Sea Scrolls in English*, 2nd ed. (Harmondsworth, Middlesex, England: Penguin Books, 1975); Howard F. Vos, *Archaeology in Bible Lands* (Chicago: Moody Press, 1977), chapter 6; Yigael Yadin, *The Message of the Scrolls* (New York: Simon & Schuster, 1957).

brought the northern kingdom to an end (see chapter 17). Sargon's successor, Sennacherib, pushed into southern Palestine, into the territory of Judah and not only besieged and took Lachish[8] (2 Kings 18:14; 19:8), but also came up against Jerusalem. The Lord delivered the city of Jerusalem from the hosts of Sennacherib (2 Kings 19:35; Isa. 37:36). A few years later, Esarhaddon subjugated Manasseh (2 Chron. 33:11). Let us now look more closely into the reign of these monarchs.

Sargon Against Ashdod; Archaeological Light (Isaiah 20:1)

Isaiah indicates that Sargon's army came against the city of Ashdod (Isa. 20:1), which is in the plain of Philistia in southwestern Palestine. Confirmation of this is found in the records of Sargon, in which he says, "Azuru, king of Ashdod, plotted in his heart to withhold tribute and sent (messages) of hostility to the kings round about him. . . . Against Ashdod, his royal city, I advanced in haste. Ashdod, Gimtu (Gath), and Asdudimmu, I besieged, I captured" (LARA, 2:13–14, paragraph 30; PANET, 286). For a discussion of the archaeological confirmation of the existence of Sargon, see chapter 17.

Sennacherib's Invasion of Judah (2 Kings 18:13ff.); Archaeological Confirmation of Hezekiah's Payment of Tribute

When Sennacherib made his invasion into Judah (701 B.C.), he took many of the cities (2 Kings 18:13) and finally threatened Jerusalem. Hezekiah then paid tribute to Sennacherib, including thirty talents of gold and three hundred talents of silver (2 Kings 18:14). The inscriptions of Sennacherib tell us of this tribute in the following words, "In addition to 30 talents of gold and 800 talents of silver, (there were) gems, antimony, jewels, large sandu-stones . . . ivory, maple, boxwood, all kinds of valuable treasures . . . which he had them bring after me to Nineveh, my royal city. To pay tribute and to accept servitude he dispatched his messengers" (LARA, 2:121, paragraph 240; also see BAB, 472; PANET, 288). The biblical and the Assyrian records agree exactly in the reference to thirty talents of gold, but the biblical figure of three hundred talents of silver at first appears to be contradicted by the eight hundred talents of silver recorded in the Assyrian inscription. It is quite possible, however, that Sennacherib counted some other payment or valuables in his figure of eight hundred talents of silver, which is more than the three hundred talents given in the Bible. It has also been suggested that the numbers were really equivalent to one another, the divergence being due to textual corruption (BAB, 473). Schrader explains it as due to the difference between the Babylonian and the Palestinian talent (RBA, 100).

Archaeological Confirmation of Sennacherib's Failure to Capture Jerusalem (2 Kings 19:35–36)

When Sennacherib's army came up against Jerusalem, God spoke through Isaiah the prophet (2 Kings 19:20ff.) and

---

[8]Sennacherib devoted considerable space to his conquest of Lachish on bas reliefs produced to decorate the walls of his palace at Nineveh. These are on display in one of the Assyrian rooms at the British Museum in London, and a cast of them may be seen in the Oriental Institute Museum of the University of Chicago. David Ussishkin, current excavator of Lachish, has produced a stunning book portraying Sennacherib's conquest of the city, *The Conquest of Lachish by Sennacherib* (Tel Aviv: Tel Aviv University Publications, 1982). A review of the book with detailed discussion of the Assyrian destruction of the city appears in BAR (March/April 1984), 48–65. This is followed in the same issue of the magazine by Ussishkin's article entitled "Defensive Judean Counter-Ramp Found at Lachish in 1983 Season," 66–73. Excavations indicate that the Israelites put up a fierce resistance against the Assyrians. As the Assyrians built a siege ramp on the outside of the walls, the Israelites built a counterramp inside the walls.

promised to defend the city (2 Kings 19:34; Isa. 37:35). The angel of the Lord went forth and smote the Assyrian army, leaving 185,000 "dead bodies" (2 Kings 19:35; Isa. 37:36).[9] Sennacherib returned to Nineveh without capturing the city of Jerusalem (2 Kings 19:36).

To the rationalist, this story of the angel's smiting an army and causing a great king to return to his native land without capturing a city seems beyond the realm of historical possibility. However, confirmation of the fact that Sennacherib did not take Jerusalem was found in an inscription on a prism called the Taylor Cylinder, discovered at Kouyunjik, the site of ancient Nineveh, in 1830 by J.E. Taylor, the British Vice-Consul at Basra. The Taylor Cylinder is now in the British Museum in London. An almost indentical inscription is found on the Oriental Institute Cylinder, purchased by the Oriental Institute of the University of Chicago in 1920 (PMOT, 316, figure 136). In the inscription Sennacherib says that he made other Palestinian cities yield, but when he comes to describe his campaign against Jerusalem, he fails to mention the capture of that city and its king, Hezekiah. Rather the text of the inscription tells of King Hezekiah in these words, "As for himself, like a bird in a cage is his royal city Jerusalem, I shut (him) up" (PANET, 288). Since Sennacherib did not capture Jerusalem (as indicated in the Bible), he made as good a story out of the siege as possible. Actually, Hezekiah was reposing quite safely in his "cage."

There is no evidence in the archaeolog-ical records that Sennacherib ever returned to the region of Palestine. The Bible gives us an adequate reason—the loss of his army before the walls of Jerusalem.

Archaeological Confirmation Concerning Sennacherib's Death (2 Kings 19:36–37)

The Bible states that Sennacherib finally met his death at the hands of his own sons (2 Kings 19:37; Isa. 37:38). Esarhaddon (680–669 B.C.), Sennacherib's son and successor, tells of this very event in the following inscription:

> In the month Nisanu, on a favorable day, complying with their exalted command, I made my joyful entrance into the royal palace, the awesome place, wherein abides the fate of kings. A firm determination fell upon my brothers. They forsook the gods and turned to their deeds of violence, plotting evil. . . . To gain the kingship they slew Sennacherib, their father.[10]

Archaeological Light on the Military Officers of Sennacherib: Tartan, Rabsaris, and Rab-Shakeh (2 Kings 18:17 KJV)

Archaeological discoveries in Babylonia show that the names of the military officers of Sennacherib (2 Kings 18:17) are not proper names but rather Assyrian

---

[9]The number seems excessive (one of the greatest problems in the Old Testament is the transcription of numbers). The Assyrians could and did amass large armies. For example, Shalmaneser III moved across the Euphrates westward with an army of 120,000 men in 845 (H.W.F. Saggs, *The Might That Was Assyria* [London: Sidgwick & Jackson], 253). But after the 183,000 died on this occasion, there was apparently a substantial army left to return to Assyria. If one assumes that the figure is accurate, it might be arrived at by including Assyrian fighting men, camp servants, Judean defectors or impressments into the Assyrian force, and even some captives (many of whom may have become collaborators). The parallel passage in 2 Chronicles 32:21 leaves unspecified the number of men killed. Another explanation is that the Hebrew of 2 Kings 19:35 could possibly be translated "one hundred and eighty and five thousand"—i.e., 100 + 80 + 5,000 = 5180.

[10]LARA, 2:200–201, paragraphs 501–2.

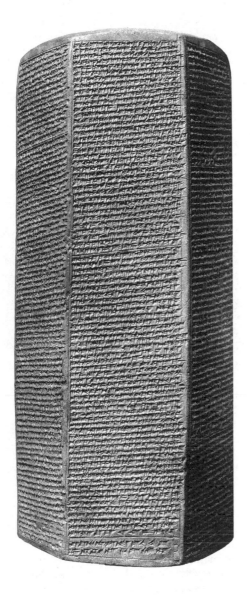

The Oriental Institute Cylinder, which gives an account of Sennacherib's campaign against Judah and against Jerusalem in particular
Courtesy of the Oriental Institute of the University of Chicago

military titles (BWMS, 43). Tartan is the Assyrian *tartanu*, indicating the second in command, the field marshall.[11] Rabshakeh is rendered *rab-shaqu* in Assyrian meaning "chief officer." Rabsaris is rendered *rabu-sha-reshi* in Assyrian and originally had the meaning of "chief eunuch" (BWMS, 43–44).

[11]BWMS, 43; cf. AOTA, 161.

Archaeological Light on Merodach-Baladan's Embassy to Hezekiah (2 Kings 20:12)

After Hezekiah's illness (2 Kings 20:1ff.), the king of Babylon, Merodach-Baladan, sent letters and a present to Hezekiah, seemingly to congratulate him on his recovery. The archaeological discoveries, however, indicate that there was a further purpose behind Merodach-Baladan's friendly gesture, a diplomatic reason. Merodach-Baladan had been able to hold out for a number of years against Sennacherib, the king of Assyria. Sennacherib himself gives us evidence of this, for he tells of going down to Babylon to subjugate Merodach-Baladan:

> In my first campaign I accomplished the defeat of Merodach-Baladan, king of Babylonia, together with the army of Elam, his ally, in the plain of Kish. In the midst of that battle he forsook his camp and made his escape alone; so he saved his life. The chariots, horses, wagons, mules, which he left behind at the onset of battle, my hands seized. Into his palace which is in Babylon, joyfully I entered. I opened his treasure house:—gold and silver, precious stones of every kind, goods and property without limit. . . . I counted as spoil. (LARA, 2:116, paragraph 234)

In another record, Sennacherib tells about many of the rebellious tactics of Merodach-Baladan:

> At the beginning of my reign, when I solemnly took my seat on the throne, and ruled the inhabitants of Assyria with mercy and grace, Merodach-Baladan, king of Babylonia, (whose heart is wicked), an instigator of revolt, plotter of rebellion, doer of evil, whose guilt is heavy, brought over to his side Shutur-Nahundu, the Elamite, and gave him gold, silver and precious stones, and (so) secured him as an ally. (LARA, 2:128–29, paragraph 257)

Thus it seems clear from these Assyrian accounts that Merodach-Baladan's real motive in sending the present to Hezekiah was to seek an alliance with him against Assyria (BAB, 475; cf. CBS, 153), even as he had similarly persuaded Shutur-Nahundu to become his ally against Assyria.

Hezekiah's Conduit (2 Kings 20:20; 2 Chronicles 32:30); Archaeological Light from the Siloam Inscription

The Bible tells us of the pool and the conduit that Hezekiah made to bring water into the city (2 Kings 20:20) from the spring Gihon (2 Chron. 32:30). This tunnel may be seen today at Jerusalem still connecting the spring of Gihon with the pool that Hezekiah made at the south end of the city, within the wall. It seems likely that Hezekiah constructed it so water would be available in a convenient place within the walls when the Assyrians would finally besiege the city of Jerusalem. The tunnel is nearly eighteen hundred feet long and about six feet in height throughout its length (MALB, 483–85).

At the south end of the conduit, where it enters the pool of Siloam, an inscription was found in 1880. The discovery is said to have been made when a small boy, wading in the water, slipped and fell. As he scrambled out, he noticed some letters carved on the wall of the tunnel (CBS, 154–55; PMOT, 326). It was brought to the attention of archaeologists, and later Sayce visited the spot and deciphered the inscription, sitting in mud and water to accomplish his task (CBS, 155). The inscription of six lines tells how the stonediggers, who began at each end of the tunnel, could finally hear each other as they approached the place where they ultimately met; it also tells that the tunnel was twelve hundred cubits long. (For a translation of this Hebrew inscription see MALB, 484; PANET, 321.) Since the tunnel is nearly eighteen hundred feet long, it gives us an indication that the cubit was about one and one-half feet at that time. The place where the two parties of diggers met can clearly be seen today, being marked by a difference in the level of the tunnel and a change in the direction of the pickmarks (BWMS, 262). The inscription is now in the Museum of the Ancient Orient in Istanbul.

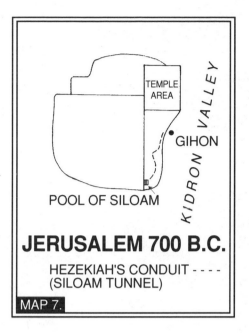

TEMPLE
AREA

GIHON

• GIHON

KIDRON VALLEY

POOL OF SILOAM

JERUSALEM 700 B.C.

HEZEKIAH'S CONDUIT - - - -
(SILOAM TUNNEL)

MAP 7.

Manasseh, King of Judah (2 Kings 21); Archaeological Light

Manasseh (687–642 B.C.) was a contrast to Hezekiah,[12] his father. He built up the high places of pagan worship that his father had destroyed and erected altars to Baal (2 Kings 21:3). Archaeological light on Manasseh comes from the inscriptions of Esarhaddon, king of Assyria (680–668) who tells of the subservience of Manasseh to his domination.[13] Esarhaddon's domination extended to Egypt as well, the conquest of which is celebrated in a rock-hewn inscription—north of Beirut, Lebanon (see picture in PMOT, 332). Manasseh's son, Amon (642–640), walked in the idolatrous ways of his father and after two years was slain, being succeeded by his eight-year-old son, Josiah.

[12]The casual student of 1 and 2 Kings may wonder why a good king like Hezekiah could have such an idolatrous son as Manasseh or how other good kings could have such bad offspring—or how bad kings could have devout sons. Of course we recognize that this sort of thing often happens in modern society, but there is another dimension to the subject that comes clear from a study of history and archaeology. Often a Hebrew king was able to suppress idolatry when foreign intervention (especially Assyrian) was weak and he could pursue an independent policy. Conversely, when Assyrian influence was strong, royal opposition to idolatry could not be so effective and might even be neutralized. Note that Manasseh was firmly under the Assyrian control, while Hezekiah had successfully opposed the Assyrians.

[13]LARA, 2:265, paragraph 690; CBS, 163–64; BAB, 476; PMOT, 333.

Chapter 19

The End of Judah, 640–586 B.C.

(2 Kings 22–25; 2 Chronicles 34–36; Jeremiah)

Josiah (640–609 B.C.), the Fifteenth King of Judah; His Reform

Josiah came to the throne as a small boy of eight (2 Kings 22:1) and ruled for thirty-one years His reign stood in striking contrast to that of his father, Amon, and his grandfather, Manasseh, with their shedding of innocent blood and fostering of degrading idolatry (2 Kings 21:16, 21). Josiah "did what was right in the eyes of the LORD" (22:2). He directed the repairing of the temple, in the course of which the "Book of the Law" was found (v. 8) and later read by Shaphan the scribe to King Josiah (v. 10). Josiah had the law read to the people of Judah and Jerusalem (23:1–2) and then made a covenant, in which the people concurred, to keep the commandments of the Lord and to walk in the way of the Lord (v. 3).

Quickened to action by the reading of the Word of God, Josiah proceeded to put away the idols and idolatry that had been promoted by his father and grandfather. He had all the vessels that had been made for Baal worship brought out to the region of the Kidron (east of Jerusalem) and burned (23:4). He put down the surviving idolatrous priests (v. 5), broke down the houses of the Sodomites (v. 7), and defiled both the high places of pagan worship (v. 8) and the place of child sacrifice where Josiah's predecessors had sacrificed their sons and daughters "in the fire to Molech" (v. 10).

Josiah's reforms were characterized not merely by the purging out of idolatry and paganism but also by a positive and aggressive movement to foster spiritual growth and worship of a true nature. He commanded the people to keep the Passover, and this proved to be a high point in their spiritual awakening, for there had been no Passover such as this one in all the days of the judges and the kings (2 Kings 23:20–21). Josiah had turned to the Lord "with all his heart and with all his soul and with all his strength" (v. 25).

The Finding of the Book of the Law (2 Kings 22:8); Archaeological Light

The Book of the Law found during the repair of the temple was probably the Pentateuch and certainly was at least the book of Deuteronomy. Critics hold that the book of Deuteronomy was written largely in the seventh century B.C.[1] and, except for some traditions that may have been handed down, it has no vital connection with the time of Moses. According to this view, after the book of Deuteronomy was found in the temple in 621 B.C. during the repairs, it underwent a series of editorial expansions between 621 and about 400 (PIOT, 181, 187).

The Bible definitely indicates that Deuteronomy is a record of the words of God to Moses (1500–1400 B.C.) and of the words of Moses to the people. This is shown by many statements telling of God's speaking to the great lawgiver and by Moses' direct messages to Israel (Deut. 1:1; 5:1; 10:1; 27:1; 29:1; 31:1). Thus the internal biblical evidence does not support the idea that the book of Deuteronomy first came into definite form as a forgery in the seventh century shortly before it was found during the temple repairs of 621.

Archaeological discoveries throw interesting light on the possible reason for the repairmen's finding the Book of the Law during their labors on the temple. It is possible that this was the copy of the Pentateuch that had been placed in the cornerstone of the temple several hundred years earlier in the days of Solomon when he directed the building of the temple (c. 967). From archaeological discoveries we now know that it was customary to place documents in the foundations of ancient buildings, just as papers and documents are placed in the cornerstones of buildings at the present time. Nabonidus, king of Babylon in the middle of the sixth century B.C. (555–539), was quite an antiquarian—in fact, almost an archaeologist. He delighted in digging into foundations of buildings ancient in his time and finding the records placed there centuries earlier. He tells of his work on the temple of Shamash at Sippar,

in Mesopotamia, which had been restored by King Nebuchadnezzar but had fallen into decay in his day. He describes his activities in detail:

> When I had brought out Shamash from within it, and made him dwell in another house, that house I tore down, and I made a search for its old foundation record; and I dug to a depth of eighteen cubits, and the *foundation record* of Naram-Sin the son of Sargon (I), which for 3200 years no king that preceded me had discovered, Shamash the great Lord of Ebabbara, the temple of the dwelling of his heart's delight, permitted me, even me, to behold. (translation in PMOT, 306)

If a copy of the law had been placed in the foundation of Solomon's temple (tenth century B.C.), as is likely from the archaeological evidence already cited, then this document would necessarily date back nearly three hundred years before the time of the supposed forgery. It would obviously invalidate the critical theory that the book of Deuteronomy was forged in the seventh century, "found" in the temple later in the seventh century, and passed off by priests as the work of Moses. The implications of the archaeological evidence do not support this critical view of Deuteronomy.

Josiah's Reform Concerning Molech (2 Kings 23:10): Archaeological Light on Molech

As noted previously, Josiah's reform included the defiling of the place of child sacrifice, where his predecessors had sacrificed their sons and daughters "in the fire to Molech" (2 Kings 23:10). The usual view of Old Testament scholars has been that *Molech* was a variant of the Hebrew word *melek*, meaning "king," and was applied to one of the pagan gods as a proper name (Baal, for example, actually

---

[1]For several aspects of the critical view of Deuteronomy, see chapter 9, the sections entitled "Critical View of the Date of Deuteronomy" and "Critical View of the Legislation of Deuteronomy," pages 101–3.

is the word for "Lord"). On the basis of archaeological discoveries, the Old Testament scholar Eissfeldt proposed another explanation of Molech. In North Africa a number of Latin inscriptions have been found that contain the name *molchomor*, a term applied to a type of sacrifice. In view of the fact that parts of North Africa were settled by the Phoenicians, who spoke a Semitic language, and in view of the fact that *molchomor* must be a Semitic rather than a Latin word, Eissfeldt believes that it is made up of two Phoenician words, the first of which is probably *molk*, a variant form of which would be *molech* (molek). Since the compound word referred to a type of sacrifice, Eissfeldt concluded that Molech of the Old Testament was not a god but rather a sacrifice. Burrows states as his opinion that, while some of Eissfeldt's theory is questionable, he has definitely established that there was a Semitic sacrifice called *molk* (BWMS, 227). R.K. Harrison argues, however, that whenever it mentions Molech, "the OT clearly referred to a specific deity."[2]

The Decline and Fall of Assyria, 626–612 B.C.; Archaeological Light from Records of Ashurbanipal

During Josiah's reign (640–609 B.C.), Assyria went into political decline, and finally its capital of Nineveh was captured in 612 by the Babylonians under Nabopolassar in alliance with the Medes (POTH, 341). The last great king of Assyria was Ashurbanipal (668–627 B.C.), who was a ruthless warrior but also a scholar. As a young boy Ashurbanipal had studied the languages that were ancient to him, in particular Sumerian. He tells of his labors in these words:

I have read the artistic script of Sumer and the dark (obscure) Akkadian, which is hard to master, (now) taking pleasure in the reading of the stones (i.e., steles) (coming) from before the flood, (now) being angered (because I was) stupid and addled by the beautiful script. . . . At the same time I was learning royal decorum, walking in the kingly ways, I stood before the king, my begetter, giving commands to the nobles. (LARA, 2:379, paragraph 986)

(Those whose brains have been "addled" by Greek and other ancient languages may take comfort from Ashurbanipal in his struggle with Sumerian.)

Ashurbanipal did a great service in collecting the clay tablets of his time and putting them in his extensive library at Nineveh. Many of these documents are copies of tablets that were ancient in his day, and thus the learning of Mesopotamia of early times has been brought down to us. In the middle of the nineteenth century, Ashurbanipal's library was found by Layard and Kassam. The tablets included such important documents as the Babylonian record of the Flood.[3]

The discouraging description of Ashurbanipal's last days gives us a picture of the beginning of decline in Assyria. In a clay tablet, he says, "Enmity in the land, strife in the house, do not depart from my side. Disturbances, evil words, are continually arrayed against me. Distress of soul, distress of body have bowed my form. I spend my days sighing and lamenting. . . . Death is making an end of me, is weighing (me) down" (LARA, 2:378, paragraph 984).

After the death of Ashurbanipal (627 B.C.), Assyria's decline culminated in the fall of the capital city of Nineveh in 612 to a coalition of Babylonians, Medes, and Scythians (FLAP, 219). Part of the Assyrian army fled to the west toward Harran and made it a temporary capital. The king of Egypt, Pharaoh Neco, came to the aid of the Assyrian remnant and their king,

---

[2]"Molech," ISBE (1986), 3:401.

[3]For further details on Ashurbanipal's library, see chapter 3.

Ashur-uballit, who stood at bay for several years at Carchemish, once the great city of the Neo-Hittite empire (FLAP, 129).

Death of Josiah at the Hands of Neco (2 Kings 23:29); Archaeological Light on the Problem Concerning Josiah's Action

The Bible recounts that Pharaoh Neco, king of Egypt, went *against* the king of Assyria in the region of the Euphrates (2 Kings 23:29 KJV). Thereupon Josiah went out against Neco, and Neco killed him. Historians of past generations were puzzled as to why Josiah, king of Judah, went against Neco when Neco was on his way to take action against Assyria, the ancient enemy of Israel and Judah. The discovery of a clay tablet published by Gadd of the British Museum explains the reason. It shows that Nineveh had already fallen, and that Neco was not going against the remnant of the Assyrian army but was actually going to its aid (as indicated above). Josiah, not wishing to have any aid reach the Assyrians, went out to Megiddo to stop Neco but was killed by the Egyptian. The word translated *against* in 2 Kings 23:29 (KJV) is a Hebrew word that also has the meaning "on behalf of," and so in this context it is clear that Pharaoh Neco was actually going up to the Euphrates region *on behalf of* the king of Assyria, to help him against the Babylonians under Nabopolassar and Nebuchadnezzar.

Neco actually suffered overwhelming defeat at the hands of Nebuchadnezzar, and the city of Carchemish, crushed, lay under its own debris until it was excavated a hundred years ago.[4] The excavations revealed what violent treatment the

city received at the hands of Nebuchadnezzar's army (BWMS, 252).

Jehoahaz, the Sixteenth King of Judah (609 B.C.) (2 Kings 23:30–33)

Jehoahaz, son of Josiah, made king after the death of his father at the hands of Neco (2 Kings 23:29–30), reigned only three months. He was deposed by Neco (v. 33), evidently on Neco's return from the north (TCK, 181; TMN, 182), and taken to Egypt, where he died (v. 34). In order to visualize the succession of kings in Judah, refer to the list in chapter 15, page 152, from time to time.

Jehoiakim, the Seventeenth King of Judah (609–597 B.C.) (2 Kings 23:34–24:6)

After Jehoahaz had been deposed by Neco (2 Kings 23:33), another son of Josiah was put on the throne of Judah by Neco. His name was changed from Eliakim ("God establishes") to Jehoiakim ("the LORD establishes"). This king paid tribute of silver and gold to his master Neco, king of Egypt (v. 35), but soon, when Nebuchadnezzar, the new king of Babylonia (605–562 B.C.) controlled Palestine, Jehoiakim shifted his allegiance to him (2 Kings 24:1).

Jeremiah and Jehoiakim (Jeremiah 36)

Jeremiah had received the word of the Lord from the thirteenth year of Josiah, i.e., 627 B.C. (Josiah 640–609), and had also ministered during the time of Jehoiakim and Zedekiah, the latter being the last king of Judah (Jer. 1:1–2). In the days of Jehoiakim, the Lord gave Jeremiah a message that pointed out the sins of the people of Judah and their need to turn

---

[4]A British Museum team excavated there in 1878–1881, again in 1911–1914, and thereafter sporadically until 1920. They traced the history of the city back to the fifth millennium B.C. Carchemish suffered repeatedly at the hands of invaders. Particularly severe was its suffering in 717 when Sargon II destroyed it, deported its Hittite inhabitants, and resettled it with Assyrians, and in 605 when Babylonians destroyed it. At that time it was the chief anchor of Pharaoh Neco's Syrian empire. See R. Youngblood, "Carchemish," ISBE (1979), 1:616–17.

from their wicked ways (Jer. 36:3). Jeremiah had the message written down on a roll by his amanuensis, Baruch (v. 4). The roll was later brought before Jehoiakim and read to him. The king took it, cut it with his pen-knife, and cast it into the fire on the hearth (v. 23). But the word of God was not so easily destroyed. Jeremiah dictated a second time to Baruch, causing the words that had been on the first roll to be recorded again (vv. 27–28, 32).

Jehoiakim's treatment of the roll of Jeremiah was in accordance with his other wicked acts described in Kings, where he was said not only to have shed blood but also to have "filled Jerusalem with innocent blood" (2 Kings 24:4).

Jehoiachin, the Eighteenth King of Judah (597 B.C.) (2 Kings 24:6–16); Archaeological Evidence of Jehoiachin's Name

When Jehoiakim died in 597 B.C., his son Jehoiachin came to the throne (2 Kings 24:6), probably beginning his reign on April 22, 597.[5] He was king for only three months. When Nebuchadnezzar came against Jerusalem in 597, Jehoiachin surrendered and was taken to Babylon (vv. 11, 15). This constituted what is usually called the second deportation, the first one apparently being in 605. Some writers inclining to the liberal view have given up the idea of a first deportation in the period 606–604, even though there is evidence for it. I see no valid reason for assuming it to be fictitious. The evidence for this first deportation is discussed in chapter 20 in the section entitled "The Three Deportations That Began the Exile," pages 193–94.

Archaeological evidence of the name of Jehoiachin was found in the excavation of Tell Beit Mirsim, thirteen miles southwest of Hebron, believed to represent the site

of the biblical town of Kiriath Sepher (Josh. 15:15–16; Judg. 1:11–12). The work was directed by W.F. Albright and M.G. Kyle in 1926, 1928, 1930, and 1932. In the upper stratum (dated a little after 600 B.C.) the excavators found two stamped jar handles with the same seal impression, reading, "Belonging to Eliakim steward of Yokin" (AAPB, 125). Yokin is a shortened form of the name rendered "Jehoiachin" in the Bible, so the seal impression says in effect, "Belonging to Eliakim steward of Jehoiachin." An identically inscribed jar handle was found in the excavation of Beth Shemesh by Elihu Grant in 1930. Careful examination showed that all three jar handles had been impressed with the same seal (AAPB, 125; KEK, 200; cf. BAB, 116). Evidently Eliakim was charged with the administration of Jehoiachin's property while the king was in exile in Babylon.

Archaeological Confirmation of Jehoiachin's Exile in Babylon (2 Kings 25:27–30); His Ration Receipts

The Bible states that Jehoiachin was a political prisoner in Babylon for thirty-seven years. At the end of that period, Evil-Merodach, king of Babylon, brought him out of prison, changed his prison garments, and gave him a daily allowance of food for the rest of his life (2 Kings 25:27–30). Confirmation of this aspect of Jehoiachin's life was found on a clay tablet from Babylon that lists the payment of rations of oil, barley, and other food, to captives and skilled workmen around Babylon; it lists Youkin (Yokin), king in Judah, equivalent to Jehoiachin, and his five sons as recipients of these issues of food.[6] It is thrilling to be able to find even

---

[5]TCK, 182; TMN, 187, based on R.A. Parker and W.H. Dubberstein, *Babylonian Chronology 626 B.C.–A.D. 45* (Chicago: University of Chicago Press, 1942), 26.

[6]W.F. Albright, "King Joiachin in Exile," BA 5 (1942): 49ff.; citing Ernest F. Weidner, "Joiachin, Koenig von Juda, in babylonischen Keilschrifttexen," *Mélanges Syriens offerts a Monsieur René*

the "ration receipts" of King Jehoiachin from over 2,500 years ago.

Zedekiah, the Nineteenth King of Judah (597–586 B.C.); the End of Judah and the Destruction of Jerusalem (2 Kings 24–25)

After taking Jehoiachin off the throne of Judah, Nebuchadnezzar made the uncle of Jehoiachin the nineteenth king of Judah; his name, Mattaniah, was changed to Zedekiah (2 Kings 24:17). Zedekiah later rebelled against Nebuchadnezzar, and the latter again invaded Judah, in 588 (the ninth year of Zedekiah, who began to reign in 597 B.C.; cf. 2 Kings 25:1). The siege of Jerusalem began on January 15, 588 B.C. (TMN, 190) and was temporarily lifted by Pharaoh Hophra of Egypt, who invaded Palestine and sent his fleet against Phoenicia (cf. Jer. 37:5–11; Ezek. 17:15–17). Finally in the eleventh year of Zedekiah, on July 18, 586 B.C., Jerusalem fell to the Babylonians (2 Kings 25:1–4), and on August 14 the Babylonians began the final destruction of the city (TMN, 190). A great number of the people were taken to Babylon in this third and final deportation; only the poor of the land were left as farmers for the country of Judah (2 Kings 25:11).

Archaeological Light from the Lachish Letters on the Detractors of Jeremiah (Jeremiah 38:4)

As the fall of Jerusalem approached in the days of King Zedekiah, Jeremiah faithfully proclaimed the message, given him by the Lord, that the Babylonians (Chaldeans) would come and take the city of Jerusalem and destroy it (Jer. 37:8). The royal officials[7] of Zedekiah's court denounced Jeremiah to the king and asked

that he be put to death for "discouraging [lit., weakening the hands of] the soldiers" (38:4), presumably because his prophecy of the fall of Jerusalem would give the soldiers fighting against the Babylonian army a defeatist attitude.

In the excavation of the site called Tell ed-Duweir, now identified with the biblical town of Lachish, J.L. Starkey found (in 1935) a group of eighteen potsherds bearing on their surface several military messages written by an army officer to his superior officer stationed at Lachish.[8] W.F. Albright pointed out[9] that in one of these letters (No. 6) the army officer complained that the royal officials (*sarim*) had sent out circular letters that were said to "weaken the hands" of the people. The army officer who wrote this Lachish letter used the expression "weaken the hands" to describe the effect of the over-optimism of the royal officials, whereas the officials referred to in the book of Jeremiah (38:4) had used the same expression in describing the effect of Jeremiah's realistic prophecy concerning the approaching fall of Jerusalem. The royal officials were deemed guilty of the very action they sought to ascribe to Jeremiah.

Archaeological Confirmation Concerning Lachish and Azekah from the Lachish Letters (Jeremiah 34:7)

In the days of Jeremiah when the Babylonian army was taking one town after another in Judah (589–586 B.C.), the Bible states that the two cities of Lachish and Azekah had not yet fallen (Jer. 34:7). Striking confirmation of the fact that these two cities were among those still holding out is furnished by the Lachish letters. Letter No. 4, written by the army officer at a military outpost to his supe-

---

Dussaud, Paris, 1939, I, 923–35. "Joiachin" is a shorter form of "Jehoiachin." See also FLAP, 225–27.

[7]Hebrew, *sarim*.

[8]R.S. Haupert, "Lachish—Frontier Fortress of Judah," BA 1, 4 (December 1938): 30; MLPP, 137.

[9]W.F. Albright, "A Brief History of Judah from the Days of Josiah to Alexander the Great," BA 9, 1 (February 1946): 4.

The mound of Lachish

rior officer at Lachish, says, "We are watching for the signals of Lachish according to all indications which my Lord hath given, for we cannot see Azekah."[10] This letter not only shows how Nebuchadnezzar's army was tightening its net around the land of Judah, but also evidences the close relationship between Lachish and Azekah, which are similarly linked in the book of Jeremiah.

Biblical Names in the Lachish Letters (Jeremiah 36:10)

The Lachish letters, written in the time of Jeremiah, contain a number of names that occur in the Bible. It is not certain whether the names in the Lachish letters refer to the same individuals as given in the Bible, but it is significant that at least three of the names in the letters appear in the Old Testament only in the days of Jeremiah: Gemariah (Jer. 36:10; 29:3), Jaazaniah (35:3), and Neriah (36:4). Other names include Mattaniah and Jeremiah, which occur in other periods as well as that of Jeremiah; the name "Jeremiah" in the letters does not necessarily refer to the prophet. Thus we have military dispatches written at the time Jeremiah was living in Judah and even giving names mentioned by the prophet. It is no wonder Haupert remarks that we have had no archaeological discovery up to recent years that has had a more direct connection with the Bible than the Lachish letters. They provide us with a virtual "supplement to Jeremiah."[11]

---

[10]W.F. Albright, "The Oldest Hebrew Letters: the Lachish Ostraca," BASOR no. 70 (April 1938): 14; AOTA, 163; FLAP, 192–95; MLPP, 138 Cf. W.F. Albright, "The Lachish Letters After Five Years," BASOR 82 (April 1941): 21.

[11]Haupert, *Lachish*, 32.

Excavations at Lachish;
Reinterpretation of the Lachish Letters

Lachish, now identified with Tell ed-Duweir, thirty miles southwest of Jerusalem, was the second most important city in the kingdom of Judah. That fact had led to the ferocious attack of Sennacherib of Assyria on that city in the days of Isaiah, in 701 B.C., as described above. The first excavation at the site took place in 1932–1938, under the leadership of J.L. Starkey. C.H. Inge and G.L. Harding continued to dig there from 1938 to 1940, and Yohanan Aharoni of Tel Aviv University led an Israeli dig there in 1966 and 1968. In 1973 David Ussishkin of Tel Aviv University began the latest excavations at Lachish.

For our present purposes, the most interesting results of the excavations concern the attacks by Sennacherib in 701 and Nebuchadnezzar in 589. Ussishkin has been able to demonstrate that Level III was the city Sennacherib attacked.[12] At that time Lachish was a large garrison city surrounded by massive battlements. The inner gatehouse was the largest of its kind ever found in Israel (BAR, 52). The Assyrians built a siege ramp on the southwest of the city, and the Judeans built a counterramp against them.[13] After conquering the site, apparently the Assyrians forced all the inhabitants to leave and then burned Lachish to the ground (BAR, 53). Probably King Josiah rebuilt Lachish,

for it was again a strong bastion to meet the Babylonian onslaught.

One of the most interesting discoveries dating to the period of the Babylonian attack was that of the Lachish letters, discussed partially above. In 1935 Starkey found eighteen ostraca in a guardroom between the outer and inner gates of the city, in a layer of ash deposited by the fire Nebuchadnezzar had kindled when he destroyed the city. Probably the Chaldeans breached the walls late in 589 B.C. after the olive harvest, because numerous burned olive pits appeared in the nearby ruins. Nebuchadnezzar then laid siege to Jerusalem in January of 588. In 1938 three other letters were found at Lachish. All of these texts were written in black carbon ink on pieces of broken pottery (See EAEHL, 3: 645–46). The standard interpretation subscribed to over the years is that these letters were written by a subordinate officer at an outpost to the commander at Lachish, and that is the position taken above. But Yigael Yadin has presented a new interpretation that they were rough drafts of correspondence that the commander at Lachish was about to send to Jerusalem. Such an interpretation would explain why, e.g., the sender or addressee is so frequently omitted and why some of the texts are so fragmentary. Yadin marshaled an impressive list of arguments for his position, which certainly is appealing.[14]

[12]David Ussishkin, "Destruction of Judean Fortress Portrayed in Dramatic Eighth-Century B.C. Pictures," BAR (March/April 1984), 51.

[13]See David Ussishkin, "Defensive Judean Counter-Ramp Found at Lachish in 1983 Season," BAR (March/April 1984), 66–73.

[14]See Oded Borowski, "Yadin Presents New Interpretation of the Famous Lachish Letters," BAR (March/April 1984), 76–77.

Chapter 20

The Exile, c. 605–536 B.C.

(2 Kings 25; Jeremiah; Daniel; Ezekiel)

The Three Deportations That Began the Exile (Daniel, Ezekiel, 2 Kings), 606–586 B.C.

Bible scholars in the past have usually held that there were three deportations of the people of Judah, who were taken from Palestine to Babylonia by Nebuchadnezzar in 605, 597, and 586 B.C. Some critics have doubted the fact of a deportation in 605; Price, for example, says that the writer of Daniel 1:1 implies that there was a deportation in the third year of Jehoiakim (c. 606–605), but that "to such a captivity at that time no other reference is found" (POTH, 358). There is, however, very good evidence for the deportation of 605, in that the book of Daniel specifically indicates such a siege of Jerusalem, with a deportation of some of the people, including Daniel and certain of the princes of the house of Judah (Dan. 1:1, 3). Moreover, as Wiseman points out, Josephus preserved an important witness of the historian Berosus (a Babylonian priest, c. 300 B.C.) concerning such a campaign. The statement indicates that while Nabopolassar was still king of Babylonia, hearing that the territory to the west had revolted, he sent his son Nebuchadnezzar (the crown prince) to put down the revolt among the Jews and others.[1]

The *Babylonian Chronicle*, coming from the court records of ancient Babylon, specifically states, "At that time Nebuchadrezzar [alternate spelling] captured the whole area of the Hatti-country" (WCCK, 69). This includes all Syria and Palestine south to the border of Egypt. In the midst of the campaign, on the eighth of Av (August 16), King Nabopolassar died (WCCK, 69), and Nebuchadnezzar hurried back to Babylon to take the throne left by his father. Twenty-three days later he "sat on the royal throne in Babylon" (WCCK, 69). In his rush Nebuchadnezzar committed the captives, including "Jews, Phoenicians, and Syrians" to some of his friends.[2] When we examine the archaeological evidence further, we find that the last two texts of Nabopolassar are dated

---

[1]Donald J. Wiseman, *Chronicle of the Chaldean Kings* (London: British Museum, 1956), 26 [WCCK].

[2]Josephus, *Against Apion*, I.19.

in the months that would correspond to May and August, 605 B.C. and that the first two records of Nebuchadnezzar are dated in September and October, 605.[3] All this integrates with the biblical indication of the first siege of Jerusalem and first deportation in 605 B.C. It does not really matter that there may not have been much of a siege of Jerusalem at that time and that Jehoiakim apparently submitted to Nebuchadnezzar voluntarily with the surrender of numerous captives or hostages (WCCK, 26). The spring or summer of 605 B.C. would be the probable time of year for the campaign of Nebuchadnezzar, and there should be no further doubt of the historicity of the event.

The first deportation, then, was in 605 B.C. and included Daniel among those who were deported (Dan. 1:1–3, 6). The second deportation occurred in 597 and included Ezekiel among the captives. The third deportation took place in 586, when Nebuchadnezzar captured Jerusalem and burned the city and the temple (2 Kings 25:9–10).

Ezekiel, the Prophet to the Exiles in Babylonia (Ezekiel 1:1ff.)

Ezekiel was carried away to Babylonia with the deportation that included King Jehoiachin in the year 597 B.C. This second deportation in the days of Nebuchadnezzar (2 Kings 24:10–16) is also specifically confirmed in the *Chronicles of the Chaldean Kings*:

> In the seventh year, the month of Kislev [December, 598], the king . . . marched to the Hatti-land, and encamped against [i.e., besieged] the city of Judah and on the second day of the month of Adar [March 15, 597 B.C.] he seized the city and captured the king. He appointed there a king of his own

choice . . . , received its heavy tribute and sent [them] to Babylon. (WCCK, 73)

Ezekiel relates that he was among the captives in Babylonia by the Kebar River (Ezek. 1:1, 3). The Kebar (Kabaru or Kabari) was one of the navigable canals that ran between Babylon and the city of Nippur to the south. Nippur was excavated by an American expedition under Peters, Haynes, and Hilprecht during the years 1888–1900 (BAB, 37).[4] Tens of thousands of clay tablets were found at this site, including a Sumerian version of the Flood. Just how close to Nippur (sixty miles southeast of Babylon) the colonies of deported Jews were located we do not know. But into this rich valley they were brought, and there they worked for the seventy years of captivity. Ezekiel, though warned of the stiff-hearted nature of his people by the Lord (Ezek. 2:4), yet was commissioned to bring to them a message of comfort and encouragement, with a prediction of the future regathering of the people and a new spiritual awakening in the Promised Land (Ezek. 11:1ff.). Ezekiel looked forward to the time of Christ's earthly kingdom, yet future, when the dry bones of Israel will come to life and the nation of Israel will be restored to the Promised Land (Ezek. 37:1–14).

Archaeological Confirmation of the Validity of Ezekiel's Method of Dating (Ezekiel 1:1; 8:1ff.)

When I first took a course in biblical criticism, I was told that the critics had not touched the book of Ezekiel and that the validity of the book was accepted by liberal and conservative alike. However, subsequently the book was attacked from several angles, but, as W.F. Albright pointed out, this critical attitude is not

---

[3]Richard A. Parker and W.H. Dubberstein, *Babylonian Chronology 626 B.C.–A.D. 45*, 2d ed. (Chicago: University of Chicago Press, 1956), 9 [PDBC].

[4]The University of Chicago and the University of Pennsylvania resumed excavations at Nippur in 1948 on a plan to work there every second year. Only the University of Chicago has sponsored the excavations there since 1965. The great temple of Inanna and the religious center of the city, as well as the residential and administrative parts of this great site, have been largely uncovered.

justified in the least, and to his way of thinking there seems to be every reason for going back to a more conservative attitude toward Ezekiel (AOTA, 164).

One of C.C. Torrey's[5] principle arguments against the authenticity of the book concerned the unusual dating of events by the years "of king Jehoiachin's captivity" (AOTA, 164). This method of dating, however, now turns out to be an "inexpugnable argument" (AOTA, 164) in favor of the genuineness of Ezekiel, as shown by archaeological discoveries. From the seal impression on three jar handles[6] bearing the reference to "Eliakim steward of Jehoiachin," it was deduced that Eliakim was the administrator of the crown property that still belonged to Jehoiachin while he was in exile. Evidently Jehoiachin was still considered king by the people of Judah, and Zedekiah was regarded as king only in the sense of being regent for his captive nephew, Jehoiachin. Thus it was quite in harmony with the attitude of the Jewish people for Ezekiel to date events according to the reign of Jehoiachin, even though he was in exile.

Any doubt that Jehoiachin was still considered king was removed by the discovery of clay tablets in Babylon that refer to "Jehoiachin the king of the land of Judah." This shows that even the Babylonians still referred to Jehoiachin, their prisoner, as the king of Judah (AOTA, 165).

Therefore, when Ezekiel tells of his vision when the elders of Judah sat before him in the "sixth year" (Ezek. 8:1), he is dating the event according to Jehoiachin's captivity (FLAP, 225–27), or as most Jews probably regarded it, his "reign" in absentia. (By way of further interest, it may be pointed out that this vision of the sixth year would have been in the year 592 B.C., which is the very date of the tablet that mentions Jehoiachin.)

The ususual system of dating in the book of Ezekiel, then, is not an evidence of its lack of authenticity, but, in the light of the archaeological evidence, "proves its authenticity in a most striking way" (AOTA, 165).

The Colony That Remained in Palestine (2 Kings 25; Jeremiah 39–41); Gedaliah

When Nebuchadnezzar captured Jerusalem, he carried away about twenty-five thousand persons, mostly inhabitants of Jerusalem, into captivity in Babylonia (POTH, 352). This constituted the third deportation. The poor of the land, however, were left to be the vinedressers and husbandmen of Palestine (2 Kings 25:12). There was little likelihood that these folk would organize a rebellion against the Babylonian control of the land, after the political leaders had been either killed or deported (vv. 11, 19–21).

Nebuchadnezzar appointed a Jew named Gedaliah to rule over the Jews who remained in Palestine (2 Kings 25:22). This man set up his capital at Mizpah (v. 23), about seven miles north of Jerusalem. Here Jeremiah came to be with him after the chief military officer of Nebuchadnezzar had released the prophet and counseled him to return to Gedaliah (Jer. 40:1, 5).

Archaeological Evidence of the Desolation of Palestine at the Time of the Exile

The invasions of Nebuchadnezzar in 605, 597, and 589–586 B.C. caused much damage and destruction in Judah. Archaeological evidence shows that many of the cities of Judah were destroyed and not rebuilt, a fact particularly evidenced in the excavations at Azekah, Beth Shemesh, and Kiriath Sepher, and also by

---

[5]Torrey was formerly a professor at Yale University.

[6]For a description of these jar handles, see chapter 19, the section entitled "Archaeological Confirmation of Jehoiachin's Exile in Babylon," page 189–90.

surface examination elsewhere (BWMS, 107). The excavation of Lachish also gave evidence of Babylonian destruction there (see chapter 19). The last invasion, in 589, culminated in the siege and destruction of Jerusalem followed by the final deportation in 586.

Nebuchadnezzar's Control of Judah; Archaeological Evidence of His Building Activity in Babylon (Daniel 4:29–30)

For twenty years, Judah had suffered from the invasions of Nebuchadnezzar II, beginning with the campaign of 605 B.C. and ending with the capture of Jerusalem and the last deportation in 586. For another twenty-five years, Judah was subject to the rule of Nebuchadnezzar; his reign lasted from 605 to 562 (PDBC, 10).

Daniel, one of the captives deported by Nebuchadnezzar in the invasion of 605 B.C. (Dan. 1:1–3, 6), lived in Babylon for nearly three quarters of a century. He gives us a good thumbnail sketch of Nebuchadnezzar's building activities. Daniel relates that one day Nebuchadnezzar considered the great city and then remarked, "Is not this the great Babylon I have built as the royal residence, by my mighty power and for the glory of my majesty?" (Dan. 4:30). The archaeological excavations in Babylon have produced inscriptions that tell of Nebuchadnezzar's great building activities. The East India House inscription, now in the British Museum, has six columns of Babylonian writing telling of the stupendous building operations the king carried on in enlarging and beautifying Babylon. He rebuilt more than twenty temples in Babylon and Borsippa and directed construction work on the docks and defenses of the city.[7] Many of the bricks taken out of Babylon in the archaeological excavations bear the name and inscription of Nebuchadnezzar stamped on them. One of the records of Nebuchadnezzar sounds almost like the boast that Daniel recorded, as noted above (Dan. 4:30); it reads, "The fortifications of Esagila and Babylon I strengthened and established the name of my reign forever" (BAB, 479; PMOT, 302).

Significance of Daniel's Reference to Nebuchadnezzar's Building Activity; Failure of Archaeology to Support the Critical View in This Matter

Daniel's indication (4:30) that Nebuchadnezzar was responsible for the extensive building operations of Babylon was abundantly confirmed, as noted in the preceding section, by the excavation of Koldewey beginning in 1899 and continuing until the First World War. The German excavators found a vast system of fortifications, buildings, canals, palaces, and temples (FLAP, 224). Nebuchadnezzar was responsible not only for rebuilding Babylon but also for adding a whole new section on the west bank of the Euphrates and for linking the two parts of the city with a bridge across the Euphrates. The latter was an especially great achievement for his day.[8]

Many critical scholars hold that the book of Daniel was not written in the time of Daniel (sixth century B.C.) but that it was composed some four hundred years later, about 168–165 (PIOT, 765). However, on the basis of the critical view, it is difficult to explain how the supposed late writer of the book of Daniel knew that the glories of Babylon were due to Nebuchadnezzar's building activities. Pfeiffer, though setting forth the critical view, acknowledges that "we shall presumably never know" how the writer of Daniel knew that Babylon was the result of Nebuchadnezzar's building projects, as

---

[7]For a picture of this inscription, see PMOT, 213.

[8]For a discussion of Babylon, see especially James G. Macqueen, *Babylon* (London: Robert Hale, 1964), chap. 6; and James Wellard, *Babylon* (New York: Saturday Review, 1972), chap. 13.

The city of Babylon, reconstructed on the basis of the excavations, with the Ishtar gate in the foreground   Courtesy of the Oriental Institute of the University of Chicago

the excavations have proved (PIOT, 759). For one who accepts the time of Daniel's life as the period of the writing of the book, there is no problem.

Discovery of Ancient Fragments of the Book of Daniel

Among the Dead Sea Scrolls there are eight fragments of Daniel.[9] The forms of the letters are similar to those of the Isaiah manuscript, pointing to the first or second century B.C. as the date for these fragments of the Daniel text. It is significant that the text is substantially the same as that in the Hebrew Bibles that we have had all along, the chief differences having to do with the spelling of words. This provides another piece of evidence

---

[9]See James A. Sanders, "The Dead Sea Scrolls—A Quarter Century of Study," BA (December 1973), 136; and G. Ernest Wright, BA (May 1949), 33.

for the care with which the text of the biblical books has been brought down to us.

Moreover, a manuscript of Daniel dating about 120 B.C. brings into question the alleged Maccabean date (mid-second century B.C.) of its composition.[10] Gleason Archer has discussed at length the critical questions concerning the date of Daniel's composition (ASOTI, 379–93), including new evidence from the Dead Sea Scrolls; he concludes, "In the light of this newly discovered linguistic evidence, therefore, it would seem impossible to maintain any longer a second-century date for the book of Daniel" (ASOTI, 393).

The End of Gedaliah; Archaeological Light from Mizpah

The rule of Gedaliah as the governor of Judah by Nebuchadnezzar's appointment (2 Kings 25:22), did not last long. A Jew by the name of Ishmael, who probably considered himself a "patriot," and Gedaliah a "quisling," leading a group of ten men in a conspiracy, killed Gedaliah at his headquarters in Mizpah (v. 25) and also the other officials who were with him (Jer. 41:2–3); they cast their bodies into a pit at Mizpah (v. 9).

The site called Tell en-Nasbe, about seven miles north of Jerusalem, was excavated by the Pacific School of Religion of Berkeley, California, under the direction of F.W. Badé. The excavators found several jar handles stamped with what was apparently the word *Mizpah*, which led them to identify the site with the Mizpah of Scripture (BAB, 132). At Tell en-Nasbe, Badé found a pit filled with rubbish and potsherds, the latest material dating from a little after 600 B.C., indicating that the cistern was closed at approximately the time of the Exile. This led him to surmise that this might even be the pit into which

Gedaliah was cast after he had been murdered by Ishmael (BAB, 133). Muir says that in one cistern there was a large number of human skeletons, and he asks, "Were these the victims of Ishmael's treachery?" (MHTE, 207). The fact that cisterns were sometimes used as a convenient means of disposing of bodies was indicated at Gezer, where Macalister found fifteen skeletons in a cistern (BAB, 223).[11]

The Flight to Egypt (2 Kings 25:26; Jeremiah 41–43)

After Ishmael had slain Gedaliah at Mizpeh (Jer. 41:2), he took the important people who remained in Mizpeh and fled with them to the east, toward the country of the Ammonites, on the east of the Jordan (v. 10). However, Johanan and the other military leaders heard of Ishmael's doing and went to find him (vv. 11–12); they located him and recovered the people whom Ishmael had abducted, but Ishmael escaped (vv. 13–15). Because of fear of retaliation from the forces of Nebuchadnezzar, Johanan with his cohorts made plans to go to Egypt (vv. 17–18). He first consulted Jeremiah, who told the group that the Lord would not have them to go down into Egypt (42:19). Johanan and his companions, feeling that Jeremiah had not spoken aright (43:2), proceeded to take the whole group who had formerly been at Mizpeh, including Jeremiah, down to Egypt (vv. 5–7).

Jeremiah in Egypt; Archaeological Light from Tahpanhes (Jeremiah 43:8–10)

Johanan brought the group to the town of Tahpanhes, in the eastern delta of Egypt. Here the Lord directed Jeremiah to act out a prophecy: he was to take stones and hide them in the brick pavement at

[10]Edwin M. Yamauchi, "The Dead Sea Scrolls," *Wycliffe Bible Encyclopedia* (Chicago: Moody Press, 1975), 159.

[11]A summary of the Tell en-Nasbe excavations may be found in EAEHL, 3:912–18.

A nilometer on the island of Elephantine in the Nile River, used to measure the flood level of the Nile in ancient times

Archaeological Evidence of a Colony of Jews in Egypt a Century and a Half After the Time of Jeremiah

At the beginning of the twentieth century, a fascinating discovery was made on the island of Elephantine, located at the first cataract in the Nile, some 583 miles south of Cairo (BAB, 3). As early as 1895, evidence of papyrus documents had been found on the island by native diggers, and in 1904, the Service of Antiquities in Egypt made excavations that uncovered many papyri, including documents written in the Aramaic language by a colony of Jews in the period 500–400 B.C. (PMOT, 320–32). One of the documents was a letter written to the Persian governor of Jerusalem in the year 407 or 408, asking for permission to rebuild the temple on the island of Elephantine. Whether these were actually some of the descendants of the Jews who came down with Johanan and Jeremiah we cannot say, but at least they may well have been some of the same. Albright believed that the Elephantine documents were written by Jews probably connected with the migration to Egypt described in Jeremiah 41–44, not long after 586 B.C. (ARBDL, 36).

Events in Babylon, c. 562–560 B.C.; Archaeological Light on Jehoiachin and Evil-Merodach (2 Kings 25:27–30)

Nebuchadnezzar died in 562 B.C. He was succeeded by his son, Evil-Merodach (POTH, 366), who released Jehoiachin from prison and gave him an allowance of provisions (2 Kings 25:27–30). We have already noted the discovery of clay tablets at Babylon listing the payment of rations of oil, barley, and other food to workmen and political prisoners. Among those listed as recipients of these provisions was Jehoiachin of Judah (see chapter 19, the section entitled "Archaeological Confirmation of Jehoiachin's Exile in Babylon," pages 189–90).

the entrance of the palace in Tahpanhes. This was to be an indication that Nebuchadnezzar would come into Egypt and set up his pavilion there (Jer. 43:8–10).

The site of Tahpanhes survives today as Tell Defenneh, about twenty-seven miles south-southwest of Port Said. Sir Flinders Petrie excavated there in 1883–1884 and laid bare a large brick building in front of which was a pavement identified with the one mentioned in Jeremiah.[12] Fulfillment of the prophecy that Nebuchadnezzar would invade Egypt finally occurred in Nebuchadnezzar's thirty-seventh year, as one of his inscriptions indicates (PANET, 308). Presumably Nebuchadnezzar did not intend to add Egypt to his empire but to launch a punitive expedition to humble Egypt and keep the Egyptians out of Asia.

[12]See Carl E. DeVries, "Tahpanhes," ISBE (1988), 4:715–16.

Archaeological evidence of King Evil-Merodach (Amel-Marduk in Babylonian) was found on a vase at Susa in Persia, reported by the French archaeological expedition there.[13] This vase bore an inscription that read, "Palace of Amel-Marduk, King of Babylon, son of Nebuchadnezzar, King of Babylon." The people of Persia (called Elam in ancient times) had apparently carried this vase from Babylonia to Persia at the time of one of their military invasions of the Mesopotamian area (BAB, 479).

Last Events in the Neo-Babylonian Empire, c. 560–539 B.C.; Nabonidus and Belshazzar (Daniel 5)

Evil-Merodach ruled for only two or three years (562–560 B.C.) and was then assassinated by his brother-in-law, Neriglissar (Nergalsharezer), who was the Nergalsharezer of Jeremiah 39:3. After a rather successful administration of four years (560–556), Neriglissar died, leaving the throne to his infant son, Labashi-Marduk, who was deposed by the priestly party in nine months and replaced by Nabonidus (Nabu-na'id), a Babylonian of the priestly group.

Nabonidus (556–539 B.C.) tells us in his inscriptions that he had been a trusted general in the army of his predecessors. As king, Nabonidus maintained the stability of the empire and spent much time in directing the building and strengthening of the fortifications on the Euphrates River. One of this great joys came in the rebuilding of ruined temples. His record telling of the rebuilding of the temple of Shamash at Sippar (PMOT, 306) and the finding of the foundation record of Naram-Sin has already been cited (see chapter 19, the section entitled "The Finding of the Book of the Law," pages 185–86).

Whereas the secular sources indicated Nabonidus as the last king of the Neo-Babylonian Empire, the Bible indicates that Belshazzar was the last ruler (Dan. 5). This apparent contradiction and difficulty has been resolved by the archaeological discoveries of recent years. It is dealt with in the following section.

Archaeological Confirmation Concerning Nabonidus and Belshazzar (Daniel 5)

A college student once wrote me the following letter:

> I am a history major at the university. This semester I am taking a course in Ancient History.
>
> As my religious beliefs are orthodox and some of Dr. ——'s are not, there are naturally quite a few points where we do not agree. The particular point which she and I are discussing at the present time concerns the book of Daniel. Dr. —— believes that Daniel errs in his book when he speaks of Belshazzar as king of the Chaldeans in Daniel 5:1. She says that Nabonidus was king of Babylon at the time of its fall and not Belshazzar. She takes the position that Belshazzar was never king, and, from the way she has spoken, I believe she even doubts his actual existence. She also has taught that Daniel errs when he says that Babylon was taken by siege. According to other accounts there was not a siege of Babylon. It was just handed over to Cyrus.
>
> I feel as though I should have proof for my beliefs whenever it is possible to obtain it. I am writing to you to ask you if you would be willing to give me your point of view on the matter or refer me to some source which, in your opinion, states the facts correctly.

I replied to the above letter basically as follows: The biblical statements concerning Belshazzar have been used for a long time by critics to demonstrate that the Bible is not accurate. It is quite true that up to one hundred years ago our historical sources (outside of the Bible) showed that Nabonidus was the last king of Babylon and was not killed when the city

---

[13]De Morgan, *Délégation en Perse*, 14:60, cited in BAB, 479.

was taken by the Persians but was given a pension by his conquerors. Ancient historians such as Berossus (c. 250 B.C.) and Alexander Polyhistor give us this information that Nabonidus was the last king of Babylon. On the other hand, the Bible indicates that Belshazzar was the last ruler of Babylon and that he was killed when the city was taken (Dan. 5:30). Modern liberal commentators, such as Hitzig, have taken the view that the name Belshazzar was a pure invention on the part of the writer of Daniel 5.[14]

Archaeological discoveries, however, show that the Bible is accurate in regard to its indications concerning Belshazzar. About the middle of the nineteenth century a great number of clay tablets were excavated in the region that was ancient Babylonia and were sent to the British Museum. During the last half of the nineteenth century many of these tablets were examined by Theophilus G. Pinches, a prominent Assyriologist of London. One of them contained the name Belshazzar, showing that such a man actually existed. Another tablet was found to bear the names of Belshazzar and Nabonidus (PANET, 310), indicating that there was some connection between these two people, and still another tablet referred to Belshazzar as the king's son (PMOT, 307). Furthermore, another tablet proved to be a contract containing an oath taken in the name of Nabonidus and Belshazzar.[15] In ancient Babylonia oaths were taken in the name of the reigning king. This tablet, then, gave indication that Belshazzar was actually a co-ruler with his father, Nabonidus.

In subsequent years, the work of Raymond P. Dougherty, then professor of Assyriology at Yale University, furnished further illumination on the situation concerning Belshazzar.[16] Dougherty showed that during the latter part of his reign Nabonidus spent a great deal of his time in Arabia (cf. PANET, 306), probably for the purpose of consolidating that part of his empire, though some scholars have suggested that he was doing what we would call archaeological work, and others have suggested that he stayed in Arabia because he liked the climate. In any event the clay tablets show us the reason for the raising of Belshazzar to the position of ruling monarch—namely, the absence of his father from Babylon. The English scholar Sidney Smith published an inscription that evidently refers to Nabonidus; it reads, "He entrusted the kingship to him," indicating the bestowal of royal authority on Belshazzar.[17]

I know of no first-rate critic today who urges this old objection concerning Belshazzar. An example of the way in which liberals recognize the facts in the case may be taken from the book *What Mean These Stones?* by Millar Burrows (BWMS, 276–77). The author points out that "the solution of this apparent discrepancy was apparent when evidence was found that during the last part of his reign Nabunaid (Nabonidus) lived in Arabia and left the administration of the government to his son Belshazzar."

The detailed facts are that Nabonidus, in one sense the last king of Babylon, was not killed by the invading Persians but was given a pension by his conquerors. On the other hand, Belshazzar, elevated to the position of ruler of Babylon by his father, was killed when the city of Baby-

---

[14]Hitzig, *Commentary on Daniel*, 75.
[15]This tablet was published by Pinches in the *Expository Times* (April 1915).
[16]R.P. Dougherty, *Nabonidus and Belshazzar* (New Haven: Yale University Press, 1929) [DNB].
[17]Ibid., 108.

lon was taken, as indicated in Daniel 5:30. The matter concerning Belshazzar, far from being an error in the Scriptures, is one of the many striking confirmations of the Word of God that have been demonstrated by archaeology.

Chapter 21

The Return from Exile, 536–458 B.C.

(Ezra, Haggai, Zechariah)

The End of the Neo-Babylonian Empire (612–539 B.C.); the Fall of Babylon (539)

Nabonidus (556–539 B.C.), the last king of the Neo-Babylonian Empire (612–539), was ruling with his son, Belshazzar, when Cyrus of Persia swept across western Asia and captured Babylon in the year 539. One of Cyrus' own clay cylinders tells that the priests of Babylon opened the gates of the impregnable city and let him come in. Cyrus felt that he was the man of destiny for his day (For Cyrus' account of his capture of the city of Babylon, see PANET, 315–16).

When Cyrus captured Babylon, he had effectively launched the Persian Empire. Coming to the throne of the principality of Anshan (north and east of the head of the Persian Gulf) in about 559 B.C., he had rebelled against his Median overlord and had conquered the Medes during the 550s, had overrun Lydia in 546, and now had subdued the Neo-Babylonian Empire in 539. The empire he established lasted for some two hundred years, until Alexander the Great conquered it in 331 B.C. One of Cyrus' early acts after taking Babylon was to permit the Jews to return to Palestine after their seventy-year captivity.

Archaeological Light on Cyrus' Policy (2 Chronicles 36:22–23; Ezra 1:1–4)

The Bible indicates that after Cyrus gained control of Babylon (on October 29, 539 B.C.) he made a proclamation permitting those people of Judah who had been deported by Nebuchadnezzar to go back to Palestine and rebuild the temple (2 Chron. 36:22–23; Ezra 1:1–4). Thus Cyrus reversed the policy of deportation that had been used by Tiglath-Pileser III (745–727 B.C.), Sargon II (721–705), and other Assyrian conquerors, as well as by the Babylonian king, Nebuchadnezzar (see chapters 17 and 20).

Archaeological evidence that Cyrus pursued a liberal and tolerant policy toward deported peoples, such as the Jews whom he found in Babylonia, was discovered during the nineteenth century by Rassam, who found the Cyrus Cylinder. This cylinder states concerning such groups, "I [also] gathered all their [former] inhabitants and returned [to them] their habitations. Furthermore, I resettled upon the command of Marduk, . . . all the gods . . . in their [former] chapels"

(PANET, 316). The cylinder tells of Cyrus' taking the city of Babylon without violence and, later, of returning people to their former dwellings. Not only was Cyrus a humane man, he was also a wise administrator. Certainly he realized that disaffection of subject peoples and their ill will toward the central administration would be eliminated if they were free to return to their ancestral homes. Presumably almost none of them did return; we do not have their records. We know about the Jewish action because of their religious devotion and the preservation of the account of resettlement in the Bible. Cyrus' humaneness and administrative wisdom were also buttressed by his polytheistic superstition or faith. He wanted the subject peoples and their gods to be well disposed toward him, and he wanted their prayers. "May all the gods whom I have resettled in their sacred cities ask daily Bel and Nebo for a long life for me and may they recommend me [to him]; to Marduk," he wrote on the Cyrus Cylinder (PANET, 316).

Preparations of the Jews to Return from Captivity (Ezra 1:5–11)

The decree of Cyrus allowing the Jews to return to Palestine was made in his first year, 539–538 B.C. (Ezra 1:1); the actual return must have gotten under way at least by 537 or 536. Those who prepared to return were given vessels of silver and gold, as well as animals and precious things (v. 6), and Cyrus even had the vessels that Nebuchadnezzar had taken from the temple in Jerusalem restored to Sheshbazzar, one of the leaders of the Jews (vv. 7–8).

The Return Under Sheshbazzar and Zerubbabel (Ezra 2); Archaeological Light on the Names of the Leaders

Prominent among those who led the people back to Palestine were Sheshbazzar (Ezra 1:11) and Zerubbabel (Ezra 2:2). A detailed listing of the various people whom they led back appears in Ezra 2, with a summary of the total at the end of the chapter, amounting to nearly 50,000 (congregation of 42,360, servants numbering 7,337, and singers numbering 200—giving a total of 49,897; see Ezra 2:64).

Archaeological light has been found on the names of these two leaders of the Jews who spent their early years in Babylonia; for it is now known from discoveries in this area that the names of Zerubbabel and his uncle, Sheshbazzar, were good Babylonian names (Zer-Babel and Shin-ab-usur) (ARDBL, 36).

Gifts for Rebuilding the Temple; the Altar Set Up (Ezra 2:3)

When the Jews returned to Jerusalem and saw the condition of the temple, which had been burned by Nebuchadnezzar's troops more than a generation before (2 Kings 25:9), some of the fathers gave freely for its restoration (Ezra 2:68). Their gifts amounted to more than a thousand "drachmas" of gold and five thousand pounds of silver (v. 69). (For an explanation of "drachmas," see "Archaeological Confirmation of the Reference to the Drachma in Nehemiah," pages 213–14.)

At the time of the return many of those whose ancestral home had been elsewhere than Jerusalem had apparently gone to their home town (Ezra 2:70), but now in the seventh month, October (according to Jewish system, see article on "Calendar," ISBE), the people gathered themselves together "as one man" in Jerusalem (Ezra 3:1), and the altar was erected so that they could offer burnt offerings according to the law of Moses (v. 3).

Materials for Rebuilding the Temple; Archaeological Light on the Use of Cedar Wood (Ezra 3)

In preparation for rebuilding the temple, payment was sent to the people of Sidon and Tyre in Phoenicia for bringing cedar trees for the construction work (Ezra 3:7). Archaeological discoveries illuminate the use of cedar wood from the Lebanon mountains in Phoenicia for the building of important structures. Long before the restoration of the temple in Jerusalem, a ruler in the city of Lagash[1] in Babylonia by the name of Gudea (c. 2100 B.C.) rebuilt a temple of Ningirsu, and for this purpose he sent to the Amanus mountains for cedar wood. The Amanus mountains were a part of the same general range as the Lebanons, lying along the Mediterranean to the north of the Orontes River. Gudea said, "From Amanus, the mountain of cedar, cedar wood, the length of which was 60 cubits, cedar wood, the length of which was 50 cubits, *ukarinnu*-wood, the length of which was 25 cubits, for the dwelling he made; (from) their mountain they were brought.[2]

Archaeological light on the use of cedar wood for construction also comes from Egypt. About 1100 B.C. a man named Wenamon was sent from Egypt to the Lebanon region to secure "timber for the great and august barge of Amon-Re," as Wenamon tells us in the record he left.[3]

The archaeological discoveries also show that Nebuchadnezzar (605–562 B.C.) had been to the Lebanon mountains. In speaking of the beautiful trees there, he said, "Mighty cedars they were, tall and strong, of wonderful beauty, whose dark appearance was remarkable—the mighty products of mount Lebanon. . . ."[4] A little later Darius I of Persia brought cedar of Lebanon to Susa (the biblical Shushan) for use in his royal palace (FLAP, 243). And, of course, Solomon had bought cedar of Lebanon from Hiram of Tyre for use in the first Hebrew temple (2 Kings 5:6 et al.).

The Foundation of the Restoration Temple Laid (Ezra 3)

After sending for the Lebanon cedar wood, the builders of the temple proceeded to lay the foundation (Ezra 3:10). When the foundation had been laid, the people sang praises and gave thanks to the Lord (v. 11), but many of the old people wept aloud (v. 12). These were the people who had seen Solomon's temple before it was destroyed in 586 B.C. by the troops of Nebuchadnezzar (2 Kings 25:9). Barton believes that these old people did not weep because the restoration temple was any smaller than that of Solomon, but rather because it was less ornate. He feels that the second temple was built on the lines of the first, which were probably still traceable in the debris, and that the builders used much of the stone from Solomon's temple, which still lay on the temple hill (BAB, 243).

The Adversaries from Among Those Brought in by "The Great and Noble Asnapper" (Ezra 4:1–10 KJV); Archaeology and Asnapper

Adversaries arose among some of those living in the land of Palestine who were descendants of foreign peoples deported from other countries to Palestine in the days of Esarhaddon and Asnapper (Ezra 4:2, 10). These people came to Zerubbabel and asked to be allowed to help build the temple, saying that they had sought the

[1]Lagash, the city of Gudea, is represented today by the site of Telloh, which was excavated by de Sarzec at intervals from 1877 to 1901 and later by Genouillac beginning in 1928; large quantities of clay tablets were found, one room alone containing an archive estimated at thirty thousand tablets (BAB, 36).

[2]Sarzec, *Découvertes en Chaldée*, p. ix, col. v. 28ff.; Thureau-Dangin, *Les Inscriptions de Sumer et d'Akkad* (Paris, 1905), 109; idem, *Sumerischen und akkadischen Konigsinschriften* (Leipzig, 1907), 68ff., all cited in BAB, 455.

[3]J.H. Breasted, *Ancient Records of Egypt* 4:278ff. [BARE].

[4]BAB, 478, translated from Pognon, *Les inscriptions babyloniennes du Wadi Brissa*, Pl. xiii f, and *Recueil de traveaux relatifs à la philologie et à l'archeologie égyptiennes et assyriennes* 28:57; see also Langdon, *Neubabylonishcen Königsinschriften*, 174ff.

God of the Jews. Zerubbabel and the fathers of Israel declined their offer of help (v. 3); they may have remembered that idolatry had been one of the chief causes of the downfall of Judah and feared that to associate with these people, whose religion was a mixture of paganism and perhaps some truth, would be another subversive factor in the new start that was being made in the reestablishment of the worship in Jerusalem (POTH, 381).[5]

Asnapper (Osnappar in NIV, Osnapper in KJV, et al.) is referred to in Ezra 4:10 as "the great and honorable Ashurbanipal" who brought into Palestine these peoples who sought to help the Jews build the temple. He is evidently the famous Ashurbanipal (668–626 B.C.) who collected the great library at Nineveh and who studied the ancient languages such as Sumerian, discovering that he was "addled" by the beautiful script (see chapter 19). To him we owe a debt of gratitude for the extensive library that was found by Layard and Rassam in the nineteenth century and from which came such important records as the Babylonian creation account and the flood record.

Archaeology and the Validity of the Letters of the Adversaries (Ezra 4:11–16); Significance of Elephantine Papyri in This Demonstration

The adversaries of the Jews wrote a letter to the Persian king, telling him that these Jews who had come to build Jerusalem would not pay their taxes to him after the city was built (Ezra 4:13). This section of Ezra is written in Aramaic. Most critical scholars have denied the essential authenticity of these Aramaic letters recorded in Ezra (AAPB, 170), but

archaeology has given a definite answer to the critical view. Specific evidence comes from the Elephantine papyri, which are letters written in Aramaic by a colony of Jews on the island of Elephantine in Egypt during the period 500–400 B.C. (see chapter 20, the section entitled "Archaeological Evidence of a Colony of Jews in Egypt. . . ," page 199). The similarity of the Aramaic in the Elephantine papyri and in Ezra shows that the Aramaic of Ezra may easily date back into the fourth century, if not even to the end of the fifth century (AAPB, 170). Albright points out that these edicts and letters of Ezra 4:7ff. are almost certainly the original text, as has been demonstrated from ancient parallels by Eduard Meyer and H.H. Schaeder (1930) (ARDBL, 36). Thus the critical view that holds that Ezra, Nehemiah, and Chronicles were all written about 250 B.C. (PIOT, 812) is not sustained. The Elephantine papyri show that Ezra need not be dated late on the ground that a late type of Aramaic is used (ASOTI, 413–16).

Cessation of the Work on the Temple Until 520 B.C. (Ezra 4)

Ezra 4 is an account of efforts of the people living in the land to prevent the Jews from rebuilding the temple. They kept on trying to discourage them or to "frustrate their plans" and kept on troubling them. They even "hired counselors" (or "bribed officials") to discredit them or to order a stop to the work altogether. The result was cessation of the work through the remainder of the reign of Cyrus and down into the reign of Darius, a period of some fifteen years (Ezra 4:5).[6]

---

[5]See also Howard F. Vos, *Ezra, Nehemiah and Esther* (Grand Rapids: Zondervan, 1987), 42ff. [VENE].

[6]For discussion of the opposition to the Jews detailed in Ezra 4 and the historical references included there, see VENE, 42–47.

The Encouragement of Haggai and Zechariah to Resume Work on the Temple (Ezra 5); the Temple Completed (Ezra 6)

In the second year of the reign of Darius (520 B.C.) the prophets Haggai and Zechariah encouraged the people to resume the building of the temple, which had been started some sixteen years earlier, about 536. Haggai pointed out that the people had become unduly interested in their own paneled houses, but now it was time to think of going to the mountain, getting wood, and building the house of the Lord (Hag. 1:4, 8). When the people began to rebuild the temple under the leadership of Zerubbabel and Jeshua (Ezra 5:2), Tattenai, the Persian ruler of the district, raised a question about who had authorized the Jews to build the temple. When the Jews stated their case, Tattenai wrote to Darius (v. 7), explaining that Cyrus had given them permission to rebuild their "house of God" (v. 13). Darius caused a search to be made in the palace and found the decree of Cyrus (6:1–3ff.). Then Darius ordered that the Jews be left alone so that they might continue the work (v. 7), and he even authorized that supplies be given from the royal treasury to help in the work (v. 8).

The work on the temple proceeded, and it was finally completed in the sixth year of Darius, which was the year 515 B.C., some twenty years after it was begun, in about 536. A great dedication service was held (6:16–17), and the observance of the Passover was restored (6:19–20).

The Sixty-Year Silence in the Book of Ezra

The sixth chapter of Ezra ends with the completion of the restoration temple in 515 B.C., and the seventh chapter begins with events in the life of Ezra in the year 438 B.C. Thus there is approximately a sixty-year gap in the historical account. This is probably due to the fact the Ezra's purpose seems to have been to deal with the reestablishment of the temple, the religious institutions, and the religious life of Judah. Apparently the next important step in this progression came in the life of Ezra in 458, and for that reason he does not deal with the intervening period.

The Period of Esther

Darius reigned 521–486 B.C. He was succeeded by Xerxes (485–465), who invaded Greece, in 480 and was initially successful, but his forces were nearly annihilated at Plataea in 479. The Ahasuerus of the book of Esther is identified with this Xerxes. The book of Esther opens in the third year of the reign of Ahasuerus (Xerxes), 483, at which time he gave a great feast in connection with preparation for the Greek invasion. King Ahasuerus commanded that Vashti, the queen, be brought before the people at the feast, but Vashti refused. The king then had Vashti deposed as queen, at the advice of his counselors (Esther 1:10–22).

The deposing of Vashti as queen occurred in the year 483 B.C. During the next four years Ahasuerus (Xerxes) was engaged in his battles against the Greeks. After his defeat at Plataea in 479, he returned to his capital at Shushan. It seems likely that the remaining events in the book of Esther (Est. 2–10) come in this period of the life of Ahasuerus, after 479. During this time Esther became the queen of Persia and was able to save her people, the Jews, from the machinations of Haman, who earlier had persuaded Ahasuerus to have the Jews killed (Est. 3:8–9, 13).

Archaeological Light on Susa, the Capital of Persia in the Days of Esther

The winter capital of Persia in the days of Darius and Xerxes (Ahasuerus)[7] was at Susa, known as Shushan in the Bible (Est. 1:2; Neh. 1:1). It is located about 150 miles northeast of the head of the Persian Gulf. In the summer the court moved to Ecbatana or Pasargadae in the mountains.

Susa has been excavated longer than any other site in Iran. Marcel and Jeanne Dieulafoy conducted the first systematic excavation there from 1884 to 1886. In 1897 the French delegation in Persia went out to start work at Susa under the leadership of Jacques de Morgan and continued until World War I. De Morgan found the Code of Hammurabi there in 1901. R. de Macquenen assumed directorship at the dig for the delegation after the war, to be followed by Roman Ghirshman. After Ghirshman's retirement in 1967, M. Jean Perrot took over leadership of the Susa excavation.

Susa is a very large site. Four gigantic mounds, covering an area of three hundred acres, stand up out of the plain on the east bank of the Shaur River, and a smaller mound rises west of the river.[8] Of special interest is the great Apadana mound, the southern part of which is covered with the magnificent palace of Darius (820 x 490 feet). This is normally described as a collection of rooms surrounding three open courts, a characteristic arrangement of Mesopotamian residences. But Frankfort casts doubt on this interpretation of the finds and questions whether a Mesopotamian element was introduced into otherwise typical Persian architecture.[9] The northern part of the Apadana mound was occupied by the great Apadana or audience hall or throne room. Originally built by Darius I, it burned and was later reconstructed by Artaxerxes II (404–359). The central hall had thirty-six majestic columns with bell-shaped bases and bull capitals, and the porticoes on two sides brought the total number of columns to seventy-two. The palace was decorated on the interior with glazed-brick panels that served as murals. Subject matter included Persian archers and spearmen, human-headed lions wearing Babylonian crowns, winged bulls, sphinxes, and griffons (FLAP, 243). Many of the remains from the site are now housed in the Susa rooms at the Louvre Museum in Paris.

---

[7] The Hebrew name Ahasuerus is fairly close to the Persian Khshayarsha; Xerxes was a name that the Greeks assigned to him.

[8] For a description of this site, see Sylvia Matheson, *Persia: An Archaeological Guide* (Park Ridge, N.J.: Noyes, 1973), 147–52.

[9] Henri Frankfort, *The Art and Architecture of the Ancient Orient*, rev. ed. (Harmondsworth, England: Penguin Books, 1970), 354.

Chapter 22

Rebuilding the Walls of Jerusalem

(Ezra, Nehemiah, Malachi, c. 458–435 B.C.)

The Persian Kings of the Fifth and Fourth Centuries B.C.

Since Palestine was subject to Persia, it will be helpful to list the Persian kings of the fifth and fourth centuries B.C. for reference in dealing with the backgrounds of this period of Bible history (that is, the period of Ezra and Nehemiah, as well as the last of the Old Testament prophets, Malachi):

Darius I	521–486
Xerxes (Ahasuerus)	485–465
Artaxerxes I	464–424
known as Longimanus	
("Longhand")	
Darius II	423–405
know also as	
Darius Nothus	
Artaxerxes II	404–359
Artaxerxes III	358–338
Arses	338–336
Darius III	335–330

Darius I was the Persian king who gave permission to resume the building of the temple at Jerusalem (Ezra 6:1–3, 7) and Xerxes was the Ahasuerus of the book of Esther (see the preceding chapter).

The Return of Ezra c. 458–457 B.C. in the Reign of Artaxerxes I, 464–424 (Ezra 7)

The first six chapters of Ezra deal with events that took place more than a generation before the time of Ezra. In these chapters, Ezra tells of the return under Sheshbazzar and Zerubbabel (Ezra 1:11; 2:2) about 536 B.C., of the laying of the foundation of the temple (3:10), the efforts of the adversaries to stop the work (4:1ff.), the encouragement of Haggai and Zechariah to complete the rebuilding of the temple (5:1ff.), and the completion of the temple in the year 515 (Ezra 6:15).

As has been noted, there is about a sixty-year silence in the book of Ezra between chapters six and seven, including the years 515–458 B.C. (see page 207); during this time the events of the book of Esther took place.

In chapter 7, Ezra begins with the events of his own life in the year 458 B.C. He tells that in the seventh year (458) of the reign of Artaxerxes, king of Persia, he went from Babylon to Jerusalem (Ezra 7:6–8), taking with him quite a company of people (8:1–20).

Ezra received the support of King Artaxerxes I, who made a decree that any of the people of Israel who were still in the region of Babylon would be permitted to return to Jerusalem with Ezra (7:12–13). Artaxerxes even made contributions of silver and gold to Ezra and his companions for the temple at Jerusalem (7:15, 20).

Arrival of Ezra in Jerusalem; Significance of the Twelve Bullocks; Revival and Reform (Ezra 8–10)

When Ezra and his companions arrived in Jerusalem (Ezra 8:32), they brought the treasures they had carried from Babylonia into the temple (v. 33), and also offered sacrifices, including twelve bullocks for all Israel (v. 35). The offering of the twelve bullocks for "all Israel" is an indication that the twelve tribes were in existence. This does not support the theory that ten of the tribes became lost and some of these lost tribes migrated across Europe to England and are the ancestors of the English people of today. The ten tribes were never lost, as shown by the offering of these twelve sacrifices representing all of the twelve tribes. Furthermore, the archaeological discoveries show that a large percentage of the people were not taken into captivity. Sargon, for example, tells us that he deported 27,290 of the inhabitants of Samaria.[1] This represented only a small fraction of the people in the northern kingdom; thus many people of the various tribes were never carried away, so no tribes could become "lost."

Ezra learned that the people of Israel who were living in the land had not kept themselves separated from the pagan people and their abominations (Ezra 9:1) and had also intermarried with the daughters of these people (v. 2). He prayed to the Lord and confessed the iniquities of the people (vv. 5–6), who then, taking cognizance of their sins, acknowledged that they had trespassed

in taking strange wives (10:1–2) and set the matter aright.

The Return of Nehemiah in 444 B.C. (Nehemiah 1–2)

Nehemiah, a Jew, was a cupbearer in the court of Artaxerxes I (Neh. 1:11), at Shushan, where the capital of the Persian Empire was located. (Archaeological discoveries at Susa have already been noted in the preceding chapter.) In the twentieth year of Artaxerxes, 445–444,[2] Nehemiah heard from his brother Hanani that the walls of the city of Jerusalem were in a broken-down condition (vv. 1–3). Nehemiah was grieved with this news, and his sadness was noticed by King Artaxerxes, who asked what the reason might be (2:1–2). Nehemiah told the king of the condition of the walls of Jerusalem and of his desire to return and build them. Artaxerxes gave Nehemiah permission and also letters of commendation to the Persian officials whom Nehemiah would meet when he got beyond the Euphrates River in his thousand-mile journey to Palestine (vv. 7–9). Nehemiah was also accorded an escort of horsemen from the army of the king, apparently arranged at the suggestion of Artaxerxes, for we have no mention of Nehemiah's requesting such a guard (v. 9).

Archaeological Confirmation of the Time of Nehemiah's Return

Nehemiah tells us that it was in the reign of Artaxerxes that he returned to Jerusalem to direct the rebuilding of the walls (Neh. 2:1). The question might arise as to whether this was Artaxerxes I or one of the other Artaxerxes who succeeded him (see the list of Persian Kings on page 209). Some scholars have tried to place the return of Ezra in the reign of Artaxerxes II (404–359). Confirmation con-

---

[1]LARA, 1:26, paragraph 55; PANET, 285.

[2]According to Nehemiah 1:1, the message from Palestine arrived in Chislev (Kislev), equivalent to December of 445 B.C. Thus Nehemiah's return to Jerusalem occurred in 444 B.C.

cerning the time of Nehemiah's return is found in the Elephantine papyri (see the section concerning the colony of Jews in Egypt, page 199), which show that it was in the reign of Artaxerxes I. These papyri were written in the generation after Nehemiah (about 408–407) and refer to some of the very persons mentioned as the contemporaries of Nehemiah in his book (BWMS, 83; FLAP, 238). Thus the return of Nehemiah occurred before 408 and of necessity in the reign of Artaxerxes I, since Artaxerxes II did not begin to rule until 404.

Archaeological Confirmation of Sanballat and Tobiah, Nehemiah's Adversaries (Nehemiah 2:10, 19; 4:1–3, 7–8; 6:1ff.)

Even before Nehemiah told of his arrival in Jerusalem (Neh 2:11), he said that Sanballat and Tobiah were grieved when they heard of his coming to seek the welfare of the children of Israel (v. 10). Sanballat and Tobiah proved to be the adversaries of Nehemiah and his people in their work to rebuild the wall of the city (v. 19; 4:1–3ff.). Archaeological confirmation of Sanballat is also found in the Elephantine papyri, which refer to Sanballat, governor of Samaria, and his two sons (AAPB, 170; BWMS, 108). In writing to the governor of Judea, the Jews of Elephantine tell of their desire to rebuild their temple; they conclude by saying, "Also the whole matter we have set forth in a letter in our name to Delaiah and Shelemiah the sons of Sanballat, governor of Samaria."[3]

Archaeological light on Sanballat's henchman, Tobiah, is also forthcoming from Egypt. The Zeno papyri were discovered at Gerza in the oasis of Egypt called the Fayum (AAPB, 170). They were written in the third century B.C., in the reign of Ptolemy II Philadelphus (285–246 B.C.),

and frequently deal with Palestine; one of these documents was actually written by a Tobias, a governor of Ammon in the region of Palestine to the east of the Jordan; this Tobias was undoubtedly a descendant of Nehemiah's adversary, "Tobiah the Ammonite" (Neh. 2:10; BWMS, 111).

Archaeological light on the family of Tobiah was also found in Transjordan itself. At Araq el-Emir, almost directly east of present-day Amman, are the ruins of a building that was the castle of the family of Tobias (BWMS, 133). The tombs of the Tobiad family are nearby, and the name Tobiah can be seen, deeply cut into their external wall in an archaic Aramaic script (AAPB, 171). Albright believed that the type of script could date back to 400 B.C., the time of Tobiah I (AAPB, 222, n. 111).

Nehemiah's Inspection Tour of the Walls of Jerusalem (Nehemiah 2:12–16)

After Nehemiah had been in Jerusalem only three days (Neh. 2:11), he made an inspection tour of the walls of the city by night (v. 12). Apparently he did not want to have any of the emissaries of Sanballat and Tobiah observing his actions so that they might lay plans to hinder the work of rebuilding the walls.

Nehemiah went out of Jerusalem by the Valley Gate, near the southwestern corner of the city and rode eastward along the wall in the Hinnon Valley, coming to the Dung Gate (Neh. 2:13) in the southern wall, and then to the Fountain Gate, which was probably near the Pool of Siloam, where the Siloam Conduit emptied out (see chapter 18, the section entitled "Hezekiah's Conduit," page 182).

When Nehemiah reached the Fountain Gate and the King's Pool, he says, "There was not enough room for my mount to get through; so I went up the valley by night, examining the wall" (Neh. 2:14–15).

---

[3]A. Cowley, *Aramaic Papyri of the Fifth Century* B.C. (Oxford: Clarendon, 1923), 114, Aramaic Papyrus No. 30 [CAP].

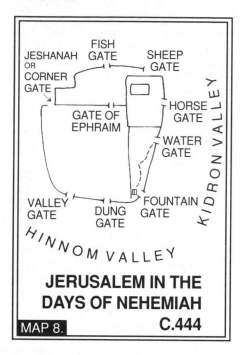

JESHANAH OR CORNER GATE
FISH GATE
SHEEP GATE
GATE OF EPHRAIM
HORSE GATE
WATER GATE
VALLEY GATE
DUNG GATE
FOUNTAIN GATE
KIDRON VALLEY
HINNOM VALLEY

JERUSALEM IN THE DAYS OF NEHEMIAH

MAP 8.　　　　C.444

interpretation he turned back, retracing his steps to the Valley Gate and entering the city again at this point from where he had gone out some time earlier (Neh. 2:15). We are not told why Nehemiah did not complete the circuit of the walls. Burrows suggests that he may have been able to see the condition of the rest of the wall without continuing his excursion, or that perhaps the breaches in the wall were the most serious on this side, or that he wished to gain only a general impression of the condition of the wall and, in order to avoid attracting attention, chose a relatively unfrequented part of the wall.[5] According to another interpretation of Nehemiah 2:15, Nehemiah just continued his survey, moving around the north of the city and thus returning to the point from which he had started. This is the intimation of the NASB, the REB, and the Jewish Publication Society translation.

Rebuilding the Walls and Gates of Jerusalem (Nehemiah 2:17–20; 3:1–32)

After surveying the wall of Jerusalem on his night tour of inspection, Nehemiah made a proposal to the people, saying, "Come, let us rebuild the wall of Jerusalem" (Neh. 2:17). Sanballat and Tobiah mocked and ridiculed them, but, undaunted, they went ahead with the construction work. Different sections of the wall and different gates were assigned to particular groups. The repair and rebuilding of the various gates with adjoining sections of wall is described in detail in Nehemiah 3. The names of the gates are given as follows:

The question as to what the valley was and why Nehemiah could not continue to ride his donkey has intrigued Bible scholars. Burrows points out that the term valley (Hebrew *nahal*, ravine) is often applied to the Kidron Valley (2 Sam. 5:23; 1 Kings 2:37; 15:13; 18:40; 23:6, 12, et al.). He believes that Nehemiah had, up to this point, been following the base of the wall along the southern side of the city but now came to the eastern wall, which was on the crest of a steep slope that was almost like a cliff and did not leave room at the foot of the wall for even a donkey to find his way. For this reason, Nehemiah proceeded along the stream bed at the bottom of the Kidron Valley.[4]

After Nehemiah had gone north along the Kidron Valley for a way and had inspected the wall, according to one

1. Sheep Gate (v. 1)
2. Fish Gate (v. 3)
3. Jeshanah Gate (v. 6), elsewhere called the Old Gate or Corner Gate

---

[4]Millar Burrows, "Nehemiah's Tour of Inspection," BASOR 64 (December 1936); 18–20; VENE, 92–94.

[5]Ibid., 21.

4. Broad Wall[6] (v. 8), running from the Jeshanah Gate to the Tower of the Ovens
5. Tower of the Ovens (v. 11)
6. Valley Gate (v. 13)
7. Dung Gate (v. 14)
8. Fountain Gate (v. 15)
9. Water Gate (v. 26)
10. Horse Gate (v. 28)
11. East Gate (v. 29)
12. Inspection Gate (v. 31)

Sanballat and his henchman, Tobiah, mocked the Jews again, Tobiah remarking that if a fox went up on the wall, he would break it down (Neh. 4:3). Nehemiah looked to the Lord and continued the work, finding it necessary when the opposition grew fierce to have the builders wear their swords while they labored on the wall with their hands (v. 18). In spite of all the opposition, the walls were completed in fifty-two days (6:15). Then the people assembled and Ezra read the word of God to them (8:1–8).

Archaeological Confirmation of the Reference to the Drachma in Nehemiah (7:70)

In connection with some of the gifts that were given for the work of rebuilding at Jerusalem, one gift of one thousand drachmas is recorded (Neh. 7:70). The Hebrew word translated "dram" in the KJV and "daric" in the ASV is actually the Hebrew word for drachma and is so translated in the NASB, the NIV, and other newer versions. Some scholars have doubted the validity of this reference to

the drachma, a Greek coin, in the book of Nehemiah on the basis of a preconceived idea that the system of Greek coinage would not have been spread abroad until after the conquests of Alexander the Great (c. 330 B.C.). This would be over a century too late for the time of Nehemiah (c. 450). Some scholars, including C.C. Torrey, have used this reference to the drachma as an argument for dating the composition of Nehemiah much later than the time when Nehemiah actually lived (ARDBL, 37; AOTA, 154). This line of argument supported the critical view of Nehemiah, which holds that Ezra, Nehemiah, and Chronicles were all written by the same man, who is usually referred to as "the Chronicler" and is dated about 250 B.C. (PIOT, 812–13, 830).

Information on the drachma came to hand when the site of Beth Zur, several miles south of Jerusalem, was excavated in 1931.[7] The excavators found in the Persian level (c. 530–330 B.C.) six drachma coins (AAPB, 227), proving that the drachma was known in Palestine in the Persian period and that Nehemiah could have mentioned it about 450 B.C. without being "ahead of himself." This confirmation was effectively pointed out by W.F. Albright, who stated that the critical arguments for the late date of the "chronicler" have been disproved by such discoveries as the Elephantine papyri[8] and the evidence for the use of the drachma standard in Palestine during the period 450–330.[9] Albright commented that Pfeiffer was "far behind the van of Old Testament scholarship" when he assigned the "Chronicler" to the period of 250 B.C. and described the

---

[6]Nahman Avigad, in his recent excavations in the Jewish Quarter, on the Southwestern Hill in Jerusalem, uncovered a two-hundred-foot section of this wall, which was about twenty-three feet thick. He ascribed the wall to the building activities of Hezekiah. See Nahman Avigad, "The Upper City," in *Biblical Archaeology Today* (Jerusalem: Israel Exploration Society, 1985), 471.

[7]O.R. Sellers, *The Citadel of Beth-zur* (Philadelphia: Westminster, 1933), 69–71ff. [SCB].

[8]See this book, chapter 21, for the significance of the Elephantine papyri.

[9]See W.F. Albright's review of Pfeiffer, PIOT, in JBL (June 1942), 126. Cf. AJA (April–June 1944), 185, which points out that an Attic drachma imitation was found near Hebron and that Athenian silver money had become almost international currency in the fifth century B.C.

memoirs of Ezra as "confused and legendary"[10] (see also ASOTI, 410–16).

Later Years of Nehemiah

During the years following 444 B.C., Nehemiah was not in Jerusalem all of the time. His brother Hananiah was put in charge of the city (Neh. 7:2), but in the year 433–432 (the thirty-second year of Artaxerxes, Neh. 13:6–7), Nehemiah found it necessary to return to Jerusalem and set some things aright. The Levites had not been given their portion (v. 10), the Sabbath was not observed by some (v. 15), and intermarriage with pagan people had been practiced by others (vv. 23ff.).

Malachi; the End of the Old Testament; the Four Hundred Silent Years

The prophet Malachi fits into the time of Nehemiah. The references to offerings (Mal. 1:7, 10) and to the temple (3:1) show that the temple had already been rebuilt (515 B.C.) and the worship established. The sins that Malachi rebuked are similar to those denounced by Nehemiah, among them intermarriage with pagans (Mal. 2:11). Pfeiffer dated Malachi too early (460 B.C., PIOT, 614). Raven suggested that Malachi may have written in 432, when Nehemiah was at the court at Susa (ROTI, 249), possibly indicated by the fact that when Malachi refers to the governor of the Jews, he does not mention Nehemiah but merely refers to "the governor" (Mal. 1:8). On various bases, Archer concludes that the date of Malachi was about 435 (ASOTI, 431–32), and he is probably right.

With the writing of Nehemiah and Malachi, the Old Testament books come to an end, shortly before 400 B.C. The intervening period of silence that came to an end with the writing of the New Testament books is often called the "Four Hundred Silent Years," for there was no recorded prophetic utterance until the days of John the Baptist. Persia (539–331 B.C.) and Greece (331 and after) were the great powers during this time. References to these powers during this period of four hundred years are not entirely lacking in the Bible, inasmuch as the Persians facilitated Jewish return to Palestine and Daniel gave specific prophecies concerning them. We will study this era in the next chapter.

[10]Albright, review of Pfeiffer, 126.

Chapter 23

Palestine Under Persia, Greece, and Egypt in the Intertestamental Period, c. 435–200 B.C.

The Close of the Old Testament, c. 435 B.C.

The Old Testament books had all been written by the time of the later years of Ezra, about 425–420 B.C., the last books being Nehemiah and Malachi, whose internal evidence points to the period 435–430. Critics hold that some of the books of the Old Testament were written later than 400, placing Ezra, Nehemiah, and Chronicles about 250 (PIOT, 812, 830), Daniel about 168–165 (PIOT, 765), and Esther about 125 (PIOT, 742). Many archaeological and linguistic discoveries present a formidable argument against the dating of these books in the late period. Events once supposed by critics to have been late are now known to have been early, for example, the return of Nehemiah has been shown to have been before 400, rather than after, through the evidence of the Elephantine papyri.[1]

Conservatives have held in the past that the Old Testament was completed by about 425–420 B.C., and true conservatives still maintain that. Liberals have presented no conclusive evidence to alter this view. Furthermore, there are specific reasons for adhering to this early date. We may cite, in addition to archaeological evidence, the following reasons for holding to the date of 425–420, in the days of Ezra, as the time when the Old Testament was completed:

1. *The testimony of Josephus.* The Jewish historian Josephus (first century A.D.) indicated that the canon of the Old Testament was completed in the reign of Artaxerxes Longimanus (464–424 B.C.; he is Artaxerxes I; see list on page 209), which would be in the time of Ezra.[2] As Green remarks,

> Strenuous efforts have been made to discredit this statement of Josephus, but without good reason. It has been said that it is not based on reliable historical information, nor the general belief of his time, but is

[1]See the preceding chapter; cf. also the significance of the discovery of the drachma in showing that Nehemiah need not be dated late on the ground of the mention of this Greek coin; see chapter 22, pages 213–14.

[2]W.H. Green, *General Introduction to the Old Testament: The Canon* (New York: Scribners, 1898), pp. 37, 38 [GIC]. For a new study of the canonicity of both the Old and New Testaments, see F.F. Bruce, *The Canon of Scripture* (Downers Grove, Ill.: InterVarsity, 1988).

merely a private opinion of his own. It is obvious, however, that this cannot be the case. Josephus was a man of considerable learning, and had every facility for acquainting himself with the history of his own nation, upon which he had written largely in his "Antiquities." His priestly origin afforded him special opportunities for becoming familiar with the religious opinions of his countrymen . . . he gives no intimation that what he here says is simply his own opinion. It is stated as a certain and acknowledged fact.[3]

2. *The character of Ezra.* Ezra was especially concerned with the sacred books; he is called "the scribe" (Neh. 8:1, 4, 9, 13), and also "a teacher well versed in the Law of Moses" (Ezra 7:6). His concern with the books of Scripture would make him a likely and appropriate person to have collected the books of the Old Testament.

3. *The nature of Ezra's time.* Ezra's time was such that the collection of the sacred books may have appropriately been made then. After the Exile, the people were founding anew the religious institutions of the nation. What would be more natural than to gather the volumes of the sacred library? (ROTI, 33).

The Jews in Palestine During the Intertestamental Period (After 420 B.C.)

There is a paucity of material on this period of history in Palestine after 420 B.C. Our two main sources are the Jewish historian, Josephus, and the apocryphal books of the Old Testament.[4] From the indications in the last books of the Old Testament (Nehemiah, Ezra, and Malachi) and from Josephus, we know that there was no longer a king ruling in Jerusalem, as there had been before the Exile. The House of David had disappeared from sight,[5] and now the leader was the high priest, and his family was the royal family. The life of the people of Palestine from this time on was ecclesiastical rather than political. The priests ruled by the law, which was impressed upon the people by public reading, evidenced already in the days of Ezra, when he read the Book of the Law to the assembled multitude in Jerusalem (Neh. 8:1ff.). Gregg says that the priests held the people to the law and the people held the priests to the law; this was a step toward democracy because it elevated the law to the place of king and made both the priests and the people guardians of the rights defined by the law. The people as well as the priests then had a voice, making for democracy, in the opinion of Gregg (GBT, 49–50). The political situation in Palestine during this period after 420 B.C. is dealt with in the next section.

Palestine Subject to Persia
Until 331 B.C.

The main period of Persian history began with Cyrus' capture of Babylon in 539 B.C. (see chapter 20; for a list of the main Persian kings see chapter 22, page 209). During the rule of Cyrus (539–530), the Jews were allowed to return from captivity to the land of Judah (southern

---

[3]Green, *General Introduction*, 38.

[4]David Gregg, *Between the Testaments, or Interbiblical History* (New York: Funk and Wagnalls, 1907), 49 [GBT]. For a new translation of the apocryphal books, see *The Revised English Bible with the Apocrypha*, 1989. For some useful books on the Intertestamental period, see William Fairweather, *The Background of the Gospels*, 4th ed. (Edinburgh: T. & T. Clark, 1926); Michael Grant, *From Alexander to Cleopatra* (New York: Scribner, 1982); Peter Green, *Alexander to Actium* (Berkeley, Calif.: University of California Press, 1990); Erich S. Gruen, *The Hellenistic World and the Coming of Rome*, 2 vols. (Berkeley, Calif.: University of California Press, 1984); Charles F. Pfeiffer, *Between the Testaments* (Grand Rapids: Baker, 1959).

[5]This does not mean, however, that God had broken the Davidic covenant. The Davidic line continued, though not on the throne, and reappeared with the birth of Christ. The Davidic line, culminating in Christ, is summarized in the genealogy of Christ (Matt. 1:1–17).

Palestine). With the permission of Darius (521–486) they were allowed to resume the rebuilding of the temple at Jerusalem, which was finished in 515 (see chapter 21). The events of the book of Esther took place during the reign of Xerxes (Ahasuerus of the book of Esther, 485–465; see this book, chapter 21). The next Persian king, Artaxerxes I (Longimanus, 464–424), allowed Ezra to return to Palestine in 458–457 and gave permission for Nehemiah to return in 444 to supervise the rebuilding of the walls of Jerusalem (see chapter 22). If the Jewish historian Josephus is correct when he states that the Old Testament was completed in the reign of this same Artaxerxes, this would indicate a date of about 425–420 at the latest, since the usual date given for the end of the reign of Artaxerxes I is either 424 or 423.[6]

With the successors of Artaxerxes I (464–424 B.C.), we enter the intertestamental period. When Artaxerxes I died, there was a struggle for the throne among three of his sons. The one who gained the day, by means of forming an army to back him, came to the throne as Darius II, also known as Darius Nothus (423–405). At this time Egypt was a part of the Persian Empire. When the Persian ruler of Egypt, Arsames, left the land temporarily to make a report to Darius II in the year 411, native Egyptians attacked the Jewish colony on the island of Elephantine, located at the first cataract (RHAP, 197). The Jewish temple on the island was destroyed; three years later, in 408, these Jews wrote to Bigvai, the Persian governor in Jerusalem, to enlist his aid in persuading the chief Persian authorities to give them permission to rebuild their temple. These very letters were found about 1900 A.D. on the island of Elephantine and are known as the Elephantine papyri; they even mention such biblical characters as Sanballat, the opponent of Nehemiah (see chapter 22, the section entitled "Archaeological Confirmation of Sanballat. . . ," page 211; see also chapter 20, the section entitled "Archaeological Evidence of a Colony of Jews in Egypt. . . ," page 199).[7]

When Darius II died in 405 B.C., two of his sons, Arsikas and Cyrus the Younger sought the throne. Arsikas gained the throne, taking the name of Artaxerxes II (404–359). Cyrus, however, did not give up hope of taking the throne of Persia. Earlier, in 408, he had been appointed Persian ruler (satrap) over the territory of Lydia in Asia Minor and had established a power base there. Cyrus was able to build up an army consisting of a great number of Greek mercenaries, and finally in the year 401 he was ready to attack his brother, Artaxerxes II, who was on the throne of Persia. Cyrus marched across Asia Minor and finally joined battle at Cunaxa, probably the modern site of Kunisch, about fifty-one miles north of Babylon.

During the battle, the forces of King Artaxerxes II gave way in a rout. Cyrus saw the king and rushed upon him, ready to give the death blow in another moment, but Cyrus himself fell, the victim of a javelin thrust. "So died Cyrus; a man the kingliest and most worthy to rule of all the Persians who have lived since the elder Cyrus: according to the concurrent testimony of all who are reputed to have known him intimately" (Xenophon, *Anabasis*, I, 9, cited in RHAP, 212). Some 10,000 of the Greek mercenaries who had been in the army of Cyrus the Younger began their trek back to the west, a journey described in the famous *Anabasis* of Xenophon. Of the original 10,000, some 8,600

---

[6]The Parker-Dubberstein date is 423 B.C. The evidence from the clay tablets shows that Artaxerxes I was recognized as king until the end of December 424, and possibly as late as the following February. Darius II was king, and tablets were dated as in his reign, by the middle of February 423 (PDBC, 16).

[7]Rogers, RHAP, 198, gives a good brief bibliography of the publication of the Elephantine papyri.

came through to the Black Sea (RHAP, 216).

Artaxerxes II was succeeded by a son, Ochos, who took the name Artaxerxes III (358–338 B.C.). He died in 338, poisoned by a physician at the behest of the court eunuch, Bagoas (RHAP, 255). Bagoas then put a son of Artaxerxes III on the throne, one named Arses, but Arses had too much a mind of his own, and Bagoas had him put out of the way also. Bagoas then put another man of the royal line on the throne, who, adopting the name Darius, set about to make sure that he had a firm grip on the throne. Seeing what Bagoas had done to others, he anticipated his schemes; Bagoas was poisoned, as he had poisoned others, and thus Darius III was able to occupy the throne with more assurance. He became king in 335, a few months after Alexander the Great became king of Macedonia. These two monarchs were to confront each other in the ensuing years.

During all of this time Palestine was also a part of the Persian Empire. The empire was divided into provinces, called satrapies, each one being governed by an officer called a satrap. Palestine fell within the boundaries of the Fifth Persian Satrapy, with its capital either at Damascus or Samaria.

The Conquests of Alexander the Great, 334–323 B.C.

In 336 B.C. Alexander the Great became king of Macedonia, the region to the north of Greece. Before his accession to the throne, his father Philip had defeated the city states of Greece at the battle of Chaeronea in 338 and had formed the League of Corinth, which he dominated. When Alexander took the reins of government, many of the Greek states were still very restless. Thebes revolted, and Alex-

ander resubjugated and utterly destroyed it, sparing only the house of the great poet, Pindar.[8] This act of ferocity cowed the rest of Greece, and Alexander was free to pursue his father's goal of launching a Panhellenic War against the Persians.

In the year 334 B.C. Alexander crossed the Hellespont and invaded Asia Minor. He had a formidable army of about 48,000 and some 16,000 support personnel, for a total of about 65,000. The cavalry units consisted of over 6,000 horses.[9]

At the River Granicus, which flows into the Hellespont, Alexander met the Persian forces of the western satraps (334 B.C.). He crossed the river unopposed and engaged the Persian forces in battle, putting them into hopeless flight. The victory was significant, for it showed the superiority of the Greek cavalry to that of the Persians. The psychological effect was important also, for the Persian Empire began to crack, with the cities of western Asia surrendering to Alexander without battle (RHAP, 272–73). After the victory at the Granicus, Alexander pushed boldly eastward, following the route of the 10,000 of Cyrus the Younger (see preceding section), traversing the difficult pass at the Cilician Gates near the northeastern corner of the Mediterranean (BCC, 433), and descending into the Plains of Issus.

There Alexander met the main army of Persia under the personal command of Darius III (335–330 B.C.) in the year 333. As the two armies joined battle, Alexander himself was in charge of one cavalry unit, 12,000 strong, which drove into the Persian left wing with great force, causing the opposing unit to yield ground at once. The rest of the Persian army made a sturdy resistance, and their superior numbers gave them great advantage, but Alexander drove into the flank of the mercenaries of Darius, and it broke in confusion. This turned the tide, though

---

[8]J.H. Breasted, *The Conquest of Civilization* (New York: Harper, 1926), 431 [BCC].

[9]Donald W. Engels, *Alexander the Great and the Logistics of the Macedonian Army* (Berkeley, Calif.: University of California Press, 1978), 18.

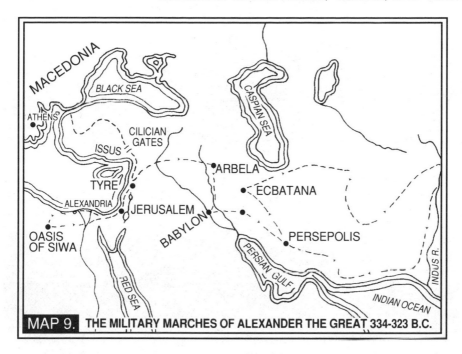

MAP 9. THE MILITARY MARCHES OF ALEXANDER THE GREAT 334-323 B.C.

much hard fighting remained to be done. At the first opportunity Alexander headed for Darius in person, knowing that he would be sitting in royal splendor in a chariot behind the center of the army. As Alexander and his unit fought in this direction, Darius was soon surrounded with the wounded and dead who fell before the Macedonians, and it was only with great difficulty that Darius was extricated by his brother and placed on a lighter chariot so that they were able to flee to the rear. He escaped none too soon, for if they had stayed a little longer, Darius would surely have been captured or killed (RHAP, 289–90). A representation of Alexander's attack on the bodyguard of Darius III at the Battle of Issus was found in the excavations at Pompeii in 1831; it is over 2000 years old, since Pompeii was destroyed by volcanic action in 79 A.D. The scene is a mosaic, made to form a floor pavement; it shows Alexander's spear

piercing the body of one of the noblemen who is protecting Darius as the Persians are hastily removing Darius from the field of battle. (For a reproduction of this mosaic, see BCC, figure 169, p. 432.)

Darius's flight from the Battle of Issus continued until he finally crossed the Euphrates River (RHAP, 291). He sent a letter to Alexander, asking for terms of peace and offering to accept the Euphrates as the boundary between their domains (BCC, 434). Alexander replied with a stiff letter, which began,

> Your forefathers came into Macedonia and into the rest of Greece and did us harm, without any previous injury from us. Now I, having been appointed leader of the Greeks and wishing to punish the Persians, have crossed into Asia. . . . My father was killed by conspirators whom you instigated, as you have boasted to everybody in your letters.

Alexander closed by saying that if Darius wished to receive his mother, his wife,

A street in the city of Tyre during the Roman period

and his children,[10] he should come before him, and whatsoever was just should be his; furthermore Darius was to address him as Lord of Asia, not as an equal, and to speak of him as lord of all his possessions; if Darius disputed his right to the kingdom, he would have to fight for it (RHAP, 296–97).

Alexander then decided to march south from Issus, going through Syria, Phoenicia, Palestine, and down into Egypt (RHAP, 294). His fame preceded his army, and as he moved south, one city after another surrendered, including Aradus, Byblus, and Sidon (RHAP, 297). When Alexander came to the city of Tyre, it was a different story.

Alexander's Siege of Tyre a Fulfillment of Ezekiel's Prophecy (Ezekiel 26)

More than 250 years before the time of Alexander, the prophet Ezekiel predicted that the city of Tyre would be destroyed (Ezek. 26:3). Specifically, he foretold that Nebuchadnezzar would besiege Tyre, breach the walls, and destroy the city (Ezek. 26:7–12). (Parenthetically, it should be noted that Tyre was a two-part city: a formidable bastion on land and a well-fortified island city about a half mile from the coast.) This part of the prophecy was fulfilled a few years after it was made, for the army of Nebuchadnezzar came up against Tyre and besieged the city for thirteen years (585–573 B.C., RHAP, 298). Before the fall of the land city of Tyre, however, the inhabitants moved most of their possessions to their island city. The ruins of the land city were left there, but the island city continued on and was a thriving metropolis when Alexander came down this part of the Mediterranean coast in 333–332.

Through Ezekiel God had also prophe-

---

[10]When Darius fled at Issus, he abandoned his mother, his wife, his two daughters, and his infant son (OHPE, 504).

sied, "They will throw your stones, timber, and rubble into the sea. . . . I will make you a bare rock, and you will become a place to spread fishnets" (Ezek. 26:12, 14). How amazing to take the worthless remains of a city and dump them in the water! Surely manpower could be put to a more useful task than that. The fulfillment, however, came in the campaign of Alexander against Tyre.

When Alexander first approached the island city of Tyre, there was a willingness to surrender. But when he demanded permission to enter the city and offer worship at the temple of the god Melkart, he was refused (RHAP, 297). The citizens of Tyre declined to accept his request on the ground that they wished to maintain neutrality in the conflict between Macedonia and Persia. Alexander began the siege of the city and found it necessary to labor for seven months before capturing it (RHAP, 298). He decided to build a causeway, using cedars from the Lebanon Mountains as piles and the debris from the old land city as material for constructing it. As the water became deeper farther out, the difficulties of the workmen increased; they were also hindered in every possible way by the people of Tyre, who had a good navy. In order to meet this challenge, Alexander left the construction of the causeway to his "army engineers" and went north to collect ships. The kings of Aradus and Byblus on the coast of Syria placed their ships at his disposal; from the island of Cyprus he was able to secure 120 ships, from Sidon about 80. With a fleet of some 220 warships, Alexander was more than a match for the sizeable, but smaller fleet of the Tyrians (RHAP, 299). After seven months, the causeway was brought up to the walls of the island city of Tyre in August 332 B.C.[11] The wall was breached from the causeway, and part of the fleet of Tyre was sunk. With the capture of the city, thousands of the inhabitants were sold in the slave market, 13,000 according to Arrian, and 30,000, according to Diodorus (RHAP, 300).

Ezekiel's prophecy concerning the throwing of the stones, timber, and rubble into the sea (Ezek. 26:12) was specifically fulfilled when Alexander's engineers built the causeway and used the remains of the ancient land city of Tyre, throwing them into the water.

Alexander's Siege of Gaza, 332 B.C.

After the siege of Tyre, Alexander proceeded down the coast of Phoenicia and Palestine, receiving the submission of the towns he encountered until he came to Gaza in southern Palestine, some 150 miles south of Tyre (RHAP, 301). Gaza had once been on the seacoast, but its harbor had silted up, and the city now lay about two miles inland on a mound over sixty feet high. Its elevation made it impossible for an army to attack it with siege machines in the usual manner. Alexander decided to build a mound beside the city, from which to attack with his siege machines. From this elevation he was able to break through the massive fortifications. After fierce combat with the gallant garrison of Gaza, Alexander took the city, and 10,000 men were slain, according to the ancient historians (RHAP, 302). The rest of the population was sold into slavery. The siege had required two months but was well worth the effort, for it raised the prestige of the Macedonian army another notch; and furthermore, valuable stores from the rich commercial city of Gaza had been added to the quartermaster department of Alexander's military machine.

---

[11]There is an excellent account in Dodge, *Alexander*, 327ff., cited in RHAP, 298. These dramatic events are summarized in A.T. Olmstead, *History of the Persian Empire* (University of Chicago Press, 1948), 506–7 [OHPE].

Josephus's Record of Alexander's Visit to Jerusalem

Josephus, the Jewish historian of the first century A.D., relates that after Alexander had taken Gaza, he made haste to go to the city of Jerusalem.[12] According to Josephus's story, the high priest Jaddua was at first frightened, but God had warned him in a dream that he should meet Alexander without fear of any evil consequences. Jaddua was to appear in his priestly garments, and the people were to be dressed in white garments. When Alexander approached Jerusalem, he saw the procession of priests and people and saluted the high priest. When one of Alexander's men asked why he treated the high priest so respectfully, Alexander replied that he had seen this very person in these very clothes in a dream while he was still in Macedonia.[13] In the dream, the high priest told Alexander to come over with his army, and he would have dominion over the Persians.

After the meeting with the high priest and the other priests, Alexander is said by Josephus to have gone to the temple in Jerusalem and to have offered sacrifice to God. When the book of Daniel was shown to Alexander, and he saw where Daniel indicated that one of the Greeks should destroy the empire of the Persians, Alexander supposed he was that person.

Whether or not this event actually occurred cannot be proved. It is likely that some of the details are in error, even if the story as a whole is substantially correct. Albright has pointed out that it is unlikely that Jaddua would have been the high priest as late as 332 B.C., since the Elephantine papyri showed that his father, Johanan, was high priest as early as 411, some eighty years earlier (ARDBL, 36–37). In any case, it is an interesting story and probably at least reflects the Jewish attitude toward Alexander.

Alexander in Egypt, 331 B.C.

From southern Palestine, Alexander made a hard march of seven days and arrived in the delta of Egypt (RHAP, 303), going from there to the city of Memphis at the south end of the delta. Here Alexander paid every honor to the cult of the Apis bull, enlisting the support of the Egyptian people. From Memphis, he went north to the Mediterranean and determined to build a city on the northwestern corner of the delta, to bear the name Alexandria. Even Alexander could not have envisaged at that time what this city would become, for by 60 B.C. it had a total population of half a million and was considered the greatest city in the world (RHAP, 306). While Alexander's architect was sketching plans for the new city, the king went two hundred miles westward along the Mediterranean coast and then due south another two hundred miles to the oasis now known as the Oasis of Siwa, where in ancient times was located the famous temple dedicated to the Egyptian god Amon.[14] One day as Alexander left the shrine of the god, the high priest of the temple addressed him as the son of Zeus-Amon (BCC, 440). This idea that he was a deity became a part of Alexander's plan for establishing his control over his empire.

Alexander at Arbela (331 B.C.); the End of His Life

Early in the spring of 331 B.C., Alexander left Egypt, marching up the coast of Palestine and Phoenicia to the city of Tyre. After completing governmental arrangements at Tyre, he left in June or July 331, going up the Lebanon Valley, and then by way of the Orontes Valley to

---

[12]Josephus, *Antiquities of the Jews*, XI.8.4 [JAJ].
[13]Ibid.
[14]For a drawing of this oasis, see BCC, Fig. 171, p. 441.

Antioch and on to the Euphrates, which he crossed with two bridges of boats, prepared by the engineers (RHAP, 317–18). He moved north and crossed the Tigris River on September 20, 331. On October 1, 331, Alexander and Darius were ready to begin the conflict (RHAP, 321) at Gaugamela, eighteen miles northeast of Nineveh. Darius had not kept up on the progress of military developments, and his army was as out of date as that of France in 1940. The Persians had devised one new weapon, a body of chariots with scythes attached to the sides for the purpose of mowing down the enemy (BCC, 436). But this was no more effective in gaining the day than was the Maginot Line in saving France in World War II. The army of Alexander crushed the Persians, and Darius III departed in ignominious flight, only to be stabbed a little later by his own treacherous attendants (BCC, 437). When Alexander arrived at the spot, he threw over the lifeless body of Darius III his own red robe in token of royal respect. Later he sent the body to Persepolis and gave it a royal burial (RHAP, 342).

After stopping at Babylon, Alexander went on to Susa and then to Persepolis, where he set fire to the Persian palace with his own hand (BCC, 437). After touching at Ecbatana in the north, Alexander proceeded across the Iranian plateau, across the Idus River, and into the frontiers of India, stopped only by the murmuring of his troops, who were not inclined to go farther eastward. He descended the Indus, touched the waters of the Indian Ocean, and finally undertook the arduous journey back to Mesopotamia, arriving at Babylon in 323 B.C., more than seven years after he had left it (BCC, 438). There he contracted a fever (perhaps malaria) and died after only a few days of illness, at the age of thirty-three.

The Division of Alexander's Kingdom; Palestine Subject to Ptolemy of Egypt, 301–198 B.C.

After the death of Alexander, a struggle followed among his generals. Macedonia finally came under the control of Antigonus, the grandson of Alexander's great general of the same name. Most of the territory in Asia that had formerly been included in the Persian Empire came under the rule of Alexander's general, Seleucus, whose line of successors is known as the Seleucid rulers, with their center at Antioch. Africa came into the possession of Ptolemy, one of the cleverest of Alexander's Macedonian leaders. His successors formed the Ptolemaic line in Egypt, with headquarters in Alexandria. Palestine ultimately fell to Ptolemy as part of his domain and remained under the Ptolemies from 301 to 198 B.C. The introduction of Greco-Macedonian culture (Hellenism) into Palestine was actively pursued by Ptolemy Philadelphus (285–246), who rebuilt such places as Ashod and Askelon, and restored the city of Rabbath-Ammon in Transjordan under the name of Philadelphia.

The Ptolemies seem to have been quite moderate in their treatment of the Jews. They encouraged a large colony of Jews to settle in Alexandria, Egypt, where they soon forgot their native tongue and required a translation of the Hebrew Bible into Greek. Produced during the period of about 250–150 B.C., this translation is called the Septuagint. Other aspects of Hellenism also made their inroads into Judaism, and some Jews came to follow a Hellenistic mindset and way of life, including a denial of the supernatural. Many Palestinian Jews also became Hellenized, and some of them became ancestors of the later Sadducees.

Chapter 24

Palestine Under Syria, the Maccabees, and the Hasmoneans in the Intertestamental Period, c. 200–63 B.C.

Seleucid Kings of Syria in the Second Century B.C.

The background of the history of Palestine in the second century B.C. is connected with the Seleucid kings of Syria, who are listed below:

Antiochus III, the Great	223–187
Seleucus IV, Philopator	187–175
Antiochus IV, Epiphanes	175–163
Antiochus V, Eupator	163–162
Demetrius I, Soter	162–150
Alexander Balas	150–145
Demetrius II, Nicator	145–139, 129–125

Palestine Passes to Syria in the Reign of Antiochus III, the Great (223–187 B.C.), in the Year 198 B.C.

For about one hundred years, Palestine had been subject to the Ptolemies of Egypt. In the year 202 B.C., Antiochus the Great of Syria pushed into the south of Palestine as far as Gaza but was driven north again by the Egyptian army under a man named Scopas. Finally at the battle of Panion (or Banias), at the sources of the Jordan in northern Palestine, Antiochus

gained an overwhelming victory over Scopas in the year 201–200. Scopas fled with the remnant of his army to Sidon, where Antiochus besieged him; the garrison was finally starved out by 199, and Scopas surrendered. By 198 all of Syria, including Palestine, was subject to Antiochus. His policy toward the Jews was friendly, following the pattern of the Ptolemies of Egypt in their treatment of the Jews in Palestine.

The Pro-Egyptian Party and the Pro-Syrian Party in the Days of Antiochus IV (175–163 B.C.)

For many years, the high priesthood of the Jews was vested in the house of Onias, but in the days of Antiochus IV the house of Tobias rose in opposition. Josephus tells how Onias got the upper hand and cast the sons of Tobias out of Jerusalem, and they fled to Antiochus IV.[1] Thus it appears that the house of Onias was pro-Egyptian and favored the orthodox Jews who clung to the faith and the practice of their religion as it had been handed down, while the house of Tobias represented the pro-Syrian party.

---

[1] Josephus, *Wars of the Jews*, I.1.1.

Antiochus IV Takes Advantage of the Rivalry in the Priestly Group

At this point something of a bidding war for the high priesthood seems to have taken place. Joshua, Onias's brother, evidently in the pro-Syrian party, paid a huge bribe for appointment as high priest and the right to build a gymnasium in Jerusalem (2 Macc. 4:8–10). Taking the Greek name Jason, Joshua proceeded to build a gymnasium to introduce athletic competition in the nude and to encourage other actions totally repugnant to the orthodox Jews. The orthodox organized under the name *Hasidim* (pious), a movement from which the Pharisees eventually came.

After three years in office (175–172), Jason was deposed by a close associate, Menelaus, who outbid him in the bribery game (2 Macc. 4:23–26), and Jason fled to Transjordan. Menelaus proved to be an even more thoroughgoing Hellenist than Jason and more unscrupulous as well. Jason waited impatiently in Transjordan for a chance to regain his lost position. Finally, in 168, when Antiochus was busy with a military campaign in Egypt, Jason raised a force and attacked Jerusalem. The disorders that followed evidently were clashes primarily between those loyal to Jason and Menelaus on the one hand and the pro-Egyptian and pro-Syrian factions on the other, but Antiochus chose to regard them as open rebellion against his rule. He sent a force to Jerusalem that broke down the walls, destroyed many houses, slaughtered countless inhabitants, and built a fortified citadel for a Syrian garrison.

Light from the Books of the Maccabees on the Situation in Palestine in the Reign of Antiochus IV of Syria (175–164 B.C.)

Much of our knowledge of the activities of Antiochus IV (175–163 B.C.) in relation to the Jews in Palestine comes from two apocryphal books called First and Second Maccabees which appear in modern English in *The Revised English Bible with the Apocrypha* (1989). Although we do not regard the apocryphal books as inspired, they are often helpful in supplying historical background and details not otherwise available. In dealing with this period of intertestamental history in the second century B.C. (c. 175–135), the books of the Maccabees provide material that otherwise would be lacking.

The Abominations of Antiochus IV (175–164 B.C.) Against the Jews

The quarrel between Onias and Jason concerning the high priesthood, and the subsequent machinations of Menelaus gave Antiochus IV the opportunity he apparently desired to wreak his hatred on the Jews in the spoliation of Jerusalem, the defilement of the temple, and a horrible persecution.

First Maccabees relates that Antiochus entered the sanctuary of the temple and took away the golden altar, the lampstand, and the other sacred vessels (1 Macc. 1:23) and then slaughtered many of the men (v. 25). Antiochus decreed that the people should forsake their own law, and as a result many of the Jews sacrificed to idols and profaned the Sabbath (vv. 43, 45). He order that idols be erected, pagan altars set up, and sacrifices of unclean animals offered (v. 50). Those who refused to act according to the word of Antiochus were to be put to death, and many of the people of Israel chose to die rather than to be defiled by unclean things (v. 65).

In 168 B.C. Antiochus IV reached a peak in his abominable crimes against the Jews. On the holy altar at Jerusalem he erected a pagan altar on which he sacrificed the flesh of swine, an animal unclean to the Jews. Both the first book of the Maccabees (1:50, 57ff.) and Josephus (JAJ, XII.5.4) tell of this sacrifice of pigs in the holy place and of the further command that the Jews were not to circumcise their children. Women who were found to have circumcised their sons were hanged on crosses and their children hanged about their necks. If any copy of the Bible was found, it was destroyed, and those with whom it was found perished miserably (ibid.).

Antiochus IV had the surname of Epiphanes, meaning "God made manifest." He was soon nicknamed Antiochus Epimanes, which means "Antiochus the madman."

The Maccabean Revolt Against Antiochus (168 B.C.)

The bitter persecutions of Antiochus IV led inevitably to a reaction among the Jews. The first effective resistance was initiated by a man named Mattathias, a priest, living at the town of Modin in Judah to the west of Jerusalem. One of the ancestors of Mattathias was named Hasmon, and from this name was derived the title Hasmonean, which was applied to the later descendants of Mattathias (cf. "The Hasmoneans," pages 228–29).

When the emissaries of Antiochus IV came to the town of Modin to compel the inhabitants to carry on pagan sacrifices and to depart from the law of God (1 Macc. 2:15), Mattathias and his five sons stood firm, refusing to bow to the coercion of the king of Syria; the father as spokesman declared categorically that he and his sons would obey the laws of their fathers and would not listen to the words of Antiochus (vv. 20, 22). When Mattathias had finished speaking, a renegade Jew came to the pagan altar that had been erected in Modin and prepared to sacrifice to the idols (v. 23). Mattathias was grieved, and his anger rose; running up to the man, he slew him, together with the emissary of Antiochus who was compelling the Jews to offer this sacrifice, which was unlawful for them (vv. 24–25). Mattathias proclaimed that everyone who had

a zeal for the law should follow him, and thereupon he and his sons fled to the hills, where they maintained themselves (vv. 27–28).

Judas Maccabaeus (166–160 B.C.)

Mattathias apparently was well along in years when he began the resistance to the decrees of Antiochus IV in 168 B.C. He died in 166 and left the work of carrying on the resistance to his five sons, appointing Simon as counselor and Judas as the military leader of the movement (JAJ, XII.6.1).

Judas proved to be a real leader. The name Maccabaeus was first applied to him. Two possible derivations of this word have been suggested: (1) It is derived from the Hebrew word *makkabah*, meaning "hammer" and (2) it is made up from the initial letters of a phrase meaning "Who is like unto thee among the mighty, O Yahweh?" (*Mi Camoca Ba'elim Yahweh*). The first explanation seems more likely.

The military genius of Judas reminds one somewhat of Joshua. In fighting against the Syrian generals, Judas used the technique of night attack and was able to scatter the armies of his Syrian opponents. Finally in 165 B.C. Judas captured Jerusalem and purified and rededicated the temple, which had been defiled by the abomination of Antiochus IV. The Jewish "Festival of Lights," or Hanukkah, or Rededication came into existence in connection with this deliverance of the Holy City.[2]

But Judas was not home free. Lysias, commander of the Syrian forces now descended on Judah, defeated Judas, and besieged Jerusalem. At that juncture, however, hearing news of an enemy force marching on the Syrian capital of Antioch, Lysias offered peace, the repeal of the laws proscribing Judaism, the removal of Menelaus from the high priest-

[2]1 Maccabees 4:52–59; John 10:22; Josephus, *Antiquities*, XII.7.7.

hood, and amnesty for Judas and his followers. The Hasidim accepted the terms because their goal of religious liberty had been achieved. Judas, however, was not satisfied with anything less than full political liberty and left Jerusalem with a small force. When the new high priest, Alcimus, seized and executed a number of Hasidim, Judas renewed the war. With greatly reduced forces, he was defeated and killed on the battlefield in 161.

Jonathan (160–143 B.C.)

The place of Judas was taken by his younger brother Jonathan. Living as a virtual freebooter in the wilderness of Tekoa and adjacent regions, as David had done, he gradually augmented his forces and was finally ready to go on the attack. At that point, dynastic quarrels in Syria made it possible for him to manipulate the situation to his own advantage, and he gained considerable power. His brother Simon became military governor of coastal Palestine from Tyre to the Egyptian border. Although a Syrian general finally killed Jonathan in 143, the Maccabean cause was too well established to be snuffed out. Simon rushed to Jerusalem and took over leadership of the nationalist movement and gained the independence of the Jews from Syria the following year.

The Hasmoneans (143–63 B.C.)

At the time of the death of Jonathan, the only one of the five sons of Mattathias who remained was Simon. He was declared by the Jews to be "their prince and high priest for ever" (1 Macc. 14:41), that is, until there should arise a prophet worthy of credence. With the naming of Simon as both prince and priest, the Maccabean leaders assumed a temporal leadership that was really a kingship, going beyond the priestly and military leadership held by the previous Maccabees. Beginning with Simon in 143 B.C., we

usually think of these leaders as forming the Hasmonean line of kings (the name of this dynasty is also called "Asmonean.") The Roman Senate recognized Simon as a friendly, independent ruler (1 Macc. 14:16–19, 24; 15:15–24). In international affairs, for the next eighty years the Romans valued the Hasmonean dynasty as a counterbalance to the Seleucid state. Domestically, the Hasmoneans depended on the aristocratic Sadducean party with its power base in the temple.

Simon was the first of the Maccabees to strike his own coinage. Archaeological excavations in Palestine have often produced such coins, giving evidence of the activities of Simon as an actual monarch (for a picture of a half-shekel of Simon see BAB, figure 192).

Simon soon fell victim to the treachery of the governor of Jericho in 135 B.C. and was succeeded by his son, John Hyrcanus (135–105), who ruled both as prince and as high priest as his father had done. Since the book of 1 Maccabees ends with the death of Simon, our sources for the next events are rather sparse, and most of our information comes from Josephus.

John Hyrcanus (135–104 B.C.) began his reign fighting for his life and his kingdom but ended it with the Jewish state at the height of its power. Avowedly expansionistic, he first reestablished control of the coastal cities of Palestine. Then he conquered the enemy east of the Jordan and followed that with the capture of Shechem and the destruction of the Samaritan temple on Mount Gerizim. Next he subjugated the Idumeans (Edomites) in the south and forced them to accept Judaism and be circumcised.

Aristobulus (104–103 B.C.), the eldest son of Hyrcanus, emerged as victor in the dynastic struggle that erupted after the death of Hyrcanus. Then he proceeded to imprison his brothers and his mother to guarantee his position as chief of state. He continued the expansionist policies of his father and extended Jewish rule into Galilee. He also continued the Hasmonean tendency to transform the religious community into a secular state, adopting the title "Philhellene" (love of things Greek) and taking the title of king.

When Aristobulus died, his widow, Salome Alexandra, released his brothers from prison and married the eldest, Alexander Jannaeus (103–76 B.C.). Jannaeus continued the expansionistic policies of his predecessors, and by the time he died he had extended the border of the Jewish state to include nearly all the territory that Solomon had ruled. He was almost constantly at war, however, and more than once came close to total disaster.

When Jannaeus died, his widow, Salome Alexandra (76–67 B.C.), succeeded him on the throne, as she had when Aristobulus, her first husband, died. Because she was a woman, she could not exercise the high priesthood. Her eldest son, Hyrcanus II, filled that position. Her more able second son, Aristobulus II, received command of the army. The Pharisees, who had enjoyed little influence under earlier Hasmonean rulers, now played an important role in the government. In general, Alexandra's reign was peaceful and prosperous. When she died at the age of seventy-three, the days of Jewish independence were nearing an end and Roman power loomed on the horizon. As a matter of fact, it was sparring between Alexandra's two sons that gave the Romans a chance to add Palestine to their empire.

Three months after the death of Alexandra, Aristobulus managed to defeat the forces of Hyrcanus at Jericho, and the latter gave up all rights to the high priesthood and the crown and retired to private life. All might have gone well for Aristobulus, had it not been for the ambition of Antipater, military governor of Idumea and father of Herod the Great. Antipater saw that he could manipulate the weak Hyrcanus but had no future under a strong leader like Aristobulus. So with the help of Aretas, king of the Nabateans, he managed to put Hyrcanus on the throne in the Jewish state.

Chapter 25

Palestine Under Roman Rule, 63 B.C. and After

(End of the Intertestamental Period and Beginning of the New Testament Period)

Pompey's March into Palestine, 63 B.C.

The Roman general Pompey finally put an end to the struggle between John Hyrcanus II and Aristobulus and made Palestine a Roman province. What happened was this. Pompey had become involved in conquests in the East, in Pontus and Armenia. In 66 B.C. one of his lieutenants visited Judea, where he heard appeals from representatives of both brothers and made some tentative decisions, pending later action of Pompey. Three years later Pompey came to Damascus and there heard appeals from the two brothers, promising a decision after a campaign against the Nabataeans (JAJ, XIV.3.2–3).

When Pompey's general, Gabinius, returned, he found that Aristobulus had locked the gates of Jerusalem against him. Gabinius then issued an arrest warrant for Aristobulus. Soon the followers of Hyrcanus opened the city gates, and Pompey launched a siege of Aristobulus's forces holding out in the citadel. When the battle was over, Palestine came under Roman rule. All non-Jewish areas (the Mediterranean coastlands, Transjordan, and Samaria) were detached from the Jewish state, and what was left was

placed under the rule of Hyrcanus II as high priest. Thus Hyrcanus (with Antipater at his elbow) controlled the Jewish state, at the pleasure of the Romans. Aristobulus was taken to Rome, where he marched in Pompey's triumphal parade, along with many Jews who were sold into slavery in the capital. In later years, as many won their freedom, they became the nucleus of the Jewish community there.

The Rise of Herod the Great

The Herods were not of Jewish stock but were descendants of Esau, the brother of Jacob. The descendants of Esau, called the Edomites, settled to the south of the Dead Sea in the region of Mount Seir and the great city that was later called Petra. About 300 B.C., the Edomites were driven out by a group of people called the Nabataeans, and they migrated to the west into the southern part of Palestine, which came to be known as Idumaea, and the people were known as Idumaeans, a Greek form of the word Edomite. The chief city of the Idumaeans, Hebron, was taken by Judas Maccabeus in 165 B.C. (1 Macc. 4:29, 61; 5:65). John Hyrcanus later subdued their territory and made the people become Jews and submit to circumcision.

The first ancestor of Herod the Great who was of any importance was a man named Antipas (died 78 B.C.). He had been appointed governor of Idumaea (the part of Palestine south of Judea) by the Hasmonean king Alexander Jannaeus (103–76, see preceding chapter). Antipas was succeeded as governor of Idumaea by his son, Antipater (the father of Herod the Great). Antipater had all of the overweening ambition of his son, Herod the Great, and saw his opportunity to gain a powerful position in the declining Hasmonean house. When John Hycranus II and Aristobulus II were both seeking to gain the throne of the Hasmoneans, Antipater took the side of John Hyrcanus II and induced him to seek the aid of the Romans. When Pompey came against Jerusalem in 63, Hyrcanus aided the Romans in their siege of the inner fortifications.

John Hyrcanus II, as ruler of Judea, and Antipater, as governor of Idumaea, continued to support the Roman general Pompey until Pompey was defeated at the Battle of Pharsalus in 48 B.C. Thereafter Hyrcanus and Antipater submitted to Julius Caesar, now the leader at Rome. Julius Caesar confirmed their political position in Judah.

Herod the Great Becomes King of Judea, 37 B.C.

Julius Caesar as head of the Roman State brought in a new order of things in Judea. He, however, was assassinated on March 15, 44 B.C., and a train of unfortunate days followed for the little territory of Judea. Antipater died in 43, poisoned by a rival. He left four sons—Phasael, Herod the Great, Joseph, and Pheroras—and a daughter, Mariamne. The second of these sons, Herod the Great, is famous in biblical history as the ruler of Judea in the days when Christ was born (Matt. 2:1).

Herod had begun his political career as a young man, ruling as governor over the territory of Galilee in northern Palestine, a post to which he was appointed by his father, Antipater (JAJ, XIV.9.1–2). Josephus says that Herod was only fifteen years of age when he came to this post, but it is quite evident that he must have been twenty-five.[1] As governor of Galilee, Herod was successful in ridding his territory of freebooters, and even more successful in raising the tribute money that was due the Roman authorities. Politically he advanced rapidly, and Mark Antony, who ruled in the East after the death of Julius Caesar, appointed Herod and his brother Phasael tetrarchs of Judea in 41 B.C. The following year Antony made Herod king of the Jews.

At that point the Parthians on Rome's eastern frontier took advantage of Rome's political and military weakness created by the period of civil war (involving first Pompey and Julius Caesar and later Augustus Caesar and Mark Antony) and invaded Syria and Palestine. They made Antigonus, son of Aristobulus II, king and high priest of the Jews (40–37 B.C.). The Jews hailed the Parthians as deliverers from the Romans, and all classes supported the rule of Aristobulus. Of course the Romans counterattacked, and Herod, with Roman help, managed to take much of Palestine. After the fall of Jerusalem (37), Antony ordered the execution of Antigonus. Now Herod became king in fact and ruled until his death in 4 B.C.[2] He remained loyal to Antony until Octavian (Augustus) defeated him (31 B.C.). Then Herod offered his total loyalty to Augustus as he had given it to Antony, and the Roman emperor accepted it.[3] Augustus

---

[1] Note in Whiston edition of Josephus, 346.

[2] It is known that the calendar is somewhat in error. Christ was born up to a couple of years before Herod died, perhaps in 6 B.C.

[3] A biography of Herod appears in Josephus, *Antiquities*, Books XV–XVII and *War* 1:18–33. See also A.H.M. Jones, *The Herods of Judaea* (Oxford: Clarendon, 1930); Stewart Perowne, *The Life and Times of Herod the Great* (New York: Abingdon, 1956).

gave Herod additional territories along the Mediterranean coast and Jericho, all of which had belonged to Cleopatra, and later the wild regions east of the Jordan. Herod held the position of an allied king with local autonomy but subject to Rome in foreign affairs. Rome used him as they did other allied kings to pacify a recalcitrant frontier province and prepare it for a stage when Rome could directly appoint governors. Those direct appointees ruled Judea in the days of Jesus and Paul.

Herod the Great, King of Judea, 37–4 B.C.: His Atrocities

Herod's rule began with crimes of violence, involving the execution of many of his enemies at the time of his conquest of Jerusalem (JAJ, XV.1.1–2). Soon thereafter he had his wife's brother, Aristobulus, the high priest, drowned in a "swimming accident" (JAJ, XV.3.3). His vengeful, jealous, and suspicious nature later led him to execute his wife, Mariamne, and her mother, Alexandra (JAJ, XV.7.4–8).

The death of Mariamne in 28 B.C. caused Herod to suffer great remorse, and he would often call for her as though she were still alive. He tried to divert his mind by ordering all kinds of feasts and assemblies, but it was to no avail (JAJ, XV.7.7). He had lost the one person whom he ever really seems to have loved. Even this remorse did not cure Herod's inclination to violence, for in 7 B.C., shortly before his own death, he had his own sons by Mariamne strangled to death (JAJ, XVI.11.7). And of course we are familiar with his massacre of the infants in Bethlehem in an effort to destroy Jesus (Matt. 2:16–18).

Herod's Lack of Understanding of the Jews

In spite of an apparent desire to understand his subject people, Herod the Great found it difficult to understand them adequately and impossible to get along with them. Two significant factors hindering Jewish acceptance of Herod were that he was not a Jew but an Idumaean and that he aligned himself with the Romans for support. A further source of estrangement lay in the fact that Herod had displaced the Hasmonean dynasty. Herod sought to win the confidence of his people by royal charity in the time of famine and by other means, but in vain. They saw in him only a usurper on the throne of David. There were innumerable plots against his life, but with almost superhuman cunning, Herod was able to defeat them and continue his rule (JAJ, XV.8).

Archaeological Light on Herod the Great's Building Activities

Herod's outstanding city constructions in Palestine were at Samaria and Caesarea. Samaria he renamed Sebaste in honor of Augustus (which in Greek is *Sebastos*) and built there a temple to Augustus, a theater, an agora with a Roman basilica, a Greek-style colonnaded main street lined with shops, and more. Harvard University excavated at the site under the leadership of G.A. Reisner in 1908–1910, and in 1931–1935 in conjunction with four other institutions. Then J.W. Crowfoot was the director (see EAEIIL, 4:1032–1050, and this book, chapter 15).

About twenty-five miles south of the modern city of Haifa, Herod rebuilt the great city of Caesarea (22–9 B.C.), about half the size of Manhattan Island, again named in honor of Augustus Caesar. This was a thoroughly Greco-Roman city, flung down on the coast of Palestine. Its temple to Augustus, hippodrome, theater, magnificent man-made harbor and port facilities, and other accouterments qualified it to be a first-class Roman capital of Palestine. Robert J. Bull of Drew University is the director of the joint expedition to

Ruins of the temple of Augustus that Herod the Great built at Caesarea in the emperor's honor

The Greco-Roman theater that Herod the Great built at Caesarea

Caesarea Maritima, which has been working at the site since 1971.[4]

In Jerusalem Herod built a theater and an amphitheater. Other examples of Herod's building activities include his reconstruction of Antipatris, northeast of modern Tel Aviv; the construction of the fortresses of Machaerus in Transjordan, of Masada along the Dead Sea, and of the Herodion, south of Bethlehem; and the palace complex at Jericho and his great palace in the western part of Jerusalem. His zeal for Hellenism and his desire to enhance his own reputation also led him to get involved in numerous building projects all over the eastern Mediterranean—in Rhodes, Greece, Lebanon, and Syria. The glory of Antioch when Paul launched his three missionary journeys from there was due in part to the beneficence of Herod.

Herod's palace in Jerusalem occupied the citadel area on the west side of the city. According to Josephus, it consisted of two main complexes surrounded by parks and gardens (Josephus, *War V*) and had three towers on the city wall, which guarded the palace's northern side. Of the three towers (Phasael, Hippicus, and Mariamne), nothing has survived except the base of the main tower, Phasael, now called the Tower of David. It is 66 feet square and approximately 66 feet high. This palace was the headquarters of Herod's government and of the Roman procurators who followed him. Here it was that Christ appeared before Pilate for his trial. Benjamin Mazar reported that excavations there revealed that the palace and gardens covered more than 4.5 acres and that the palace itself was built on a podium measuring 1,000 by 430 feet. Nothing was found of the superstructure.[5]

Herod's Rebuilding of the Temple at Jerusalem

The temple of the Jews in Jerusalem at the beginning of Herod the Great's reign was the same building that had been reconstructed some five hundred years earlier when the Jews returned from the Babylonian Captivity (see chapter 21). Herod's penchant for building new edifices prompted him to make plans to rebuild the temple at Jerusalem. In order not to offend the sensitive feelings of the Jews, Herod chose a thousand priests, many of whom were trained to be stone-cutters and carpenters, so that no profane hand would have to touch the shrine of the temple (JAJ, XV.11.2).

The main part of the temple, begun in 20 B.C., was completed within eighteen months, but the final touches were still being added in the days of the ministry of Christ. It was for this reason that the Jews, speaking to Christ, could say that it had taken forty-six years to build the temple (John 2:20). It was not completely finished until A.D. 64, only six years before it was destroyed by the legions of Titus when Jerusalem was taken in 70. The temple occupied the same ground plan as that of its predecessor, but Herod did increase its elevation to one hundred cubits (BAB, 250). The temple complex was arranged in terraces, with the temple itself at the highest point. The outer court was the court of the Gentiles, then came the court of the women and the court of the Israelites, and finally the temple precincts.

After the Six Day War in 1967, Israeli archaeologists were free to explore the Temple Mount. In February, 1968, Benjamin Mazar began excavations south and southwest of the Temple Mount on behalf of the Hebrew University and the Israel

[4]See especially, Kenneth G. Holum et al., *King Herod's Dream: Caesarea on the Sea* (New York: Norton, 1988); EAEHL, 1:270–85. The latter also describes other explorations and excavations at the site.

[5]Benjamin Mazar, *The Mountain of the Lord* (Garden City, N.Y.: Doubleday, 1975), 78–79 [MML].

THE HERODIAN LINE

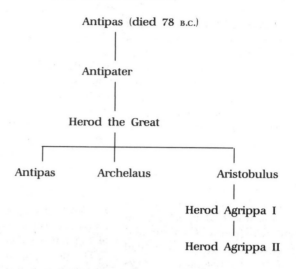

Antipas (died 78 B.C.)

Antipater

Herod the Great

Antipas   Archelaus   Aristobulus

Herod Agrippa I

Herod Agrippa II

Exploration Society. This work has continued until the present time.[6] Some of the more significant finds are the following: First, the Herodian Western Wall, often called the Wailing Wall, extends 69 feet (19 courses of masonry) below the present surface to bedrock. Second, the enormous arch near the southwestern corner of the western wall has been reinterpreted. This is called Robinson's Arch because Edward Robinson first identified it as part of a bridge from the Temple Mount across the Tyropoeon Valley to the Upper City. Excavations showed that this was the end of a monumental staircase that led up from the Tyropoeon Valley rather than the end of a bridge. Third, archaeologists uncovered along the western wall part of what was Jerusalem's main street during the Herodian period. Fourth, along the southern wall the Hulda Gates were discovered; the western gate was a double gate (43 feet wide) and the eastern gate a triple gate (50 feet wide). Fifth, these were approached by massive stone stairways. The one facing the western Hulda Gate is 215

feet wide and consists of thirty steps. The stairway leading to the eastern Hulda Gate has been torn away. Sixth, numerous ritual immersion baths, *mikvehs*, were uncovered in the area between the two stairways. It is interesting to note that these would have provided facilities for the multitude of believers to be baptized on the Day of Pentecost (Acts 2:41).

Herod Antipas (4 B.C.–A.D. 39)

When Herod the Great died in 4 B.C., his son Herod Antipas was assigned rulership over the northern province of Galilee and the transjordan area called Perea. Antipas had married a daughter of the king of Arabia, King Aretas of the Nabataeans, but he sent her back to her father and lived with Herodias, his brother's wife. It was this illicit union that John the Baptist rebuked, and for this rebuke John ultimately lost his life (Mark 6:16–18). It was to Herod Antipas that Christ was sent by Pilate during the trial, because Christ came from Galilee, the place of Herod Antipas's jurisdiction (Luke 23:6–12).

[6]The outstanding early account of Mazar's excavations may be read in his own words in MML. See especially pages 131–52 for a summary of some of the most significant finds.

A stone stairway that led to the Hulda Gate of the temple in Jerusalem

The Herodion, a fortress built by Herod the Great and the place where he was buried

The peristyle garden in the Herodion

Antipas launched numerous construction projects, including Tiberias on the sea of Galilee, named for Tiberius Caesar.

Herod Archelaus (4 B.C.–A.D. 6)

Herod Archelaus was the oldest son of Herod the Great. Upon the death of his father, he came to rule over Judea and Samaria and ruled with such an iron hand and incurred such dislike that he finally had his possessions taken from him by the Roman government and was banished to Vienna in Gaul.[7] At this time Judea was placed under the rule of a Roman procurator (see the last section in this chapter, pages 238–39).

Herod Philip (4 B.C.–A.D. 34)

A third son of Herod the Great, Herod Philip, became the tetrarch of Trachonitis, Batanea, and Gaulanitis (the area northeast of the Sea of Galilee). He apparently ruled justly and well. He built as his capital Caesarea Philippi (Matt. 16:13; Mark 8:27). Excavations at Caesarea Philippi (Banias) began in May, 1988, under the auspices of the Israel Department of Antiquities and the Nature Reserves Authority, with the participation of three American universities. Attention centered on a series of well-preserved vaults, nine of which were excavated, dating to the first century A.D. The use of these vaults, which apparently stood in the center of the New Testament city, has not yet been determined. Apparently superstructures stood on these vaults. Later in the summer, excavation was conducted at the temple of Pan at the site.[8] V. Tzaferis directed this first season of excavation.

Herod Agrippa I (A.D. 40–44)

Herod Agrippa I was the grandson of Herod the Great and Mariamne (and the son of their son, Aristobulus, whom Herod the Great had put to death in 7 B.C.). Herod Agrippa I hated his uncle, Antipas, and in 39, when Antipas was banished, he received his uncle's territory of Galilee and Perea. The next year, by currying the favor of the emperor of Rome, Herod Agrippa I received Judea and Samaria as well. He endeavored to be tactful with the Jews, taking sides against the Christians and even killing James the apostle with the sword (Acts 12:1–3).

Herod Agrippa II (A.D. 44–70 as King; Died c. A.D. 100)

When Herod Agrippa died in 44, his son, Herod Agrippa II, was only seventeen years old and was considered too young to rule. The country was placed under the care of a Roman procurator, but later Herod Agrippa II was given certain territories, including the area to the east of the Sea of Galilee. Herod Agrippa II is mentioned in the New Testament in connection with the apostle Paul, who appeared before him (Acts 25:13, 26:1ff.). When the Jews planned to rebel against the Romans, Herod Agrippa II warned against the rebellion. In spite of this warning, the Jews revolted, and when Jerusalem fell in A.D. 70, the Romans remembered Agrippa's loyalty to them, allowing him to come to Rome and live. Here he became a praetor (Roman official) and finally died in the year 100 at the age of seventy.

The Relationship of Pontius Pilate to the Government of Palestine in the New Testament Period

As noted above, the province of Judea was under the jurisdiction of Herod Archelaus from 4 B.C. until A.D. 6, when he was deposed from office. Judea was then put under a Roman provincial ruler who

---

[7]JAJ, XVII.13.1–2.

[8]See *Excavations and Surveys in Israel 1988/89* (Jerusalem: Israel Antiquities Authority, 1990), 10–11.

held the title of "procurator," and was directly responsible to the emperor. Pontius Pilate was the fifth of these procurators to rule over Judea after the deposing of Herod Archelaus and was the one who sentenced Christ to the cross (Matt. 27:2, 11ff.). Josephus tells us that Pilate held this office for ten years (JAJ, XVIII.4.2), a tenure that probably lasted from 26 to 36.

Tiberius was the emperor who appointed Pilate to his post in the province of Judea, and Pilate reciprocated in part by dedicating a small temple to the worship of the emperor in Caesarea. An inscription mentioning this dedication and naming both Pilate and Tiberius came to light in the theater of Caesarea during an Italian excavation there in 1961.[9] This is the first time that archaeological evidence of an inscriptional nature attesting to the existence of Pontius Pilate has been found.

---

[9]Kenneth G. Holum, *Caesarea on the Sea* (New York: Norton, 1988), 109–10.

Chapter 26

The Life and Ministry of Christ

(Matthew; Mark; Luke; John)

Prophecies of Christ in the Old Testament

The Old Testament abounds with prophecies that give details of the birth, life, and ministry of Christ. For example, Isaiah 7:14 predicted that he would be born of a virgin; Micah 5:2 indicated that he would be born in Bethlehem; and Isaiah 53:3 showed that he would be "a man of sorrows." His triumphal entry into Jerusalem was predicted in Zechariah 9:9, his betrayal for thirty pieces of silver in Zechariah 11:12, the use of the betrayal money for a potter's field in Zechariah 11:13, and the nailing of his hands in Zechariah 13:6 and Psalm 22:16. The fact that not a bone in his body was to be broken is indicated in Psalm 34:20, his death in the presence of criminals in Isaiah 53:8–9, his provision of atonement in Isaiah 53:4–5, and the fact of his resurrection in Psalm 16:10 ("You will not let your Holy One see decay"). The rejec-

tion of Christ is indicated in Micah's statement "They will strike Israel's ruler on the cheek with a rod" (5:1).

The Amazing Significance of the 332 Prophecies Concerning Christ

Many other prophecies, in addition to those given above, are found in the pages of the Old Testament. The great significance of the number of these prophecies was pointed out by Canon Liddon of England.[1]

Canon Liddon is the authority for the statement that there are 332 distinct prophecies in the Old Testament that have been literally fulfilled in Christ (HBCF, 156). Someone with a flair for mathematics has figured out that the mathematical probability of all these prophecies being fulfilled in one man is represented by an amazing fraction, the numerator of which would be one and the denominator represented by a figure

[1]Henry Parry Liddon, 1829–1890, educated at Oxford, vice-principal of St. Edmund's Hall at Oxford, delivered lectures in the Bampton Lectures series on the subject "The Divinity of Our Lord." In 1870 he was made canon of St. Paul's Cathedral in London and also professor of exegesis at Oxford. In 1882 he resigned his professorship and traveled in Palestine and Egypt, and in 1886 he was made chancellor of St. Paul's.

written with the number eighty-four followed by ninety-seven zeros (HBCF, 157). The chances of all these prophecies being fulfilled in one man are so overwhelmingly remote that there is no way they could be the shrewd guesses of mere men; rather, they were given by God to holy men who "spoke from God as they were carried along by the Holy Spirit" (2 Peter 1:21).

The Birth of Christ at Bethlehem (Matthew 2:1); Significance of the Prophecy

Some seven hundred years before the birth of Christ, the prophet Micah predicted that he would be born in Bethlehem Ephrathah (Mic. 5:2). Such foreknowledge is an evidence of the supernatural nature of the Bible, and the prophecy is all the more striking when we remember that there were two Bethlehems—one in northern Palestine, Bethlehem of Zebulun, and one in southern Palestine, Bethlehem Ephrath, or Bethlehem of Judah. Guided by the Holy Spirit, Micah not only stated that the birthplace of the "ruler in Israel" would be Bethlehem but he also indicated which Bethlehem it would be—Bethlehem Ephrathah. Seven hundred years later the prophecy was fulfilled in the birth of our Lord.

The Date of the Birth of Christ, Probably Between 6 and 4 B.C.

Because of an error in the ancient calendar, Christ was not born in the year one, as we now compute dates, but was actually born a few years B.C. His birth took place while Herod the Great was still alive (Matt. 2:1), and Herod died sometime between March 12 and April 11 in the year of 4 B.C.[2] Moreover, the visit of the wisemen had also occurred before the death of Herod. By the time they arrived, the holy family was no longer in the

stable but in a "house" (Matt. 2:11), and the baby was now called a "child." Herod, determined to eliminate this possible competitor for his throne, decided to kill all the boys in Bethlehem "two years old and under, in accordance with the time he had learned from the Magi" (Matt. 2:16). On this basis we could push the date of Christ's birth back to 5 or possibly the end of 6 B.C.

A second means of determining the date of Christ's birth concerns establishment of the date of the census (Luke 2:2). At the end of a lengthy discussion of this subject, Finegan concluded that it may have been in 6 or 5 B.C. He noted that while this census is only "concretely affirmed" by Luke 2:2, Justin Martyr and Tertullian (second century A.D.) stated that the record of this census was in the archives in Rome (FHBC, 234–38).

A third criterion used to peg the date of Christ's birth involves the construction of the temple. John 2:20 says that Herod's temple had been under construction forty-six years by the time Christ was thirty years of age (Luke 3:23). The temple was begun in 733 A.U.C. (ab urbe condita, from the founding of the city, i.e., Rome). If we add 46 to 733, we get 779. Subtract Christ's age at the time, 30, and we get 749 A.U.C. or 5 B.C. for the date of his birth. Since he was a little over 30 and the temple may have been in the process of being built slightly over 46 years, the date of Christ's birth could easily be pushed back to 6 B.C.

Archaeological Confirmation of the Validity of Luke's Reference to the Census at the Time of the Birth of Christ (Luke 2:1–3)

Luke tells us that at the time of the birth of Christ, Caesar Augustus sent out a decree that "a census should be taken of the entire Roman world." Luke also

---

[2]Jack Finegan, *Handbook of Biblical Chronology* (Princeton: Princeton University Press, 1964), 231 [FHBC].

indicates that this was done when Cyrenius was governor of Syria, and that everyone had to go to his "own town" for the enrollment (Luke 2:1–3).

Earlier it was believed that Luke had made almost as many mistakes as could possibly be made in these few lines, for it was thought that he was in error with regard to (1) the existence of such an imperial census, (2) Cyrenius's being governor at the time (Luke 2:2), and (3) everyone's having to go to his ancestral home. Archaeological discoveries remarkably confirmed and illuminated all of these statements of Luke, attesting his reliability in the very items noted above: (1) the discovery of the number of papyrus documents relating to census taking shows that a census was made every fourteen years, and these documents point back to a census taken 9–6 B.C.;[3] (2) though earlier references seemed to show that Cyrenius was governor of Syria in A.D. 6, which would be too late for the time of Christ's birth, an inscription was found at Rome in 1828 indicating that Cyrenius had been governor twice; and shortly before World War I, Ramsay found a monument in Asia Minor likewise implying two governorships for Cyrenius. Thus he could have been governor at the time of Christ's birth, as well as at a later period, in A.D. 6 (CNAD, 538); and (3) an edict made in A.D. 104 by the governor of Egypt (which was under Roman rule, just as Palestine was) showed that at the time of the census people were to return to their ancestral homes.[4] In summary, it is evident that archaeological discoveries testify to the validity of Luke's statements.

Evidence Outside of the Bible for the Existence of Jesus Christ

Especially since the rise of modern rationalism in the eighteenth century, some have doubted the very existence of Christ on earth. And in spite of accumulating evidence to the contrary, there are still voices who argue against Christ's historicity. Therefore we pause to restate some of the evidence.

First, there were the Roman writers. Tacitus, the "dean" of Roman historians (c. A.D. 60–120), among other works wrote the Annals, a history of the Julio-Claudian emperors from Tiberius to Nero (A.D. 14–68). In the section on Nero, Tacitus briefly described the persecution of Christians and in the process named their leader: "Christus, from whom their name is derived, was executed at the hands of the procurator Pontius Pilate in the reign of Tiberius."[5]

Second, Pliny the Younger (c. 62–113), while governor of Bithynia and Pontus in Asia Minor (modern Turkey), was faced with the issue of how to treat Christians, who were by then an illegal sect. In about 111 or 112 he wrote to the emperor Trajan for advice on the suject. In the process he bore witness to the innocent lives of Christians and their allegiance to Christ, their founder.[6]

A third witness to the person of Christ is Lucian of Samosata (c. 125–190), regarded by many as the most brilliant writer of revived Greek literature under the Roman Empire. During his later years he held a government post in Egypt. Of particular interest is his satire on Christians, published under the title The Passing of Peregrinus, in about 170. He described Christ as the originator of the cult of Christianity and mentioned that he was "crucified in Palestine" for having originated this cult.[7]

An especially important first-century Jewish historian was Josephus, who in his Antiquities (A.D. 93) made a rather

---

[3]Camden M. Cobern, New Archaeological Discoveries, 9th ed. (New York: Funk & Wagnalls, 1929), 46–47 [CNAD]; FLAP, 260.

[4]Adolf Deissmann, Light from the Ancient Past (New York: Harper & Brothers, 1922), 271 [DLAE].

[5]Tacitus, Annals, 15.44.

[6]Pliny the Younger, Correspondence of Trajan, Epistle, 10.96.

[7]Lucian, Passing of Peregrinus, 1.11.13.

evangelical-sounding reference to Jesus. He spoke about how Pilate condemned him to death and how he appeared alive again to his followers on the third day (JAJ, XVIII.3.3). Some critical scholars used to regard this passage as an insert by later Christian writers to gain respectability for their movement, but the general attitude today is that the reference is an embellished account of Josephus's more restrained reference to Jesus. They observe that Josephus, as an outstanding historian, quite likely made some reference to Christ. Moreover, later on he did speak of James as "the brother of Jesus, who was called Christ" (JAJ, XX.9.1). Writers who argue about the earlier longer passage tend to ignore this unembellished statement that has a ring of authenticity and may be accepted as a bona fide witness to Jesus' life on earth.

Of course there are numerous works of the church fathers of the first and second centuries that speak in great detail of the reality of the Christ. And the New Testament, now recognized to be a first-century document, must be accepted as a reliable witness to Jesus' historicity.

Christ's Birth at Bethlehem; the Manger; the Inn (Luke 2:7)

When Christ was born at Bethlehem, he was laid in a manger (Luke 2:7). The probable location of the birth of Christ is a matter of interest to the Christian world, and, fortunately, we do have some light on this subject. One of the church fathers, Justin Martyr (c. 110–165), indicated that in his time a cave in Bethlehem was pointed out as the birthplace of Christ.[8]

There are a number of old houses in Bethlehem today that are built over caves in the limestone rock, and these caves are used for stabling cattle even at the present time (CANT, 81).[9] Caves were certainly used for the same purpose in the time of Christ, and it is quite likely that his birth took place in such a grotto. Today the Church of the Nativity stands over a cave that has been pointed out for hundreds of years as the scene of the birth of our Lord. We can trace this tradition back to 325. In that year, the Bishop of Jerusalem, Macarius, informed the Emperor Constantine that in Bethlehem there was a cave that the people of the town venerated as the birthplace of Christ. The emperor gave orders for the construction of a church to enshrine the scene of the Nativity, and the work began in 326. This church has suffered various changes and destructions and rebuildings, but the cave still remains beneath it and can be seen today. High authorities generally believe that the cave of the Nativity is the birthplace of Christ, and there is no reason to doubt the tradition. The cave is about forty feet long and twelve feet wide (CANT, 79; FLAP, 532–35)

The Church of the Nativity as it now stands is a product of the extensive building activity of Justinian (emperor A.D. 537–565, but reportedly he was angry that the church did not turn out to be more grand, so he punished the builder (FLAP, 534). Minimal excavations under the present church were conducted in 1934 by William Harvey, and he found remains of the Constantinian church (FLAP, 535). The visitor to the church today can see under the floor of the nave

---

[8]S.L. Caiger, *Archaeology and the New Testament* (London: Cassell, 1939, 77) [CANT]. We do not have Justin Martyr's own statement on this, but another church father, Origen, c. 250, refers to Justin's writings that tell of this cave; Origen's reference is in his work, *Against Celsus*, I, 51.

[9]Morton picturesquely describes some of the caves of Bethlehem over which present-day houses are located. The caves are level with the road, and the one-room house is reached by a flight of stone steps numbering fifteen or twenty. The caves are still used as stables for animals, which enter from the road level. In most of the caves one can see a stone trough, or manger, cut from the rock, with iron rings to which the animals are tied at night. See H.V. Morton, *In the Steps of the Master* (New York: Dodd, Mead, 1937), 144 [MSM].

some of the floor mosaics of Constantine's church.

Jesus was born "in a manger, because there was no room for them in the inn" (Luke 2:7). Ordinarily there would be inns or stopping places (caravansaries) for caravans every twenty or twenty-five miles, the length of a day's journey. Bethlehem, however, is only five miles south of Jerusalem, and we might wonder why there would be an inn there. The answer lies in the fact that there was a branch route that came to Bethlehem from the Dead Sea region, and Bethlehem would have been the natural stopping place for those coming along this branch route, which made a junction with the main route at Bethlehem.

The Infancy of Christ; the Years of Silence

The name "Bethlehem" means "House of Bread," and in itself seems almost prophetic of Christ, who was the "Bread of Life." After Christ was born, an angel of the Lord told the shepherds near Bethlehem of the great event (Luke 2:9–11). The shepherds' fields where the shepherds were watching their flocks are still pointed out on the northeast of Bethlehem. After the visit of the shepherds, the Magi came from the East (Chaldea or Persia) for the express purpose of worshiping the newborn king (Matt. 2:11). During this period, Jesus was circumcised according to the Mosaic Law (Lev. 12:3), and Mary offered the pigeons for her purifying, according to Leviticus 12:8.

The suspicion of Herod the Great and the fear of losing his kingdom prompted him to order the slaughter of the innocent children in Bethlehem. This act was entirely in accord with his character as we have it delineated in our ancient sources, particularly in Josephus. A man who had his own wife and her mother put to death, his brother-in-law forcibly drowned in a swimming pool, and his own sons strangled (see chapter 25, page 233) was certainly capable of giving the order that the children under two years of age in Bethlehem should be slain (Matt. 2:16).

The Lord directed Joseph to take Mary and the Christ child to Egypt to escape the wrath of Herod (Matt. 2:13–15). After Herod the Great died, they could safely return to Palestine, but this time the Lord directed Joseph to take his family to Galilee, for Archelaus, the worst of the sons of Herod the Great, now ruled in his father's place in Judah (4 B.C.–A.D. 6; see chapter 25, page 238).

The Gospels are silent concerning the life of Christ from the time of the return from Egypt to Galilee until his baptism by John the Baptist (c. A.D. 27), except for the record of his visit to the temple in Jerusalem when he was twelve years old. After talking with the learned men in the temple, Jesus said to his concerned parents, "Didn't you know I had to be in my Father's house?" (Luke 2:49)—an indication of his own self-consciousness of his mission.

The Baptism of Christ and the Early Judean Ministry

Up to the time that Christ appeared before John the Baptist, John apparently did not know him (John 1:31). But when John saw him, he intuitively recognized Christ as the One whose coming he was to herald. After his baptism, Christ devoted himself to his public ministry and his messianic mission. Immediately following the baptism, Christ was tempted by Satan in the Judean desert in respect to body, mind, and spirit. Satan first tempted Christ to satisfy his physical hunger by turning stones into bread (Matt. 4:3), an appeal to the need of the body. The second temptation was intended to influence Christ to presume upon God by toying with his supernatural powers in casting himself down from the pinnacle of the temple (Matt. 4:5–6), an appeal to the pride of mind. The third temptation was designed to cause Christ to seek a shortcut to world sovereignty by merely yielding to one act of homage to Satan (Matt. 4:8–9), but Christ had come to do the will of God. He would adhere to the way of the Cross. At each temptation, Christ answered Satan by quoting Scripture. It is significant to note that in answering Satan, our Lord quoted from the book of Deuteronomy, a work denied to Moses by the critics and explained by them as a forgery (see chapter 9, pages 101–2).

The Gospel of John provides information about the early Judean ministry of Christ. This period includes the witness of John the Baptist, in which he pointed out the Lord as "the Lamb of God, who takes away the sin of the world" (John 1:29). This testimony was a commendation of Christ to two of John the Baptist's disciples, Andrew and John; they followed Christ and became the first two disciples (v. 37). They immediately told others, Andrew bringing Simon his brother (vv. 40–41). Our Lord called Phillip, who in turn sought out Nathanael (vv. 43–45), probably the same person known as Bartholomew the apostle.

During an interval in the Judean ministry, Christ went to Galilee, where he performed his first miracle of turning water into wine at the wedding feast at Cana (John 2:1–11). Afterward he returned to Jerusalem to keep the Passover, at which time he cleansed the temple, driving out the wrangling money changers and the sellers of animals from the court of the temple (vv. 14–16). When the Jews asked Jesus by what sign he did this, he replied with the enigmatic answer, "Destroy this temple, and I will raise it again in three days" (v. 19), referring to his body. Even here Christ had reference to the conflict that would end in his rejection and death, though the disciples did not really comprehend this until after his resurrection (v. 22). A short time later, Nicodemus came to Jesus by night and learned the truths of the new birth (John 3).

The Galilean Ministry (27–29)

On the way from Judea to Galilee, Jesus passed through Samaria, and there talked to the woman at the well (John 4), explaining to her that he would give living water, a picture of salvation. From there, Christ journeyed on to Galilee, probably ministering there for about two years. During this time, Jesus healed the nobleman's son (John 4:43–54) and visited Nazareth, where he read the Scriptures in the synagogue, declaring that they spoke of him. But he was not received by his own people; the Nazarenes drew him to the brow of the hill on which their city was built and would have thrown him down, but "he walked right through the crowd and went on his way" (Luke 4:29–30).

Christ went from Nazareth to Capernaum, on the shores of Galilee, and there made his headquarters (Matt. 4:13), for it is later referred to as "his own town" (Matt. 9:1). At this time, the Lord enabled Simon to make the miraculous catch of fish (Luke 5:1–9), and Christ said then that he would make them to be "fishers of men" (Matt. 4:19). Much of Christ's activity was carried on in Capernaum and the vicinity. Here he healed Peter's wife's mother (Matt. 8:14ff.), healed the paralytic (Mark 2:1ff.), and called Matthew from his task of tax collector to the position of disciple (Matt. 9:9ff.)

Edward Robinson first identified the site of Capernaum (Tell Hum) on the northwest shore of the Sea of Galilee in 1838. Small excavations there in 1856 and 1881 prompted looting of stones, and the Franciscan Order purchased the site in 1894 to protect it. H. Kohl and C. Watzinger excavated the synagogue beginning in 1905, and since 1968 V. Corbo and S. Loffreda have been excavating there. Attention has especially focused on the synagogue, which probably dates to the

Excavated fishermen's quarters at Capernaum

Octagonal church at Capernaum that covered an early Roman house, believed to be that of Peter

third century A.D. and therefore could not be the one in which Jesus ministered. The structure of two stories was built of white limestone and measured about sixty-six feet long and sixty feet wide, with a side room that could serve as a school and social hall. In 1981 excavations below the floor of the synagogue uncovered

247

what were believed to be remains of the synagogue in which Jesus preached. In front of the synagogue stood a residential area (now cleared), and in front of that stood an octagonal church, which the excavators have dated to the mid-fifth century. Below the church was a house dating to the first century; the excavators believe this house to have been the house of Peter. Progress is now being made on uncovering some of the residential section behind the synagogue.[10]

It was in Galilee, on a hill overlooking the northwestern shore of the Sea of Galilee, that Christ gave the great Sermon on the Mount (Matt. 5–7), which presents principles of character and conduct for those who are members of the kingdom. By Galilee Christ fed the five thousand (Matt. 14:13–21) and then gave the great discourse on the bread of life (John 6:22–71). From time to time there were disputes with the Pharisees, in which Christ rebuked their inward sin, which was veneered with an outward and pretended purity (Matt. 15:1–20; Mark 7:1–23).

At Caesarea Philippi, near the sources of the Jordan, some fifty miles north of Galilee, Peter gave his great confession: "You are the Christ, the Son of the living God" (Matt. 16:16). Christ at this time said that he would build his church upon the rock, the rock being symbolic of the truth that Peter had confessed.[11] It is significant that one of the early sermons in the church, recovered through archaeological discovery, is entitled "Peter the Rock." It goes to great lengths to explain that Peter was not the rock (CNAD, 279). A few days after Peter's confession of Christ, the Transfiguration took place, probably on a slope of Mount Hermon, during which there was a foreview of the coming glory of Christ (Matt. 17).

Christ's Last Journey to Jerusalem

While Christ was still in the vicinity of Galilee, he sent out the seventy disciples to prepare the way in the towns to which he would come (Luke 10:1ff.). The messengers were to announce to the people whom they met that the kingdom of God was near (Luke 10:9), referring to the impending visit of Christ who was to come after these disciples. During the course of his journey from Galilee, Jesus came into Perea, the region to the east of the Jordan. Here he answered the lawyer's question "Who is my neighbor?" by giving the parable of the Good Samaritan (Luke 10:25ff.)

A little later, Jesus went to Jerusalem on the visit described in John 10:22–29, for the Feast of Dedication, which was held in December in commemoration of the cleansing of the temple and restoration of worship by Judas Maccabeus in c. 165 B.C. after it had been defiled by Antiochus Epiphanes (in 168 B.C.; see chapter 24, pages 227–28). At this time Jesus set forth again the clear claim to his deity in the statement, "I and the Father are one" (John 10:30), and the Jews picked up stones to stone him.

Leaving Jerusalem, Jesus went to the place where John had first baptized (John 10:40) but was called back to Bethany on the occasion of the death of Lazarus (John 11), after which he withdrew again from the vicinity of Jerusalem to Ephraim, a place near the wilderness (John 11:54). During this time Christ healed the lepers in the vicinity of Samaria (Luke 17:11–19), and in his discourses dealt with the subject of divorce (Matt. 19:3–12), the coming of the kingdom (Luke 17:20–37), the parable of the unjust judge (Luke 18:1–8), and the fact of his coming cru-

---

[10]See especially EAEHL, 1:286–90; James F. Strange and Hershel Shanks, "Has the House Where Jesus Stayed in Capernaum Been Found?" BAR (December 1982), 26–37; V. Corbo, *The House of Saint Peter at Capharnaum* (Jerusalem: Franciscan Printing Press, 1972); and Stanislao Loffreda, *A Visit to Capharnaum* (Jerusalem: Franciscan Printing Press, 1973).

[11]For a discussion of the meaning of the rock, see Howard F. Vos, *Matthew* (Grand Rapids: Zondervan, 1979), 118–20.

cifixion and resurrection (Matt. 20:17–19), which the disciples found so hard to believe.

Subsequently, Jesus came to Jericho, where he healed blind Bartimaeus (Matt. 20:29–34) and called Zacchaeus to come down from a sycamore tree to hear the words of life (Luke 19:1–10). Soon afterward, Jesus arrived in Bethany, just east of Jerusalem, six days before the Passover (John 12:1), and then began the events that quickly led to the betrayal, trial, and crucifixion of our Lord.

Archaeological Discoveries in Egypt Relating to the Greek Language of the New Testament

During the nineteenth century, scholars assumed that many words in the New Testament were peculiar to the Bible and were not found in the ordinary language of the first century A.D. Kennedy found about 550 such words in the New Testament, which he considered to be "biblical" words (CNAD, 119). Some even suggested that New Testament writers invented words in order to convey certain ideas. Such a practice would, however, really hinder the message of the New Testament from reaching the people, for they would readily understand only those words that were familiar to them and would have difficulty in understanding the meaning of "invented" words.

Archaeological discoveries in Egypt during the later years of the nineteenth century brought a startling discovery. Thousands of papyrus documents—including letters, wills, receipts, tax records and the like—were found in the excavations in Egypt, where the hot dry sands had preserved them for some two thousand years. The significance of these papyrus documents was brought to the attention of the scholarly world by a young German scholar named Adolph Deissmann in 1895, when he pointed out that these records of everyday life were written in the same type of Greek as that used in the New Testament (CNAD, 30). This demonstrated that the New Testament was not written in some artificial language containing many "invented" words, but was actually written in the language in common use and therefore would be intelligible to everyone. God's purpose in making the gospel known to everyone is seen even in the type of Greek used—*koine* (common) Greek.

The significance of this great discovery is seen in the fact that dozens of words once thought peculiar to the New Testament are now known to have been good everyday words in the first century A.D., known to and used by all people of the Greek-speaking world, which in those days included the entire Roman Empire and the Near East all the way to the Indus River in India. We have seen that years ago Kennedy listed 550 such "biblical" words, whereas Deissmann, as a result of his study of the papyri, reduced this to a list of only about fifty words not yet found in other writings (CNAD, 119).

The papyri have not only demonstrated that some words thought to be invented were in standard use, but they have also clarified the meanings of many words inadequately understood before and have breathed new life into the meanings of others. A few examples will demonstrate the contribution of the papyri in this connection.

In the Sermon on the Mount Jesus condemned externalism and told those who made a public show of piety that they had their reward in the recognition accorded them (Matt. 6:2, 5, 16). In the papyri the construction used here was a technical term for granting a receipt and indicated payment in full, with no expectation, in this case, for any further reward in heaven. Thus the NIV translates the clauses in these three verses, "they have received their reward in full."[12]

Second, Peter urged in 1 Peter 2:2 that believers crave "sincere" milk (KJV), or "pure spiritual" milk (NIV), of the word. Of course no one has seen or tasted "sincere" or "spiritual" milk. In the papyri the word signifies "unadulterated" and refers to wheat unadulterated or unmixed with barley, or oil unmixed with impurities (DBS, 256). Now the meaning of the 1 Peter reference is clear.

Third, the word translated "forgiveness" in the New Testament is used in the papyri in the economic sense of remission of debt, but it is also used in a very beautiful and refreshing connotation that might not occur to us. In Egypt it was used in the irrigation of land and was the technical expression for releasing of water by opening the sluice gates. So forgiveness may be viewed as the divine opening of the sluice gates of mercy and the pouring of life-giving water over the dry and thirsty soul (DBS, 89–101).

Fourth, Hebrews 11:1 takes on a whole new significance as a result of the contribution of the papyri. We are not quite sure what to think when we read that "faith is the substance of things hoped for" (KJV). In the papyri the word translated "substance" is a legal term used to denote the collection of papers bearing on the possession of a piece of property; we would use the word "deed."[13] Now we come up with the glorious translation, "Faith is the title-deed of things hoped for," and faith loses some of its abstract or nebulous character.

In addition to what the papyri do for word meanings, they also contribute to our understanding of Greek grammar. In the past, scholars sometimes observed that passages in the New Testament seemed to have been written in bad grammar, compared to what appeared in classical literature. Critics occasionally commented that grammatical errors could be expected from unlettered fishermen who had become apostles. But we all recognize that grammatical usage changes. For example, in the past few years it has become acceptable in English usage to split infinitives. When we engage in a careful study of the papyri, we find that numerous shifts in grammatical usage took place between the classical and New Testament periods and that what appears in the New Testament is good grammar judged by the standards of its own time.

Zacchaeus the Tax Collector (Luke 19:1–10); Archaeological Light on Tax-Collectors and Taxes in Ancient Times

When Jesus was at Jericho, he called Zacchaeus down from a sycamore tree into which Zacchaeus had climbed in order to better see the Lord as he passed by (Luke 19:1–5). Zacchaeus was a tax collector; by his own confession (that he would make restoration if he had taken too much) he showed the traits of the tax collector of ancient times, who extorted all of the money he could from the people. Several papyri have been found concerning the extortions of tax collectors, and they bring vividly to mind the popular feeling that there must have been against Zacchaeus, as well as against Matthew, who was also a tax collector (Matt. 9:9) (CNAD, 29).

A study of taxation under the Romans reveals that opposition to tax collectors did not necessarily arise from overcharging on allowable rates. The real problem sometimes came with payment; in extending credit, agents might engage in what amounted to loan sharking. Moreover, in Palestine Jewish tax collectors employed by the Roman government were looked on as agents for an oppressive, occupying power, in some sense

---

[12]G. Adolph Deissmann, *Bible Studies* (Edinburgh: T. & T. Clark, 1903), 229 [DBS].

[13]George Milligan, *Here and There Among the Papyri* (London: Hodder & Stoughton, 1922), 72.

disloyal to their own people. Thus they might be hated even if they were scrupulously honest.

The need for tax collectors in the ancient world is revealed by the documents excavated in Egypt. The custom house receipts of a town named Socnopaei Nesus show that there was a heavy tariff rate on both exports and imports and that the individual merchants and tradesmen of every kind had to pay heavy taxes. There were taxes on land and farm stock, on goats and pigs of the temple, and on every item, in fact, that was taxable. In Bible times a very heavy force of collectors must have been necessary (CNAD, 85), and for this reason we should not be surprised to encounter tax collectors such as Zacchaeus and Matthew in the New Testament.

Archaeological Light on the Apparent Contradiction Concerning the Healing of Blind Bartimaeus (Matthew 20:29; Mark 10:46; Luke 18:35)

Just before the Lord met Zacchaeus at Jericho (Luke 19:1ff.), he healed the blind in the same vicinity (Luke 18:35ff.). Matthew (20:29) says that this healing took place as Christ *left* Jericho, whereas in Luke (18:35) the indication is that it took place *on the way into* Jericho. Some have suggested that these were two different events, and that is a possibility.

Archaeology, however, has thrown additional light on this apparent discrepancy. Early in the twentieth century Ernest Sellin of the German Oriental Society conducted excavations at Jericho (1907–1909). He showed that the Jericho of Jesus' time was a double city (CNAD, 361). The old Jewish city was about a mile away from the Roman city. In addition to what Sellin found, Josephus spoke of a theater (JAJ, XVII.vi.3), and amphitheater (viii.2), and a hippodrome (vi.5) there. So far, excavators at Herodian Jericho have uncovered part of the Hasmonean palace and the adjacent swimming pools (where

Herod drowned Aristobulus) and a good part of the palace of Herod the Great and his son Archelaus (EAEHL, 2:565–70). The great structures to which Josephus referred and the residential area await the work of the archaeologists.

It is possible that Matthew wrote about the Jewish city that Christ had left, whereas Luke wrote about the Roman one, at which Christ had not yet arrived. Thus, on his way from the old to the new city, Christ met and healed the blind Bartimaeus. Therefore, if these three passages in Matthew, Mark, and Luke refer to the same event, there is not any contradiction; and if they refer to different healings, there would of course be no contradiction either.

The Trial and Crucifixion of Christ

As noted previously, Christ arrived in Bethany near Jerusalem "six days before the Passover" (John 12:1), probably on a Friday evening. On Saturday evening, a supper was given in honor of Jesus; at this time Mary anointed his feet with costly pure nard (John 12:3), showing her love for him. On the next day, Palm Sunday, Jesus made his triumphal entry into Jerusalem, where the multitude hailed him as "King of Israel" (John 12:12–13), and that evening he returned to Bethany (Mark 11:12).

On Monday, Jesus and his disciples were again on the way into the city. A fig tree, having nothing but leaves, was cursed by the Lord and withered away (Matt. 21:18–22); as to whether the record of the cleansing of the temple at this point (vv. 12–13) is a second cleansing or is the same act as described by John at the beginning of the ministry of Christ is difficult to determine.

Tuesday of the Passion Week was a most eventful day. When Christ appeared at the temple, the scribes, priests, and elders, representing the Sanhedrin, asked him by what authority he acted (Matt. 21:23). Jesus met this effort to ensnare him with a counterquestion, "John's baptism—where did it come from? Was it from heaven, or from men?" His questioners were stymied, for they realized that if they said that the baptism of John was from heaven, Christ would ask why they did not believe him concerning his testimony about Christ; but if they said that John's baptism was of men, they would have to fear what the people might do and say, for John was esteemed by the people. Other ensnaring questions, such as the question of tribute to Caesar (Matt. 22:17), were also effectively answered by the One who is the source of all wisdom. Our Lord then turned the sword of verbal condemnation on his prosecutors and denounced them as hypocrites making only a pretense (Matt. 23:13–14), as fools and blind (23:17), and as a brood of vipers (23:33).

On this same day as the apostolic company was leaving the temple, the disciples pointed to the magnificence of the temple, which brought forth Christ's prophecy that not one stone should be left upon another (Matt. 24:2), a prophecy that was fulfilled within forty years. The remainder of Matthew 24 contains Christ's predictions of events yet to be fulfilled, including his second coming (v. 30). To this discourse on the future (Olivet Discourse, Matt. 24), Christ added the great parables of Matthew 25 on the wise and foolish virgins, the talents, and the sheep and goats—the last one dealing with the judgment of the nations. On Tuesday evening Christ forewarned the disciples of his approaching crucifixion (Matt. 26:2).

Jesus may have spent Wednesday in retirement in Bethany, in preparation of his spirit for the last great conflict (although some scholars arrange the events of this day a little differently).

On Thursday, the fourteenth of Nisan, Jesus gave instructions to the disciples to make preparations for the observance of the Passover (Matt. 26:17–19); they followed the man bearing the pitcher of water and were shown the upper room prepared for their use (Mark 14:13–16). At evening Jesus and the Twelve gathered, and he washed their feet (John 13:2–20); this was followed by the observance of the Passover, now instituted as the Lord's Supper (Matt. 26:26). Here in the Upper Room, Christ foretold his betrayal (John 13:21ff.) and Peter's denial (v. 38), followed by his wonderful words of comfort in John 14, "Do not let your hearts be troubled," and the promise of giving the Counselor or Comforter, the Holy Spirit (John 14:16ff.). He then gave the lesson on the vine and the branches (John 15), and closed with the wonderful intercessory prayer of John 17.

It was still Thursday evening when Jesus and his disciples came to the Garden of Gethsemane, on the east side of Jerusalem (Matt. 26:36). Following the agony in the garden, Jesus was arrested by Roman soldiers, sent by the chief priests (Matt. 26:39–47) and led there by the traitor Judas. Our Lord's surrender was voluntary, demonstrated by the fact that the Father would have sent more than twelve legions of angels if he had but asked (v. 53; in the Empire Period of Rome a legion numbered between 5,000 and 6,000 men; this would mean between 60,000 and 72,000 angels). But this was not a battle against flesh and blood but against sin.

It would have been about midnight Thursday when Jesus was hurried to the house of Caiaphas, the high priest (Matt. 26:57). The whole trial of Christ abounds with illegalities. To mention only a few, it was held at night, there was lack of a definite charge, an interrogation of the accused was made, and there was haste in condemning Christ. He was then brought before Pilate (Matt. 27:11), who against his own convictions and through fear of a charge of disloyalty to Caesar yielded up the One whom he had declared guiltless. Pilate sent Jesus to Herod Antipas, who had jurisdiction over Galilee but happened to be in the city at that time (Luke 23:6–11). Jesus did not answer the questions of Herod or the false accusations heaped upon him by the priests and scribes as he stood before them (v. 9); Herod and his men mocked Christ, putting a robe on him, and then sent him back to Pilate.

During the morning hours of Friday, Pilate finally yielded to the mob, who shouted that if he released Jesus he would not be the friend of Caesar (John 19:20). Christ, bearing the crown of thorns made by the soldiers (Matt. 27:29), was led out to Calvary, and there, between two thieves, was crucified (Matt. 27:35, 44). From the sixth to the ninth hour (12:00 to 3:00 P.M.) there was darkness (Matt. 27:45); it was as though nature herself were veiling her face from the greatest crime ever perpetrated. The Holy One of Israel was being made sin for us.

It was three o'clock by the time Christ had given up his spirit. The Sabbath began at evening, and in order that his body might not remain on the cross on the Sabbath, Joseph of Arimathea sought and obtained permission from Pilate to bury Jesus (Matt. 27:57–60). The body of Christ was placed in Joseph's own new tomb, and the door was closed with the rolling stone. Some of the priests and Pharisees asked that it be sealed and were given permission to seal the stone (Matt. 27:66).

Location of Calvary

Ever since the British hero General Charles George Gordon identified a certain hill just north of the Damascus Gate in Jerusalem as Calvary in 1883, the popular acceptance of this site has grown. In recent years over a hundred thousand tourists and pilgrims have visited there annually. The proposed hill of Calvary stands just north of the present city wall, and by some effort one can imagine that it looks like a skull. On its western side, just 820 feet north of the Damascus Gate is a cave that many have come to believe was the actual burial place of Christ. In 1894 the Garden Tomb Association of Great Britain bought the cave and the surrounding garden, and the tomb is now called the Garden Tomb. Protestants, who have no special rights in the use of the Church of the Holy Sepulcher, have been especially enamored with this site as the location of Calvary and the tomb of Christ. By no means have all Protestants been convinced of its validity, however. The best that some can say is that a visit to the Garden Tomb is satisfying because it permits one to visualize an early empty tomb without the kind of decorative impediments of the Church of the Holy Sepulcher.

Among arguments in favor of Gordon's Calvary are that it resembles a human skull, is close to the city, and is not far from the Damascus Gate and that a cemetery containing a tomb identified as that of Christ is located nearby. Answers to these points include the following: The spot has not looked like a skull for more than a couple of centuries; the continued use of sand and stone from the mound has brought it to its present appearance. Moreover, the city walls and the great North Road are not in the same locations as in New Testament times. In Jesus' day the city wall ran far south of where it does now.

This is where the subject stood until the last few years. Now it must be viewed in a different light. After the Israeli occupation of East Jerusalem and the West Bank in 1967, it has been possible for Israeli archaeologists to work in East Jerusalem. Amihai Mazar made a study of the burial caves north of the Damascus Gate and concluded that the whole area had been an Iron Age cemetery (during the general period of the eighth to the seven centuries B.C.).[14] Gabriel Barkay, who teaches at Tel Aviv University and the American Institute of Holy Land Studies, has made a new study of the case for the Garden Tomb and has concluded that it was first hewn in the Iron Age II period, during the eighth to the sixth centuries B.C., and was not used again for burial purposes until the Byzantine period. So it is not the tomb in which Jesus was buried.[15]

The traditional site of Calvary and the tomb of Jesus is in the Church of the Holy Sepulcher, now located deep inside the old city of Jerusalem. But was it outside the city in New Testament times? As a result of various discoveries in recent decades, the line of the wall has now been established; the wall was about 500 feet to the south and 350 feet to the east of the church.[16] If the church was outside the wall, the next issue is the legitimacy of the claim that Jesus was buried there.

The church as it now stands is essentially a Crusader structure, begun after the Crusaders captured Jerusalem in 1099. The prior history of the site requires a considerable amount of space to describe it in full (for details, see FLAP, 527–32), but the main outline can be briefly put. By and large the Crusader church replaced a church erected by Constantine and dedicated in 335, though parts of the edifice had been destroyed and rebuilt. Apparently what Constantine constructed was a rotunda covering the tomb of Jesus, before which (on the east) lay a garden open to the sky and surrounded by a portico of columns. In the southeastern corner of the garden stood the rock of Calvary. Then on an axis with the tomb and to the east of the garden Constantine put up a basilica church (Bahat, 36; FLAP,

527–28). Reportedly all Constantine had to do when he built his church was to remove a small temple built by Hadrian to Venus/Aphrodite on that site when he rebuilt Jerusalem early in the second century A.D. Local Christians had identified this as the place of Christ's death and burial to Queen Helena, Constantine's mother, when she visited Jerusalem in A.D. 326 (Bahat, 35). Eusebius, the noted church historian, who preached in the church soon after its construction, reported how after the removal of the temple of Venus the tomb of Christ reappeared.[17] The Crusader church covered the site of the tomb, the garden, Calvary, and Constantine's basilica.

In recent times the Crusader Church of the Holy Sepulcher became quite decrepit. A restoration plan was finally agreed on in 1959 by the religious bodies having access to the church, and the following year Virgilio Corbo of the Franciscan School in Jerusalem was appointed archaeologist for the project. The Franciscan Printing Press published the three-volume report, the *Holy Sepulcher of Jerusalem*, in 1981–1982. The restoration involved a considerable amount of excavation under the church. Beneath the north wall of the rotunda lies a tomb traditionally attributed to Joseph of Arimathea (Bahat, 31). After completing his study on the Church of the Holy Sepulcher, Finegan concluded, "We may with confidence seek beneath the roof of this structure the true place of Golgotha and the sepulcher of Christ" (FLAP, 532).

The Resurrection and Ascension of Christ

On the morning of the first day of the week (Sunday), the two Marys came to the

---

[14]Amihai Mazar, "Iron Age Burial Caves North of Damascus Gate Jerusalem," *Israel Exploration Journal* 26 (1976): 1–8.

[15]Gabriel Barkay, "The Garden Tomb—Was Jesus Buried Here?" BAR (March/April 1986), 57.

[16]Dan Bahat, "Does the Holy Sepulcher Church Mark the Burial of Jesus?" BAR (May/June 1986), 38.

[17]Charles Coüasnon, *The Church of the Holy Sepulcher Jerusalem* (London: The British Academy, 1974), 13–14.

tomb and found that Christ had risen (Matt. 28:1ff.). Ten appearances of Jesus after his resurrection are recorded in the Gospels, five of them occurring on the resurrection day. Among the significant ones are his meeting with the disciples on the Emmaus road (Luke 24:12–35) and with the Eleven on the day of his resurrection (vv. 35ff.), his appearance at the Sea of Galilee when the disciples were fishing (John 21:1ff.), and his meeting them at the mountain in Galilee where he gave the great commission to go into all the world and preach the gospel (Matt. 28:16–20). The last appearance of Christ on earth was on the slopes of the Mount of Olives, near Bethany, where he ascended to heaven (Luke 24:50–51). As he went up, two angels appeared and assured the disciples that he would return (Acts 1:11), an event for which we wait and pray.

Archaeological Evidence Against New Testament "Form Criticism"

A new type of biblical criticism has developed since 1919 under the leadership of Martin Dibelius and Rudolph Bultmann, both of Germany (AAP, 242). It is called "form criticism"[18] because it holds that the oral traditions of the church developed into definite literary "forms," such as the miracle stories, parables, and sayings of Jesus (ASAC, 294). Form critics usually hold that much of the content of the Gospels was adapted or in other cases invented to correspond to situations that developed in the church after the days of the apostles (AAP, 242). This means, according to form criticism, that much of the material in the Gospels really reflects a later period in the church and merely appears to describe the early apostolic era. The gospel of John, to cite an example, is held by this school (e.g., Bultmann) to contain practically no original historical material, but to reflect a period in the second century A.D.

In 1942 historian A.T. Olmstead[19] reacted against this critical view of John. He insisted that the narratives of John were written down in Aramaic before A.D. 40 and were later rendered in Greek (AAP, 243). (Truly conservative scholars hold to 85–90 as the date of John's gospel, on the basis of internal as well as external evidence; TINT, 173.) While Olmstead probably went too far in the reverse direction from those who hold to a second-century date for John, it is refreshing to see an objective historian object to these subjective extremes of form criticism. More recently Bishop John A.T. Robinson (Anglican), lecturer in theology at Cambridge University, rejected many of his earlier radical views and concluded in 1977 that the New Testament books were written between A.D. 47 and 70.[20]

Archaeological discoveries have given definite evidence that the background of the gospel of John reflects a knowledge of the situation in Palestine prior to A.D. 70. This evidence is well summarized by W.F. Albright (AAP, 244–48). Only two items from this body of evidence will be given here: First, very often in the gospel of John the Aramaic term *rabbi*, rendered in Greek as *didaskalos*, "master, teacher" (John 1:38; 20:16), is applied to Christ. Rabbinic scholars have held that the use of this term was a borrowing from current usage in the second century, when it appeared in the Mishnah[21] and other sources. This would mean that the employment of "master" was an evidence of the late date of the gospel of John.

---

[18]Known in German as *Formgeschichte*. For brief descriptions, see AAP, 242ff.; ASAC, 298; TINT, 118ff.; Donald Guthrie, *New Testament Introduction*, 3rd ed. (Downers Grove: InterVarsity, 1970), chap. 6.

[19]At the Oriental Institute of the University of Chicago until his death in 1945.

[20]John A.T. Robinson, *Can We Trust the New Testament?* (Grand Rapids: Eerdmans, 1977), 63.

[21]The Mishnah (or text) is one of the two main parts of the Talmud, the other being the Gemara, or commentary.

Excavations by E.L. Sukenik, however, produced an early ossuary[22] in 1930 from Mount Scopus (across the Kidron Valley from Jerusalem) on which the Greek word *didaskalos* ("master") was applied as the title of a man named Theodotion, whose personal name was written in Aramaic characters (AAP, 244). This discovery shows that one may not charge the gospel of John with an anachronism in the use of the term "master" (*didaskalos*).

Second, some scholars formerly held that personal names used in the gospels, particularly in John, were fictitious and had been selected because of their meaning and not because they referred to historical persons. Such speculations are not supported by the ossuary inscriptions, which preserve many of the biblical names. Those occurring include Miriam (Mary), Martha, Elizabeth, Salome, Johanna, and Sapphira (Acts 5:1), as well as Jesus (equivalent to the Old Testament Joshua), Joseph, and an abbreviated form of the name Lazarus (AAP, 244). While no one would insist that the biblical characters bearing these names are necessarily the same as those recorded on the ossuaries, nonetheless the ossuary inscriptions show that these names fit in the early New Testament period and that the form critic is left without archaeological support for using this criterion of personal names for his late dating of New Testament material, particularly the gospel of John.

As noted before, conservative scholars hold that the gospel of John was written about 85–90.[23] In addition to the ossuary evidence, discoveries of papyrus manuscripts also support this date, as against a later date in the second century, held by adherents of form criticism. In 1935 C.H. Roberts identified a fragment of the Gospel of John that had been excavated several years earlier by Grenfell and sent to the John Rylands Library in England (often referred to as "Rylands John"). This fragment contains only five verses (18:31–33, 37–38), but it is most significant because papyrus experts agree in assigning it to the first half of the second century. Kenyon points out that the copy of the gospel from which this fragment came would have circulated in Egypt in the period 130–150. This means that the original Gospel of John must have been composed sometime earlier than 130, which would bring us so near to the traditional date that "there is no longer

---

[22]An ossuary is a bone chest in which bones of those long dead were placed so that the tomb could be reused for another burial. An inscription bearing the name of the person to whom the bones belonged was usually inscribed on the ossuary.

[23]This is based on a number of factors. The church fathers gave indications that John was written after the other gospels: Irenaeus (c. 140–203) placed it after Matthew, Mark, and Luke, and Clement of Alexandria (c. 155–215) said that John wrote "last of all." Jerome (c. 340–420) gives a similar indication. The way in which the gospel of John refers to "the Jews" implies that it was written after that nation had become confirmed enemies of the church and many years after the author had been absent from Palestine. The lack of reference to the destruction of Jerusalem in 70 seems to require that the gospel be dated sometime before that event, or sufficiently afterward to allow for it to have become somewhat incidental. Since the evidence would point to a date sometime after 70 rather than before, it would likely be sometime between 85 and 90. (Other factors noted below would preclude its being much later.) Irenaeus declares that John wrote this gospel at Ephesus and that he lived until the time of the Roman emperor Trajan, who began to rule in 98. Since John did not get to Ephesus until about 69 or 70 (following Paul's last visit there in 65 or 66; cf. TINT, 170), it must have been written sometime after 70, inasmuch as no reference is made to the Jewish troubles of 66–70 or the destruction of the temple in 70. Since John lived until the time of Trajan (98), it appears logical on the basis of all these indications to date the Gospel 85–90. Westcott, the well-known New Testament scholar of the nineteenth century, substantially agreed to this date, placing it late in the first century. For development and documentation of this material, see TINT, 172–73.

any reason to question the validity of the tradition."[24]

Other evidence for the early date of John and the other Gospels appeared in the discovery of some papyri fragments that were published by H.I. Bell and T.C. Skeat of the British Museum. The document from which these fragments came must have been written in the first half of the second century A.D. and contains material that Kenyon assigns to the first century. It records the stories of the healing of the leper (Mark 1:40–42) and the question of paying tribute to Caesar (Matt. 22:17–18; Mark 12:14–15; Luke 20:21–25), and reflects the language of not only the first three Gospels but also of John (KBMS, 22–23). Here also, Kenyon says, is "confirmatory evidence of the existence of the Fourth Gospel by about the end of the first century" (KBMS, 23).

Kenyon points out that if the fourth Gospel was written by A.D. 90, and if it was preceded by Matthew and Luke, and earlier by Mark, about 65, then there was not time enough for the elaborate process required by Dibelius's form criticism. This theory presupposes, first, the diffusion of stories about Jesus, then their collection and classification into groups according to their literary form, and finally the formation of continuous narratives in which they were utilized. Kenyon aptly remarks that there simply is "not time for elaborate processes of literary workmanship and development" (KBMS, 52). The discoveries thus show that the speculations of the school of form criticism are not supported[25] and that the Gospels must have been written in the first century A.D.

The General Critical View of the Date of the Gospels; the Bearing of Archaeology

As we have seen in the preceding section, an integral part of the theory of form criticism is the late dating of the Gospels. This was first developed by F.C. Baur (1792–1860) and others in the Tübingen school of German criticism. They set forth the view that the Gospel of John could not have been written until 160 (BAB, 588).

The same evidence that refutes form criticism's late dating of the Gospels is applicable to a more general theory holding to their late date. This would include the archaeological evidence showing an early background for John, such as the indications on ossuaries of the early use of the term "master" and of New Testament names, as well as Rylands John and the Gospel fragments published by Bell and Skeat (see preceding section). All of this evidence points to the existence of the Gospel of John by the end of the first century, which is the date held by true conservatives.

In regard to the Synoptic Gospels (Matthew, Mark, and Luke), it is refreshing to see that one of the greatest French liberal scholars of the last generation, Maurice Goguel, puts them in the first century in his work *The Early Church.*[26] Most significant of all, of course, is not the opinion of the scholars, but rather the internal evidence from the Gospels, the evidence from the archaeological discoveries and papyrus documents, which point to the early date and validity of the Gospels.

Something has been said about the contribution of the early papyrus fragment of the Gospel of John to the dating

---

[24]Frederic G. Kenyon, *The Bible and Modern Scholarship* (London: Murray, 1948), 21 [KBMS]. Sir Frederic Kenyon was formerly Director of the British Museum; his field of specialization is in New Testament manuscripts.

[25]There is other evidence against form criticism that for the sake of conciseness cannot be treated here. For summary, see TINT, 118–21.

[26]*L'Eglise primitive (Jésus et les origines du Christianisme)* (Paris: Payot, 1947); cf. review written by C.C. McCown in JBL 68, 3 (September 1949): 270.

of the books of the New Testament. There are two other contributions the papyri make in this regard. This first concerns the argument based on historical grammar. We are familiar with the fact that language keeps changing, and even the less technically educated person can, for instance, spot the difference between the English of Shakespeare's or Thomas Jefferson's day and contemporary American prose. Just so, the person who has studied the papyri knows what the Greek style and vocabulary was like in the first century and knows that the New Testament uses the language of the first century, not the second or third. The conclusion of Millar Burrows in this regard is significant: "Unless we resort to the wholly improbable hypothesis of a deliberate and remarkable successful use of archaic language, it is evident therefore that the books of the New Testament were written in the first century" (WMTS, 54).

Second, the biblical papyri, dating from the second or third centuries help to destroy the old critical view that the oral traditions, and especially the miraculous nature of Christ's ministry, evolved over time and finally came to their present form in the third or fourth century.

The Dead Sea Scrolls and the Ministry of Christ

Soon after the Dead Sea Scrolls began to make their impact, a literature developed that sought to rob Christ and Christianity of all their uniqueness. Some found Christ to be merely the "reincarnation of the Teacher of Righteousness" of the Qumran community, and the church to be merely an extension of the community there. A detailed and definitive answer to these assertions is not possible in a few words here, nor is it necessary. William S. LaSor in his definitive work *The Dead Sea Scrolls and the New Testament* has carefully handled all aspects of these issues. He showed that John the Baptist either was not a Qumranian or, if he ever had been, he had broken completely with the community's viewpoint. He demonstrated the tremendous difference between the church and the Qumran community. And answering some of the earlier assertions, LaSor concluded that the "Teacher of Righteousness" was really totally unlike Jesus Christ. Contrary to claims of likeness, there is no record of his crucifixion, burial, resurrection, or promise of return.[27]

[27]William S. LaSor, *The Dead Sea Scrolls and the New Testament* (Grand Rapids: Eerdmans, 1972), 152, 247–54. See also R.K. Harrison, *Archaeology of the New Testament* (London: English Universities Press, 1964), chapter 6, "Qumran and the New Testament." Charles F. Pfeiffer in his *Dead Sea Scrolls and the Bible* (Grand Rapids: Baker, 1969) has a helpful chapter entitled "Qumran Messianism."

Chapter 27

The Beginning of the Church

(Acts 1–12)

The Day of Pentecost; the Beginning of the Church (Acts 1–2)

After the ascension of Christ (Acts 1:9), Matthias was chosen to replace Judas among the apostles (vv. 15–26). The next important event occurred on the Day of Pentecost. Pentecost was one of the Old Testament festivals, referred to in the Pentateuch as the "Feast of Weeks" (Exod. 34:22), because it was celebrated seven weeks, or fifty days, after the Passover (Lev. 23:16). On that day, two loaves were presented, along with the offering of lambs and other animals (v. 18). It was to be a day of rejoicing, as well as a day in which Israel remembered that they had been bondservants in the land of Egypt, a reminder to observe the statutes of the Lord (Deut. 16:11–12).

When the disciples gathered on this Day of Pentecost, it was fifty days after the resurrection of Christ, or just ten days after his ascension (since his postresurrection ministry was forty days). The Holy Spirit came upon the disciples, and they spoke with other tongues, so that the strangers who were in Jerusalem could understand what they were saying (Acts 2:6). Thus we see that there was a specific purpose for the speaking in tongues—it was to enable the visitors in Jerusalem to understand the message.

The coming of the Holy Spirit on Pentecost is generally recognized as marking the beginning of the church.[1] The apostles were now changed, and the outpouring of the Holy Spirit on them enabled them to become effective wit-

---

[1] Those who hold that the church began in Old Testament times would say, rather, that Pentecost was a turning point in the church. Both views present a definite aspect of truth: to say that the church began in Old Testament times is to emphasize the fact that people in all ages are saved by the shed blood of Christ. It is evident that a change took place in the operation of the Holy Spirit beginning with Pentecost. From then on the Holy Spirit indwells the believer, whereas in Old Testament times he came upon individuals for special tasks. As to salvation, it is clear that whether the church began at Pentecost or in Old Testament times, in all ages people have been saved only by the substitutionary death of Christ. Old Testament saints looked forward to the promised Seed, whereas those in the Christian era look back to him and his finished work on Calvary. Peter states the truth of the unity of the plan of salvation when, referring to Old Testament believers, he says, "It is through the grace of our Lord Jesus that we are saved, just as they are" (Acts 15:11).

259

nesses of the resurrection of Christ as the fundamental fact in Christianity and to extend the church by preaching the gospel according to the Great Commission.

Archaeological Evidence of Jews in Many Countries in the New Testament Period

Among the people who heard the disciples speak in tongues on the Day of Pentecost were those from Phrygia, Egypt, Rome, and many other places (Acts 2:10). Many of them, perhaps most of them, were descendants of Palestinian Jews who years earlier had gone to other countries and there lived and learned the language of their adopted land. Archaeological evidence of Jews in these other lands has been forthcoming in the excavations. Ramsay's work in Asia Minor in the region of ancient Phrygia showed that there were many Jews in that area in the New Testament period. Some two thousand families of Jews had been brought from Babylon to Phrygia about 200 B.C. and had populated the district; with succeeding generations they increased in numbers and influence, and many of them grew rich. With the passage of time, they even forgot their own language (CNAD, 417). It was undoubtedly for Jews of this type who may have been visiting Jerusalem that the miracle of the tongues at Pentecost occurred; it was necessary in order that these Jews could understand the message.

Egypt is also mentioned among the countries represented by the hearers of the disciples on the Day of Pentecost (Acts 2:10). The presence of Jews in Egypt in the New Testament period has been shown by several excavations, including evidence from a large oasis called the Fayum, about forty miles south and a little west of Cairo (CNAD, 65). Here was a Jewish colony, named Samaria, where the Jews were, among other things, bankers, tax gatherers, and police officers (CNAD, 79). The entire fourth quarter of the great

city of Alexandria, named for Alexander the Great, was a Jewish district.

The Bible refers to Rome as one of the places represented on the Day of Pentecost (Acts 2:10). Evidence for Jews living at Rome in that era appeared in the excavation of several early cemeteries in that city that proved to be Jewish. One cemetery on the Via Portuensis yielded 119 inscriptions, some of them showing the seven-branched lampstand, and others giving such Jewish names as Jacob, Judas, Anna, and Rebecca (CNAD, 517–18).

Peter's Message on the Day of Pentecost (Acts 2:14–39)

After the apostles had spoken in different tongues on the Day of Pentecost, those who had heard were amazed, and some mocked, saying they had had too much wine (Acts 2:12–13). Peter stood up and addressed the group. He pointed out that Jesus of Nazareth, whom God had raised, was the One foretold by David (v. 25), the One who would not see corruption (Ps. 16:10, a prophecy of the resurrection of Christ). Peter then called on Israel to repent, to be baptized in the name of Jesus Christ for the remission of sins, and to receive the Holy Spirit (Acts 2:38). Many gladly received the message, and about three thousand were baptized and added to those who already believed. This constituted the beginning of the church.

Peter's Second Sermon; the Opposition That Followed (Acts 3–4)

After Peter and John healed the lame man at the Beautiful Gate (Acts 3:1–11), a group of people gathered at Solomon's porch, and Peter took the opportunity to address them (3:11–12). He called on Israel to repent that their sins might be blotted out, pointing to Christ as the One whom God had raised up, the One sent to turn them from their iniquities (vv. 19, 26).

The priests and Sadducees were greatly disturbed at this preaching of Jesus and the resurrection (Acts 4:1–2), and they seized the disciples and confined them. But the seed had already been sown, and in spite of the detention of the disciples, about five thousand men had believed (v. 4). Peter was given opportunity the next day to address the Jewish council known as the Sanhedrin; he preached to them the truth of the crucifixion and resurrection of Christ, in whom alone there is salvation (vv. 10–12). The Jewish leaders ordered them to preach no more in the name of Christ (v. 17), but Peter and John candidly answered, "We cannot help speaking about what we have seen and heard" (v. 20).

Mutual Aid in the Early Church; the Sin of Ananias and Sapphira (Acts 4:32–37; 5:1–11)

It seems that, in order to meet an emergency in the early church, there was a temporary practice of pooling the resources of the believers. Those who had property sold it and brought the proceeds to the apostles, who distributed according to every person's need.[2]

A man and his wife, Ananias and Sapphira, sold some property and brought only a part of the money to the apostles, keeping back a part, yet pretending to have brought all of it. There was no compulsion for them to have brought anything. Their sin lay in the fact that they lied, pretending that they had brought it all (Acts 5:2). Upon hearing the charge against him, Ananias fell down and died. When his wife, Sapphira, came in, she likewise lied about the matter, and died when confronted with the fact of her sin.

Archaeological Light on the Name Sapphira (Acts 5:1)

Until earlier in this century, no evidence of the name Sapphira had been found outside of the Bible. In 1933, a report was published of the discovery of several ossuaries and other objects contemporary with New Testament times on which was written the name Sapphira (HSAB, 84), showing that it was a perfectly good name and fits into this period.

The Second Persecution of the Church (Acts 5:17ff.)

The works and words of the apostles caused more and more people to turn to

---

[2]Some have thought that this temporary pooling of resources by members of the early church at Jerusalem gives justification to communism as a legitimate form of government. An examination of the situation shows just the opposite. First, it was a *temporary* measure designed to meet an immediate need. Doubtless many Jews who became Christians were unable to continue their former means of employment because of prejudice on the part of employers (and for other reasons as well), and there was need for helping them over this transition stage while the church was in the process of being established and until there could be set up a regular "fund" to take care of such contingencies. Not only did the local converts have financial needs, but also many pilgrims who had come to Jerusalem for the Feast of Pentecost were in great distress. Some of them wished to stay longer for spiritual enrichment and had no resources to do so, and others feared to return home and face the economic and social discrimination they would encounter there. Second, as shown by the case of Ananias and Sapphira, there was no compulsion on them or anyone else to put anything in the common pool. Those who did so gave *voluntarily*, an entirely different situation from the communistic idea, which sets aside the rights of voluntary giving and virtually, by decree, makes the property of the thrifty the property of the indolent. Third, this was a *local* practice carried on, as far as we know, only at Jerusalem to meet an immediate need—the poverty of some of the new believers. There is no evidence that such communism was practiced at Philippi, Corinth, Ephesus, or other more affluent places. This temporary measure was merely an outworking of true Christian charity and bears no resemblance to the political communism prevalent in many countries of the world in much of the twentieth century. The idea of one man's enterprise being penalized by another man's laziness is foreign to the Scriptures. It is clearly stated that "if a man will not work, he shall not eat" (2 Thess. 3:10).

the Lord (Acts 5:12–14). This in turn aroused the ire of the high priest and his company, and they put the apostles in prison (vv. 17–18). When they were brought before the council, the apostles were asked why they had not ceased to teach in the name of Christ. Peter and the other apostles gave their unanswerable reply: "We must obey God rather than men" and then continued to exalt Christ as the One who could forgive sins (vv. 28–31). The council considered putting the apostles to death, but one of the Pharisees, Gamaliel, warned that if this movement were of men, it would fail, but if it were of God, they could not overthrow it (vv. 38–39). Gamaliel's wise council influenced them to abandon their thought to kill the apostles, and they were content to beat them and let them go with the admonition that they should not speak in the name of Jesus. The apostles went out, rejoicing that they were considered worthy to suffer for his name, and they did not stop teaching and preaching the good news of Jesus Christ (v. 42).

The Appointment of Deacons (Acts 6:1–7)

A complaint arose within the church because certain of the widows were being neglected in the provision that should have been made for them. The apostles realized that if they busied themselves too much with the necessary everyday routine, they would neglect the preaching of the Word of God. They therefore decided to appoint deacons, who would take care of serving the needy. This first deacons' board consisted of seven members, one of whom was Stephen (Acts 6:5).

The Third Persecution, Initiated by the Synagogue of the Freedmen and Others (Acts 6:8–15)

Stephen set a good example, not restricting himself to serving the needy but also doing great spiritual wonders among the people. This aroused the wrath of those in the synagogue of the Freedmen and other groups of Jews, who stirred up the people so that they again brought one of the believers, this time Stephen, before the Jewish council (Act 6:12).

Archaeological Evidence of the Synagogue of the Freedmen (Acts 6:9)

In 1913, Captain Weill excavated at Jerusalem and found an inscription stating that a certain "Theodotus" (Greek translation of the name Nathanael) had "constructed the synagogue. . ." (for translation, see BAB, 564). The father of Theodotus had a Latin name, Vettenos (shown by the inscription), which probably means that the father was one of the Jews captured by Pompey (63 B.C.; see chapter 25), taken to Rome, and later liberated, becoming a "libertine" or freedman and returning to Jerusalem. Thus it seems likely that this inscription, bearing a name appropriate for a freedman, may come from this very synagogue of the freedmen who initiated the persecution against Stephen (BAB, 564). It is interesting to note that, according to the inscription, the synagogue Theodotus constructed had a hospice connected with it "for the needy from abroad." These needy might have included freed Jews returning from Rome with plans to resettle in Palestine. This name Vettenos is the type of name that would be given by a man named Vettius to his slave; Clermont-Ganneau has suggested that this Vettius might be the very man of the same name who acted for Cicero, the Roman orator, as his agent in money matters (MCEP, 197).

Stephen's Message (Acts 7)

When Stephen was brought before the council, the council set up false witnesses against him, who charged that he spoke blasphemous words against the holy place and the law (Acts 6:13–14). Stephen was then asked by the high priest if these things were so; his answer forms the

Seventh chapter of Acts. He began with the call of Abraham, telling how God had brought him into the Promised Land and had watched over him and all of his descendants, showing his favor to Joseph, Jacob, Moses, and a host of others. But Israel had been stiffnecked and had persecuted the prophets and slain those who proclaimed the Righteous One to come, the very One whom they had murdered.

The First Appearance of Saul, Later Called Paul (Acts 7:58)

The words of Stephen cut his accusers to the quick, and they threw him out of the city and stoned him (Acts 7:57–58). One of the witnesses of the stoning of Stephen was a young man named Saul, at whose feet the murderers of Stephen laid their clothes. Stephen's calm committal of himself to his Lord must have made an impression on Saul—but what type of impression we do not know. Outwardly, it seemed merely to spur Saul on to a greater persecution of the Christians, for he continued to try to destroy the church, committing believers to prison whenever he could.

The Ministry of Philip; Archaeological Light on Candace (Acts 8)

In the meantime, the ministry of the church went forward. Philip went to Samaria and preached Christ (Acts 8:5). He was carrying out the commission of Christ, to take the Gospel beyond Jerusalem and Judea to Samaria and more distant regions (v. 8). Sometime later Philip was traveling in the south, toward Gaza, and there he met an Ethiopian eunuch, a man of authority in the government of Queen Candace of Ethiopia. Archaeological light on the group of queens called Candace was found by McIver in his excavations in Nubia, 1908–1909. In the Christian period these Nubians still called their queen Candace; they gave her milk to drink, regarding obesity an attribute of royalty (BAB, 30). In the British Museum there is a large relief showing one of these queens named Candace.

Philip found the Ethiopian eunuch reading the fifty-third chapter of Isaiah and tactfully asked him if he understood what he read. Then, receiving an implied invitation, he proceeded to explain the Scripture passage and to lead the man to a knowledge of Christ (Acts 8:35–36).

The Conversion of Paul (Saul) (Acts 9)

Saul set out for Damascus, planning to look for Christians whom he might bring bound to Jerusalem (Acts 9:1–2). As he journeyed along the road to Damascus, a light engulfed him; he fell to the ground and heard a voice calling to him, "Saul, Saul, why do you persecute me?" Saul asked, "Who are you, Lord?" and received the answer, "I am Jesus whom you are persecuting" (vv. 4–5). Saul asked what he should do, and the Lord told him to go on into Damascus. When Saul arose and opened his eyes, he could see no one. He was brought to Damascus to the house of Judas on Straight Street. There he stayed three days and was then met by a man named Ananias, who put his hands on him, and immediately the scales of blindness fell from his eyes. (Later Saul's name was changed to Paul.)

Peter's Ministry to the Gentiles (Acts 10)

The Lord revealed to a Roman army officer, a centurion named Cornelius, that he should send to Joppa for Peter (Acts 10:5). When the messengers arrived at Joppa, Peter went with them to the home of Cornelius at Caesarea, some distance to the north of Joppa (v. 24). To the household of Cornelius Peter preached Christ as the One who could give remission of sins (v. 43), and they believed. With the preaching of the Gospel to this household, the ministry to the Gentiles was definitely begun.

263

The Church at Antioch; First Use of the Name "Christian" (Acts 11:19–30)

The persecution of Stephen had resulted in the scattering of many believers, some of whom came to Antioch and preached the Word to the Jews (Acts 11:19–20). The Jerusalem church heard the good news of the church at Antioch and sent Barnabas to visit the believers there (v. 22). From Antioch, Barnabas went on to Tarsus and brought Paul back to Antioch, where they both taught the people for a whole year (v. 26). It was here at Antioch that the believers were first called Christians.[3] During the famine that occurred in the reign of the Roman emperor Claudius (41–54), the Christians at Antioch took up an offering and sent it for the relief of the believers in Judea (vv. 28–30).

The Imprisonment of Peter; Death of Herod Agrippa I (A.D. 40–44) (Acts 12)

At this time (c. 40–44) Herod Agrippa I put James the brother of John to death, and imprisoned Peter (Acts 12:1–3). The believers prayed for Peter, and the Lord sent an angel who brought Peter out of prison (v. 7). Herod reigned for only a short time, dying in 44. The Antioch church now prepared to send Paul and Barnabas on the first missionary journey (Acts 13:1–3).

Antioch, the Great Apostolic Center

Antioch was not only the place where believers were first called Christians; it was also the city that became the early headquarters of Christianity and from which the church sent the apostle Paul on all three of his missionary journeys. It was the third most important city of the Roman Empire—after Rome and Alexandria. Metzger estimated the population of Antioch to have been about a half million during the first Christian century and believed that about one-seventh of them were Jews.[4] The city was located on the Orontes River in Syria, about sixteen miles from the Mediterranean. Its seaport was Seleucia.

In 1931 the Syrian government gave permission to Princeton University and the National Museum of France to excavate at Antioch for a period of six years. By means of these excavations and historical references, it has been possible to reconstruct some of the main features of the city as it appeared during the New Testament period.

As one entered the gate in the northeast wall, he would have found himself on an open roadway thirty feet wide paved with Egyptian granite. All along both sides of this four-and-a-half-mile-long thoroughfare (running from northeast to southwest) stood covered colonnades, each thirty feet wide. As a result of this construction, a pedestrian could walk the entire length of the city protected from sun and rain. Houses and public buildings could be entered between the columns of the walkway. Augustus and Tiberius, with the assistance of Herod the Great of Judea, built this street with its walks in the period from 23 B.C. to A.D. 37.

Side streets intersected the main street, and the more important were colonnad-

---

[3]Modern believers must often wonder how the term *Christian* originated and what it implied. In the Greek the term is *Christianos*. The adjective ending (*ianos*) originally applied to a slave belonging to a great household and subsequently was regularly used to denote adherents of an individual or party. So a Christian might be regarded as a slave of Christ or simply an adherent of Christ (J. Dickie, "Christian," ISBE, 1:657). Head, working from the papyri, observes that a *Kaisarianos* was an imperial slave or soldier belonging to the divine Caesar; the parallel form, *Christianos*, would signify a slave or soldier belonging to the divine Christ (Eldred D. Head, *New Testament Life and Literature as Reflected in the Papyri* [Nashville: Broadman, 1952], 50). As bondslaves we have been bought with a price (1 Cor. 6:19–20); as Christian soldiers we are to "fight the good fight of faith" (1 Tim. 6:12; cf. Eph. 6:11–17).

[4]Bruce M. Metzger, "Antioch-on-the-Orontes," BA 11 (December 1948): 81.

ed. Public fountains stood at the corners of the streets, where women and children could get the family water supply. There were numerous squares where children played, shopkeepers sold their wares, philosophers taught, and entertainers performed. In the middle of the city the main thoroughfare opened into a plaza where a striking bronze statue of Tiberius stood, erected by the grateful city for all the emperor's benefactions.

In the river to the north of the city lay an island some two miles long by two miles wide. There had stood the palaces of the Seleucids, and Roman royal residences had succeeded them. On the island was also a hippodrome with an arena over sixteen hundred feet long, built in the first century.

Along the southeast bank of the river and south of the island was located the city's original quarter as established by Seleucus Nicator in 300 B.C. Here barges discharged cargoes at stone quays. Near-by stood an agora (covering four city blocks) and a temple of Zeus.[5]

An especially interesting find, presumably unearthed at Antioch, is the famous Chalice of Antioch, now in the Metropolitan Museum of Art in New York, reportedly found in 1910 by workmen who were digging a well. The chalice is of two parts: a plain inner cup of silver, about seven and a half inches high and six inches in diameter, and an outer gilded holder with twelve figures displayed on the outside. Much has been written about the date and interpretation of this piece. The outer cup has been said to represent Christ and his disciples, and the inner cup has even been identified as the Holy Grail, used by Christ at the Last Supper. Dates as early as the first century have been assigned.[6] Perhaps the best that can be said about this chalice is that it is an early piece of Christian art of some century later than the first and that Christ or some of the disciples may be intended by the artistic representations.

---

[5]See Glanville Downey's *Ancient Antioch* (Princeton: Princeton University Press, 1963) and his *History of Antioch in Syria* (Princeton: Princeton University Press, 1961).

[6]For a discussion see H. Harvard Arnason, "The History of the Chalice of Antioch," BA (December 1941), 49–64, (February 1942), 10–16; Floyd V. Filson, "Who Are the Figures on the Chalice of Antioch?" BA (February 1942), 1–10.

Chapter 28

Paul's Journeys

(Acts 13–28)

Paul's First Missionary Journey
(Acts 13–14)

The church at Antioch in Syria was led by the Lord to commission Paul and Barnabas to go on the first missionary journey (Acts 13:1–3). They left Antioch and went some sixteen miles to the seaport of Seleucia (v. 4) on the Mediterranean. There they took a ship to travel across a seventy-nine-mile stretch of the Mediterranean to the island of Cyprus, where they landed at the port of Salamis (v. 5). At Salamis they preached in the synagogues (see map 10).

The harbor at Seleucia, from which Paul's first and third missionary journeys were launched

Archaeological Work at Salamis

Salamis was the great port on the eastern side of Cyprus, and it was the chief city of the island during the Roman period. Unfortunately, because of destructive earthquakes in the region, it may be impossible ever to visualize the city as it was when Paul and Barnabas preached there about A.D. 45. For instance, an earthquake destroyed the city in 76/77. Rebuilt under the emperors Trajan and Hadrian, it was again hit by a severe earthquake in 332 and another ten years later—this time accompanied by a tidal wave. Again, during the seventh century, Arab raids destroyed the city, and it was finally abandoned in favor of Famagusta, about five miles to the south.

Although digs did take place at Salamis in the nineteenth century, serious work did not begin there until the Cyprus Department of Antiquities launched annual campaigns at the site beginning in 1952. Much of what they uncovered dated either to the city's early history (eleventh to seventh centuries B.C.) or to the Byzantine period (fourth century A.D. or later). Two finds are of interest to the New Testament student, however. Not far from the harbor stood the theater of Salamis.

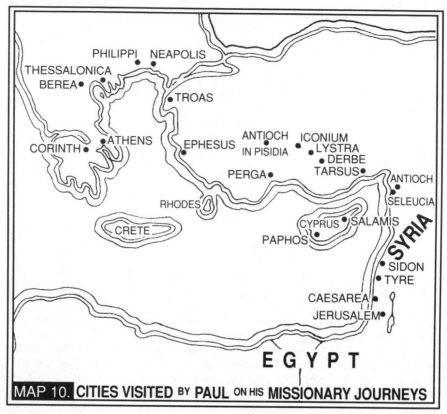

MAP 10. CITIES VISITED BY PAUL ON HIS MISSIONARY JOURNEYS

Discovered in 1959, it had an orchestra area about 87 feet in diameter and a cavea of 50 rows of seats. The structure is estimated to have seated over 15,000 people. It was built early in the first century A.D. and was therefore in use when Paul and Barnabas came through.

In the late 1960s the department worked extensively at the stone forum, located several hundred yards south of the theater. Considered to be the greatest in the Roman Empire, this town center was 750 feet long and 180 feet wide. Along the sides were 27-foot-high columns spaced 15 feet apart and topped with Corinthian capitals. Behind the colonnades stood the usual shops of a Greek agora. At the south end of the forum or agora stood the temple of Zeus, of which only the high podium remains. The cella measured about 50 feet square. Unfortunately, Turkish occupation of the site since 1974 has made it impossible for the Department of Antiquities to continue to work there.[1]

Archaeological Light and Confirmation Concerning Sergius Paulus
(Acts 13:6–12)

Paul and Barnabas, with their companion John Mark (the author of the gospel of Mark), left Salamis and traversed the island of Cyprus to the western end, coming to the city of Paphos (Acts 13:5–6). There they met the ruler of the area, the proconsul named Sergius Paulus. In

[1]See Vassos Karageorghis, *Salamis in Cyprus* (London: Thames & Hudson, 1969); idem, *Salamis* (Nicosia: Department of Antiquities, 1970).

1912 Ramsay found a block of stone at Antioch with this inscription on it: "To Lucius Sergius Paullus, the younger, one of the four commissioners in charge of the Roman streets. . ." (CNAD, 539). Another inscription told of a woman named Sergia Paulla. According to Ramsay, these two people probably were the son and daughter of the Sergius Paulus who was proconsul of Cyprus in the days of Paul. Ramsay even believes that the inscription about the daughter hints that she may have been a Christian, training her children in the Christian faith. (He infers this from the indication that her husband dropped out of public life, perhaps because he had become a Christian, CNAD, 540.) Concerning the spelling of Paulus, Ramsay said, "The spelling of the Latin name is always 'Paullus' but the Greeks always spelled it with one 'l,' Paulos. This rule is almost universal. Thus even in orthography Luke's accuracy is confirmed" (CNAD, 539, footnote 91).

Confirmation of Sergius Paulus's Title (Acts 13:7)

Luke indicates that the title of Sergius Paulus was that of proconsul (English, "deputy," Acts 13:7). The discoveries show that this was the correct designation of the title of the ruler of Cyprus in the time that Paul and Barnabas were there. Cyprus was originally an imperial province in the Roman State, but in 22 B.C. Augustus transferred it to the Roman Senate, and it was therefore placed under the administration of proconsuls. The archaeological confirmation of this is indicated in the Cyprian coins that have been found.[2] Before Paul and Barnabas left Paphos, Sergius Paulus believed, being astonished at the doctrine of the Lord (v. 12).

Paul and Barnabas Journey to the Mainland of Asia Minor; Ministry at Antioch (Acts 13:13–50)

When their ministry was finished on the island of Cyprus, the apostle Paul and his companions crossed the Mediterranean to the mainland of Asia Minor, coming to Perga, which was twelve miles inland from the coast. It was at this point that John Mark left Paul and Barnabas and returned to Jerusalem (Acts 13:13).

Paul and Barnabas journeyed on north to the city of Antioch in Pisidia and there ministered to the Jews in the synagogue. Paul preached, telling how Jesus Christ had come from the seed of David, had been crucified, had risen again, and was the One who justified those who believe in him (Acts 13:14–44). Opposition to Paul grew on the part of the Jews (vv. 45, 50), and so he and Barnabas turned to the Gentiles, and preached the Word to them (vv. 46–49).

Archaeological Light on the Region Between Perga and Antioch; Possible Reason for John Mark's Return to Jerusalem (Acts 13:13)

When Paul wrote to the Corinthians later and pointed out his earnestness in preaching the Gospel, he indicated that in his journeys he had been "in danger from rivers, in danger from bandits. . ." (2 Cor. 11:26). Conybeare and Howson, well-known New Testament scholars, suggest that Paul was referring to the journey between Perga and Antioch when he told of these perils, particularly from bandits. This is supported by the archaeological discoveries that have been made in the region of Pisidia, the territory in which Antioch is located. Ramsay pointed out a number of archaeological inscriptions in the Pisidian area that refer to the armed policemen and soldiers who kept the peace in this region, while other

---

[2]C.M. Kerr, "Paulus, Sergius," ISBE (1929 ed.). See also the revision of this article in the 1986 edition of ISBE by J.J. Hughes.

inscriptions "refer to a conflict with robbers, or to an escape from a drowning in a river."[3] It may have been for this reason that John Mark decided to go home when Paul and Barnabas reached Perga (Acts 13:13), for the next region they had to traverse in order to come to Antioch in Pisidia was this very region that was shown by the archaeological inscriptions to require armed soldiers to keep the peace. Perhaps the prospect of an encounter with brigands helped John Mark to decide to return home at this juncture. It may, of course, have been for other reasons as well.

Excavations at Antioch of Pisidia

As the 1924 University of Michigan excavations have shown,[4] life at Antioch in Paul's day centered around two paved squares, the Square of Tiberius and the Square of Augustus. The former lay at a lower level, and scattered around on its three thousand square feet of paving stones were many incised circles and rectangles on which residents in their idle hours could play all kinds of games. From the lower square, twelve steps about seventy feet long led into the Square of Augustus through a magnificent triple-arched gateway. The façade of this propylaea was faced with two pairs of Corinthian columns that flanked two enormous reliefs of Pisidian captives (representing Augustus's victories on land) and had a frieze with tritons, Neptune, dolphins, and other marine symbols (commemorating Augustus's victories on the sea, especially at Actium).

At the east end of the Square of Augustus a semicircle was cut out of the native rock, before which rose a two-story colonnade with Doric columns below and Ionic above. In front of the center of the semicircle stood a Roman temple, the base of which was cut out of native rock and the superstructure built of white marble. It had a portico of four Corinthian columns across the front. The frieze of this temple, apparently dedicated to the god Men and to Augustus, consisted of beautifully executed bulls' heads (the symbol of Men) bound together with garlands of all sorts of leaves and fruits. What the rest of the city was like the excavators were not able to determine.

Paul's Ministry in Iconium; the Flight to Lystra and Derbe (Acts 14)

After Paul and Barnabas turned from the Jews to preach to the Gentiles at Antioch, the Jews stirred up many of the chief people of the city of Antioch, and Paul and Barnabas were expelled from the region (Acts 13:46, 50). They went on to the town of Iconium, which was east of Antioch. There they spoke in the synagogue, and again the Jews stirred up opposition to the point that Paul and Barnabas were about to be stoned. They fled to the towns of Lystra and Derbe, farther to the southeast (Acts 14:1–6; see map 10).

Archaeological Confirmation Concerning Luke's Indication of the Relationship of Iconium, Lystra, and Derbe (Acts 14:6)

When Luke, the author of the book of Acts, describes Paul's departure from Iconium, he says, "They . . . fled unto Lystra and Derbe, cities of Lycaonia" (Acts 14:6). This implies that Lystra and Derbe were in the territory of Lycaonia and Iconium was not (see maps 10 and 11). Roman writers such as Cicero, however, indicated that Iconium was in Lycaonia, and on the basis of such evidence, many

---

[3]W.M. Calder, "Pisidia," ISBE (1929 ed.), 4: 2401.

[4]David M. Robinson, "A Preliminary Report on the Excavations at Pisidian Antioch and at Sizma," AJA 28 (October 1924): 435–44; William M. Ramsay, *The Bearing of Recent Discovery on the Trustworthiness of the New Testament* (Grand Rapids: Baker, reprint 1979), chapter 4 [RBRD].

MAP 11.   **INDICATIONS CONCERNING LYCAONIA**

critical scholars have held that the book of Acts was not written by Luke but was an untrustworthy work written much later.

A monument found in 1910 in Asia Minor by Sir William Ramsay showed, however, that Iconium was considered to be not a Lycaonian, but rather a Phrygian city. Further discoveries demonstrated that the Iconians had distinguished themselves as being citizens of a Phrygian city. Luke's accuracy was definitely confirmed.

The Conclusion of Paul's First Missionary Journey (Acts 14); Archaeological Light on Zeus and Hermes

Paul and Barnabas preached the gospel at Lystra and healed a lame man (Acts 14:7-10). This miracle caused the people of Lystra to consider the apostles to be gods, and they called Barnabas, Jupiter, and Paul, Mercury (vv. 11-12). Jupiter and Mercury were the Roman equivalent for the Greek gods Zeus and Hermes.

Archaeological light on the worship of Zeus and Hermes in the region of Lystra was found on two inscriptions discovered in the neighborhood of Lystra in 1909. One of these monuments was erected to "priests of Zeus," and another one tells of two men who, "having made in accordance with a vow at their own expense [a statue of] Hermes Most Great along with a sun-dial dedicated it to Zeus the sun-god" (RBR, 48–49).

When the people of Lystra, thinking that Paul and Barnabas were gods, prepared to make sacrifices to them, Paul talked to them, urging them to turn from these vanities to the living God (Acts 14:13, 15). Their ministry in Lystra was interrupted by Jews from Iconium and Antioch who caused Paul to be stoned and left for dead; Paul got up, however, and they retraced their steps through Lystra, Iconium, and Antioch in Pisidia, encouraging the believers in these regions (vv. 22–23). Continuing their return journey, they came back to the home base at Antioch in Syria, where they gave their "missionary report," relating the things that God had done with them, and "how he had opened the door of faith to the Gentiles" (v. 27).

The Jerusalem Council (Acts 15)

While Paul and Barnabas were in Antioch in Syria, after returning from their first missionary journey, certain men from Judea came to Antioch, teaching that believers must be circumcised according to the law of Moses before they could be saved (Acts 15:1). This was nothing but legalism; it put the believer under law rather than grace. Paul and Barnabas disputed with these legalists; they determined to go to Jerusalem and ask the elders there about the question. In the council held at Jerusalem, Peter pointed out that we are saved through the grace of the Lord Jesus Christ (v. 11). Then James declared as the official position of the council that the Gentiles should not be put under any obligation to the law as a means of salvation, but that it would be well for the Gentiles to abstain from meat sacrificed to idols so that this would not be a stumbling block to the Jewish Christians (vv. 19–29).

Paul's Second Missionary Journey (Acts 15:36–18:22); the Call to Macedonia

Some time after the Jerusalem Council, Paul proposed to Barnabas that they make a journey to visit the believers in the cities where they had preached on the first missionary journey (Acts 15:36). Barnabas wanted to take John Mark with them, but Paul remembered how John Mark had left them in the middle of the first journey and decided not to take him. When Paul and Barnabas separated over the issue, Barnabas took John Mark with him, and they went to Cyprus (v. 39); but Paul chose Silas, and they went overland to the north and west again, visiting Derbe and Lystra, the home of Timothy (Acts 16:1ff.).

Paul and Silas, continuing across Asia Minor, traveled to the northwest and finally reached Troas. There Paul had a vision, in which a man appeared to him and said, "Come over to Macedonia and help us" (Acts 16:9). In response to the vision, Paul and Silas sailed from Troas and came to Neapolis in Macedonia and then went on to the city of Philippi. At this point in the book of Acts, the first person plural pronoun "we," is used, indicating that Luke[5] had joined the party on the journey from Troas to Neapolis and Philippi (vv. 10–12).

Archaeological Confirmation Concerning Luke's Reference to a "District" of Macedonia (Acts 16:12)

When Paul and his companions came to Philippi, Luke refers to it as being in "that district" of Macedonia. He uses the Greek word *meris* for the word translated "district." F.J.A. Hort, a well-known New Testament scholar, believed that Luke was wrong in this usage, and asserted, "*Meris* never denotes simply a region, province, or any geographical division: when used of land, as of anything else, it means a portion or share." Since a writer would not be expected to use the expression "that share of Macedonia" when he meant "that district of Macedonia," Hort suggested that there had been a primitive error in the text and a conjectural emendation.[6]

Archaeological excavations in the Fayum in Egypt, however, have shown that the colonists there, many of whom came from Macedonia where Philippi was located, used this very word *meris* to describe the divisions of the district. Thus these documents show that Luke knew more about the geographical terminology of Macedonia than one of the greatest experts on the Greek language in recent times. All scholars now agree that this word *meris* was used by Luke in a legitimate sense that is particularly associated with Macedonia (CNAD, 546). Thus archaeology corrected Hort and again showed the accuracy of Luke.

Archaeological Confirmation of Luke's Reference to the Rulers of Philippi as "Magistrates" (Praetors) (Acts 16:20)

While Paul was in Philippi, he and his companions led Lydia, a seller of purple, to a knowledge of the Lord Jesus (Acts

---

[5]That Luke was the author of Acts is indicated by, among other evidences, the similar beginning of the gospel of Luke and the book of Acts and the similar Greek style of the two books.

[6]In other words, according to Hort, a scribe found an obvious error in the text, conjectured what he thought it said originally, and changed (emended) the text to read *meris*, which, according to Hort, was incorrect also. See Westcott and Hort, *Greek Testament*, vol. 2, Appendix, 96.

The Agora at Philippi, where the mob scene of Acts 16 took place

16:14–15). Some time later, Paul cast a demon out of a girl who was possessed (vv. 16–18). This angered the masters of the girl, who had used her for soothsaying, and they had Paul and Silas brought before the magistrates, who had them beaten and committed to prison (vv. 20–24).

Luke, the author of Acts, refers to the rulers of Philippi as "magistrates" (*praetors*). This term was not technically correct for the officials of Philippi, inasmuch as the town normally would have been governed by two *duumvirs*.[7] The archaeological inscriptions have shown, however, that the title of *praetor* was used as a "courtesy title" for the supreme magistrates of a Roman colony. As usual, Luke moved on a plane of educated conversation rather than on the plane of technicality.[8]

While Paul and Silas were in prison at Philippi, an earthquake shook the foundations of the building, and the doors were opened. This gave Paul and Silas an opportunity to lead the jailor to a knowledge of Christ (Acts 16:25–34). The next day, the magistrates sent an order to have the two men freed, and when they learned that they were Roman citizens, they were all the more eager to have them leave (vv. 38–39).

Archaeological Work at Philippi

The French School at Athens worked at Philippi from 1914 to 1938, and the Greek Archaeological Service has been active there since World War II. As usual, attention has focused on a limited number of major structures in the middle of town. The agora, center of Greek life, where the mob scene and judgment of Acts 16 took place, is a large rectangular area 300 feet long and 150 feet wide. On its northern side stood a rectangular podium with steps leading up to it on either side. This apparently was the place where magistrates dispensed justice. Although the agora was largely rebuilt during the reign of Marcus Aurelius in the second century

[7]Roman officials in towns of the empire who paralleled the two consuls in Rome.
[8]Hogarth, *Authority and Archaeology*, 351–52; also Ramsay, *St. Paul the Traveller* (Grand Rapids: Baker, reprinted 1979), 218; CNAD, 546–47.

A.D., the general plan presumably is essentially the same as it was in Paul's day. Along its north side ran the Egnatian Way, the Roman highway across northern Greece. The acropolis of Philippi, over one thousand feet high, towers above the town. On its eastern slope are the well-preserved remains of a Greek theater, which in its original form dates back to the fourth century B.C. when Philip of Macedon founded the town; but it was radically altered in the Roman period.

The early success of the Gospel at Philippi is evident from the fact that imposing ruins of great churches may be seen. At the south side of the agora stand the remains of a sixth-century church known as Basilica B. Just north of the agora, across the modern highway, lie the ruins of a large fifth-century church known as Basilica A. East of the agora in an area of recent excavation may be seen the remains of another fifth-century church flanked by a third-century bath (FLAP, 350–51).

In the past few years excavations have gone forward at the east end of the agora and at the city's east wall and gate. Archaeological work is slow, and as is true with most other sites in Bible lands, excavation at Philippi has uncovered only a fraction of the ancient town.

Archaeological Light and Confirmation Concerning Thessalonica

After they left Philippi, Paul and Silas went on to the city of Thessalonica (Acts 17:1). Archaeological light and confirmation have been discovered concerning several items connected with Thessalonica. Two examples follow. First, Luke's use of the word "politarch" for the rulers of Thessalonica was once thought to be an inaccuracy, but the discovery of seventeen inscriptions at Salonika (modern name of Thessalonica) containing this term shows the accuracy of this usage.

Second, the use of the word meaning "turn upside down" (*anastatoō*) in connection with the accusation made by the adversaries at Thessalonica is illuminated by an ancient letter found in Egypt, written by a spoiled child to his father, who had gone up to Alexandria.[9] In this letter, this child described how his mother had been terribly disturbed; he writes, "And she said, 'He quite upsets me. Off with him!' " The same word appears here for "upset" (*anastatoō*) as is used in the accusation against Jason and the others who were said to have "turned the world upside down." A study of this picturesque word shows that just as a spoiled child upset his mother and drove her to distraction, so Jason, Paul, and the others were upsetting the complacency of the unsaved in Thessalonica, and are described as "turning the world upside down."

Archaeological Research at Athens

From Thessalonica, Paul journeyed to Athens (Acts 17:15). A knowledge of the archaeological remains of Athens enables us to fill in the colorful background of his visit to this city.

When Paul arrived in Athens, he probably headed straight for the agora. There, at the hub of public life, he could learn best where he might lodge and how to arrange his affairs. In fact, he reasoned there "daily" about the Christian faith with individuals he was able to engage in conversation (Acts 17:17). The agora was excavated by the American School of Classical Studies from 1931 to 1940 under the leadership of T. Leslie Shear and from 1946 to 1960 by Homer A. Thompson. In 1969 new excavations began at the north end of the agora, and they continue to the present time.

Now one can visualize the Athenian agora as Paul knew it. Along the east side stood the great stoa of Attalos, built by

---

[9]J.H. Moulton, *From Egyptian Rubbish Heaps* (London: Charles H. Kelly, 1916), 37–39.

Attalos II, king of Pergamum, in the second century B.C., and rebuilt by the excavators as the agora museum. Some 385 feet long and 64 feet wide, it was faced with a two-story colonnade of forty-five columns on each level—Doric on the first story and Ionic on the second. Behind the colonnade were twenty-one shops on each level. Directly opposite the stoa in the middle of the agora stood the odeion, or music hall, of Agrippa, built about 15 B.C. and seating one thousand people. Extending across the agora from the south end of the stoa of Attalos sprawled the middle stoa (450 feet long), which was connected to the south stoa by a small east stoa. At the west end of the south stoa was the *heliaia*, or law court, adjacent to which was the southwest fountain.

The west side of the agora was the political side. At the south was the round *tholos*, the office of the *prytany*, a committee of the city council. The official set of standard weights and measures was kept there. North of that was the public record office, behind which rose the home of the Council of Five Hundred. North of this complex was the temple of Apollo and the stoa of Zeus, a favorite haunt of Socrates. On the hill behind the temple of Apollo stood the temple of Hephaestus (god of the forge), one of the best preserved of all Greek temples (104 feet long by 45 feet wide). Across the north of the agora extended the "Painted Stoa," a kind of historical picture gallery with scenes of Athenian struggle with the Persians at Marathon, among others. Here philosophers held forth, one of the better known of which was Zeno, founder of the Stoic school.

A few hundred feet east of the Greek agora lay the Roman market. Made necessary by the expansion of Athenian commercial affairs, it particularly housed wine and oil shops. This center was built by Julius Caesar and Augustus Caesar. The structure consists of an interior courtyard 269 by 187 feet and paved with

marble, surrounded by an Ionic colonnade, through which entrance was gained to the shops. At the east end of the market stands the Tower of the Winds, a hydraulic clock arranged with sundials. This is an octagonal tower in white marble measuring 26 feet in diameter and about forty feet in height. Excavation of this market was undertaken by the Greek Archaeological Society in 1890 and carried on intermittently until 1931; much is yet to be done there.

At the south end of the Greek agora stands the Areopagus or Mars Hill, where Paul probably spoke to many of the intelligentsia of Athens. This 377-foot hill stood just west of the Acropolis. And as he delivered his Mars Hill speech, Paul must have gestured toward the Acropolis when he spoke of "temples built by hands" (Acts 17:24).

Undoubtedly Paul visited the Acropolis. A visitor to Athens could hardly have avoided it. Besides, Acts 17:23a may be translated, "For as I went about and examined objects of your religious devotion, . . ." indicating that the apostle went sight-seeing in the city. The magnificent *propylaea* with its adjacent Nike temple and statue of Athena, the Erechtheum, and the Parthenon must have inspired Paul's admiration. The Parthenon was, of course, still in perfect condition. Built of white Pentelic marble, it measured 238 feet in length and 111 feet in width. Its encircling row of forty-six fluted Doric columns stood at a height of 34 feet. Encircling the structure above the colonnade was the Doric frieze with 92 panels depicting legendary and mythological scenes dear to the hearts of Greeks. Inside the colonnade the Ionic frieze encircled the temple below the roof. This continuous frieze, 524 feet in length, consisted of six hundred figures and portrayed the annual Panathenaic procession up to the Parthenon to honor Athena. The pediment on the east end of the temple depicted the birth of Athena, and the one on the west portrayed the struggle between Athena and Poseidon for control of Attica. Inside was the great gold-and-ivory statue of Athena. To the north of the Parthenon stood the Erechtheum, temple of Athena and Poseidon-Erechtheus with its beautiful porch of the maidens (caryatids).

On the southeast slope of the Acropolis lay the great theater of Dionysus, where the leading dramatists of ancient Greece aired their productions. The theater seated about 17,000 people. Just east of it stood the Odeion of Pericles, probably used for musical events.

From 1884 to 1891, Greek archaeologists examined the whole Acropolis area down to bedrock. The Greek Archaeological Society also excavated the remains of Pericles' odeion in the 1920s. Several German scholars studied the theater of Dionysus. The American School of Classical Studies excavated the north slope of the Acropolis from 1931 to 1939 under the direction of Oscar Broneer.

Some distance to the southeast of the Acropolis stood the great temple of Zeus. It was excavated by the Greek Archaeological Society from 1886 to 1901 and by the German School from 1922 to 1923. Begun in the latter part of the sixth century B.C., it was still open to the sky in Paul's day and was not completed until the second century A.D. The structure had 104 Corinthian columns of Pentelic marble 56 feet high. These were arranged in two rows on the sides and three rows at the ends and rested on a foundation 354 feet long and 135 feet broad. The height was over 90 feet to the top of the pediments.[10]

Paul at Corinth; Archaeological Light

From Athens Paul journeyed to Corinth, the great commercial center of Greece in New Testament times. The city gained significance from its location on the Isthmus of Corinth, across which goods flowed in quantity, not having to follow the longer and more dangerous route around the southern tip of Greece. The economic opportunities there and the biennial Isthmian Games held nearby brought throngs of businessmen, athletes, and sports enthusiasts to whom Paul could minister; and he stayed at Corinth for eighteen months (Acts 18:11), being second only to Ephesus in length of evangelistic effort. As a result of the work of the American School of Classical Studies, conducted at Corinth since 1896, except for war years, we now know something of what the city was like when Paul ministered there.

At the center of the city stood the agora—the agora being the hub of activity in any Greek city. It measured about 600 feet in length (east-west) and 300 feet in width (north-south). Following the natural configuration of the land, the southern section stood about six feet higher than the northern part of the agora. At the dividing line of the two levels stood the bema or podium where public officials could address crowds and render judgment. No doubt Paul stood before Gallio here (Acts 18:12–13). The bema was flanked by a row of central shops. A south stoa extended some 500 feet along that side of the agora. Among other things, it housed the city council and office of the supervisors of the Isthmian Games.

The road from the port of Lechaion entered the agora on the north. On the west side of the road at the entrance to the agora stood a basilica, which along with basilicas on the south and east of the agora provided court facilities where the litigious Corinthian Christians could have been involved in court cases (1 Cor.

[10]For a detailed discussion of the agora, see John M. Camp, *The Athenian Agora* (London: Thames & Hudson, 1986). For further information on the agora and other excavations in Athens, see Paul MacKendrick, *The Greek Stones Speak*, 2nd ed. (New York: Norton, 1981), 429–40; FLAP, 352–58.

Reconstructed Stoa of Attalos in the Athenia agora

The bema or judgment seat at Corinth, where Paul stood before Gallio

The inscription of Erastus in the theater at Corinth, thought to be the Erastus Paul knew (Rom. 16:23)

6). On the east side of the road near the agora entrance a stone was found bearing the inscription "Synagogue of the Hebrews," thought by some to be the lintel of the synagogue in which Paul may have preached (Acts 18:4). A little farther away along the Lechaion Road stood shops of the meat and wine merchants, in one of which was found an inscription indicating it was a *makellon*, the word used in 1 Corinthians 10:25. This must be the very meat market where, Paul said, believers could shop with a clear conscience, not worrying whether the meat sold there had at one point been offered to idols.

On a rocky terrace adjacent to the northwest corner of the agora stood the temple of Apollo, dating to the sixth century B.C. It measured 176 feet long by 69 feet wide, and the 38 columns of the peristyle rose almost 24 feet in height. These fluted Doric columns were more impressive than many in Greece because they were made of single blocks instead of being built up with drums of stone. In the side of the hill northwest of the temple was the 14,000-seat theater of Corinth. In the pavement near the stage area one can still see an inscription saying that the *aedile* Erastus laid the pavement at his own expense. Scholars commonly believe that this is the same Erastus, one of Paul's converts, to whom the apostle referred in Romans 16:23, when he wrote the epistle to the Romans from Corinth.

Some five miles east of ancient Corinth on the Saronic Gulf the American School of Classical Studies has been excavating the site of the Isthmian Games. There, near the end of the modern Corinth Canal, one can see remains of the temple of Poseidon, a theater, and part of the stadium. The stadium of Paul's day lay some 800 feet away in a natural depression. The Isthmian Games were held every two years and probably drew larger crowds than the Olympic Games. The Isthmian Games provided the backdrop for Paul's comments about the race in 1 Corinthians 9:24–27.[11]

Archaeological Light on the Date of Paul's Sojourn at Corinth—A.D. 50 (Acts 18:12)

While Paul was at Corinth, the Jews had him brought before the ruler of the city, Gallio the proconsul (Acts 18:12). Archaeological discovery has given us a definitely fixed point for Paul's sojourn in Corinth, for an inscription found at Delphi shows that Gallio was proconsul of Achaia in 52. (BWMS, 86). The account of Paul's trial before Gallio suggests that Gallio had recently come to office.[12] Since Paul had already been there eighteen months (v. 11), it is likely that he came to Corinth about A.D. 50.[13]

1 and 2 Thessalonians Written from Corinth, A.D. 50–51 (Acts 18:12)

Paul wrote 1 and 2 Thessalonians from Corinth, as internal evidence in these epistles shows (TINT, 193, 198). It is likely that these letters were written within a few months of each other, probably during the years 50–51.

The Conclusion of the Second Missionary Journey (Acts 18:18–22)

After Paul left Corinth in 51–52, he stopped at Ephesus and then continued on to Palestine, landing at Caesarea (Acts

[11]For documentation, see Jerome Murphy-O'Connor, "The Corinth That Saint Paul Saw," BA (September 1984), 147–59; idem, *Corinth* (Wilmington, Del.: Michael Glazier, 1983); FLAP, 358–63; Jack Finegan, *The Archaeology of the New Testament* (Boulder: Westview, 1981), 142–52 [FANT].

[12]The biblical context seems to indicate that the coming of Gallio induced the Jews to bring Paul to trial. If this is so, it means that Paul's trial before Gallio occurred early in the latter's proconsulship (TINT, 194).

[13]BAB, 560–61; BWMS, 86; CNAD, 502; TINT, 194; Deissmann, *St. Paul*, 246–47, 280–81.

18:22). He concluded the second missionary journey at the home base of Antioch in Syria.

Paul's Third Missionary Journey (Acts 18:23–21:16); Archaeological Light on His Stay at Ephesus

Paul's third missionary journey began at Antioch in Syria (Acts 18:22–23). From there he went north and then west, through the territory of Galatia and Phrygia (v. 23), where Iconium and Antioch of Pisidia were located, and then on to the city of Ephesus (Acts 19:1ff.) in the western part of Asia Minor (see map 10, page 268).

Ephesus was a great city when Paul arrived. With a population in the hundreds of thousands, it probably ranked fourth in size in the Empire behind Rome, Alexandria, and Antioch of Syria. The importance of the city at that time was threefold: political, economic, and religious. It had become the de facto capital of the province of Asia, and the Roman governor resided there. Its economic prowess lay in the fact that it stood astride the great route to the interior of Asia Minor and the north-south road through western Asia Minor. Religiously, Ephesus was a leading center for the worship of Diana, or Artemis. Ephesus was therefore a very strategic center for evangelization. From this one spot not only the whole province of Asia but also many other parts of the Roman Empire could be reached with the Gospel.

The archaeological history of Ephesus began on May 2, 1863, when the British architect John T. Wood started his search for the temple of Diana, one of the seven wonders of the ancient world. He did not discover the ruins of the temple until December 31, 1869, and then worked five more years at the temple site. The temple platform was 239 feet wide and 418 feet long. On that stood the temple itself, which measured 180 feet wide and 377 feet long, its roof supported by 117 sixty-foot columns. These columns were six feet in diameter, and 36 of them were sculptured at the base with life-sized figures.

The Austrian Archaeological Institute began to excavate in the ancient city of Ephesus in November 1897 and excavated there continuously for sixteen years. Members of the institute resumed work there between the world wars (1926–35) and have continued annually since 1954. To date they have uncovered only about 25 percent of the ancient city. In recent years they also have done some work on the temple of Diana.

The excavation of Ephesus is one of the most impressive of all archaeological projects in Mediterranean lands. If one walks through the Magnesian Gate into the city of Ephesus in a westerly direction, on his right are the east baths (from the second century A.D.). A short distance farther on the right stands an odeion, or covered concert hall (A.D. 150), which increasingly is being interpreted as the meeting place of the town council (capacity about 1400). Next to it is the town hall, built about the time of Christ's birth. Facing these two civic structures on the left is a long basilica (built about the beginning of the first century A.D.), which served as a court building. This was the northernmost structure of the Roman state agora.

When one reaches the end of the basilica, he enters the open roadway of Curetes Street (which runs northwest). This is lined on both sides with inscribed statue bases and excavated structures. Immediately on the left is a plaza, at the back of which stands a temple of Domitian, built during his reign near the end of the first century, when John was living there. On the right is the Memmius monument (erected at the end of the first century B.C.) in honor of a grandson of the dictator Sulla.

Here at the beginning of Curetes Street is a gateway formed by two pillars adorned with reliefs of Hermes or Mer-

The great theater at Ephesus, where the mob scene of Acts 19 took place

cury. As one descends the street, he will soon see on the right a fountain of Trajan and then the temple of Hadrian (both of the early second century). Behind the temple of Hadrian stand the baths of Scholastica (built c. A.D. 100 or earlier). Across the street from the temple of Hadrian on a hillside rise villas of the first century A.D., now partially restored.

Passing other minor structures, one comes to the junction of Curetes and Marble streets. On the left in a little plaza is the early second-century A.D. library of Celsus (now restored). On the right of this plaza is a monumental gate that leads into the Hellenistic commercial agora. The gate, too, has been completely restored. An inscription above the gate dates to the reign of Augustus Caesar; thus the gate was there while Paul lived in the city.

We now walk down Marble Street. Behind the wall on the left of Marble Street (which goes north) spreads the great Hellenistic commercial agora 360 feet square and surrounded with shops,

including some where silversmiths marketed their wares. On the right of the street rises Mount Pion and the great Hellenistic theater where the mob scene of Acts 19 took place. Measuring some 495 feet in diameter, the theater held about 25,000 people. The cavea of the theater was divided into three bands of twenty-two rows of seats each, and twelve stairways divided the cavea into huge wedge-shaped sections. Much restoration work has been done on the theater and its stage area.

From the theater, the Arcadian Way, 1,735 feet long, led westward to the harbor. This marble-paved street, 36 feet in width, was lined on both sides by a colonnade behind which were shops. At both ends of the street were monumental gateways. While this street, in the form the excavators found it, dates from about A.D. 400, there was a magnificent street on the site during the first century. As one walks from the theater to the harbor, one passes a late-first-century gymnasium and bath. If one returns to the theater and walks on an extension of Marble Street, he will pass, on the right, the city stadium built during the reign of Nero while Paul was there.

Ephesus is sacred to the memory of the apostle John, as well as to Paul. On the hill of Ayasoluk, overlooking the temple of Diana, the apostle John lived and was buried according to Christian tradition of the second century. At first marked by a memorial, the grave was enclosed by a church in the fourth century. The emperor Justinian (527–565) took down the old church and erected a domed basilica over the tomb. Restorations at the site of the church have been going on in recent years (for documentation on Ephesus see FLAP, 345–49; FANT, 155–71).

Paul remained in Ephesus for over two years (Acts 19:10) and during that time wrote the first epistle to the Corinthians, probably in the spring of 54 or 55 (TINT, 205). When Paul left Ephesus, he went into Macedonia (Acts 20:1), and there evidently wrote the second epistle to the Corinthians, probably some seven or eight months after writing 1 Corinthians. The second epistle would have been written late in 54 or 55 (TINT, 209).

From Macedonia, Paul went on to Greece, where he spent three months (Acts 20:2–3). While he was there, he wrote Galatians (TINT, 217), seeking to set right the Galatian people who had come under the influence of Judaizers. During that same sojourn in Greece, Paul was in Corinth for a time, where he wrote the epistle to the Romans, probably in 56 (TINT, 226).

Paul left Greece, returning through Macedonia to Philippi (Acts 20:6), and went on to Troas. From there Paul and his company sailed down the coast of Asia Minor, passing near Ephesus (v. 17), where Paul gave an account of his ministry to the Ephesian elders, pointing out that he had never hesitated to declare "all the counsel of God" (v. 27). Paul's return journey took him on across the Mediterranean, past the island of Rhodes and the island of Cyprus, to Tyre (Acts 21:7), and then to Caesarea, from where Paul and his companions went to Jerusalem (vv. 8, 15).

Paul Imprisoned at Caesarea; His Voyage to Rome (Acts 21–28)

While Paul was in Jerusalem, after his return from the third missionary journey, some of the Jews in Jerusalem thought they saw him bring Gentiles into the court of the temple (Acts 21:20–29). They stirred up a riot in order to kill Paul, but order was restored by the Roman guard (vv. 31ff.). Paul gave his defense before the assembled mob (22:1–21) and later before the Jewish council of the Sanhedrin (23:1–6). Some of the Jews conspired to kill Paul (vv. 12ff.), but when the Roman authorities at Jerusalem learned of the plot, they sent him to Caesarea (for a discussion of excavations at Caesarea, see chapter 25), where he was imprisoned for more than two years (24:27). Paul appealed his case to Caesar (i.e., the Roman emperor, who was Nero at that time, 25:11) and was sent by ship from Palestine to Italy (Acts 27:1–28:16).

Paul was in Rome for two years (Acts 28:30). He probably arrived in 59 and was released in 61 (TINT, 185). The book of Acts must have been written in about 61, for it closes with the record of Paul's detention at Rome for these two years.

During the two-year stay at Rome, Paul wrote the Prison Epistles: Ephesians, Philippians, Colossians, and Philemon. They were probably written in the following order: Colossians, Philemon, Ephesians, and Philippians (TINT, 228), during the years 60–61 (TINT, 233, 251). Paul's second imprisonment is treated in chapter 29.

Chapter 29

The Development
of the Early Church

*(Paul's Later Life: Pastoral Epistles; General Epistles;
Book of Revelation; Development of the Church)*

Paul's Release from Prison (A.D. 61) and Further Travels

Paul's first imprisonment lasted two years, probably from 59 to 61, during which time he wrote the Prison Epistles. The book of Acts ends with a description of this imprisonment and the statement that Paul was detained in Rome for two years (28:30). However, we can trace Paul's travels after his release from this first imprisonment in 61 from early church sources and certain of his expressed purposes, including his plan to see the Philippians (Phil. 2:23–24) at Philippi in Macedonia and to visit Philemon at the town of Colosse in Asia Minor (Philemon 22).

Leaving Rome in 61, Paul probably took the main highway across Italy to Brundisium (modern Brindisi) on the Adriatic Sea, then crossed the Adriatic to Apollonia or to Dyrrhachium, where he took the main highway across Greece (the Egnatian Way) to Philippi in Macedonia. Prob-ably he did not stay long in Philippi, but hurried on to Ephesus and visited Colosse and other cities of Asia Minor in this vicinity (TINT, 261). These travels probably took most of the year (61–62), after which Paul may have made a voyage to Spain. The probability of a voyage to Spain is indicated by Paul's purpose to visit that country, expressed when he wrote to the Romans in about 56 (Rom. 15:24). Also, the early church writer Clement of Rome seems to imply that Paul went to Spain (Clement *ad Cor.* 5), and the fact of such a journey is stated in the Canon of Muratori.[1] It is thought that Paul may have remained in Spain for two years, probably 62–64 (TINT, 261–63). Robertson thought that Paul may have been in Spain when Rome was burned on July 19, 64.[2]

Paul's First Epistle to Timothy and His Epistle to Titus (64–65)

Some time after Paul left Spain, he wrote the first epistle to Timothy, about

---

[1]The Canon of Muratori is a fragment of a document, so named because it was discovered by an Italian named Muratori in the Ambrosian Library at Milan in 1740. It dates from A.D. 170 or a little later (TINT, 22).

[2]A.T. Robertson, "Paul the Apostle," ISBE (1929 ed.), 4:2286.

64 or 65 (TINT, 263). Timothy was carrying on ministerial duties in the church at Ephesus, acting as Paul's temporary representative in his apostolic capacity (TINT, 262). Paul wrote to encourage Timothy to oppose false teachers and not give heed to myths (1 Tim. 1:4). He also wrote to instruct him in the qualifications of church officers (1 Tim. 3) and to exhort him to faithfully discharge his pastoral duties (1 Tim. 4:6ff.).

A short time later, probably during the year 65 (TINT, 266), Paul wrote the epistle to Titus. Titus was Paul's representative on the island of Crete, not actually being the "bishop of Crete," as Eusebius calls him (TINT, 265). The subject matter of Paul's words to Titus ranges in content from urging him to complete the organization of the work at Crete (Titus 1:5) to warning him against false teachings and teachers (3:9–10).

Defense of the Pauline Authorship of the Pastoral Epistles (1 and 2 Timothy and Titus)

Critics have said that the Pastoral Epistles (1 and 2 Timothy and Titus) could not have been written by Paul because they differed in style and language from the other Pauline epistles. Cobern suggests that the difference may be due to the fact that ancient writers used scribes, and a different scribe would produce a different style (CNAD, 102). It is not necessary, however, to posit the idea of various scribes producing varying style and vocabulary in the Pastoral Epistles, because a comparison shows that these epistles did not have a vocabulary that differed greatly from the other epistles Paul wrote. An actual count shows that 1 Timothy has 82 new words not found elsewhere in the New Testament; 2 Timothy has 53 such words; and Titus 33—a total of 168. On the other hand, the epistles from Romans through Philemon contain 687 such words.[3]

Why is there some difference in vocabulary between the Pastoral Epistles and the other letters of Paul? The answer lies in the fact that different subjects require different words. When Paul wrote the Pastoral Epistles, he would obviously use different words in dealing with ministerial duties and responsibilities from those he would use when he wrote concerning justification by faith or when he dealt with the errors of Gnosticism.[4]

1 and 2 Peter (A.D. 65–67)

In about 65 Peter wrote his first epistle to the believers in Pontus, Galatia, Cappadocia, Asia, and Bithynia—all provinces of Asia Minor. It is possible that Peter had visited these regions of Asia Minor, or converts of Paul may have evangelized the area (TINT, 283–84). Peter wrote to comfort these Gentile believers in their trials (1 Peter 1:7) and to remind them that they had been redeemed, not with silver and gold, but with the "precious blood of Christ" (1 Peter 1:19).

The second epistle of Peter was written in about 66 or 67 (TINT, 291). He urges believers to go on in the faith, adding to their faith the godly virtues that should characterize believers, including brother-

---

[3]John Rutherford, "The Pastoral Epistles," ISBE (1929 ed.), 4:2261.

[4]A detailed discussion of the supposed problems of authorship of the Pastoral Epistles appears in Everett F. Harrison, *Introduction to the New Testament*, rev. ed. (Grand Rapids: Eerdmans, 1971), 351–63, with the conclusion that they came from Paul's pen. Harrison also mentions the testimony to Paul's authorship in the early church. Donald Guthrie in his *New Testament Introduction*, 3rd ed. (Downers Grove: InterVarsity, 1970), 584–622, provides an even more exhaustive discussion of the authorship of the Pastorals and likewise tends to support the traditional view of Pauline authorship. Certainly the idea that the Pastorals were composed in the second century is totally unacceptable, because, as noted earlier (chapter 26), the argument from historical grammar, developed from the contribution of the papyri, requires that all the New Testament books were written during the first century (BWMS, 53–54).

ly kindness (2 Peter 1:7). Peter also warns against false teachers who bring in heresies, even denying the atonement of Christ (2:1) and his return in glory (3:4).

Answer to the Critical Opinion Concerning 2 Peter

Critics have held that Peter did not write 2 Peter because of differences in style and vocabulary between the two epistles. A possible answer to this supposed difficulty is supplied by the internal evidence of 1 Peter, which shows that Peter used Silvanus as a scribe or amanuensis to write the epistle (1 Peter 5:12). This means that Silvanus could have suggested and made stylistic improvements in Peter's dictation (TINT, 285–86). If Peter used another amanuensis or wrote with his own hand when he composed the second epistle, this would explain the differences between the two letters. We should not be surprised that the Greek of 2 Peter "jars on us" (CNAD, 115), since Peter and John are referred to in the New Testament as "unschooled" (Acts 4:13). There are some differences between the vocabularies of 1 and 2 Peter, but the work of Dods and Zahn show that there are also some very remarkable similarities.[5] The likelihood of 2 Peter's being a forgery is well answered by H.C. Thiessen's question, "Would a forger risk detection by neglecting closer attention to the style and language of I Peter?" (TINT, 288).

Hebrews (A.D. 67–69)

Whether Paul wrote the epistle to the Hebrews cannot be proved or disproved conclusively (TINT, 300–301), but there is some indication of the time of its composition. The internal evidence of the book makes it clear that the temple had not yet been destroyed (this occurred in A.D. 70), being shown by the references to priests offering gifts (8:4), to the offering of sacrifices from year to year (10:1), and to other activities of the temple referred to in the present tense. The people addressed had evidently been Christians for a long time. Putting all these factors together, it seems likely that the book of Hebrews was written about 67–69 (TINT, 304). The writer of Hebrews sets forth Christ as superior to the angels, to Moses and Joshua (Heb. 3–4), and to the earthly priests of the Old Testament.

Paul's Last Epistle—2 Timothy; the End of His Life (A.D. 67–68)

When Paul wrote to Titus in about 65, it is evident that he planned to spend the winter in Nicopolis (Titus 3:12). Since there were eight places named Nicopolis, it is not possible to ascertain which one was the location of Paul's sojourn, but the prevailing opinion holds to the Nicopolis in Epirus (now divided between Greece and Albania). Paul probably left Nicopolis when the Neronian persecution became severe and fled across Macedonia to Troas in Asia Minor, where he was shown hospitality by Carpus. He seems to have departed from Troas suddenly, for he left his cloak, some books, and the parchment manuscripts of the Old Testament there (2 Tim. 4:13). We are not certain of Paul's travels from this point on, but we know that he was arrested and taken to Rome for trial (TINT, 268).

During this second imprisonment at Rome, Paul wrote 2 Timothy, in about 67–68 (TINT, 269), exhorting Timothy to be strong in the grace that is in Christ (2 Tim. 2:1) and warning him to watch out for apostasy—for people who would not endure sound doctrine (4:3).

---

[5]Dods, *An Introduction to the New Testament*, 210–11; Theodor Zahn, *Introduction to the New Testament*, 2:289–90, cited in TINT, 288. For a more extended discussion of the authorship of 2 Peter, see Harrison, *Introduction to the New Testament*, 411–26. Harrison defends Petrine authorship.

Paul apparently was put to death by the Roman government shortly before the death of Nero, who died June 8, 68. Thus the end of Paul's life may be placed in the spring of 68. According to tradition, he was led out along the Ostian Way and was beheaded there. A grove is still pointed out in the countryside beyond Rome as the traditional scene of the execution of the great apostle.

Jude (A.D. 75), 1, 2, and 3 John (A.D. 85–90)

The epistle of Jude was probably written in about 75 (TINT, 296), to warn concerning false teachers and their teaching, urging believers to "contend for the faith" against those who deny our only Master and Lord Jesus Christ (Jude 3–4). Many of the church fathers held that Jude quoted from the apocryphal books known as the Assumption of Moses (v. 9) and the book of Enoch (v. 14), and it was rejected as canonical on this ground. Philippi, however, denied that Jude quoted from these apocryphal books, asserting that Jude wrote from oral tradition, and this is quite possible. Moorehead points out that even if Jude did cite two passages from noncanonical books, it does not mean that he accepted those books as true; Paul quoted from three Greek poets—Aratus, Menander, and Epimenides[6]—but that does not mean he endorsed all that those poets wrote. When Jude cited the prophecy from Enoch that the Lord would come (v. 14), this does not mean that he accepted the whole book as true, but rather that he received this particular prediction as from the Lord (TINT, 294–95).

The three epistles of John were all written in the period from 85 to 90. John was probably living in Ephesus at this time, as indicated by Irenaeus (TINT, 308), and he seems to have written his first epistle to the churches in the surrounding area, such as Smyrna, Pergamos, Thyatira, Sardis, Philadelphia, and Laodicea. John wrote to these believers, pointing out the provision for daily cleansing from sin by confession to the Lord (1 John 1:9), showing that the walk of the believer should not be in sin (3:9), warning against apostasy (2:18), and assuring the believers that they may be certain of their salvation (5:1, 13).

The second epistle of John is a letter addressed to "the chosen lady" (v. 1), probably a believer and her family who lived in one of the towns in Western Asia Minor near Ephesus. John commended these people for walking in the truth (v. 4), warned them against spiritual deceivers (v. 7), and expressed a hope to visit them soon (v. 12).

The third epistle of John was written to a friend of Paul named Gaius (v. 1). Paul knew men by that name residing at various places, including Macedonia (Acts 19:29), Derbe (Acts 20:4), and Corinth (Rom. 16:23; 1 Cor. 1:14). We do not know whether he was one of these individuals or perhaps another not mentioned in any other part of the New Testament. John wrote to this Gaius to express his joy in hearing of Gaius's walk in the truth (v. 3); to commend him for his hospitality to visiting ministers (vv. 5–6); to tell of his plans to rebuke the trouble-maker, Diotrephes (vv. 9–10); and to express his hope of seeing him personally in the near future (vv. 13–14).

The Book of Revelation (A.D. 95)

The true title of this book is given in the opening verse, "The Revelation of Jesus Christ," and it is often referred to as "the book of the Revelation," or "the book of Revelation," or just "Revelation." In any event it is not the revelation of John, for it is not John but rather Christ who is revealed in this book written by John.

The book of Revelation may be dated

---

[6]Acts 17.28; 1 Corinthians 15:33; Titus 1:12.

The temple of Artemis at Sardis in Asia Minor, with a little chapel built into it at the left, showing the triumph of the Gospel there

about 95, on the basis of indications in the church fathers Irenaeus, Clement of Alexandria, and Eusebius to the effect that John's banishment to the island of Patmos was in the latter part of the reign of the Roman emperor Domitian (81–96). Under Domitian, Christians were persecuted for not worshiping the emperor, a situation seemingly implied in John's statement that he was on the island of Patmos "because of the word of God and the testimony of Jesus Christ" (Rev. 1:9) (TINT, 323).

The book of Revelation falls into three great divisions that are unequal in length: (1) Chapter 1 concerns John's vision of Christ in the midst of the seven lampstands, commanding John to write about the seven lampstands, which are the seven churches (Rev. 1:13, 19–20). (2) The second section (chapters 2–3) records the messages from the Lord to each of the seven churches: Ephesus, Smyrna, Pergamum, Thyatira, Sardis, Philadelphia, and Laodicea. (3) The third division comprises the bulk of the book of Revelation (chapters 4–22). This last section deals with events yet future to our time, including details on the rule of the Antichrist, the dark days of the Tribulation, the coming of Christ in glory to establish justice and righteousness on earth (19:11–16), his thousand-year rule in the Millennium (20:1–6), the white throne judgment at the end of the Millennium (20:11–15), and the ushering in of the eternal ages with the new heaven, the new earth, and the new Jerusalem (21:1–2). The book closes with the prayer that is anticipatory of the coming again of Christ, "Amen. Come, Lord Jesus" (Rev. 22:20).

Answer to the Objections Concerning the Linguistic Nature of the Book of Revelation; Archaeological Light

The book of Revelation is inferior to the gospel of John in its linguistic qualities (CNAD, 115; TINT, 322). Some have tried to explain this fact by positing that Revelation was written by John in the 60s, before he had learned much Greek, and then, after a lapse of some thirty years during which his Greek improved, he wrote the gospel of John in the 90s.[7] This explanation does not fit the facts very well, for it seems that the gospel of John was probably written in about 85–90 (TINT, 173) and the book of Revelation a few years later, about 95 (TINT, 323).

What, then, is the explanation of the difference in the vocabulary and style of the gospel of John and Revelation? Several factors supply the answer:

1. Many constructions in Revelation that were once thought to be bad Greek are now known from the archaeological discoveries to have been forms in common every-day usage. For example, in Revelation 14:19, the expression "the great winepress" is so construed that the word "winepress" is in the masculine and the word "great" is in the feminine gender. This would constitute a violation of the grammatical principle that a modifying adjective should agree with its noun in gender (such a violation of a grammatical idiom is called a "solecism"; an example in English would be the construction, "between you and I," instead of "between you and me"). The New Testament archaeological discoveries made in Egypt have shown, however, that the construction with two different genders between a noun and its modifier (as in Revelation 14:19) is also found with this same word in the papyri.[8] A number of other textual discoveries show that many of the supposed blunders and solecisms of New Testament writers are merely grammatical forms common among the middle classes of the first century A.D.

2. A second objection to the language of Revelation was that it contained expressions characteristic of the Hebrew language; however, the papyri show that in this case as well, many forms of speech once supposed to be Hebraic or Semitic were not such at all but were expressions used by the non-Jewish population of the apostolic period (CNAD, 115).

3. It is quite true that there are some expressions in Revelation that are Hebraistic in style, but as H.C. Thiessen points out, this is only what we might expect in a book that makes a copious use of Old Testament imagery (TINT, 320).

4. A careful study shows that there are significant similarities between the book of Revelation and the other writings of John, such as "the Word," "he who overcomes," "water of life," "show," "little lamb," and others (TINT, 320).

Other differences between Revelation and the gospel of John may be explained by such factors as change of subject matter and circumstances and difference of amanuensis (TINT, 320).

Archaeological Light on Date of the Book of Revelation

Nikolaus Morosow set forth the eccentric theory that the book of Revelation was written as an astrological exercise by John Chrysostom on or about September 30, 395.[9] Chrysostom was one of the church fathers who lived in the fourth century; he died shortly after 400. The answer to this fantastic idea of Morosow is furnished by archaeological discoveries in Egypt. At a site called Oxyrhynchus,[10] Grenfell and Hunt found a beautiful edition of the book of Revelation written on vellum, dating from the main part of the fourth century. This shows that the book of Revelation had been in circulation for some time previously, long before the

---

[7]S.A. Cartledge, *A Conservative Introduction to the New Testament* (Grand Rapids: Zondervan, 1943), 198 [CCIN].

[8]CNAD, 111; citing Moulton, *Prolegomena*, 60, who speaks of this loss of gender distinction.

[9]Nikolaus Morosow, *Die Offenbarung Johannes*, 1912, 100–110; cited in CNAD, 104–5.

[10]About 120 miles south of Cairo, CNAD, 6.

impossible date suggested by Morosow (CNAD, 104–5).

Moreover, as has already been noted, the argument from historical grammar indicates that all New Testament books were written during the first century A.D. By way of review, this argument, based on discoveries in the papyri from Egypt, observes that the New Testament books as we have them are now known to have been written in the grammar and vocabulary of the popular Greek of the first century, not in the language of some subsequent period.

Archaeological Light on Places of Worship in the New Testament Period: Synagogues, Catacombs, Churches

Synagogues. The synagogue of the Jews was not abandoned at first by Christians in the early part of the New Testament period. Christ himself, as was his custom, went into the synagogue at Nazareth and read the Scriptures on the Sabbath (Luke 4:16ff.). When Paul went from town to town on his missionary journeys, he customarily went to the synagogue first and told the Good News to the assembled Jews (as at Salamis, Acts 13:5; Antioch in Pisidia, 13:14; Iconium, 14:1). Evidence of first-century synagogues is now coming to light. First, as noted in the discussion of Capernaum (chapter 26, pages 246–48), some remains of what appears to have been the Capernaum synagogue of Jesus' day have been found under the floor of the extensively preserved third-century synagogue there. Second, Yigael Yadin found a fairly well-preserved synagogue at Masada that was certainly in use at the time of the destruction of the temple in A.D. 70. Yadin thought that its earliest use may date back to the days of Herod the Great.[11] Third, V. Corbo found a synagogue at the Herodium (Herod's great fortress seven miles due south of Jerusalem), which was introduced during either the first revolt (A.D. 66–70) or the second revolt 132–135) (EAEHL, 2:502–10). There are, of course, many more synagogues excavated at biblical sites and dating from the second, third, or fourth centuries (e.g., Capernaum, Chorazin, or Sardis), but it is not the purpose of this book to attempt a history of the synagogue in the ancient Near East.

Catacombs. The catacombs at Rome were constructed for underground burial, but at times when the persecutions were severe, they were used as places of refuge and worship (BWMS, 207). Several of the catacomb passages connect with small chapels, which were likely used in connection with the burial services during ordinary times but may well have served as regular meeting places when it was not safe to meet above ground. These chapels are probably the oldest preserved places of Christian worship.

Catacombs were used by Christians as burial places during the first to the fourth centuries, the end of their use coming at the time of the invasion of Rome by Alaric the Visigoth (CNAD, 385). During the tenth to the sixteenth centuries, the catacombs were almost completely forgotten. In the sixteenth century one of the catacombs was accidentally discovered, but the true discoverer of the catacombs was de Rossi (1822–1894), who thoroughly explored them and published his results in three splendid volumes (CNAD, 386).

A study of the area has shown that the passageways of the various catacombs near the city of Rome would total 550 miles if they were extended in a straight line, according to de Rossi (CNAD, 384), and it is estimated that there are nearly two million graves in them. They covered a surface area of about 615 acres (FLAP, 455). The oldest inscription that can be dated in the catacombs was made in 72 (CNAD, 394), and the use of the catacombs continued unabated through the second and third centuries, with a de-

---

[11]Yigael Yadin, *Masada* (New York: Random House, 1966), 181–87.

cline in the fourth century when Christianity became the state religion and catacomb burials were no longer necessary. At least thirty-five Christian catacombs are known at Rome (FLAP, 455).

The painting on the walls of the passageways and rooms of the catacombs show us what the early Christians thought and believed. The most common scenes pictured are the raising of Lazarus, the escape of Noah from the deluge, the escape of Daniel from the lions, and the escape of Jonah from the great fish. All of these scenes have the one underlying motif of escape or deliverance and are an evidence of the fact that the early Christians were looking to Christ for deliverance. These scenes often appear in the oldest catacombs, such as the Catacomb of Domitilla, the Catacomb of Priscilla, and the Catacomb of Lucina, all of which are accepted by scholars as dating back to the first century (CNAD, 384) or, at the latest, to the middle of the second century A.D.[12] Just before the outbreak of World War II, my wife and I spent a month in Rome, devoting most of our time to an examination of the catacombs. Our study strikingly demonstrated that the early Christians who used them left a wholehearted testimony to a trust in Christ and his saving power.

Churches. Both because of the persecution of Christians and the fact that they often came from the lower classes of society in the early days of the church, we would not expect to find remains of very early church buildings. Moreover, it was common for groups of believers to meet in homes (see, e.g., Rom. 16:5, 14–15), and wealthy believers sometimes either made their property available for church services or gave it to the church for its use. Private homes provided greater secrecy than public structures in the event of persecution (see, e.g., FLAP, 495).

The earliest church yet to be excavated and dated with certainty was uncovered at Dura, a ruin on the Euphrates River, about halfway between Aleppo and Baghdad. Although there was some excavation at the site earlier, the definitive work took place from 1928 to 1937 under the sponsorship of Yale University and the French Academy of Inscriptions. During the 1931–32 season, excavators found in a house a chapel that had been made by joining two rooms and installing a platform. An adjacent room served as a baptistry. The numerous scenes on the walls included those of Jesus walking on the water to meet Peter, the Marys before the tomb of Jesus, the temptation of Adam and Eve, David and Goliath, the healing of the paralytic, and more—all in an extraordinary state of preservation. A dated inscription on the wall fixed construction or renovation to A.D. 232.[13]

When we move into later centuries, there is an abundance of ruins of churches in Bible lands. There are some remains of Constantine's fourth-century Church of the Nativity at Bethlehem (under the present church) and his basilica at the site of Mamre near Hebron. There are the Capernaum church over the presumed house of Peter (mid-fifth century), basilicas at Philippi dating to the fifth and sixth centuries, baths at Hierapolis converted into a Christian church during the

[12]Paul Styger's researches into the origins of the catacombs seem to indicate that the oldest Christian catacombs go back to about A.D. 150, a date that is still very early in the history of the church. In the case of the Catacomb of Domitilla, it appears from the inscriptions that this property was made available to a group of pagans who used it as a burial place in the first century and that their descendants accepted Christianity about the middle of the second century and established three underground burial places on the property as Christian burial chambers. Cf. FLAP, 462, and Paul Styger, *Die römischen Katakomben, archäoligische Forschungen üier den Ursprung und die Bedeutung der altchristlichen Grabstätten*, 1933.

[13]See Clark Hopkins, *The Discovery of Dura-Europos* (New Haven: Yale University Press, 1979), 90–96; Marie-Henriette Gates, "Dura-Europos: A Fortress of Syro-Mesopotamian Art," BA (September 1984), 166–81.

The magnificent temple of Bacchus at Baalbek

fifth century, unexcavated churches at Sardis dating to the fifth and sixth centuries, and many, many more.

Christianity Confronts Paganism; the Great Temple Complex at Baalbek

Although the advance of the Gospel during the first Christian centuries was phenomenal, paganism did not just roll over and play dead. Numerous older pagan worship centers were maintained, and new ones sprang up all over the Roman Empire; a few grandiose projects were launched. Perhaps the greatest of these was at Baalbek, located on a superb site fifty-three miles east of Beirut.

Probably as early as the reign of Augustus, the massive temple complex at Baalbek was begun. Inscriptions show that work on the temple of Jupiter was well under way during Nero's reign. And the temple of Bacchus apparently was begun about the middle of the first century A.D. For over two centuries construction went on at the site to produce a magnificent complex exuding a sense of power, size, and glorious magnificence.

A huge substructure—from 24 to 42 feet above the ground—was built for the temples to fulfill a psychological function—to render them more imposing by lifting them high above the neighboring landscape. Worshipers would enter the temple complex through a tower-flanked propylaea 165 feet wide and 38 feet deep, with columns brought from faraway Aswan in Egypt. They would then pass through a hexagonal court into a great altar court 350 feet square. On either side of the altar were large stone basins (actually tanks) 68 feet long by 23 feet broad and 2 feet 7 inches high for ritual washing.

From this court a magnificent stairway led to the temple of Jupiter. Surrounded by a colonnade of fifty-four columns, the cella, or holy of holies, was 290 by 160 feet, over five times as large as that of the Parthenon. Six of the great one-hundred-ton Corinthian columns of the peristyle remain standing. Sixty-five feet high, they

291

are the tallest in the Greco-Roman world. Atop the columns is a 16-foot entablature ornately decorated with lions' and bulls' heads.

Adjacent to the temple of Jupiter on the south and at a lower level is the temple of Bacchus with a cella 87 by 75 feet, originally surrounded by a peristyle of forty-six columns 56 feet high. Beautifully preserved, no better example of a Roman temple interior survives. East of the Acropolis was a round temple, rare in Syria, that was probably a temple of Venus, constructed about A.D. 250.

Huge stones appear in the temple complex substructure, the three largest being about 64 feet long, 14 feet high, and 11 feet thick and each weighing over a thousand tons. The largest stone of all never made it out of the quarry and may be seen about a mile south of the modern town. It measures 70 by 14 by 13 feet.

A German archaeological mission under the leadership of Otto Puchstein and Bruno Schulz dug at Baalbek from 1900 to 1904, thoroughly studying the acropolis area. From 1943 to 1975 the Lebanese Antiquities Service under the direction of Maurice Chehab and architect H. Kalayan conducted restoration work at the site.[14]

Palestine from New Testament Times to the Present

In A.D. 66 the Jews revolted against the Romans, and after four years of fierce warfare (described by Josephus), the Romans captured Jerusalem and destroyed the temple in A.D. 70. The tenth Roman legion was left at Jerusalem to maintain order (BAB, 162). Evidence of their occupation of Jerusalem appears even today when, from time to time, tiles are found bearing the inscription of this legion. In 132 a revolt of the Jews was led by a man named Simeon, who was called Bar Cochba, or Kokhba (Aramaic, meaning "son of the star"). This insurrection was not put down until 135 by the forces of the Roman emperor Hadrian. Hadrian determined to erase the Jewish city of Jerusalem from the map, and to accomplish this he rebuilt the city, making it a Roman colony and naming it Aelia Capitolina. He built a pagan temple to Jupiter on the site of the Jewish temple (BAB, 162). Jerusalem in this form continued on until the time of Constantine (c. 325).

The emperor Constantine made Christianity a legal religion of the Roman Empire. As at least a nominal Christian, he took an interest in the Holy Land. His mother, Queen Helena, made a trip to Palestine and sought to identify many scenes of gospel events. On the site selected by her as the location of the tomb of Christ a church was built in about 325. After many destructions and vicissitudes, it stands today and is still know as the Church of the Holy Sepulchre. Pilgrimages were frequent during the 300 years (300–600) after its construction, and many monasteries and churches were built in Palestine during this time. Queen Helena was also instrumental in the construction of churches at Bethlehem and Mamre near Hebron.

In 615 Chosroes II of Persia overran Palestine. The Persians controlled Palestine until 628, when it was regained by the Byzantine kings of the Roman Empire. It remained under Byzantine control for only a few years, 628–638, when the Muslims conquered it.[15]

After 638 Palestine was ruled by Muslims from various areas and dynasties in the Near East, including the Caliphs of Medina, Damascus, and Baghdad; the Fatimid Caliphs of Egypt, and the Seljuk Turks. Seljuk mistreatment of Christian

---

[14]While there are numerous works on Baalbek, most of them are not now readily available. Probably the best current work is Friedrich Ragette, *Baalbek* (Park Ridge, N.J.: Noyes Press, 1980).

[15]Palestine continued under the Muslims from 638 to 1917, except for a period of 89 years (1099–1188) when the Crusaders from Europe governed the area.

pilgrims to the Holy Land and pressure on the borders of the Byzantine Empire led to the organization of Crusades in Western Europe. The first Crusade resulted in the establishment of the Latin Kingdom of Jerusalem, which lasted from 1099 to 1188. Archaeological materials from the Crusader period are often found on the top or at least near the surface of many tells and ruins in Palestine.

Crusader involvement in the construction of the Church of the Holy Sepulchre has already been noted. A second major Crusader bastion on which archaeologists have concentrated is at Caesarea (see EAEHL, 1:282–85). Probably pride of place goes to the magnificent Crusader construction at Acre, however. There between 1955 and 1965 the great Refectory of the Order of St. John was cleared. The large two-aisled hall is under the present government hospital. It had three chimneys to facilitate its use as a refectory. The hall is built in the transitional style, from Romanesque to Gothic. Three huge columns, each about nine feet in diameter, support the heavy cross-rib vaults of the ceiling. Presumably the structure was erected about 1148, when Louis VII, leader of the Second Crusade, lived in Acre (EAEHL, 1:20).

After the fall of the Latin Kingdom in 1188, Palestine again came under Muslim control. The Sultans of Egypt controlled Palestine until 1517, when the Ottoman Turks captured it and survived as the rulers of Palestine during a long period of misrule.

The Allied Forces took Palestine during World War I, and in 1917 Palestine was freed from the domination of Muslim rulers. General Allenby was able to deliver Jerusalem without firing a shot in the Holy City. The League of Nations gave Great Britain a mandate to administer Palestine, and the Holy Land was opened up for the return of the Jews to their ancestral home by the provisions of the Balfour Declaration.[16] Seemingly the impossible occurred when the State of Israel was proclaimed on May 14, 1948, under United Nations auspices. Certainly the return of the Jews to Palestine is a foreshadowing of the time when the Lord "will reach out his hand a second time to reclaim the remnant that is left of his people . . . and gather the exiles of Israel; he will assemble the scattered people of Judah from the four quarters of the earth" (Isa. 11:11–12).

Prospects for the Future in Archaeology

Edward Chiera,[17] in his fascinating book on the clay tablets,[18] estimated that 99 percent of the Babylonian clay tablets remain undug, and A.T. Olmstead[19] pointed out, shortly before his death in 1945, that something like half a million clay tablets that have already been excavated are yet to be read and appraised.[20] It has been estimated that there are some five thousand ruin heaps in Palestine (including tells), only a few hundred of which have been excavated at all, and of these only about thirty have been the scenes of major digs. The Iraq Department of Antiquities has records of over 6,500 tells (mounds of buried cities) in the

[16]The Jewish population of Palestine was largely exterminated during the first (A.D. 66ff.) and second (132–135) Jewish revolts, and Arabs occupied the land during medieval and modern times. Extensive Jewish repatriation began with Theodor Herzl and the Zionist movement in the 1890s.

[17]Late Assyriologist at the Oriental Institute of the University of Chicago.

[18]George Cameron, ed., *They Wrote on Clay* (Chicago: University of Chicago Press, 1938), 233.

[19]Near Eastern specialist and historian at the Oriental Institute of the University of Chicago.

[20]A.T. Olmstead, "History, Ancient World, and the Bible," JNES 2, 1 (January 1943): 32. Although Olmstead wrote long ago, the situation has not improved since his day because more tablets have been found than have been translated since the time he compiled his estimate.

country; well over 6,000 of them have not yet been excavated at all. Nor has the day of "diminishing returns" been reached in Near Eastern archaeology—that is, in excavating one does not find a mere duplication of materials and information that is already known from previous excavations. Considering all of this, one is thrilled at the propects for the future in the field of archaeological research.

The Usefulness of Archaeology Today

In the meantime, there is already available abundant material that should be appropriated and put into use by Bible students in their study and teaching of the Scriptures. I once thumbed through the book of Genesis and mentally noted that each of the fifty chapters was either illuminated or confirmed by some archaeological discovery—the same would be true for most of the remaining chapters of the Bible, both the Old and New Testaments. With such an amount of material at hand to help us understand the Scriptures better and to show their validity, we need only to use it in order to enable others not only to appreciate the historical sequence of events in the Bible but also to realize afresh the significance of the great spiritual truths revealed in it. This book has been an effort in that direction.

BIBLIOGRAPHIES

BIBLIOGRAPHY

Some General Works on Archaeology and the Bible
(usually reliable but holding a variety of theological positions)

Albright, W.F. *The Archaeology of Palestine*. Harmondsworth, Middlesex, England: Penguin Books, 1949.

_____. *The Archaeology of Palestine and the Bible*. Cambridge, Mass.: ASOR, 1974.

_____. *Archaeology and the Religion of Israel*. Baltimore: Johns Hopkins Press, 1942.

_____. *From the Stone Age to Christianity*. Baltimore: Johns Hopkins Press, 1940.

_____. *Yahweh and the Gods of Canaan*. Garden City, N.Y.: Doubleday, 1968.

Barton, George A. *Archaeology and the Bible*. 7th ed. Philadelphia: American Sunday School Union, 1937.

Burrows, Millar. *What Mean These Stones?* New Haven: American Schools of Oriental Research, 1941.

Finegan, Jack. *Light from the Ancient Past*. 2nd ed. Princeton: Princeton University Press, 1959.

_____. *Archaeological History of the Ancient Near East*. Boulder, Colo: Westview, 1979.

Kenyon, Frederic. *The Bible and Archaeology*. New York: Harper, 1940.

Kitchen, Kenneth A. *Ancient Orient and Old Testament*. Chicago: InterVarsity, 1966.

Mazar, Amihai. *Archaeology of the Land of the Bible*. New York: Doubleday, 1990.

Price, Ira M., O.R. Sellers, and E. Leslie Carlson. *The Monuments and the Old Testament*. Philadelphia: Judson, 1958.

Robinson, George L. *The Bearing of Archaeology on the Old Testament*. New York: American Tract Society, 1941.

Schoville, Keith N. *Biblical Archaeology in Focus*. Grand Rapids: Baker, 1978.

Thomas, D. Winton, ed. *Archaeology and Old Testament Study*. Oxford: Oxford University Press, 1967.

Thompson, J.A. *The Bible and Archaeology*. 3rd ed. Grand Rapids: Eerdmans, 1982.

Unger, Merrill F. *Archaeology and the Old Testament*. Grand Rapids: Zondervan, 1954.

Vos, Howard F. *Archaeology in Bible Lands*. Chicago: Moody Press, 1977.

Wright, G. Ernest. *Biblical Archaeology*. Philadelphia: Westminster, 1961.

Works Opposing the Critical View of Scripture
(based on archaeology, linguistics, etc.)

Allis, Oswald T. *The Five Books of Moses*. Philadelphia: Presbyterian and Reformed, 1943.

Archer, Gleason L., Jr. *A Survey of Old Testament Introduction*. Rev. ed. Chicago: Moody Press, 1974.

Green, W.H. *The Unity of the Book of Genesis*. New York: Scribner, 1910.

_____. *The Higher Criticism of the Pentateuch*. New York: Scribner, 1896.

Guthrie, Donald. *New Testament Introduction*. 3rd ed. Downers Grove: InterVarsity, 1970.

Hamilton, Floyd E. *The Basis of Christian Faith.* 3rd ed. New York: Harper, 1946.

Harrison, Everett F. *Introduction to the New Testament.* Rev. ed. Grand Rapids: Eerdmans, 1971.

Harrison, Roland K. *Introduction to the Old Testament.* Grand Rapids: Eerdmans, 1969.

Kyle, M.G. *The Deciding Voice of the Monuments in Biblical Criticism.* Oberlin: Bibliotheca Sacra, 1924.

————. *Moses and the Monuments.* Oberlin: Bibliotheca Sacra, 1920.

————. *The Problem of the Pentateuch: A New Solution by Archaeological Methods.* Oberlin: Bibliotheca Sacra, 1920.

Orr, James. *The Problem of the Old Testament.* New York: Scribner, 1917.

Raven, John H. *Old Testament Introduction.* New York: Revell, 1910.

Thiessen, Henry C. *Introduction to the New Testament.* Grand Rapids: Eerdmans, 1943.

Unger, Merrill F. *Introductory Guide to the Old Testament.* Grand Rapids: Zondervan, 1951.

Wilson, Robert D. *A Scientific Investigation of the Old Testament.* Revised by Edward J. Young. Chicago: Moody Press, 1959.

————. *Is the Higher Criticism Scholarly?* 9th ed. Philadelphia: The Sunday School Times, 1948.

Young, E.J. *An Introduction to the Old Testament.* Grand Rapids: Eerdmans, 1949.

Works on the Dead Sea Scrolls

Bruce, F.F. *Second Thoughts on the Dead Sea Scrolls.* 2nd ed. Grand Rapids: Eerdmans, 1961.

Burrows, Millar. *Burrows on the Dead Sea Scrolls* (a combination of his *Dead Sea Scrolls* and *More Light on the Dead Sea Scrolls*). Grand Rapids: Baker, 1978.

Charlesworth, James H., ed. *John and the Dead Sea Scrolls.* New York: Crossroad, 1990.

Cross, Frank M. *The Ancient Library of Qumran and Modern Biblical Studies.* Grand Rapids: Baker, 1958.

Davies, Philip R. *Qumran.* Grand Rapids: Eerdmans, 1982.

LaSor, William S. *The Dead Sea Scolls and the Christian Faith.* Chicago: Moody Press, 1962.

————. *The Dead Sea Scrolls and the New Testament.* Grand Rapids: Eerdmans, 1972.

Murphy-O'Connor, Jerome, and James H. Charlesworth, eds. *Paul and the Dead Sea Scrolls.* New York: Crossroad, 1990.

Pfeiffer, Charles F. *The Dead Sea Scrolls and the Bible.* Grand Rapids: Baker, 1969.

Sanders, James A. "The Dead Sea Scrolls—A Quarter Century of Study." BA (December 1973).

deVaux, R. *Archaeology and the Dead Sea Scrolls.* London: Oxford University Press, 1973.

Vermes, Geza. *The Dead Sea Scrolls in English.* 2nd ed. Harmondsworth, Middlesex, England: Penguin Books, 1975.

Vos, Howard F. *Archaeology in Bible Lands.* Chicago: Moody Press, 1977. Chapter 6.

Yadin, Yigael. *The Message of the Scrolls.* New York: Simon & Schuster, 1957.

Yamauchi, Edwin M. "The Dead Sea Scrolls." In *Wycliffe Bible Encyclopedia.* 2 vols. Chicago: Moody Press, 1975. 1:434–42.

Works on the Monuments and the Bible

Breasted, James H. *Ancient Records of Egypt.* 5 vols. Chicago: University of Chicago Press, 1906.

Luckenbill, D.D. *Ancient Records of Assyria and Babylonia.* 2 vols. Chicago: University of Chicago Press, 1926.

Pritchard, James B., ed. *Ancient Near Eastern Texts Relating to the Old Testament.* 2nd ed. Princeton: Princeton University Press, 1955.

Works on Bible Geography

Adams, J. McKee. *Biblical Backgrounds.* Revised by Joseph A. Callaway. Nashville: Broadman, 1965.

Aharoni, Yohanan. *The Land of the Bible.* London: Burns & Oates, 1967.

————, and Michael Avi-Yonah. *The Macmillan Bible Atlas.* New York: Macmillan, 1968.

Baines, John, and Jaromir Malek. *Atlas of Ancient Egypt.* New York: Facts on File, 1980.

Beitzel, Barry J. *The Moody Atlas of Bible Lands.* Chicago: Moody Press, 1985.

Cornell, Tim, and John Matthews. *Atlas of the Roman World.* New York: Facts on File, 1982.

Levi, Peter. *Atlas of the Greek World.* New York: Facts on File, 1980.

May, Herbert, ed. *Oxford Bible Atlas.* 2nd ed. New York: Oxford University Press, 1974.

Orni, Efraim, and Elisha Efrat. *Geography of Israel.* 3rd ed. Jerusalem: Israel Universities Press, 1971.

Pfeiffer, Charles, and Howard F. Vos. *The Wycliffe Historical Geography of Bible Lands.* Chicago: Moody Press, 1967.

Pritchard, James B., ed. *The Harper Atlas of the Bible.* New York: Harper & Row, 1987.

Ramsay, William M *The Historical Geography of Asia Minor.* New York: Cooper Square, reprint 1972.

Rasmussen, Carl G. *Zondervan NIV Atlas of the Bible.* Grand Rapids: Zondervan, 1989.

Roaf, Michael. *Cultural Atlas of Mesopotamia.* New York: Facts on File, 1990.

Smith, George A. *The Historical Geography of the Holy Land.* London: Hodder and Stoughton, 1897.

Wright, G.E., and F.V. Filson. *The Westminster Historical Atlas to the Bible.* Rev. ed. Philadelphia: Westminster, 1956.

A Few of the More Useful Encyclopedias

Blaiklock, Edward M., and R.K. Harrison, eds. *The New International Dictionary of Biblical Archaeology.* Grand Rapids: Zondervan, 1983.

Bromiley, Geoffrey W., ed. *International Standard Bible Encyclopedia.* Rev. ed. 4 vols. Grand Rapids: Eerdmans, 1979–88. This replaces the 1929, 5-vol. set. Both editions are used in this book.

Buttrick, George A., ed. *Interpreter's Dictionary of the Bible.* 4 vols. Nashville: Abingdon, 1962.

Douglas, J.D., ed. *Illustrated Bible Dictionary.* 3 vols. Leicester, England: Inter-Varsity, 1980.

Tenney, Merrill C., ed. *Zondervan Pictorial Encyclopedia of the Bible.* 5 vols. Grand Rapids: Zondervan, 1975.

BIBLIOGRAPHIES

Archaeology and the New Testament

Blaiklock, E.M. *The Archaeology of the New Testament*. Grand Rapids: Zondervan, 1970.

Cobern, C.M. *The New Archaeological Discoveries and Their Bearing upon the New Testament*. 9th ed. New York: Funk and Wagnalls, 1929.

Deissmann, Adolf. *Light from the Ancient East*. New York: Doran, 1927.

Harrison, R.K. *Archaeology of the New Testament*. London: English Universities Press, 1964.

Finegan, Jack. *The Archaeology of the New Testament: The Life of Jesus and the Beginning of the Early Church*. Princeton: Princeton University Press, 1969.

————. *The Archaeology of the New Testament: The Mediterranean World of the Early Christian Apostles*. Boulder, Colo.: Westview, 1981.

McRay, John. *Archaeology and the New Testament*. Grand Rapids: Baker, 1991.

Unger, Merrill F. *Archaeology and the New Testament*. Grand Rapids: Zondervan, 1962.

BIBLIOGRAPHY

Arranged Alphabetically by the Abbreviations Used in This Book

AAP   Albright, W.F. *The Archaeology of Palestine.* Harmondsworth,
Middlesex: Penguin Books, 1949.

AAPB   ————. *The Archaeology of Palestine and the Bible.* Cambridge,
Mass.: ASOR, 1974.

AARB   Adams, J. McKee. *Ancient Records and the Bible.* Nashville:
Broadman, 1946.

AARI   Albright, W.F. *Archaeology and the Religion of Israel.* Baltimore:
Johns Hopkins Press, 1942.

AASOR   *Annual of the American Schools of Oriental Research.*

AFBM   Allis, Oswald T. *The Five Books of Moses.* Philadelphia: Presbyterian
and Reformed, 1943.

AFOTC   Alleman, H.C., and E.E. Flack, *Old Testament Commentary.*
Philadelphia: Muhlenberg, 1948.

AJA   *American Journal of Archaeology.*

AJSL   *American Journal of Semitic Languages.*

AOTA   Albright, W.F. "The Old Testament and Archaeology." In AFOTC.

ARDBL   ————. "Recent Discoveries in Bible Lands." In Young's *Analytical
Concordance to the Bible.* 20th ed. New York: Funk and Wagnalls,
c. 1936.

AS   *American Scholar.*

ASAC   Albright, W.F. *From the Stone Age to Christianity.* Baltimore: Johns
Hopkins Press, 1940.

ASOTI   Archer, Gleason L., Jr. *A Survey of Old Testament Introduction.* Rev.
ed. Chicago: Moody Press, 1974.

BA   *Biblical Archaeologist.*

BAB   Barton, G.A. *Archaeology and the Bible.* 7th ed. Philadelphia:
American Sunday School Union, 1937.

BAHE   Breasted, J.H. *A History of Egypt.* New York: Scribner, 1912.

BAR   *Biblical Archaeology Review.*

BARE   Breasted, J.H. *Ancient Records of Egypt.* 5 vols. Chicago: University of
Chicago Press, 1906.

BASOR   *Bulletin of the American Schools of Oriental Research.*

BBH   Blaikie, William G. *A Manual of Bible History.* Rev. ed. London, New
York: Nelson, 1923.

BBHM   ————. *A Manual of Bible History.* Revised by Charles D.
Matthews. London: Nelson, 1940; reissued by Ronald Press, New
York: 1942.

BCC   Breasted, J.H. *The Conquest of Civilization.* New York: Harper, 1926.

BDB   Brown, Driver, Briggs. *A Hebrew and English Lexicon of the Old
Testament.* New York: Houghton Mifflin, 1906.

BHE   Brugsch. *History of Egypt.* 1891.

BJ   Blaikie, William G. "The Book of Joshua." In *The Expositor's Bible*. New York: Funk and Wagnalls, 1900.

BOI   Breasted, J.H. *The Oriental Institute*. Chicago: University of Chicago Press, 1933.

BS   Blaikie, William G. "The First Book of Samuel." In *The Expositor's Bible*. New York: Armstrong, 1901.

BSS   ————. "The Second Book of Samuel." In *The Expositor's Bible*. New York: Armstrong, 1893.

BWMS   Burrows, Millar. *What Mean These Stones?* New Haven: American Schools of Oriental Research, 1941.

CAH   *Cambridge Ancient History*. 2nd ed. New York: Macmillan, 1924.

CANT   Caiger, S.L. *Archaeology and the New Testament*. London: Cassell, 1939.

CAP   Cowley, A. *Aramaic Papyri of the Fifth Century*. Oxford: Clarendon, 1923.

CBE   Chadwick, G.A. "The Book of Exodus." In *The Expositor's Bible*. London: Hodder and Stoughton, 1896.

CBS   Caiger, S.L. *Bible and Spade*. London: Oxford University Press, 1936.

CCIN   Cartledge, S.A. *A Conservative Introduction to the New Testament*. Grand Rapids: Zondervan, 1943.

CCIO   ————. *A Conservative Introduction to the Old Testament*. Grand Rapids: Zondervan, 1943; reissued by University of Georgia Press, Athens, Ga., 1944.

CG   Calvin, John. *Commentaries on the First Book of Moses, Called Genesis*. Revised by John King. Edinburgh: Calvin Translation Society, 1847.

CHJ   Case, Shirley Jackson. *The Historicity of Jesus*. Chicago: University of Chicago Press, 1912.

CNAD   Cobern, C.M. *The New Archaeological Discoveries and Their Bearing upon the New Testament*. 9th ed. New York: Funk and Wagnalls, 1929.

CREP   Cobern, C.M. *Recent Explorations in Palestine*. Meadville, Pa.: Tribune, c. 1915.

DBS   Deissmann, G. Adolf. *Bible Studies*. Edinburgh: T. & T. Clark, 1903.

DDBH   Duncan, J. Garrow. *Digging up Biblical History*. New York: Macmillan, 1931.

DG   Driver, S.R. *The Book of Genesis*, Westminster Commentaries. 4th ed. London: Methuen, 1905.

DNB   Dougherty, R.P. *Nabonidus and Belshazzar*. New Haven: Yale University Press, 1929.

DS   Diodorus of Sicily. E.T. by C.H. Oldfather. 10 vols. New York: Putnam, 1933.

DTH   Driver, S.R. *A Treatise on the Use of the Tenses in Hebrew*. Oxford: Clarendon, 1892.

EAEHL   Avi-Yonah, Michael, ed. *Encyclopedia of Archaeological Excavations in the Holy Land*. 4 vols. Englewood Cliffs, N.J.: Prentice Hall, 1975–78.

EBLT   Ellis, William T. *Bible Lands Today*. 1926.

EDC   Engberg, R.M. *The Dawn of Civilization*. Chicago: University of Knowledge, 1938.

EHR _____. *The Hyksos Reconsidered.* Studies in Ancient Oriental Civilization (SAOC). Chicago: University of Chicago Press, 1939.

ELAE Erman, A. *Life in Ancient Egypt.* Translated by H.M. Tirard. London: Macmillan, 1894.

EQ *Evangelical Quarterly* (Edinburgh).

FANT Finegan, Jack. *The Archaeology of the New Testament.* Boulder, Colo.: Westview, 1981.

FHBC _____. *Handbook of Biblical Chronology.* Princeton: Princeton University Press, 1964.

FLAP _____. *Light from the Ancient Past.* 2nd ed. Princeton: Princeton University Press, 1959.

GBT Gregg, David. *Between the Testaments.* New York: Funk and Wagnalls, 1907.

GHCP Green, W.H. *The Higher Criticism of the Pentateuch.* New York: Scribner, 1895.

GIC _____. *General Introduction to the Old Testament: The Canon.* New York: Scribner, 1898.

GIT _____. *General Introduction to the Old Testament: The Text.* New York: Scribner, 1899.

GHH Garstang, John. *Joshua, Judges.* London: Constable, 1931.

GOSJ Glueck, Nelson. *The Other Side of Jordan.* New Haven: American Schools of Oriental Research, 1940.

GRJ _____. *The River Jordan.* Philadelphia: Westminster, 1946.

GS *The Geography of Strabo.* E.T. by Horace Leonard Jones. 8 vols. London: Heinemann; New York: Putnam, 1932.

GSJ Garstang, John, and J.B.E. Garstang. *The Story of Jericho.* Rev. ed. London: Marshall, Morgan and Scott, 1948.

GT Gaussen, L. *Theopneustia: The Plenary Inspiration of the Holy Scriptures.* Cincinnati, 1859; reissued by Moody Press, Chicago.

GTG Griffith-Thomas, W.H. *Genesis.* London: Religious Tract Society, n.d.

GUG Green, W.H. *The Unity of the Book of Genesis.* New York: Scribner, 1910.

HBCF Hamilton, F.E. *The Basis of Christian Faith.* 3rd ed. New York: Harper, 1946.

HBG Heidel, Alexander. *The Babylonian Genesis.* 2nd ed. Chicago: University of Chicago Press, 1951.

HCH Harper, R.F. *The Code of Hammurabi, King of Babylon about 2250 B.C.* Chicago: University of Chicago Press, 1904.

CHOT Hengstenberg, E.W. *Christology of the Old Testament.* Translated by Theodore Meyer. Edinburgh: T. & T. Clark, 1863.

HDB Hastings, James. *Dictionary of the Bible.* Rev. ed. New York: Scribner, 1927.

HDGG Hart-Davies, D.E. *The Genesis of Genesis.* London: Clarke, 1932.

HEBL Hilprecht, H.V. *Explorations in Bible Lands During the 19th Century.* Philadelphia: Holman, 1903.

HHMM Harper, W.R. *Introductory Hebrew Method and Manual.* Revised by J.M.F. Smith. New York: Scribner, 1921.

HSAB *The Haverford Symposium on Archaeology and the Bible.* Edited by Elihu Grant. New Haven: American Schools of Oriental Research, 1938.

BIBLIOGRAPHIES

ILN *Illustrated London News.*

ISBE *International Standard Bible Encyclopedia.* Edited by James Orr. 5 vols. Severance, 1929. Reprinted by Eerdmans, 1939. (Revised ed., edited by Geoffrey W. Bromiley. 4 vols. Grand Rapids: Eerdmans, 1979–88. This edition is also referred to in this book.)

JAJ Josephus. *Antiquities of the Jews.* Translated by William Whiston.

JBL *Journal of Biblical Literature.*

JFB Jamieson, Robert, A.R. Fausset, and David Brown. *A Commentary Critical and Explanatory on the Whole Bible.* Rev. ed. 1 vol. Grand Rapids: Eerdmans, 1935.

JNES *Journal of Near Eastern Studies.*

JSAT Jack. J.W. *Samaria in Ahab's Time: Harvard Excavations and Their Results.* Edinburgh: T. & T. Clark, 1929.

JSKL Jacobsen, Thorkild. *The Sumerian King List.* Chicago: University of Chicago Press, 1939.

KA Kroeber, A.L. *Anthropology.* New York: Harcourt, Brace, 1948.

KBA Kenyon, Frederic. *The Bible and Archaeology.* New York: Harper, 1940.

KD Keil, C.F. and F. Delitzsch. *Biblical Commentary on the Old Testament.* Edinburgh: T. & T. Clark, 1872.

KDVM Kyle, M.G. *The Deciding Voice of the Monuments in Biblical Criticism.* Oberlin: Bibliotheca Sacra, 1924.

KEK ————. *Excavating Kirjath-Sepher's Ten Cities.* Grand Rapids: Eerdmans, 1934.

KMM ————. *Moses and the Monuments.* Oberlin: Bibliotheca Sacra, 1920.

KNJ Knight, G.A. Frank. *Nile and Jordan.* London: Clarke, 1921.

LARA Luckenbill, D.D. *Ancient Records of Assyria and Babylonia.* Chicago: University of Chicago Press, 1926.

LAS ————. *The Annals of Sennacherib.* Chicago: University of Chicago Press, 1924.

LC Lange, John Peter. *A Commentary on the Holy Scriptures: Critical, Doctrinal, and Homiletical.* New York: Scribner, 1870.

LCG ————. *Commentary on Genesis.* New York: Scriber, 1870.

LDSS Ladd, George Trumbull. *The Doctrine of Sacred Scripture.* 1883.

MACR Möller, Wilhelm. *Are the Critics Right?* New York: Revell, n.d. [c. 1899].

MALB Mazar, Amihai. *Archaeology of the Land of the Bible.* New York: Doubleday, 1990.

MBCA Marston, Charles. *The Bible Comes Alive.* London: Eyre and Spottiswoode, 1938.

MCEP Macalister, R.A.S. *A Century of Excavation in Palestine.* New York: Revell, 1925.

MCG Murphy, J.G. *Critical and Exegetical Commentary on the Book of Genesis.* Boston: Estes, 1873.

MEG Macalister, R.A.S. *The Excavation of Gezer.* New York: Revell, 1912.

MHTE Muir, James C. *His Truth Endureth.* Philadelphia: National, 1937.

MLPP McCown, C.C. *The Ladder of Progress in Palestine.* New York: Harper, 1943.

MNBE Marston, Charles. *New Bible Evidence.* New York: Revell, 1934–35.

MRAB	MacRae, Allan A. "The Relation of Archaeology to the Bible." In MSCF.
MSCF	*Modern Science and Christian Faith*. Wheaton: Van Kampen, 1948.
MSM	Morton, H.V. *In the Steps of the Master*. New York: Dodd, Mead, 1937.
NCA	Neatby, T. Miller. *Confirming the Scriptures*. London: Marshall, Morgan and Scott, n.d.
NOTP	Noordtzy, A. *The Old Testament Problem*, printed in issues 388, 389, 390 of *Bibliotheca Sacra*, and reprinted as booklet, 1940–41, by Dallas Theological Seminary.
NPRE	Naville, E. *The Store-City of Pithom and the Route of the Exodus*. London, 1903.
OHA	Olmstead, A.T. *History of Assyria*. New York: Scribner, 1923.
OHPE	_____. *History of the Persian Empire*. Chicago: University of Chicago Press, 1948.
OHPS	_____. *History of Palestine and Syria*. New York: Scribner, 1931.
OIA	Oesterley, W.O.E. *An Introduction to the Books of the Apocrypha*. New York: Macmillan, 1935.
OIC	*Oriental Institute Communications*. Chicago: The Oriental Institute of the University of Chicago, n.d.
OJJ	Oesterley, W.O.E. *The Jews and Judaism During the Greek Period*. London: SPCK; New York: Macmillan, 1941.
OPOT	Orr, James. *The Problem of the Old Testament*. New York: Scribner, 1917.
ORHI	Oesterley, W.O.E., and Theodore H. Robinson. *A History of Israel*. Oxford: Clarendon, 1932.
PAK	Poebel, A. "The Assyrian King List from Khorsabad," JNES, 2, 1 (January 1943).
PANEP	Pritchard, James B., ed. *The Ancient Near East in Pictures*. 2nd ed. Princeton: Princeton University Press, 1969.
PANET	_____. ed. *Ancient Near Eastern Texts Relating to the Old Testament*. 2nd ed. Princeton: Princeton University Press, 1955.
PC	*Pulpit Commentary*.
PDBC	Parker, R.A., and W.H. Dubberstein. *Babylonian Chronology, 626 B.C.–A.D. 45*. Chicago: University of Chicago Press, 1942.
PEEA	Pember, G.H. *Earth's Earliest Ages*. New York: Revell, c. 1876.
PEOT	Peet, T. Eric. *Egypt and the Old Testament*. Liverpool: University Press of Liverpool, 1924.
PGH	Piper, Otto. *God in History*. New York: Macmillan, 1939.
PIOT	Pfeiffer, R.H. *Introduction to the Old Testament*. Rev. ed. New York: Harper, 1948.
PMOT	Price, Ira Maurice, et al. *The Monuments and the Old Testament*. Philadelphia: Judson, 1958.
POTH	Petrie, Flinders. *Palestine and Israel*. London: SPCK, 1934.
PSB	Prescott, W.W. *The Spade and the Bible*. New York: Revell, 1933.
PSBA	*Proceedings of the Society of Biblical Archaeology*.
RBA	Robinson, George L. *The Bearing of Archaeology on the Old Testament*. New York: American Tract Society, 1941.
RBR	Robinson, Edward. *Biblical Researches in Palestine*. 3rd ed. Boston: Crocker and Brewster, 1868.

RCP	Rogers, R.W. *Cuneiform Parallels to the Old Testament*. 2nd ed. New York: Abingdon, 1926.
RENG	Ryle, H.E. *Early Narratives of Genesis*. London: Macmillan, 1904.
RGGT	Robertson, A.T. *New Short Grammar of the Greek Testament*. London: SPCK, 1931.
RHAP	Rogers, R.W. *A History of Ancient Persia*. New York: Scribner, 1929.
RHES	Reisner, G.A.; C.S. Fisher; D.G. Lyon. *Harvard Excavations at Samaria, 1908–1910*. Cambridge: Harvard University Press, 1924.
ROTI	Raven, John. *Old Testament Introduction*. New York: Revell, 1910.
RRB	Rogers, R.W. *The Religion of Babylonia and Assyria*. New York: Eaton and Mains, 1908.
SBT	Harold R. Willowby, ed. *The Study of the Bible Today and Tomorrow*. Chicago: University of Chicago Press, 1947.
SDB	*Smith's Dictionary of the Bible*. New York: Hurd and Houghton, 1871.
SG	Skinner, John. *Genesis*. International Critical Commentary. New York: Scriber, 1910.
SHL	Smith, J.M.P. *The Origin and History of Hebrew Law*. Chicago: University of Chicago Press, 1931.
SNG	Spurrell, G.J. *Notes on the Text of the Book of Genesis*. Oxford: Clarendon, 1896.
SSWE	Steindorff, George, and Keith C. Seele. *When Egypt Ruled the East*. Rev. ed. Chicago: University of Chicago Press, 1957.
STTP	Spinoza, Benedict de. *Tractatus Theologico-Politicus*. In *The Chief Works of Benedict de Spinoza, 1670*. Translated by R.H.M. Elwes. London: George Bell, 1883.
TCK	Thiele, E.R. "The Chronology of the Kings of Judah and Israel." JNES 2, 3 (July 1944): 137–38.
TINT	Thiessen, H.C. *Introduction to the New Testament*. Grand Rapids: Eerdmans, 1943.
TKB	Trumbull, H. Clay. *Kadesh-barnea*. New York: Scribner, c. 1884.
TMN	Thiele, Edwin R. *The Mysterious Numbers of the Hebrew Kings*. New rev. ed. Grand Rapids: Zondervan, 1983.
TSTS	Theissen, H.C. *Lectures in Systematic Theology*. Rev. ed. Grand Rapids: Eerdmans, 1979.
UNBG	Urquhart, John. *The New Biblical Guide*. Chicago: Blessing, n.d.
VENE	Vos, Howard F. *Ezra, Nehemiah, Esther*. Grand Rapids: Zondervan, 1987.
WA	Woolley, C.L. *Abraham*. New York: Scribner, 1936.
WBE	Wilson, John A. *Burden of Egypt*. Chicago: University of Chicago Press, 1951.
WCCK	Wiseman, Donald J. *Chronicle of the Chaldean Kings*. London: British Museum, 1956.
WCI	Wright, G.E. *The Challenge of Israel's Faith*. Chicago: University of Chicago Press, 1944.
WDICJ	Wood, Bryant G., "Did the Israelites Conquer Jericho?" BAR (March/April 1990), 44–59.
WDP	Woolley, C.L. *Digging Up the Past*. New York: Scribner, 1931.
WFWA	Wright, G.E., and F.V. Filson. *The Westminster Historical Atlas to the Bible*. Rev. ed. Philadelphia: Westminster, 1956.

WPHI   Wellhausen, Julius. *Prolegomena to the History of Israel*. Edinburgh: Black, 1885.

WSC   Wright, G. Frederick. *Scientific Confirmations of Old Testament History*. Oberlin: Bibliotheca Sacra, 1913.

WSEB   *The Westminster Study Edition of the Holy Bible*. Philadelphia: Westminster, 1948.

WSI   Wilson, Robert Dick. *A Scientific Investigation of the Old Testament*. Revised by Edward J. Young. Chicago: Moody Press, 1959.

WST   Warfield, B.B. *Studies in Theology*. New York: Oxford University Press, 1932.

WUC   Woolley, C.L. *Ur of the Chaldees*. Revised by P.R.S. Moorey. London: Herbert, 1982.

YAB   Yahuda, A.S. *The Accuracy of the Bible*. London: Heinemann, 1934.

YLP   _____. *The Language of the Pentateuch in Its Relation to Egyptian*. New York: Oxford University Press, 1933.

INDEX

INDEX